Millennium Dawn

Planet Earth faces many global crises. Global war, militarism, terrorism, and the proliferation of weapons of mass destruction proceed unchecked. Global poverty, disease, illiteracy, and waste of human potential have encompassed one fourth of the world's population and continue to grow. World fresh water supplies and agricultural lands are disappearing at alarming rates. Global warming and other forms of environmental destruction are at an advanced state and continue unchecked.

This book presents an analysis of our total human situation on planet Earth and provides the basis for a redeemed world order based on democracy, peace, prosperity, and a new human maturity. It provides the basis for tremendous hope in the future by distilling the latest thought in philosophy, spirituality, the social sciences, economics, and politics.

Martin demonstrates in detail the range of potentialities within human beings for rapidly transforming both themselves and their institutions toward a decent, just, and sustainable world order. In doing so he offers an original philosophical synthesis of human spirituality, social maturity, and political-economic potential. This book provides a truly holistic vision for dealing with our global crises that is at the same time both practical and realistic.

Glen T. Martin is Professor of Philosophy and Religious Studies at Radford University in Virginia. He is Secretary-General of the World Constitution and Parliament Association (WCPA), President of International Philosophers for Peace...(IPPNO), and President of the Institute On World Problems (IOWP).

Dr. Martin has lectured, published, and traveled in many countries of the world in the service of world peace and a transformed future for humankind. He is author or editor of six books directed toward the actualization of planetary maturity within a just, free, and democratic world order. He has also published dozens of articles on a variety of topics in political commentary, comparative philosophy, the spirituality of human liberation, economic democracy, democratic world government, and global social issues. His personal home page is found at www.radford. edu/~gmartin.

PRAISE FOR MILLENNIUM DAWN

The book is a masterpiece. It does several impressive things: it critically re-examines traditional political philosophies, it adds to the discussion a sensitive application of spiritual thinkers, it probes the real world we face, and it offers a unified comprehensive, thorough and hopefully original vision. – *Dr. Robert Ginsberg, Professor of Philosophy and Comparative Literature, Penn State University, Delaware County*

This is a major work on the most vital problem of the 21st Century written in the light of contemporary science, metaphysics, ethical and political theory and the philosophy of religion. It draws and comments upon a wide range of ideas as expressed by recent thinkers from Mahatma Gandhi to Levinas and Habermas. But it is not simply a theoretical discussion: it assesses and recommends practical reforms and procedures indispensable to the salvation of humankind, not just in the religious sense of that word, but from the mortal dangers which threaten us at the present time from the destruction of the ecological environment, from the proliferation of weapons of mass extermination, from global terrorism, and from the impoverishment of the peoples of the world by unregulated market forces.

The key principle developed by professor Martin is that of unity in diversity (which is considered throughout in all its varied applications, scientific and philosophical, ecological, social and political) in the regulation of inter-personal and international affairs. The book ought to be required reading for all politicians and religious leaders, as well as for academicians and the public in general. – *Dr. Errol E. Harris, John Evans Professor of Moral and Intellectual Philosophy (Emeritus), Northwestern University*

Ever since humanity stepped into the nuclear civilization, thinkers and philosophers have expressed their serious concern and deepest anguish over the disastrous "crossroads" that we all face. Only a few people have come up with concrete proposals and plans. Dr. Glen T. Martin is one such scholar-philosopher-activist, who has dedicated his life to seeking and establishing a viable alternative to for the survival of humanity and lasting peace on Earth. The result of this quest is found in Millennium Dawn.

This book strives with great seriousness of purpose to present an integrated answer to some complex questions of human existence and performance. It is bound to provoke constructive thinking in millions of people, who have the potential to play a role in the creation of a new world order on the bed-rock of justice, equality, fraternity, and unity. – *Sri E. P. Menon, world peace activist; Executive Trustee, India Development Foundation, Bangalore, India*

In this meticulously researched and documented study, philosopher and peace activist Glen T. Martin discusses the crises situations currently threatening human survival on Earth. He exposes their underlying causes, considers historical trends pointing to advancements toward a heightened planetary maturity, and outlines in theoretical and practical detail the means to achieving a universally just and sustainable prosperity in which all humanity must share.

The result is a cohesive and comprehensive philosophical perspective on an issue too pressing to be ignored. For those who care to consider the ways in which rapacious capitalist exploitation and archaic nation-state sovereignty have evolved to a point that makes them a global menace, and to those interested in weighing the evidence supporting world government under the *Constitution for the Federation of Earth*, Martin's book is mandatory reading. – ***Dr. Richard Perkins,*** *Department of Philosophy, Canesius College, Buffalo, New York*

Professor Martin has created a monumental intellectual synthesis that lays bare the causes of today's world crisis and unerringly outlines the foundations for human liberation in spiritual, political, and economic terms. The book is a masterpiece destined to become a bible for a new generation concerned about redeeming our planet from impending destruction. It offers a vision of hope that needs to be adopted worldwide.

Martin's vision of a transformed world order is practical and immediately achievable. With perfect insight Martin writes that "the economics of absolute property rights that now dominates the world through monopolies on land, technology, money creation, and information will be transformed over time to an economics of conditional property rights in which the common good and prosperity of the diverse peoples of the Earth will be ensured."

Martin understands that raw poverty can be eliminated in ten years and all the world's citizens would be living a sustainable quality lifestyle in two generations. The elimination of monopolies, as laid out by professor Martin, is so simple, the efficiency gains so enormous, and attaining the goals of socialism so obvious, that I trust millions of concerned citizens will engage in what he calls "transformative praxis," dedicated to rapidly creating a new world of peace, justice, and prosperity for everyone. – ***Dr. J.W. Smith***, *founder, Institute for Economic Democracy, author of Economic Democracy: The Political Struggle of the Twenty-First Century*

MILLENNIUM

DAWN

Millennium Dawn

The Philosophy of Planetary Crisis

and Human Liberation

Glen T. Martin

Institute for Economic Democracy Press

IED

Institute for Economic Democracy

PO Box 309, Appomattox VA 23958

In cooperation with the
Institute On World Problems
313 Seventh Ave., Radford, VA 24141, USA
www.worldproblems.net

The Institute for Economic Democracy is a Non-Profit Organization
dedicated to publishing quality books for progressive social change.
Group discounts, Classroom/ University Bookstore discounts
www.ied.info/cc.html

Copyright © 2005 by Glen T. Martin
All rights reserved.
For any properly cited individual quotation up to 500 words,
no permission is necessary.

Printing 1.2
Publisher's Cataloging-in-Publication Data
Martin, Glen T.
    Millennium dawn : the philosophy of planetary crisis
    and human liberation / Glen T. Martin.
    p. cm.
    Includes bibliographical references and index.
    ISBN 0-9753555-0-3 (hc)
    ISBN 0-9753555-1-1 (pbk)

    1. Life. 2. Meaning (Philosophy) 3. Civilization,
Modern--Philosophy. 4. Human evolution. 5. Social
evolution. 6. Cosmology. I. Title.

BD431.M37 2005   128
                  QBI04-800134

Book cover designed by Michael Dorfman and William Kovarik

First Edition 2005
Printed in the United States of America

*This book is dedicated to the hundreds
of millions of the world's poor,*

*some of whom I have known personally
in Nicaragua, Ghana, Togo, India, and Bangladesh,*

*who have not given up their humanity
or their love,*

*despite being forced to live lives of
relentless suffering and hardship.*

*In them, is the hope
and the light of the world.*

x

Table of Contents

Part Three:

Economic and Social Liberation

Part Four:

Practical Utopia

and Democratic World Government

Foreword

This book is comprised of fourteen chapters, several of which are written to stand on their own. Each of these chapters attempts, so to speak, to "tell the whole story" in its own way. As such, each of these comprehensive chapters (such as Chapter Three or Thirteen) can be read independently according to the reader's immediate concerns. They can also be copied or reproduced as independent units. The book is written not only for philosophers but for the general educated reader. Everyone is, or should be, a philosopher – concerned about the meaning of life and our future on this planet.

In our age of fragmentation, I believe there is a great need to attempt to "tell the whole story" as much as possible. The result of this attempt is a slight repetition among some chapters. I believe this is a necessary and healthy feature of the book. As Ludwig Wittgenstein wrote in the Preface to his classic, *Philosophical Investigations* (1968), "this book crisscrosses the terrain from a variety of perspectives," creating an ever more synoptic and integrated view of the territory.

At the same time, different chapters have significantly different emphases. They attempt to tell the whole story while developing different themes. Therefore, the series of chapters forms a clear developmental pattern, from unity in diversity, to spirituality, to critical theory, to world government, to transformative praxis. The entire book tells the whole story much more fully than any of the chapters could do.

My purpose in writing this book was not profit, professional promotion, or personal satisfaction. My purpose is to disseminate these ideas as widely as possible and activate transformative praxis toward a new world order. The reader is encouraged to contact me for permission to reprint any of the chapters you find useful in your own struggles for a just world order.

I particularly wish to thank Dr. William Kovarik of Radford University, Dr. Richard Perkins of Canisius College, and Dr. J.W. Smith of the Institute for Economic Democracy for their invaluable contributions to the preparation of the manuscript for this book. I am very grateful to each of them.

I also want to thank a number of others who made unique and valuable contributions to this project, some of whom may not know the extent of their contribution: Eugenia Almand, Dr. Terence Amerasinghe, Dr. Dominique Balouki, Dr. Robert Ginsberg, Dr. Errol E. Harris, Dr. Peter Heller, Gary Hicks, Sarwar Kamal, Dr. Roger Kotila, Dr. Rashmi Mayur, E.P. Menon, Dr. Mujibur Rahman, and Phyllis Turk. I also want to thank Michael Dorfman who modified the NASA photo for the book cover. I am, of course, entirely responsible for the final result.

Chapter One: Introduction

Humanity at the Crossroads
Between Liberation and Self-Destruction

"Truth rises with a song." Melody pulsates in every life that is informed with purpose. Periods of fulfillment ring with sweet music. But at the great turning points of history, the beat of a march must be heard. In the face of upheavals and wild calamities the philosopher will be poorly armed if he does not believe that true insight bears within it the rhythm of a march. There is a vision that can be harder, fiercer, more urgent than anything on earth and which is nothing but man's return to his original moment. For why should not this return be a perpetual possibility? When the great original choice was to be made, man failed and the fabric of existence was destroyed. But ever since this eternal refusal, man's original uncorrupted state has constantly presented itself afresh. Not a moment passes but we could, if we dared, be restored to our pristine state of perfection. True vision therefore does not come to man after years of pondering; for it is nothing more nor less than clairvoyant perception of truth, a faculty which, like eyes and heart, has been vouchsafed to him from the first.

Erich Gutkind

*The need for profound human change emerges not only as an ethical or religious demand, not only as a psychological demand arising from the pathogenic nature of our present social character, but also as a condition for the sheer survival of the human race. Right living is no longer only the fulfillment of an ethical or religious demand. For the first time in history the **physical survival of the human race depends on a radical change of the human heart.** However, a change of the human heart is possible only to the extent that drastic economic and social changes occur that give the human heart the chance for change and the courage and vision to achieve it.*

Erich Fromm

At the dawn of the twenty-first century we stand at the end of the line. We must transform ourselves and our social, economic, and political world toward planetary maturity within the relatively near future, or we die – and the promise of the two-million-year-old human project comes to an end through nuclear holocaust, environmental collapse, endless wars, mass starvation, or planetary chaos. The time available for human immaturity has run out.

1. Our Historical Situation and Human Evolution

This book attempts to link the philosophical meaning of the human project with the multifaceted global crisis of the twenty-first century. The greatest philosophical questions of the ages – What is God? What is a human being? What is the meaning and purpose of life? What are justice, democracy, or freedom? – are today no longer theoretical luxuries of those rare persons called philosophers. These questions become a matter of desperate need, a vital life-line through which we struggle to survive and fulfill the hope and promise of our two-million-year-old human project.

We are at the end of the line, aware of the limited carrying capability of our tiny planet, aware of its fragile ecological balance that is rapidly being destroyed, aware of the immense misery of poverty and deprivation that encompasses at least a third of the world's inhabitants, and aware of our ability to entirely destroy the human world through nuclear holocaust, biological weapons, or other means, aware of the totalitarian and rapacious nature of our global economic institutions and the corresponding system of autonomous nation-states that are rapidly destroying cultures, ecosystems, and human beings in their greed for profits and power.

The chapters that follow describe the reasons why we are at the "end of the line." And they outline the promise of a new maturity and its liberating possibilities for the coming of age of humankind. They call for critical thought and action focusing on the resources at our disposal for altering the current suicidal trajectory of history. In terms of these resources, I have attempted to integrate critical thought in the sense of our possibilities for maturing politically, socially, and economically with another aspect of philosophical reflection in the sense of maturing spiritually from our adolescent condition of isolated, selfish egos to deeply aware, loving, communal persons who place the common good and the welfare of all above egoistic competitiveness and selfishness. I believe that human evolution has developed immense capacities for spirituality and critical rationality that are within us waiting to be realized, capacities entirely sufficient to deal with our present set of global crises.

But evolution alone is no longer sufficient. This can be expressed by saying that by the twentieth century the destiny of the planet and the future of humanity had been "delegated" to us. Do we wish to continue blindly and semi-consciously into the nightmare of global cataclysms and collective suicide awaiting us within the next century, or will we take responsibility for what has been delegated to us through nonviolent revolutionary thought and action for a transformed world? Do we wish to take the next step in human maturity, intelligently assessing our situation and dealing with it in a responsible, cooperative, and compassionate manner, which is the essence of human maturity? What has been "delegated" to us is not the task of inventing ourselves *ex nihilo*. We need but choose to realize the social and spiritual potentialities already within us and already prepared within our more-than-two-million-year history.

We know today that for vast aeons our human ancestors lived within the womb of nature, innumerable generations living and dying over hundreds of thousands of years leaving no signs of a self-conscious awareness of themselves as human beings. This vast prehistory might be called the "age of simple unity," a unity of awareness submerged within nature like that of the animals – the squirrels, the birds, and the fish. On the scale of evolution, we emerged from this age of womb-like unity only yesterday, perhaps 15,000 to 40,000 years ago, evinced in the astonishing phenomenon that people all over the world simultaneously began to create those early cave drawings – symbolic representations, used perhaps in early initiation rituals within the cavern depths, of the animals, the hunters, and the shamans wearing their animal masks.

A new consciousness emerged with these cave drawings during a period that some have called the "age of magic" (see Swimm and Berry, 1992). Perhaps the most significant event in the evolution of human consciousness, this transformation represents the early emergence of the power of picturing, and the beginnings of human self-consciousness, akin to that which emerges in the young child the first few months after birth. In this event, human beings discovered power, power over nature and other people, that became their obsession down to our present age. What this means will become clear as we proceed.

After this second age, the process of spiritual evolution accelerated with the simultaneous discovery of agriculture all over the world about 10,000 BCE. Agriculture and the beginnings of civilization soon led to another distinct transformation in human consciousness, giving birth to a third era often called the "age of mythology." All of nature becomes alive, and human beings relate to nature as a Thou, as a living consciousness in interaction with their emerging self-consciousness (see Frankfort, et. al., 1973). Young children today seem to pass through a phase similar to that which characterized the human species for perhaps six or eight thousand years prior to the emergence of our own epoch, an event that occurred during the famous Axis Period in human history.

From about the sixth century to the second century BCE, all over the world great individual philosophers or religious teachers arose who articulated world-views critical of the mythological era. These radical innovators promoted a separation of the self-conscious subject from nature as object, emphasized a detached reasoning according to an impersonal *logos* found in nature, and insisted upon human agency: ethical and personal responsibility. This era included Confucius, Lao Tzu and Chuang Tzu in China, Gautama Buddha and the author of the *Bhagavad Gītā* in India, the Hebrew Prophets in Israel, Zoroaster in Persia, and the Pre-Socratic philosophers in Mediterranean Greece.

The separation from nature beginning in the cave paintings during the age of magic results now in an acute subject-object split in which the world becomes an independent object for human consciousness and human beings become an object for themselves. Each human being can objectify his or her self, marking within each of us a split between the existential immediacy of our selves and our self-conscious ego objectifying that self. The self, now split between what it is and its egoistic self-objectification, forever struggles to heal that rupture, and the fear of suffering and death that accompany it; it struggles ceaselessly to become one and at peace. But in most people it struggles wrongly, attempting to possess itself through self-mastery, to possess others as confirmation of its insecure ego, or to possess property and economic security against the certainty of its death. The drive for power replaces the fullness of life.

This phenomenon operates not only on the individual level, but on the level of collectivities as well: groups and nations face the world as a threat to their insecure collective egos in a posture of defense, aggression, alliances, or suspicion. This inner split, full of fear, anxiety, and disquiet, culminates in the phenomenon of modern capitalism, the social, economic, and political anti-system characterizing the past five centuries that is premised on the acquisitive, greedy, anxiety-ridden, and grasping self, on the individual level and on the level of collectivities.

Many advanced thinkers concerning spiritual matters today believe human beings are on the verge of a breakthrough to a new era in human consciousness, a fifth age beyond the era of the fractured human ego. We are ready to move beyond the era of the grasping, greedy self to a redeemed self in communion with the world and with other human beings, and capable of living in peace and simplicity on our beautiful planet. In the twenty-first century, the evolutionary process has made us capable of planetary maturity. But we must consciously decide to take the next step before it is too late. There exist many signs in literature, poetry, philosophy, and art of an awareness that the ego must die, and that we are in the process of another transformation (e.g., Gebser, 1985).

The redeemed self does not give up its uniqueness and individuality, but fully realizes uniqueness and individuality for the first time – and becomes ever more deeply in contact with the ecstatic fullness of life. In addition, many advanced thinkers on social issues today believe that human beings are on the verge of a social transformation from a history of systems of domination and exploitation to new self-aware economic and social systems premised on human dignity, human needs, and harmony with the precious environment that sustains life on this planet. These thinkers have developed systemic critiques of the present world system and have proposed alternative economic and social systems based on sustainable, critically aware premises that could lead to a genuinely transformed world order.

These two sets of thinkers rarely see eye to eye and tend to operate with quite different assumptions. I argue that both transformations are necessary if we are to survive and flourish, but neither is sufficient alone. This book attempts to explicate their interpenetration and mutual implication. Planetary maturity encompasses both.

This process of spiritual and social transformation in our day includes a series of fundamental paradigm changes, although it goes much deeper into human consciousness and history than that of a paradigm or model by which we operate. Yet several new paradigms have burst upon the intellectual life of the twentieth century that humanity has yet to appropriate. Let me mention here just four (Martin, 1999, pp. 1-18). First, the emergent evolutionary paradigm: the ideas of Errol E. Harris, Pierre Teilhard de Chardin, Alfred North Whitehead, Nicholas Berdyaev, Samuel Alexander, Eric Gutkind, and others that something great and precious is emerging with human life out of the evolutionary process. Human beings are integral to the evolution of the universe and the natural order. This is replacing the older paradigm, often asserted within the Existentialist movement, for example, in which human life and consciousness seemed to be a meaningless cosmic accident.

Secondly, the ecological paradigm of the interdependence of organism and environment is replacing the older paradigm of the domination of the human ego over nature. A mature understanding of organisms and their inseparability from their environment finds ways to promote successful interdependence and sees domination and exploitation as self-destructive. Thirdly, the sub-atomic paradigm of the inapplicability of so-called causal necessity at the micro-level of matter and energy is replacing the older paradigm of a possible human control over causal determinism according to known mechanical laws. This new paradigm revealed by twentieth-century science unveils our universe as a *mysterium magnum* within which the traditional distinctions between idealism and materialism, between matter and spirit, or between time and eternity may have vanished.

Fourth, the Einsteinian paradigm that has revealed the interrelation of the space-time-energy matrix at the macro-level supersedes the Newtonian paradigm of absolute, separate dimensions of space, time, and matter in motion. The Einsteinian universe exhibits a wholeness beyond anything our pictorial imaginations can encompass and points the way, we will see, toward a philosophy of wholeness that is integral to a mature view of the universe. The false power derived from the ability of the human ego to objectify and picture the world is coming to an end.

With all these paradigmatic shifts, and others that are emerging, we are realizing what is perhaps most fundamental of all: the universe cannot be pictured by the human ego-imagination. What began at Lascaux and Altamira and the other cave painting sites during the age of magic is coming to an end with the paradigm shifts of the twentieth century. We are realizing that the universe we live in cannot be pictured by the human mind; it cannot be imagined or grasped, any more than the egoistic self-image can picture the reality of ourselves. The magical attempt to grasp and manipulate the world by creatures who assume they can stand apart from the world and control it draws to a close in our era. These paradigm shifts point toward the awakening in human beings of a new awareness, a new oneness, and a new compassion, beyond the adolescent fetishes and pseudo-realities we once thought we could manipulate with our ego-imaginations.

Things are one at a much greater level of unity than the ego can imagine, and we are part of that oneness, as the great mystics of all ages and cultures have repeatedly told us. As we will see, all things resonate at a level of oneness that does not preclude diversity, individuality, or freedom, but instead makes these possible. Our task is to realize that oneness with nature and with one another toward which the emerging paradigms are pointing. And our task is to realize that oneness in our economic and social systems as well, a oneness that makes possible freedom and diversity and openness into an as yet to be determined future.

These paradigms also have their roots in a history of our modern era of the last five centuries, and in an historical development of humankind that goes back well over two thousand years. This history has prepared the way for the social forms of mature, democratic social and economic institutions, with their respect for human rights, human dignity, and community, that must emerge worldwide in the next century if we are to survive and flourish on this planet. This means that human beings will begin to take responsibility for not only themselves but for the common good of their communities and the planetary society with which they are inseparably interdependent. The task may seem immense, for it means transforming the institutions presently dominant in history that have been built around this false ego-consciousness, institutions that will condition future generations to live according to their dictates.

On the other hand, we are not without immense resources, as I hope to make clear in this book: a new human maturity is just around the corner if we but have the wisdom to actualize it. The most pervasive and destructive of the global institutions with which we must cope are the modern "neo-liberal" economic system and its alliance with the dangerous and regressive system of "sovereign" nation-states. For neither of these is predicated on planetary wholeness and the common good of all citizens of planet earth. In Part Three of this book, we will examine our modern economic system in some depth and attempt to show that its assumptions and mode of operation promote neither the welfare of all nor human survival on this planet. Yet here too there exist global movements of concerned citizens acutely aware of these dangers and working to transform our present world system in the direction of social and economic maturity.

Today we face the most immense concentrations of wealth in human history, billions of dollars, concentrated in private hands, unaccountable to the common good, and institutionalized to maximize ever further accumulations of private profit. Transnational corporations, with assets larger than some nation-states, are institutionalized around the sole goal of a perpetual increase of their already unimaginable wealth. If we define "madness" as the inability to cognize adequately and respond to the matrix of objective, intersubjective, and subjective environments that encompass our lives, even to the point where this leads to suicide or the probability of self-destruction, then the dominant ethos of our era appears quite mad.

Why is it that so few people in the first-world have compassion for the immense suffering that goes on in the third-world? Why is it that so few people in the first-world even seem to care about the future of our planet or future generations of human beings that must live with the devastation we are creating? Why is it that first-world nations cannot think creatively about the future but remain trapped in the illusion that ever more military prowess will somehow create security or prosperity within our fragile world?

In the face of the threat to human existence that human beings encounter at the dawn of the twenty-first century, I do not exaggerate by saying that we live in a kind of mad, global circus; a kind of lethal ga-ga land, a Coney Island society run by the clowns of investment and finance and policed with all seriousness by the adolescent minds in the Pentagon, CIA, and third-world dictatorships. To many, the entire dominant global system (or, better, "anti-system") looks like an insane asylum: economic madmen, political terrorists, or military lunatics playing mindless and deadly games of power and profit maximization while the entire human project, two million years of human evolution, runs down the drain of history toward imminent self-destruction.

As many thoughtful people have pointed out, the development of nuclear weapons systems alone, putting the world for decades into a nightmarish balance of ever possible instantaneous holocaust, cannot be described as anything but insane. Yet we can also understand this madness as but the childish bravado of human beings and social institutions badly in need of growing up.

The present economic, social, and political anti-system of the world entirely omits one fifth of the global population who live in what the U.N. calls "absolute poverty," a condition of imminent starvation and misery unimaginable to most people in the first-world. Another two fifths of the human population barely scrape by, being used by the dominant anti-system for cheap labor and resources in order to feed the mindless luxuries and useless, unsustainable excesses of the first-world. Meanwhile, the global population continues to explode. Some predictions forecast ten to twelve billion people on our planet by the year 2025 (Caldicott, 1992).

The drastically expanding earth population is causing massive social dislocation around the world as populations exceed the agricultural and economic carrying capability of their environments. This contributes to the continuing growth of unimaginable poverty for much of the world's population despite the so-called "green" agricultural revolution and often increased economic activity in much of the world. The Earth's present population acts as a drain on the earth's limited resources that will be catastrophic unless this phenomenon is turned around in the near future.

The world had only about one billion people in the year 1800. By 1925, the population had doubled to two billion. By 1960, only 35 years later, the world had three billion people (Corson, ed., 1990, p. 24). At the dawn of the third millennium we have exceeded six billion and are currently adding eighty million persons per year to the population of our planet. What madness prevents the world from working urgently together to prevent this coming suicidal catastrophe? What madness urges us to continue building weapons of mass destruction instead?

At the same time, global warming is an established scientific fact. The ambient temperature of the earth is rising. The glaciers are melting. Violent storms and droughts are increasing. Phytoplankton in the oceans (the base of the entire food chain) are dying from unknown causes, perhaps from the warming of the seas. Growing desertification is taking place worldwide, along with a yearly massive loss of fertile agricultural lands, daily extinction of species, and an on-going deforestation of the earth, including destruction of the trees that produce much of the oxygen we breathe and bond the carbon dioxide that our industrial processes and automobiles produce. These facts are recorded in book after book (Brown et al., 1999; Harris, 1993; Flavin et al., 2002).

Despite this, the pouring of industrial and automotive wastes into the atmosphere and the burning of fossil fuels continues without any serious measures being contemplated for their elimination. Auto sales are at all time highs. Oil exploration and the building of pipelines continues at unprecedented levels. Scientists have established the fact that global warming is steadily changing the ecological balance of the planet. Yet no substantial changes are contemplated for the dominant systems of human activity that are a major contributor to this process. The shrinking of glaciers in Alaska, Greenland, Tibet, and elsewhere has reached rapid and unprecedented levels, and the number of icebergs breaking off from both polar caps has steadily increased throughout the last half of the twentieth century. They have discovered recently that the North Pole is now open water and no longer an ice cap (Brown, 2001, p. 27).

Scientists have stated over and over again that the effects of global warming are likely to cause major climate changes worldwide. Some areas will experience widespread drought and desertification while others will be subject to severe and irregular weather patterns, making stable crop production difficult or impossible. About one third of the world's population live within sixty kilometers of the sea. (Caldicott, 1992, p. 25). Melting polar regions will also raise sea levels and flood coastal areas globally, displacing hundreds of millions of people worldwide and flooding precious coastal farming areas. Yet serious discussion of the system that produces these effects is off limits for much of the mass media and the governmental and business executives who are determining policy.

The list of serious environmental problems goes on and on. Forests, which produce much of the oxygen we breathe, are disappearing at the rate of an area half the size of California every year. Phytoplankton in the oceans, the other major source of oxygen, are dying at alarming rates. The ozone layer that protects all life from lethal solar radiation is in the process of disintegration. Soil erosion from the farming methods of agribusiness or from the enforced poverty in the third-world amounts to untold billions of tons per year, leading to a growing desertification worldwide.

Meanwhile, the world spends nearly a trillion dollars per year in military expenditures, almost half of that by the United States alone, an investment primarily to be sure the present world anti-system remains in place and is not altered in the direction of sanity, human decency, or a modicum of rationality. These and other facts will be documented and discussed in the course of this book, but it may not be an exaggeration to say the present "world order" is a kind of cruel and sadistic circus run by substantially mad men and women, mostly men, who refuse to examine their self-destructive behavior. More charitably put, it appears clear that such a "world order" is childish at best, an adolescent nightmare badly in need of maturing to a level in which we begin to take responsibility for ourselves, for our planetary home, and for the welfare of future generations.

But this worldwide anti-system is not so anarchic as I have depicted. For those who run this global asylum, themselves inmates, are working diligently to further consolidate and institutionalize their non-system in fundamental ways. They are running the U.S. economy at the expense of the rest of the world (Hudson, 2003). Second, they are trying to transform international law to protect transnational corporations from the legal systems of national governments through global regulations like the *North American Free Trade Agreement*, the *Free Trade Agreement of the Americas, World Trade Organization* regulations, or other economic, trade or, "structural adjustment" regulations imposed on the world by the International Monetary Fund and the World Bank. Such trade regulations or imposed economic adjustments are written to protect the rapacity of corporations from the environmental and labor laws in the countries that their business operations exploit, and to free capital from the trade restrictions of individual nation-states (Chossudovsky, 1998).

Third, the Pentagon announced in its 1996 document called "Vision 20/20" the goal of global military control of the world: through the ability to entirely destroy a third-world army with impunity (as it did with Iraq in 1991 and 2003) and through the militarization of space that would give absolute control to the United States over the entire world, perhaps ending forever the hope of the world's majority for a decent life free from poverty, exploitation, misery, and death (Shorr, 1999, pp. 14-16). An even marginally sane world order would be working night and day to eliminate all weapons of war on Earth. Can there be any greater madness than the attempt to place these weapons in orbit?

Yet, for many thoughtful persons, the terrible terrorist attacks on the United States of 11 September 2001 have driven home again the need for reexamining our world order. The world faces multiple crises of a planetary magnitude, some of which are outlined above: global destruction of our environment, global militarism, war-making, and weapons of mass destruction, global poverty, misery and social disintegration, and the global population explosion. If these crises did not seem to affect us directly in the relatively prosperous and secure first-world countries, 11 September should serve as a wake-up call that we cannot separate ourselves from the immense misery of the world order around us.

We live on a tiny, interrelated and interdependent planet. We are all in this mess together, and the way into the future cannot be more war, militarism, surveillance, and destruction of human trust and liberty. It cannot be more divisiveness and fracturing of our fragile, interdependent world, for this will only perpetuate the cycle of violence and destruction at a time when only the cooperative efforts of people and governments around the world can address these multiple global crises.

After several chapters enumerating the gruesome details of world militarism, social chaos, population explosion and environmental destruction, the 1995 *Report of the Commission on Global Governance* emphasizes that there can be no future for the world without global cooperation and unity among citizens, non-governmental organizations, cultures, corporations, and governments in addressing these problems. Global conflict, violence and more brutal imperial relationships will only exacerbate these crises (Klare, 2002). We must examine the foundations of our current world order to find an alternative path ahead, for the causes of these planetary crises are not separate from the causes of global terrorism, fear, and hatred. But these past and impending calamities do not signal the end of the matter by any means. As stated above, all over the world there appears to be an awakening going on, spiritually and socially, and people are beginning to take responsibility for the human destiny that has been "delegated" to us.

Imperial systems – Egypt of the Torah, Rome of the Christian New Testament, the Holy Roman Empire of the European Middle Ages, Spain of the Conquistadors, Holland, Portugal, Britain and France of the age of slavery and colonialism, the United States in this era of neo-colonialism – always insist on their eternity, legitimacy, and right to endure. They arrogate to themselves the place of God and repress all struggles for freedom and justice within their spheres of domination. They attempt to displace the deep historicity of the divine-human spirit emerging from the world historical processes with proclamations of their eternity, moral self-justification, and role as the carriers of civilization. Witness the speeches given by every president of the United States since the Second World War: the U.S. is good, and stands for civilization, freedom, and justice in the world.

Such simplistic formulas, establishing a dualism between one segment of the human population and the rest of the world, create ideological simplifications that discourage genuine thought about the roots of our multiple world crises and possible planetary solutions. For we are beginning to understand that no solutions are possible that are not planetary in scope. Ethnocentrism must give way to a planetary perspective.

For those who take their stand in world solidarity with the processes of awakening, transformation, and liberation emerging from the depths of existence, there can be no compromise with imperial systems striving to freeze history into their patterns of domination and limitation. All imperial systems are limited in scope and do not embrace the welfare of the entire planet. The struggle for the liberation of nature, like the struggle for human liberation against economic and imperial domination – the struggle for freedom, justice, and peace for all persons on this planet – is also the struggle in world solidarity with the awakening divine-human spirit emerging from the deepest heart of the universe. We are witnessing the struggle of human beings for a new social and spiritual maturity.

2. The Central Themes of the Following Chapters

Part One, Chapters Two and Three below, attempts to show the necessary integration of spiritual and social, political, and economic transformation by approaching the issue from two quite different thematic principles. Chapter Two argues that the most fundamental principle arising from the conceptual revolutions or paradigm shifts of the twentieth century (the ecological, the Einsteinian, the micro-particle, and the sociological) is the "principle of unity-in-diversity." This principle, arising out of our scientific understanding of the universe itself, serves as a fundamental paradigm for comprehending personal maturity and social-economic maturity.

This principle is elucidated in Chapter Two as a foundation for the subsequent chapters. I argue that this principle is a paradigm around which we can and should be organizing our thinking and acting in all areas of human existence. Evidence for this new paradigm is abundant, and examples of it are to be found everywhere at the dawn of the new millennium. These examples can serve as a great source of clarity and hope for our thinking and acting.

Chapter Three expresses the new holism embodied in this book in terms of the principle of "deep nonviolence." I characterize "nonviolence" here not primarily as a method of making social change without perpetuating the cycle of violence but instead as a principle pointing to a transformed world that has substantially reduced not only war and terrorism but the violence of domination, exploitation, falsehood, and dehumanization. The chapter tries to show that a truly nonviolent world order cannot be realized without the inclusion of truly critical social theory (the tradition associated with Karl Marx and others), nor can the tradition of critical social theory lead us to a liberated world order in the absence of a spiritual transformation toward "compassion." Finally, it explores the role of nonviolent direct action in this equation.

Part Two, comprising Chapters Four through Six, constitutes a sequence that attempts to build an argument concerning spirituality at the dawn of the twenty-first century. Chapter Four traces the breakthroughs in the understanding of religion that have emerged from twentieth-century scholarship. It shows that much of our popular sense of religion remains "pre-Copernican," out of tune with the growing intellectual and scientific maturity of human beings within history. On this basis Chapter Five then attempts an assessment of contemporary work on spirituality and mysticism in order to reveal the immense possibilities that are open to us in the light of a "post-Copernican," mature understanding of religion and spirituality. Finally, Chapter Six grounds our possibilities for spiritual and religious "breakthrough" in concrete social-scientific understandings of the processes of human growth and maturity.

Part Two, therefore, attempts to take spirituality out of the realm of rumor, confusion, and psycho-babble and ground our possibilities in a coherent philosophy of spiritual awakening based on modern scholarship and social-scientific thought, as far as this is possible. Spiritual awakening appears, therefore, as the next step in a human maturity for which human beings are quite ready and not as some esoteric transcendence reserved for a few geniuses and hermits scattered here and there throughout world history.

Part Three, Chapters Seven through Nine, forms another unit that explores a critical understanding of the present global economic system and attempts to articulate the principles of an alternative system. Chapter Seven formulates the philosophical basis for a transformed socialist theory, drawing on the insights regarding ethical and spiritual maturity presented in Part Two. Chapter Eight examines the tradition of "critical theory" stemming from the work of Marx and others with a focus on the maturing of critical theory, the overcoming of earlier dogmatisms and misunderstandings concerning the work of Marx, and the continuing evolution of the role and function of critical theory throughout the twentieth century. Chapter Nine then presents a contemporary understanding of the phenomenon of the world economic system of the past five centuries and the possibility of a transformed socialism in the light of human spiritual maturity and the maturing of critical theory itself.

Part Four, Chapters Ten through Twelve, attempts to apply the previous themes philosophically to our planetary world system. It shows the necessity for non-military, democratic world government and its connection with what I call the "three sources of transformative spirituality": the ethical, the mystical and the eschatological. Chapter Ten sets the stage for this development by explicating the principle of unity-in-diversity (introduced in Chapter Two) in relation to world order and further grounding that principle in the insights of human spirituality. Chapter Eleven shows the complete compatibility of critical theory and mature socialism with the proposed *Constitution for the Federation of Earth*. Chapter Twelve presents an in-depth investigation of the principle of unity-in-diversity in relation to non-military, democratic world government.

The final section of the book, Part Five, comprising Chapters Thirteen and Fourteen, returns to some of the themes of Part One, the themes of praxis and the question of *how* we go about deeply transforming ourselves and our world order. These themes are now, however, treated in the light of the argument of the entire book, including the new understanding of human spirituality from Part Two, of critical theory and mature socialism from Part Three, and of the meaning and dynamics of democratic world government from Part Four. Chapter Thirteen presents specific proposals for a liberated world political and economic system. The concluding Chapter Fourteen attempts to underline the existential and ethical sense of truth that has formed the basis for this volume and repudiate those forms of post-modern relativism and skepticism that destroy action and hope. It ends with ten concrete recommendations for a praxis of hope that can form the basis for action toward a transformed world order at the dawn of our new millennium.

3. Three Sources of the Transformative Imperative

From this outline of chapter themes, it should be clear that the chapters below are not directed toward criticism and delegitimation of the present world order alone. They also explore the vision of what I call the "practical utopia" that is available to us as a regulative ideal for social and spiritual transformations, and they explore our real possibilities social and spiritual transformation. For the resources that our long evolution has bequeathed to us are immense. And because of events and breakthroughs in the twentieth century, we are in a position at the cusp of the twenty-first century for the first time to tap these resources and create a truly new world. Unless we find fulfillment, personal spiritual fulfillment and social-economic fulfillment, in a world of peace, justice, and freedom, there is little hope for the planet or for our children.

That is why this book is a call to transformative maturity, not mere reform. Authentic ethical-spiritual awareness is nonviolently revolutionary, as I hope to show, and militates toward mature human fulfillment in the spiritual and social-economic dimensions. For these two dimensions are deeply interrelated. The critically informed understanding that social-economic relations deeply condition our consciousness and the dimensions of law, culture, religion, politics, and ideas are absolutely essential to a maturity oriented praxis. Critical social and economic theory can reveal the hidden structures of oppression and dehumanization in contemporary society, structures that are veiled by self-justifying ideology. But critical theory does this through a criterion of liberation that it cannot fully justify through the limited forms of critical reason. What I call a "utopian demand" for a transformed human reality permeates the human condition in a way that cannot be reduced to any scientific form or rationally discernible dialectic of history (Jay, 1984; Boswell and Chase-Dunn, 2000). I hope to show that this "utopian" criterion of liberation requires the realization of compassion and the spiritual-intellectual maturity of the whole human being.

Our institutions, in a complex way, condition human consciousness, mass producing the immaturity, alienation, and commodification of this era, and yet they are also influenced by the progressive and liberating forms of human thought. Ultimately, the liberating forms of thought have history on their side, for growing up, as Aristotle insisted, is ultimately an evolutionary process not entirely within our control but driven by the inherited potential within us. Yet given the current global crises faced by our world, human initiative becomes vitally important. The complex influences between our institutions and our consciousness work both ways, in dialectical reciprocity. Immature institutions reproduce immaturity in the new generation; mature institutions can promote maturity within the new generation.

In terms of human spirituality, three sources of emancipatory praxis are elucidated in this book: First, the mystical breakthrough to the One, the vast fullness-emptiness of things that activates a compassionate identification with the other (drawing on thinkers like Jiddu Krishnamurti, Raimon Panikkar, and Meister Eckhart). Second, the ethical realization of the other person as an end in his or her self (Immanuel Kant), as an infinity that cannot be appropriated to my totalization of the world (Emmanuel Levinas), or as standing in the relationship of community with me in a way that puts me in revolutionary conflict with all systems of domination, dehumanization, and exploitation (Enrique Dussel). Third, the utopic-eschatological call that can inform awareness, whereby history is summoned to fulfillment and fruition in a transformed world of peace, justice, freedom, and love (Errol E. Harris, Pierre Teilhard de Chardin, Nicolas Berdyaev, Gene Gebser, Eric Gutkind, Enrique Dussel, and others).

These sources of human emancipation can be conceptually distinguished, but I believe that in our everyday awareness they blend into one another. They represent aspects of a new maturity that I hope to elucidate in this book. In our ethical-spiritual lives, which are often punctuated by "moments of awakening," one or another of these sources of our deepest humanity may be most distinct, but probably all of them are present in some degree, interfused, in the background of our everyday awareness. We have only to begin attending to these aspects of our experience (which are systematically ignored by our present educational, cultural, social, and economic institutions) for them to begin to emerge more clearly.

We can see something of this interfusing of the sources of emancipatory praxis if we look at the eschatological call itself, that has two fundamental dimensions that should be distinguished and will be explored further in this book. These dimensions might be called the "internal" and "external" sources of the call. First, the utopic-eschatological ideal arises from our experience of the ethical, the infinity of the other person, or authentic community. We discover in our awareness a perpetual critique of all that dominates and dehumanizes human beings and the corresponding ideal of a transformed world. We might liken the ethical dimension to the "natural law" tradition in Western thought, expressed in one way by St. Paul's claim that God has written the moral law on our hearts (Romans 2:14-15).

But the same natural ethical law includes within it, as Kant pointed out, an ideal for a world of a universal kingdom of ends in themselves, a world of peace, justice, and freedom where the dignity of human beings, instead of their "price," determines personal relationships and institutional structures. These ideas have radical implications, since the intrinsic nature of our present system is to use those who are poor and have only their labor to sell as exploitable tools for the enrichment of those who are wealthy enough to own some of the means of production.

The second, the "external" source of the utopic-eschatological call, arises from an awareness related to the mystical but including within itself an intuition of the world process insofar as the One beyond time and the temporal dimension share a common divine source. This "external" call was heard by the great spokespersons of the eschatological dimension, including some Hebrew Prophets, Jesus, Meister Eckhart, and Nicolas Berdyaev, and it can be heard today by those who approximate this awareness. I discuss the implications of these modes of human awareness at some length in the chapters that follow, with an eye to how these potentialities within all ordinary human beings can be realized in the face of our present global crisis.

Each of these sources of emancipatory praxis can be demoted to a merely evolutionary imperative (as opposed to a "categorical" imperative). This demotion was even done by Immanuel Kant in his social-political thought and as is often done by many practitioners of Zen or other forms of contemporary spirituality. It is also done by contemporary critical social theorists such as Michael David Levin or Jürgen Habermas. This demoting of the imperative that confronts us in authentic mystical, ethical, or eschatological awareness partly reflects an understanding of the concept of "deep transformation" as something that applies only to social-political conditions not currently present in the societies in which these theorists operate. I think these persons are mistaken in this, but that is not the central point here.

The central point is that human growth and maturity comes in stages, as I will detail in Chapter Six. As each of us can confirm in our personal lives, growth is transformative and comes in breakthroughs and jumps, not merely in incremental changes. The central point is that to be merely evolutionary in our approach, and not transformative, is to miss something fundamental about our human situation and about our historical situation at the dawn of the twenty-first century. This misses the cosmic significance of the human project itself, of the present moment, and of the spiritual dimension of human life.

Many practitioners of mysticism, or proponents of authentic ethics or critical social theory, do not find the system quite so bad as I have described it. They flourish within zones of imperial domination where the "open veins of Latin America," the starving and maimed children of Iraq and their agonized mothers, the genocidal despair of the people of East Timor, or the crushing misery of child labor and exploitation in Africa and Southeast Asia are not immediately apparent.

But awareness of infinity in the face of the other (for Emmanuel Levinas) or awareness of the imperative to do what is right regardless of my inclinations (for Kant) issues in "absolute" responsibilities. I will argue that a mature person faces just such "absolute" responsibilities. In the face of the present world system of blood, despair, misery, and death, these absolute responsibilities can only be deeply transformative responsibilities: the world system must be fundamentally transformed from a system of death to a system of life.

The chapters below contain much discussion of Karl Marx, Jürgen Habermas, and other critical thinkers in the post-Marxist revolutionary tradition. I argue that critical theory or some form of rationally grounded, mature socialism is a necessary but not a sufficient condition for emancipatory praxis. The revolutionary inspiration that led Marx to live in poverty and devote his life to the cause of humanity was not only critical and theoretical but also a consequence of some degree of awareness of one or more of these spiritual sources of human liberation.

Marx was an atheist steeped in the Bible. As an atheist he might not associate the source of his compassion and solidarity with the victims of class society with a command from God. Yet the Christian-Marxist thinker José Miranda argues that Marx believed in God precisely because he believed in justice (1986, p. 191). In terms of my argument concerning "spiritual maturity" in Chapter Five, this is plausible. The metaphors by which we point to emancipatory intuitions may be theistic, as in

Christianity, Judaism, or Islam, or non-theistic, as in Buddhism, Marxism, or some forms of atheism. The point is not to bicker about the metaphors themselves but to understand their significance as metaphors and to realize a transformed world.

As Enrique Dussel expresses this principle in *Ethics and Community*, this emancipatory imperative is the imperative revealed by God in the Bible when the Bible is taken in terms of the transformative theme at its heart (1993, pp. 15-16). But I am arguing here that this is also available to all persons through something like a "natural law" written on the human heart, available to us through one or all of the sources of deep human awareness: the mystical, the ethical, and the eschatological. Different religions have emphasized different aspects of these sources in their scriptures and traditions. Christianity, for example, has emphasized the eschatological aspect of awareness, whereas Buddhism has emphasized the mystical aspect. The new human maturity actualizes the spiritual aspects of human existence hopefully free of the dogmas and bigotries that have plagued traditional religions.

It must be underlined, however, that this book is not intended to focus on the "spiritual" side of existence at the expense of the body, the material conditions of existence, or an analysis of human institutions. Just as the spiritual and mystical traditions must be enlarged to include institutions and the material conditions of existence, so too must the critical tradition of Marxism be enlarged to include the ethical and spiritual aspects of existence. And both must encompass a new understanding of the body and the material world. For the mind or spirit can no longer be conceived as a separate substance apart from the body (and nature), as many traditional religions tended to do. Nor can the mind or spirit be conceived as a mere epiphenomenon of the body, as Marxism tended to do.

Philosopher Michael David Levin (1988) argues eloquently for the need to include the body and its capabilities in our articulation of a critical social perspective directed to a just and sane world. But the human body is at once a self and a center of awareness. As Levin indicates, "listening" is more than a sensory mechanism involving the ears, just as "seeing" is more than a sensory mechanism involving the eyes. The "spiritual" need not be separated from the body-self, that can be conceived as under a variety of metaphors, including that of a "radio receiver" with the ability to receive the deepest resonances issuing from the heart of the universe. The body need not be separated from the spirit through an ontological dualism. As long ago as the thirteenth century, Thomas Aquinas initiated a rethinking of the Neoplatonic repudiation of matter and the body through arguing for a necessary individuation of the spirit provided by the flesh. In the twenty-first century, we are in a position to heal the divorce between matter and spirit through a new philosophical and spiritual maturity.

The triune awareness that provides the sources of the transformative imperative need not be epistemologically divorced from the body and its capabilities. The body contains within it, as Levin argues, following Aristotle, capacities that require development and activation for a mature, fulfilled happiness to be made possible. The mature development of our capacities means the activation of our bodily capacities for awareness of the mystical, the ethical, and the eschatological. These capacities may or may not issue from what Levin asserts as an "ontological attunement with being" in infancy. But these capacities do not require the metaphysical assertion of a non-material "spirit" to make them possible.

Neither does the transformative imperative issue from a positivistic materialism that makes of our bodily and spiritual wholeness a mere epiphenomenon of blind mechanical processes, as dogmatic Marxism tended to assert. The emancipatory imperative is an imperative for the transformation of this world, this person, and this history in their complexity and wholeness. It is fully incarnate and demands an incarnated world of peace, justice, and freedom. It would be strange if the triune aspects of awareness at the source of this imperative were themselves not a possibility of our bodily, incarnate nature. Maturity drives toward wholeness, toward integration.

The chapters in this volume attempt to explore our possibilities for social and spiritual transformation within the context of a world writhing in agony, chaos, and injustice and faced with imminent collapse. They focus on the liberating possibilities of critical rationality and spiritual awakening, two dimensions of liberating praxis ultimately in harmony with one another. And they attempt to present a picture of our human situation and our human potentialities as broadly as possible within the space of a single volume. Yet they also try to grapple directly with the nexus of concrete, global crises that we face at the cusp of the twenty-first century and suggest specific courses of action directed toward our survival and flourishing on this planet in a decent, just, and free planetary society. I hope the reader can share something of my sense of urgency and crisis and my sense of tremendous hope, since today we stand so close to realizing our true destiny and some of our highest potentialities as human beings within this holy cosmos.

4. The Theme of Transformative Praxis
But what are we concretely to do in the face of this apparent global madhouse and the immense social and economic systems that protect it? The task of human transformation and survival on the surface of it appears

overwhelming. Yet emergent evolutionary forces are at work beyond human control, even beyond the control of the human adolescents who build and deploy their nuclear weapons. In our two-million-year human history, the several transformations of consciousness have occurred spontaneously all over the globe and have happened entirely without conscious human agency.

Our age shows many signs that this is happening again and that we are being transformed beyond the age of ego-consciousness toward an age of unity, cooperation, harmony, and peace. Brian Swimme and Thomas Berry appropriately call this new age "ecozoic," implying a new interrelationship among human beings and a new sense of interdependency between human beings and their planetary environment (1992, ch. 13). We are almost being forced to give up what we never possessed in the first place, and to live with a new, non-acquisitive simplicity and unity. Yet the chapters in this volume struggle with the problem of what we can do and how we can do it. They attempt to be as concrete as possible in their suggestions for action.

The time is ripe for institutional transformation as well. The peoples of the third-world are growing ever more aware that they are forever condemned under the present world system to function as an underdeveloped service area for first-world exploiters (Boswell and Chase Dunn, 2000; Smith, 2003a). The world is ripe for another breakthrough in social-political consciousness as well. There exist many signs that economists and social thinkers are becoming aware of the need for a sane economics premised on sustainability, human dignity, and human needs. These two tendencies may well merge into an entirely new era before we know it.

In a broad way, we might say that awareness of the social demand for political democracy first exploded in the eighteenth century, just as awareness of the possibilities and dynamics of historical progress in democracy and freedom exploded in the nineteenth century with Hegel and Marx, and awareness of the new paradigms enumerated above has exploded in the twentieth century. The culmination of this process may well happen in the twenty-first century. Yet given that the process will certainly require struggle and massive activism by the peoples of the earth, what is the role of reflective and critical thought in general in this race against time toward a genuinely new age (Martin, 1999)?

Critically thoughtful persons can investigate and interpret these processes and awaken people to their significance. We can explore the implications of the emergent evolutionary paradigm and the other paradigms creating a revolution in twentieth-century thought. We can critically explore the human ego-structure and point out its devastating consequences, such as its links to institutionalized greed and war. We can elucidate the ethical and religious dimensions of human existence, of which the human project has not yet even begun to become clear, and articulate their deep, important implications for the transformation of consciousness and society. We can articulate what Levinas calls the "absolute ethical responsibility" encountered when we meet the other person as Other in the genuine encounter of "face to face." And we can organize and take action to alter existing institutions of oppression and domination and create alternative institutions premised on rationality, compassion, and the sanctity of human beings and the earth.

As individuals, we can also meditate, or practice some form of spiritual discipline, to awaken ourselves to the point where we speak with authority about the transformed consciousness confronting human beings in their evolutionary journey. And we can awaken ourselves to a vision of what I call "practical utopia," the genuine possibility of a rational and compassionate world society that lies just the other side of the present crisis of humanity. On this basis we must found our thought and action: on a critique of the present insane world system and on something wholly positive – the entirely real and common-sense utopic light that shines from the future and realizes the highest potentialities of our two-million-year-old human journey toward this future. The new human maturity is full of authentic hope.

Philosophy and critical reflection have long been associated with the ivory tower of academia, and academic institutions worldwide have evolved as hegemonic institutions elucidating and protecting the dominant ideologies of nations and power systems. As critically thoughtful and compassionate persons, we can intellectually leave the ivory tower mentality and become activists for world peace and a transformed human reality.

All over the world at present, especially in the third-world, thinkers in Asia, Africa, and Latin America are working out philosophies of liberation. The liberation of human beings from war, from the outmoded system of nation-states, from undemocratic forms of oppression and tyranny, but perhaps most fundamentally from the global economic system that is currently an anti-system of death, starvation, and misery for at least one and a half billion members of the human population. This book envisions our resources for survival and flourishing on this planet through a philosophy and a spirituality of liberation that draws on several traditions, from Marxism to Buddhism to Christianity, while attempting to see the human situation independently of any of them. Human beings are in the process of growing up.

For those of us in the first-world, it takes a minimum of courage and

decency to develop a critical consciousness and begin to take the side of
the poor and oppressed. Yet this is the beginning of a real ethical journey
into compassion, solidarity, and a truly transformed world in which all
human beings are treated with equality and respect. For our brothers and
sisters in many third-world countries, such philosophical activity risks
dismissal from a person's job, exile, torture, even death. The forces of
intellectual and social repression, taught by the military and ideological
representatives of global capital, are real and they are vicious. This alone
should indicate the moral and social significance of the philosophy of
liberation and of our solidarity with the poor and the oppressed. This
book reflects many years of reading, thought, and critical reflection as well
as my personal journey toward openness, solidarity, and transformation.

We must encourage our young people to think critically so they see
the gigantic lie of human greed and power on which the present global anti-
system is based. We must help activate in ourselves and in the peoples of
the third-world an awareness of oppression and the transformative desire to
become engaged agents of our destiny. We must be guided by the utopic
vision of a united humanity in a just, free, democratic, non-military world
based on sustainable development, cooperation rather than competition,
peace rather than so-called national self-defense, justice that eliminates
poverty, and freedom for all instead of economic and military domination
for the few. All such social changes are causes of, and consequences of,
the transformation in human consciousness presently underway. They
are causes and consequences of the process of maturing. As mentioned
above, throughout this book, but especially in the concluding section, I have
attempted to articulate the concept of transformative praxis at some depth.

There is nothing about these goals that is utopian in the negative
sense. They reflect the strictest realism in the light of our present mad
trajectory toward planetary suicide and in the light of a world of military
and economic domination by the rich and powerful over the poor and
exploited worldwide. For this system means the continued death of
untold millions in the third-world and the imminent collapse of the global
environment. If this happens, it will mean the end of the world-historical
possibilities of the two-million-year old human project, a project itself the
fruition of a four-billion-year evolution of life on planet earth.

A system predicated on life is not an unattainable utopia. It is only
real alternative to the system predicated on death. All forms of domination
and exploitation are predicated on the death of the dominated and the
exploited and on the inner spiritual death of the dominators, as the work
of Paulo Freire (1974) and others has made clear. The alternative is a
system without domination or exploitation, a system predicated on mature,

responsible men and women working together for the mutual realization of their potential as human beings and of the communities of which they form an integral part. This is hardly farfetched, but, as I hope to show in this book, the next step in the process of growing up for human beings and the human project. As the biblical God puts it: "I have set before you life or death. Choose life." It may be that we will surprise ourselves and find that it is not much more difficult than this choice.

The present moment is therefore one of cosmic significance. For the human project is a product of the anthropic trajectory of a universe perhaps fifteen billion years in the making, a product of five billion years of evolution of the precious planet on which we live, of four billion years of life on this planet, and of two million years since the emergence of our marvelous human species. We stand at the verge of a possible dawning of planetary maturity.

We must substantially fulfill our human project in the relatively near future by transforming ourselves and the world according to a practical utopian vision of deep peace, or we perish in a paroxysm of nihilism, self-destruction, and despair. We must free ourselves from the anxiety-ridden and grasping ego, and the capitalist and nation-state systems within which it is institutionalized, or we will suffocate under its lethal consequences. The power to accomplish both has been "delegated" to us through the development of technology and the planetary scope of our institutions, on the one hand, and the evolution of our spiritual resources on the other. We are at the final crossroads. The choice is still ours. Soon it will be too late, and the choice may be revoked.

PART ONE

A Holistic Philosophy
of Spiritual
and Social Maturity

Chapter Two

A Planetary Paradigm for Human Life:
The Principle of Unity-in-Diversity

*That some major change in the way we live is beginning to manifest itself is evident
from the many signs of our times, not the least of which is the exhaustion of the
principles by which we have been living. In the midst of continual technological
upheaval the sense of emptiness and loss of freedom grows. Unreality and
spiritual vacuity spread like a disease. We may recognize in these signs the
persistence of certain characteristic problems of the modern age which, if
anything, are intensifying: a science which needs neither religion nor morality; a
medicine and therapy which cannot deal with the "whole human being" because
this conception itself has been lost; a fragmentation of standards and common
life; and everywhere the growth of state power, shrinking individuals....*

*The change we are speaking about is an **epochal change** that will
be at once subtle and all-pervasive. The expressions that come to mind to
describe it are a new way of looking at things, **a new way of thinking, a new
arrangement of emphases on which is important and not important in
human life.** This kind of change has occurred only two or three times in the
course of Western civilization – at its beginning in fifth and fourth century
B.C. Athens, at the beginning of the Christian world in the fourth century
of this era, and in the Renaissance of the fifteenth and sixteenth centuries.*

Henry Leroy Finch

*The world as revealed by the natural sciences....is a physical whole, indivisible,
but differentiating itself continuously into a scale of physical forms: space-time,
energy, elementary particles, atoms, and molecules; cosmic gas, galaxies, stars,
and stellar systems. It is, further, a biotic whole, differentiating itself in individual
organisms, species, genera, symbioses, and ecosystems, to form a biosphere
that is inseparable from its physical basis. From the biosphere there emerges a
noösphere, comprehending all that has gone before....*

*Personality involves not only the awareness of self, but also the
recognition of one's relations to other persons.... Its **nisus** is not simply to
cognize the world as a whole, but just as much to make it whole, where either as
perceived or as practically manipulable, it seems incomplete and falls short of
the requirements of the organizing principle. This, in the final issue, is the urge
to discover and possess that eternal whole, which, in Spinoza's words, "feeds
the mind solely with joy and is free from all distress." The practical rational
propensity to achieve ultimate wholeness, which manifests itself in human action,
initially as the capacity and endeavour to conceive and to strive for a better state
of the self, is the groundspring of morality and the social order.*

Errol E. Harris

S ince the second half of the twentieth century only, a global awareness has begun to dawn on a significant number of persons. Throughout nature, the twentieth century has shown us the inseparability of wholes and parts in the scheme of things. From macrophysics to quantum physics to ecology to social theory, the unity and diversity of the world we live in has been demonstrated. This understanding of the interrelation of wholes and parts constitutes a new paradigm for human thinking and action that has the potential to transform civilization and liberate us into a new world.

Yet we are sunk so deeply in our dogmas and adolescent prejudices that we are unable to internalize this understanding in any ways that result in effective action. The first photos from space sent back to Earth during the 1960s activated the possibility for understanding this tiny, fragile whole of a planet on which we dwell. Buckminster Fuller called it our "spaceship Earth." But we are surrounded by fragmented institutions inherited from the distant past before human beings had any inkling of the unity-in-diversity of themselves or the universe. And our sense of self continues to be conditioned by these institutions so that we too, in our thinking and acting, find ourselves unable to grow easily to the maturity that has been the great triumph of twentieth-century scientific thought.

1. The Emergent Paradigm for Science and Human life

The emerging science of ecology demonstrated over and over the principle of unity-in-diversity in which species and individuals cannot be understood apart from the ecosystems within which they are intertwined. And it has become clear to scientists that the variety of ecosystems themselves are intertwined on the planetary level where large ocean currents, the jet stream, patterns of rainfall, seasonal changes, and the variety of living things on the planet form an interdependent web of life. Ecologist Gregory Bateson calls this principle of unity-in-diversity uncovered by the science of ecology "systems." Living things form systems, and the planet itself is one encompassing ecosystem.

But human civilization is not a system in which the whole and parts interact in a flexible and healthy way to live in harmony with one another and the planet that sustains us. "The processes of ecology are not mocked," Bateson asserts. We will destroy ourselves unless we achieve "a single system of environment combined with high human civilization in which the flexibility of the civilization shall match that of the environment to create an ongoing complex system, open-ended for slow change of even basic (hard programmed) characteristics" (1972, pp. 504 & 494).

Yet the human ego, like the related social and economic systems that emerged from the Renaissance, continues to think of itself as autonomous, as "master" of nature and the Earth, and as independent of the web of social and biological life that encompasses our tiny planet. The dominant forms of selfhood or ego also continue to define themselves over and against other human beings and their social groupings (whether races, religions, nation-states, or ideologies), thwarting Bateson's "high civilization" where human beings have united into a single, dynamic, and flexible planetary civilization. This is the next step in the process of human beings growing to maturity on planet Earth. This is the only step that could cope with the immense planetary crises outlined above in Chapter One.

The twentieth century has given us a new paradigm for nature, society, and the universe that can be named "the principle of unity-in-diversity," the deep interrelation of wholes and parts on every level of existence. Yet our institutions, like our existential sources of action, continue to be based on the "modern" Newtonian paradigm and institutions nearly five centuries old. In astrophysics, the Einsteinian paradigm replaced the Newtonian. The universe cannot be understood as a collection of discrete bodies in motion within the "container" of an absolute space and time. Today, we understand the universe in terms of "fields," interdependent fields encompassing space, time, energy, and matter.

The part cannot be understood without the whole, and its characteristics are a function of its relationship with the whole. In *The Tao of Physics* (1975), physicist Fritjof Capra points out that our notion of a universe made of independent material objects, so fundamental to the Newtonian paradigm of the eighteenth century, has been abandoned by contemporary physics:

> Thus modern physics shows us once again – and this time at the macroscopic level – that material objects are not distinct entities, but are inseparably linked to their environment; that their properties can only be understood in terms of their interaction with the rest of the world. According to Mach's principle, this interaction reaches out to the universe at large, to the distant stars and galaxies. The basic unity of the cosmos manifests itself, therefore, not only in the world of the very small but also in the world of the very large; a fact which is increasingly acknowledged in modern astrophysics and cosmology. In the words of the astronomer Fred Hoyle,
> "Present-day developments in cosmology are coming to suggest rather insistently that everyday conditions could not persist but for the distant parts of the Universe, that all our ideas of space and geometry would become entirely invalid if the distant parts of the Universe were taken away. Our everyday experience even down to the smallest details seems to be so closely integrated to the grand-scale features of the Universe that it is well-nigh impossible to contemplate the two being separated." (pp. 209-210)

Similarly, in microphysics the modern idea of the world as a collection of discrete "atoms" functioning as building blocks comes to an end. As in macrophysics, in microphysics, the concept of the "field" is also fundamental. Micro-particles cannot exist without the whole (the field), and the whole cannot exist without its elements. As Capra asserts above, the principle of unity-in-diversity of the universe extends from the macro to the micro levels. In *Apocalypse and Paradigm* (2000b), philosopher of science Errol E. Harris describes this new paradigm for microphysics:

> Every kind of particle is associated with a field, and every field with one or more kinds of particle. In short, atomism has given way to the conception of a whole (field), the structure of which determines the nature and behavior of the parts (quantum events). In quantum physics certain parameters are found to be complementary, so that neither can be measured precisely without rendering the other completely indeterminate. All that can be definitely determined is a probability amplitude within the system as a whole, which "collapses" only with measurement. In contemporary physics, such holism is pervasive.... In brief, the physical universe must be a single unified whole of interconnected events and overlapping fields. (pp. 78-79)

The science of ecology has understood the unity of life and environment on our planet, including the planet itself as an encompassing ecosystem. Macrophysics understands the principle of unity-in-diversity as fundamental to the entire universe and microphysics sees the tiniest elements of existence as embedded within this pervasive holism in the same way. The fundamental organizational principles of the universe are embodied within every part, and the diversity of parts is expressed in a tremendous diversity of particular forms.

Similarly, in social theory (from Karl Marx through Max Weber, George Herbert Mead, and Jürgen Habermas) the individual cannot be understood as an independent reality prior to social interaction and the community from which he or she springs. Instead, the social whole of the community makes possible, and is inseparable from, the diversity of the individuals within the community. These thinkers have shown that the self is relational to its very core, and that society is not founded, as British philosopher John Locke proposed in his seventeenth-century *Second Treatise on Government*, as a collection of individuals who are themselves prior to society.

We will examine more fully in subsequent chapters what contemporary German philosopher Habermas, in particular, demonstrates at great length: rootedness in community does not rob individuals of autonomy but is the specific vehicle by which moral and social autonomy is achieved. We need to achieve that "high civilization" of which Bateson speaks if we are to flourish as human beings and bequeath our glorious planet Earth intact to future generations.

The implications of the emerging planetary paradigm include nothing less than authentic planetary democracy. Democratic theory has been evolving over the five centuries of the modern period within the framework of a struggle against the non-democratic institutions and forces of that period. Today, the self is understood as relational (as opposed to inherently autonomous and prior to the social matrix that forms it) and democracy is no longer considered the legislation of abstract laws for citizens regardless of their differences. Instead, recent democratic theory involves the maximization of freedom and equality precisely through the recognition and respect for differences within a communicative context in which self and other engage in authentic dialogue regarding their respective individualities and their relations to universality (Habermas, 1994, pp. 107-148).

Human rights and dignity cannot exist without a unified social framework in which the collective force of the whole of society respects the integrity and uniqueness of each individual Unity and diversity mutually imply one another on all levels of nature, including the level of human civilization and (we will see below) the level of the mature human self. Without a planetary democratic civilization, there can and will be no genuine protection of the millions of persons victimized every year whose rights and dignity are violated with impunity. Similarly, without a planetary democratic civilization, the planetary crises discussed above, for which no solution is possible on the national or local level, will bring about the self-generated suicide of the human project (Martin, 2002). The diversity and complexity of the planetary ecosystem that sustains us can only be protected by a "flexible high civilization" whose wholeness implies the integrity of its parts.

Yet our dominant institutions that have evolved over the last five hundred years are mere fragments that are incapable of promoting the unity-in-diversity of mature democracy and incapable of dealing with the crises that are facing us on a planetary scale. The global economic system and the system of sovereign nation-states are predicated on fragmentation, division. They prevent unity among human beings and are inherently destructive of human diversity. Let us look at the features of the antiquated modern paradigm under which we are still living and operating and the impediments it creates for a new human maturity of thinking and acting.

2. The Fragmented Modern Paradigm

The modern world-order evolved as a complex system of institutions and social attitudes since the Renaissance. It includes several fundamental elements that continue to dominate and impede the emerging world civilization of the twentieth and twenty-first centuries. Fundamental among these elements are the following: (1) the system of sovereign nation-states, (2) the system of global capitalism, (3) the systemic drive to dominate, control and master nature, largely through science and technology, and (4) the system of education, culture, and social interaction producing the modern sense of self.

Each of these areas has evolved through interface and interaction with the others in that distinctive way that we call the "modern world." In order to delineate more fully the emerging planetary paradigm that is the focus of this chapter, we will look briefly at each of these facets of the fragmented modern paradigm. We will continue to go more deeply into the essential features of the modern world and the possibility of their transformation in subsequent chapters.

The notion of "sovereignty" slowly developed as European nations emerged from the Medieval period into the modern system of nation-states. This notion asserts that to be a "nation-state" is to have absolute authority over internal matters within the state and complete autonomy and independence in relation to other nation-states. In the early modern period, indigenous peoples in North and South America, Africa, and elsewhere had quite different systems of social organization and little notion of "sovereignty" of nations. But as Ward Churchill points out, European explorers like Columbus, in their quest for gold and possessions for their respective crowns, imposed upon the "discovered" peoples the so-called "doctrine of discovery." This doctrine formed an early basis for what is today called "international law," asserting that inhabited lands had to be respected as sovereign.

The peoples in the discovered lands had control over their internal affairs, and their duly-constituted authorities could enter into treaties and agreements with the European powers whom they encountered. This concession to the notion of a world organized according to the principle of sovereignty, however, had to be qualified by the realities of power relations among nations. For the European nations had technical and military superiority. Therefore, the doctrine of discovery (by which the colonizing and conquering European nations operated) asserted that the "discovered" peoples (1) had to trade exclusively with the discovering nation, (2) had to accept Christian missionaries among them, and (3) were not permitted to refuse these conditions nor to use violence against the representatives of the Crown. If these conditions were not met, the foreign power had the right to (1) conquer by force and (2) confiscate the indigenous people's land and possessions as compensation (1998, pp. 259-261).

We can see in this description of the early modern idea of sovereignty a characteristic of the system of sovereign nations that has persisted to the present. For sovereign nations are interested in economic growth, possessions, and wealth. They have evolved an international system within which they struggle for ascendancy with one another, and the more powerful nations routinely use their power and influence in world affairs to shape international trade to their advantage (Smith, 2003a). The system of sovereign nations is a system of competition among autonomous units on a planet of many such units.

From the earliest beginnings of the system of dividing the world into autonomous units called nation-states, there also developed a system by which the more powerful used their power to foster material advantage for themselves. Although the global economic system has evolved through several stages such as mercantilism, colonialism, slave-based economies, liberalism, and neo-liberal capitalism, the principle has remained unchanged that the nations use their power, influence, and position to compete with one another for resources, wealth, and economic advantage. Just as with the early doctrine of discovery, "free competition" is not to their advantage, but hegemony, spheres of influence, and systems of domination.

In light of this, the U.S. Monroe doctrine of 1827 was not a defense of freedom for the emerging nation-states of the Americas from European interference; it was a declaration of hegemony and sphere of influence intended to enhance the economic position of the early United States. Similarly, President James Monroe and others saw our neighbor Cuba (a possession of Spain) as a "ripe fruit" that would eventually fall to the expanding United States, enhancing the steady growth of national wealth and power (Chomsky, 1993, pp.143-145).

Secondly, what is today called "international law" is not law in any sense remotely like the law that exists within sovereign nations. For the law within nations is legislated by persons claiming legitimate authority to do so and is enforceable by a system of police and courts over every citizen within the nation. Citizens within nations are precisely that: citizens under the rule of law – not autonomous entities independent of their relations with their society. Internally, nation-states normally have the power to create laws binding citizens and the authority to enforce those laws. But nation-states are not "citizens" of planet Earth in any comparable way (see Kant, 1957). Being autonomous in their external affairs, no laws over them can be legitimately legislated and no enforcement system can ensure that any so-called laws are obeyed. The most nation-states can do is enter into treaties (that are misleadingly called "international law"). And these treaties are only binding as long as the nation finds that its self-interest inclines it to maintain the agreement.

The modern world system that evolved since the Renaissance emerged from a civilization that had little awareness of living on a relatively small planet functioning as a limited whole for the scope of human and other forms of life. The world seemed immense as Columbus and others ventured into the vast unknown and sought the unlimited riches and resources that the world seemed to harbor in its uncharted wilderness areas. The nation-states saw colonial possession or growth and expansion as forms of national "manifest destiny." The British empire spanned the globe and was the inheritance of British civilizational superiority. Every year, school children in Britain would celebrate "Empire Day," taking pride in their far flung empire (Jerome, 1966, ch. 8).

The United States entered into numerous treaties with the Indian tribes of North America (therefore recognizing them as sovereign nations) only to betray the treaties when its self-interest dictated in order to continue the expansion that was its manifest destiny. Finally, when the Indians were no longer the slightest military threat, Congress passed a law abolishing the sovereignty of all Indian tribes and absorbing them within the system of the United States (Churchill, 1998, pp. 269-272). Today, the United States military establishment sees the nation's "manifest destiny" as controlling and dominating the world from outer space (Parrish, 2001, pp. 14-16).

In the modern world system, the economics of capitalist competition cannot be disentangled from the system of sovereign nation-states. The vast wealth and resources that the United States coveted on Indian lands is not fundamentally different from the vast oil reserves that the United States goes to war to protect in the Middle East. Nation-states use their military might to protect and promote their economic interests. The system of sovereign nations and the global economic system are inextricably intertwined. In its earlier forms like mercantilism, the state and private wealth were not so clearly distinguished as today, with quasi-state institutions (like the British East India Company) pursuing wealth in foreign countries.

Today, the legal separation between private capital and government action makes as little difference as in the past. This larger history of the relation between capital and nation-states from the Renaissance to the present is described in detail in such books as Terry Boswell and Christopher Chase-Dunn, *The Spiral of Capitalism and Socialism*, or J.W. Smith, *Economic Democracy: The Political Struggle of the Twenty-First Century*. These works trace the ways global capital dominates the system of nation-states and uses the system in the service of its interests.

Today, as in the past, the most powerful nation-states act in the service of the dominant interests within them to protect and promote the global economic system that benefits those interests. So-called modern democratic states have evolved as class systems in which the owners of capital and wealth are a main influence on the formulation of internal laws and external foreign policy (Domhoff, 1967; Palast, 2003). As John Jay said of the early United States, "those who own the country ought to run it" – and it has been that way ever since (Chomsky, 1996, p. 90). The result is that the state, in its internal and foreign policies, acts to protect the interests of the capital- owning class that forms an integral part of the drive of nation-states to compete on a planetary scale for trade predominance, spheres of influence, and control of resources.

Historical examples abound. In the United States in 1954, the United Fruit Company, with vast holdings in Guatemala, was behind the CIA backed coup that destroyed Guatemalan democracy and instituted a series of military dictatorships amenable to U.S. economic hegemony in the region. Again, the United States multinational corporation ITT presented the State Department with a detailed plan to destroy the elected socialist government of Chile in 1973 and bring to power a military dictatorship compatible with United States economic interests in that country (Blum, 1995). The list of corporate approved or sponsored interventions by the United States government goes on and on. The evidence for this principle is overwhelming (Blum, 2000; Chomsky and Herman, 1979).

Under the capitalist system that has evolved through the modern period for the past five centuries, elites institutionalized a system within which they claim their vast concentrations of private wealth compete with other vast concentrations of wealth for the accumulation private profit. In a world of diminishing resources, intersecting ecological crises, exploding population, and sophisticated weapons with supersonic delivery systems, they tell us that we must rely on Adam Smith's "invisible hand." If only we allow every individual and corporation to compete in a "free system" of unregulated greed and lust for wealth, they tell us, then the "greatest good of the greatest number of people" will miraculously result. In reality, however, since governments interfere to promote the economic advantage of corporations within their countries, and since huge corporations strive to create monopoly conditions for themselves and eliminate competition, this system of trade is not "free" after all (Smith, 2003a).

The vast empirical evidence that this "invisible hand" has never resulted in "the greatest good of the greatest number of people" in five centuries of trade is irrelevant to the powerful promoters of the dogma of capital. The truth that life has been a nightmare for the majority of the persons on the planet for five centuries is irrelevant. "Look at how rich the ruling class is after all? That did not come about by accident but though the blessings of capitalism." The overwhelming evidence that global poverty is growing, that the global environment is being rapidly destroyed, that the global population is exploding, and that global militarism still wastes more than 800 billion United States dollars a year on weapons and militarism is irrelevant (Gallik, 1997). Any form of democratically guided planning must be excluded as taboo from the sacred circle of the marketplace. Government may interfere, everyone understands, for the benefit of the dominant interests. This does not interfere with "free trade," we are told, but protects it. What is not allowed is for governments to interfere for the benefit of everyone. For that would be "socialism," not "free trade."

Concern for future generations, for living sustainably on an overtaxed planet, or for the more than a billion starving inhabitants of the planet today cannot enter into economic considerations. The equations are all so clear on paper. Just take Economics 101 in any United States university. A perfect symmetry of mathematical calculations. If you do not plan for the future, but just let people be greedy little atoms of "rational self-interest," then a perfect world of prosperity for all is the result. It could not be clearer on paper. The living nightmare that forms the world we live in for most inhabitants of the planet is irrelevant. For we are not talking here about reason and science, but about religion and dogma, a religion with sacred fetishes every bit as powerful as those of the Medieval Church burning heretics at the stake. We will examine this phenomenon of global economics in some depth in subsequent chapters.

This system evolved over five centuries and never fully encountered the global perspective that has only emerged since the twentieth century. Today we understand that we will not survive on this planet without recognizing the inseparability of unity and diversity, of wholes and parts in the scheme of things. Economics, like the system of nation-states, must be transformed according to the paradigm of unity-in-diversity. Each of these systems is fragmentary and undemocratic to its core.

Under the emergent paradigm of the late twentieth century, unity is a fundamental consideration for economic well-being of all persons on the planet, for the health of the environment, for sustainability of the planet for future generations, and for the other species with whom we share our planetary home. As the *IPPNO Document on World Peace* (2000) points out, this necessarily means democratically guided planning to consider how best to devise an economic system that benefits and sustains every citizen of the planet and the other species with whom we share this world. It means careful consideration of the impact of technological innovations, sensitive forethought concerning the welfare of future generations, and a sense of communal stewardship toward our planetary home. It means the rule of just and enforceable law protecting every person on the planet from exploitation, brutalization, violations of their civil liberties, or other threats to their dignity as unique human beings. It means bringing economics, and nation-states, within the sphere of planetary democratic planning, responsibility, and accountability (see Martin, 1999b).

The third aspect of the modern paradigm that emerged from Renaissance thinking was the idea that human beings can use science and technology to master nature and dominate the planet for their designs. Francis Bacon was one of the early proponents of this ideology that became fundamental to fragmented modern thinking. As Herman E. Daly (1996) points out, this assumption included the idea that human beings are apart from nature and the web of life. It included the sense of nature as being an inexhaustible resource and having a near infinite ability to absorb our interference, waste products, and the consequences of our vast mining and engineering projects.

Only in the twentieth century did people begin to realize the global consequences of this attitude in the growing scarcity of water, the toxic pollution of large portions of the Earth, the disintegration of the ozone layer, global warming, the global depletion of fisheries, the deforestation and consequent erosion of arable land worldwide, and the growing phenomenon of droughts, irregular weather patterns, and violent storms (Daly, 1996; Korten, 2001). Yet even today, at the dawn of the third millennium, the World Bank is funding in some countries vast engineering projects that are destined, like past projects, to alter the ecosystems of the huge areas affected by these projects. Like the World Bank, nation-states and global corporations think in terms of mastery and exploitation of nature instead of activity in harmony with the web of life (Chossudovsky, 1999; Renner, 1996).

The notion of mastery and domination of nature is inseparable from the use of science and technology to master and dominate other human beings. The most obvious manifestation of this is the development of ever more sophisticated military capacities for crowd control, counter insurgency technologies, and warfare (Allen, 1999, 2000; Allen-Leach, 2000; Morales, 2001). The wonders of science that could be used for genuine communication, healing, and wholeness among the human population are used for spying, death, destruction, and protecting and fomenting ever deeper fragmentation.

As with the system of autonomous nation-states, and as with global capitalism, the ideology of mastery and domination of the planet by science and technology is the product of an ideology from a past age, a modern period that emerged after the Renaissance that had little or no understanding of our planetary ecology and global interdependence as these emerged in the twentieth century. Science and technology are not to blame here but the ideology of mastery and domination of a nature understood to be unlimited in its malleability. This pattern of thinking is inseparable from the system of nation-states (which themselves think in terms of domination, hegemony, and spheres of influence) and the system of capitalism whose ideology assumes that unlimited self-interest and drive to economic domination without concern for the whole or the human community can magically create human and natural health and prosperity.

The ethos of mastery and domination through science and technology has been used in the service of each of these elements of the modern paradigm, further promoting and entrenching the fragmentation tearing our planet apart: parts claiming independence from the wholes that shape and sustain them. As an ecologist, Bateson presents a list of what he calls "ideas that dominate our civilization" that he says are at the root of our contemporary global crises. These ideas hang together and can be subsumed under the four forms of fragmentation that we have been discussing:

> (a) It's us *against* the environment. (b) It's us *against* other men. (c) It's the individual (or the individual company, or the individual nation) that matters. (d) We *can* have unilateral control over the environment and must strive for that control. (e) We live within an infinitely expanding "frontier." (f) Economic determinism is common sense. (g) Technology will do it for us. (1972, p. 492)

Bateson argues that the greatest strength of an ecosystem and the greatest need of a healthy civilization is "flexibility," which he defines as an "uncommitted potentiality for change" (p. 497). An ecosystem is a unity within the diversity of the life-forms that flourish within it. The seven ideas listed by Bateson are all ideas that diminish or prevent the creative flexibility required for our survival on this planet. They are all products of an historical development that has fostered fragmentation instead of the creative flexibility of unity-in-diversity.

Although Bateson's summary is complete in other respects and dovetails with my own analysis, he leaves out one of the most fundamental sources of fragmentation that has torn the world apart for several centuries, and continues to so in an ever more damaging manner: the nation-state system that, we have seen, is a crucial aspect of the inflexibility and fragmentation of our modern world. But the root of the problem is deeper than the domination of our civilization by particular ideas. For our fragmented institutions and limited, inflexible ideas foster the development of fragmented selves, and fragmented selves, in turn, tend to reproduce fragmented institutions that are inherited by future generations.

The dawn of the third millennium requires that we grow to the maturity of unity-in-diversity, that we transcend our adolescent sense of independence for mature relational freedom. This maturity must include all of our fundamental institutions, from the nation-state system and our economic system to our use of science and technology. The potential for this transformation is easily within reach as we begin to realize who and what we are and begin to understand the nature of the universe we inhabit. Our modern paradigm, therefore, includes a fourth factor, our sense of self, created and sustained by the nation-state system, the capitalist system, and the systematic drive for mastery and domination. This is implicit in Bateson's list as well, since the overcoming of the attitude of defining ourselves against nature and against other persons would mean precisely a new sense of self. But this orientation "against" others is continually reinforced by our dominant institutions. Our sense of self is conditioned by our dominant institutions. Therefore, it too must move from fragmentation to unity-in-diversity.

3. Fragmented Selves and the Quest for Wholeness

Today, we are threatening ourselves with extinction or a vastly diminished existence upon planet Earth. Today, many raise the alarm with respect to the coming cataclysms. Many demonstrate the corporate plunder of our planet (Karliner, 1997; Tokar, 1997; Brecher and Costello, 1994; Siva, 1997). Many elucidate the human consequences of the growing environmental crisis (Harris, 1993; Renner, 1996; Seligson and Passe-Smith, 1993; Mander and Goldsmith, 1996; Brown, 2001). A substantial literature exists with respect to weapons and militarism (Sivard, 1996; Gallik, 1997; Korb, 2001; Shorr, 1999).

Eminent scientists have demonstrated the clear outlines and destructive consequences of the population explosion (Cohen, 1995). Many scholars and thinkers describe the ever-growing poverty and misery worldwide (Chossudovsky 1999; Boucher, 1999). But few think beyond the ideological and spiritual assumptions of our era to the possibility of a genuine liberation that will establish a life on Earth truly peaceful, prosperous, just, and sustainable. For to do this means to think outside the ideological box that encloses us. We must recognize that our human possibilities are not defined by the box, by our limited assumptions and our blinders, but instead that the box itself constricts and strangles our natural potential for genuine transformation and liberation.

We cannot expect a utopia exempt from human failing, weakness, error, and duplicity once we have emerged from the narrow confines of our antiquated forms of thought. We cannot expect that a perfect existence will miraculously emerge and eliminate at a single stroke the immense problems that human beings face in living successfully on planet Earth. But what will emerge is the framework for human fulfillment, the mature civilization that can begin to tackle seriously the problems of living on the planet precisely because we have emerged out of our adolescent assumptions, stupidities, and smallness of vision.

Human beings on planet Earth are ready to grow up through transformations in each of these dimensions that constrict and threaten to destroy us. History has forced us to the brink of self-destruction, or to spiritual and institutional maturity. And it will take transformations in both these dimensions (the spiritual and institutional) to unleash our immense human-divine potential for a decent life on planet Earth.

This potential for genuine transformation and liberation is nothing other than our potential for authentic civilizational and personal wholeness. We are living today with a set of assumptions and values that are disparate, fragmented, and incomplete. We have little wholeness in our lives or in our institutions and this fragmentation has led to the global crises that threaten to destroy us and our precious planet (Kahler, 1967). We remain adolescents in our thinking and acting, not because of some fixed, innate "human nature" but because the constricting box of our assumptions strangles our potential and will not let us spontaneously grow to maturity.

Human consciousness has evolved through several stages, as we saw in Chapter One, and we are today faced with the necessity for another fundamental transformation. The time is ripe at the dawn of the third millennium. It must be now, or it may be never. This is why we must examine the basic assumptions that constrict and confine us within the box and why we must delineate the dynamics of wholeness that can lift us naturally to a new level of existence where the real problems of human life can be addressed.

In the quotation at the head of this chapter, Errol E. Harris speaks of the human "nisus" or tendency toward wholeness. Despite a multiplicity of often conflicting tendencies within ourselves, human beings ultimately strive for wholeness: personal wholeness, social wholeness, planetary wholeness, even (as we will see) a cosmic sense of wholeness. However, our human potential is rarely actualized. Our thinking and acting in this regard is retarded by social and institutional forms that promote continuing fragmentation. These antiquated institutions were centuries ago the product of the nisus toward wholeness, but today they are fetters on the need for deeper and more authentic forms of wholeness.

Psychologist Carl R. Rogers calls this nisus for wholeness "creativity" and argues that this is fundamental to being human:

> The mainspring of creativity appears to be the same tendency which we discover so deeply as the curative force in psychotherapy – *man's tendency to actualize himself, to become his potentialities.* By this I mean the directional trend which is evident in all organic and human life – the urge to expand, extend, develop, mature – the tendency to express and activate all the capacities of the organism, or the self. This tendency may become deeply buried under layer after layer of encrusted psychological defenses; it may be hidden behind elaborate facades which deny its existence; it is my belief, however, based on my experience, that it exists in every individual, and awaits only the proper conditions to be released and expressed. It is this tendency which is the primary motivation for creativity as the organism forms new relationships to the environment in its endeavor most fully to be itself. (1961, pp. 350-351)

Today the fragmented institutions of our modern world and the ideas they promote constitute a box that constricts our thinking and feeling. These institutions affect our ability to create wholeness on all levels: personal, social, planetary, and cosmic. They restrict what Rogers calls our tendency to actualize ourselves, to mature, and to form new relationships with our environment that allow us to be more fully ourselves. They inhibit our movement to Bateson's "flexible high civilization."

Human maturity must be understood as something that transcends the kind of maturity described in much of the popular psychology of our day. Throughout the history of thought, from Gautama Buddha in India and Lao Tzu in China to Plato in Greece, great thinkers have envisioned a more profound human wholeness and deeper maturity than popular definitions have proposed. Drawing on this history of thought and the breakthroughs in understanding made possible only in the twentieth century, I am attempting to pose for the twenty-first century a conception of what we are as human beings and what we are capable of.

This entire book is meant to describe the outlines of our limited assumptions and to present the dynamics of a new wholeness and maturity for humankind. As such, the present chapter functions as an outline of what will be more fully discussed and elaborated in subsequent chapters. It attempts to formulate the basic parameters of the new wholeness emerging as a paradigm for human maturity for the twenty-first century and beyond.

At the outset of this chapter, H. L. Finch speaks of the "exhaustion of the principles by which we have been living" and the ever growing fragmentation, loss of freedom, and emptiness that characterize our lives.

He asserts that the "whole human being" needs to be restored and that our age represents an "epochal change" that may be described by "a new way of looking at things" or a new emphasis "on what is important and not important in human life." The deeper maturity that we can and must soon realize is connected with this discovery of a new sense of wholeness in human beings on the personal and the societal levels. This wholeness has been there all along, though we have most often failed to perceive it as such. Yet to realize this possibility we must shift perspective, or emphasis, in such a way that the gestalt by which we comprehend ourselves and our world switches, foreground to background, and we literally begin to think and live in a new way.

This gestalt-switch, which can bring us rapidly from fragmentation to wholeness, is our imminent and quite real human possibility at this point in history. This new way of seeing and thinking is not far away and, in a pointedly realistic sense, will not be that difficult, but we have to accept the idea that real change will accompany it. The real change will lead to a world of much greater peace and freedom, but it will require giving up our attachments to several pseudo-realities that we fear to lose such as the ego and its vanities, our greed and desire for unlimited accumulation of private wealth, our compulsion for mastery and domination of nature and other people, and our tendency to objectify, categorize, and dehumanize human beings who are different from us. For wholeness means a deep integration of the diverse forces and tendencies within ourselves. It also means the oneness of humanity upon planet Earth, a oneness in which the diversity of individuals, races, sexes, cultures, religions, and nations is not abolished but instead integrated through a new way of seeing and being.

4. What Personal Wholeness Is Not

In order to understand more deeply the dynamics of the unity-in-diversity within personal wholeness, let us first examine six descriptions of the modern fragmented self and its destructive consequences. I will attempt to summarize each kind of fragmented self in an opening sentence, and then explain further the kind of selfhood to which the formula refers. Each of these six forms of self should be familiar to us within the range of people we have known.

To begin, it should be clear that personal wholeness is not the obsession of the personality under a dominant compulsion, desire, emotion, or ideology. The inherent ambiguity of the self, immersed within numerous multiplicities, generates anxiety, dread, and self-doubt. This classical problem has been exacerbated in the modern world with the breakdown of traditional cultural and religious identities, a phenomenon explored by much of the sociology and psychology of our time. Whereas traditionally a person's identity was secured by his or her place in the community or by his or her religious identification as a Moslem or a Jew, today such culturally-imposed ideas of self are breaking down, leading to a worldwide social reaction that involves the rejection of modernity and an attempt to re-embrace these premodern determinants of meaning and selfhood.

Psychologist Robert J. Lifton, in *The Protean Self: Human Resilience in an Age of Fragmentation* (1993), identifies what he calls "fundamentalism" as a common response to the apparently rootless flux of our modern condition. Instead of embracing "the protean self" through a dynamic integration of multiplicity within wholeness,

> One embraces fundamentalism in order to overcome the sense of despair and individual futurelessness associated with fragmentation and nonfunctional proteanism. That new relationship to fundamentalism can help sustain the self, at least for a while; but it may also lead to further fragmentation. Always totalistic in spirit, it presses toward a purity that must be attained but is unattainable.... Fundamentalism thus creates a thwarted self, never free of actual or potential fragmentation. (p. 202)

The obsession of the personality under a dominant passion or emotion (for example, racism, fascism, or the cult of Jesus) or a dominant compulsion (for example, making money or fighting communism) or a dominant ideology (for example, Americanism or Islamic purity) does not create wholeness but instead solidifies fragmentation. A characteristic feature of such fundamentalist forms of selfhood is being against, being divided off from what is perceived as impure, alien, evil, or failure. Fundamentalist selves of all forms revolve around what theologian Matthew Fox in *A Spirituality Named Compassion* calls "dualisms" (1990, pp. 80-83).

Those with such a dominant compulsion, desire, emotion, or ideology find their identity and security in a world of multiplicity through what is excluded, hated, or feared. The compulsive seeker after money engages in a competition that excludes the "losers" as much as it excludes compassion and human connectedness. The Christian fundamentalist may reject modern science as an instrument of Satan and see non-fundamentalist Christians as impure and corrupt. Anti-Communist ideologues tend to see everyone working for progressive social change as a potential enemy. When the self coagulates around a narrow set of doctrines or emotions, to the exclusion of the rest of the multiplicity within itself and the world, then wholeness is excluded, and fragmentation with its attendant destructiveness and divisiveness becomes inevitable.

Second, personal wholeness is not the constriction or limitation of the self to an unambiguous identity or a small, thoughtless, everyday pettiness from which all the vagueness, mystery, terror, and depth of existence is removed. A human being is a dynamic compendium of energies and potentialities. Human consciousness seethes with hopes, fears, desires, images, thoughts, intuitions, inclinations, ideologies, and ideas. Human maturity and fulfillment must integrate this rich multiplicity into a unity-in-diversity characterized by ethical insight, critical thought, direction, meaning, simplicity, reverence, deep awareness, spirituality, and compassion.

Several of these qualities will be discussed in subsequent chapters, but here the point to note is that our human potential is for largeness, not narrowness and smallness, richness in diversity, depth, and meaning, not rigidness, blindness, and pettiness. Yet a common reaction to the explosion of knowledge and ideas that characterize the modern and postmodern worlds is to constrict the self into smallness, to refuse to deal with the question of the depths of existence or the apparently irredeemable diversity confronting us today.

A typical reaction to the immense diversity confronting us is contraction, contraction of the self and its ideas into something settled, finished, small, and mostly dead. But this is not human personal maturity, and it is not the path toward the realization of our human project on planet Earth. Contraction of the self does not bring wholeness and human fulfillment but only further fragmentation.

Contraction of the self is not simply a personal tragedy; as a widespread phenomenon, it has terrible social consequences. Citizens of nations and the planet become incapable of deep critical thought and political participation since a narrow self cannot deal intelligently with the great issues confronting human beings on our planet. Small selves absorb their ideas uncritically from their surroundings, playing into the hands of propaganda promoting war preparations, nationalism, or consumerism. Subject to manipulation, small unambiguous identities cut themselves off from the depth and richness of their existence and, like the fundamentalists, contribute to the fragmentation and potential self-destruction of the human project on our planet.

To be small, to be contracted into a narrow identity today, is not to be a harmless, humble person living quietly in some obscure social role. This is to be part of the global crisis of our time that may destroy human life and the precious planet that serves as our home. Such smallness is not healthy and not "normal" but makes a person a cipher within an adolescent, an insane, civilization. This idea is even more telling today at the dawn of the third millennium than when it was expressed by psychiatrist R. D. Laing in *The Politics of Experience* (1967). What I am calling a "contracted self," a so-called "normal," well-adjusted human being, is in reality "an outrageous violation" of our real possibilities for being human:

> We do not live in a world of unambiguous identities and definitions, needs and fears, hopes, disillusions. The tremendous social realities of our time are ghosts, specters of murdered gods and our own humanity returned to haunt and destroy us. The Negroes, the Jews, the Reds. *Them.* Only you and I dressed differently. The texture of the fabric of these socially shared hallucinations is what we call reality, and our collusive madness is what we call sanity....
>
> In the last fifty years, we human beings have slaughtered by our own hands coming on for one hundred million of our species. We all live under constant threat of our total annihilation. We seem to seek death and destruction as much as life and happiness. We are as driven to kill and be killed as we are to live and let live. Only by the most outrageous violation of ourselves have we achieved the capacity to live in relative adjustment to a civilization apparently driven to its own destruction. (pp. 73 & 76)

Third, personal wholeness is not a free-floating, ungrounded utilitarian or instrumental self. With the breakdown of traditional societies in the modern world, and the simultaneous calling-into-question of traditional religious and ethical values, a movement developed that has had tremendous impact on societies far out of proportion to its significance within the history of philosophy. This movement developed through several phases– for example, Enlightenment naturalism, utilitarianism, and modern instrumentalism. In many of its forms, it holds that reason is a crucial tool for human beings. However, it also holds that reason alone is not constitutive of our human essence, as much of the Western tradition believed.

Detached reason has only a limited pragmatic role to play in human life. It can explore methods or procedures by which we can realize our personal or social aims or goals, but reason cannot tell us what goods, aims, or goals to pursue. The ends of our action are determined, instrumentalism argues, by the needs and desires of individuals or of society. Reason cannot determine intrinsically valuable ends, since no such ends exist. In other words, the ends are not intrinsic or substantive goods or goals, but instead all ends are arbitrary, purely subjective, or socially conventional. Human life has no objective meaning, direction, or purpose beyond our subjectively-constituted purposes. Reason is merely an instrument for realizing these purposes (see Marcuse, 1969).

Philosopher Charles Taylor in *Sources of the Self: The Making of the Modern Identity* (1989) is strongly critical of the instrumentalist movement, which is one of the sources of the self that he traces through the modern period. The instrumentalist movement is connected with the crisis of meaning that we have been facing in the twentieth and twenty-first centuries. Reason is seen as powerless to discover some intrinsic meaning to human life. It is also the particular instrument that shows the quest for such meaning to be senseless. Taylor writes that the failure of instrumentalism can be understood in terms of "division or fragmentation." "To take an instrumental stance to nature is to cut us off from the sources of meaning in it. An instrumental stance toward our feelings divides us within, splits reason from sense. And the atomistic focus on our individual goals dissolves community and divides us from each other" (pp. 500-501).

Instrumentalism does not recognize larger wholes or substantial relationships beyond an atomistically-conceived human being having extrinsic relationships with other persons and larger social units. Diversity is irredeemable. A real unity beyond temporary associations of persons or a subjective resonance with nature is impossible. Fragmentation is the result, as Taylor points out: fractured meaning and fractured selves. For instrumentalism, little hope exists for a transformation of human beings that will allow us to encounter creatively our global crises. For instrumentalism, our possibilities for mature wholeness (which are the theme of this book) do not exist. Instrumentalism is a vision of truncated, constricted, and severely limited human possibilities. This is a false vision, as we will see, insofar as it refuses to acknowledge the depth and meaning of human existence and the immense transformative potential that each human being carries within his or her self.

Fourth, personal wholeness is not an ungrounded subjectivism forever exploring a rootless creative potential upon which is placed the burden of solving all the problems and conflicts of human life. Charles Taylor also traces what he calls "subjectivist expressionism" as one of the sources of the self throughout the modern period. He argues correctly that this movement is a counter-movement and protest to the desiccated self of instrumentalism, and he associates subjectivist expressionism in its shallower forms with aspects of the human potential movement in the United States.

The assumption here is that techniques or methods of therapy can lead people to wholeness, happiness, fulfillment, and that if these goods were realized in a population there would be positive social consequences such as peace and harmony in the world. But the situation is not nearly this simple, since the self cannot be divorced from its social, ecological, or cosmic environment, as I have attempted to show. If the self were clear, integrated, whole, then perhaps wonderful social consequences would follow. But the self, in and through itself, cannot achieve such a miraculous transformation (apart from concomitant social transformation), even if guided by therapists or gurus, themselves trapped in the fragmented modern condition. As Taylor puts the matter:

But our normal understanding of self-realization presupposes that some things are important beyond the self, that there are some goods or purposes the furthering of which has significance for us and which can provide the significance a fulfilling life needs. A total and fully consistent subjectivism would tend towards emptiness: nothing would count as fulfillment in a world in which literally nothing as important but self-fulfillment.... A society of self-fulfillers, whose affiliations are more and more seen as revocable, cannot sustain the strong identification with the political community which public freedom needs.... The "triumph of the therapeutic" can also mean an abdication of autonomy, where the lapse of traditional standards, coupled with the belief in technique, makes people cease to trust their own instincts about happiness, fulfillment, and how to bring up their children. (pp. 507-508)

Since we are linked together in a fundamental unity-in-diversity, self-fulfillment without a corresponding social and ontological fulfillment, is but another manifestation of fragmentation.

Fifth, personal wholeness is not a drive to mastery, domination, or manipulation of persons or things in the service of perceived self-interest or a dominant ideology. In his well-known book, *Obedience to Authority* (1974), psychologist Stanley Milgram reported on the results of hundreds of experiments in which subjects were asked to give ever more severe electric shocks to a victim they were told was part of a "learning experiment." The amazing results of the experiment showed a large percentage of ordinary people, from all walks of life, were willing to inflict what they believed to be tremendous pain on the victim they thought was receiving shocks as part of the experiment (p. 5).

The book also expresses his deep perplexity and consternation at the willingness of ordinary American citizens from all walks of life to commit such cruel acts in obedience to the authority of the scientist conducting the experiment. The implications for systems of authority perceived as legitimate by citizens are enormous. Milgram discounts the argument that only totalitarian systems, like that of the Nazis, foster torture, murder and, atrocities through the use of authority:

In democracies men are placed in office through popular elections. Yet, once installed, they are no less in authority than those who get there by other means. And, as we have seen repeatedly, the demands of democratically installed authority may also come into conflict with conscience. The importation and enslavement of millions of black people, the destruction of the American Indian population, the internment of Japanese Americans, the use of napalm against civilians in Vietnam, all the harsh policies that originated in the authority of a democratic nation, and were responded to with the expected obedience.... I am forever astonished that when lecturing on the obedience experiments in colleges across the country, I faced young men who were aghast at the behavior of experimental subjects and proclaimed they would never behave in such a way, but who, in a matter of months, were brought into the military and performed without compunction actions that made shocking the victim seem pallid. (pp. 179-180)

Serious questions must be raised regarding Milgram's assumption that such a thing as authentic democracy exists in the United States (or anywhere else) in which there exists truly the rule of the people and the principle of unity-in-diversity as the basis for all social institutions. As we have seen, the system of nation-states evolved around the principle of national self-interest, defeating the possibility of a democratic world-order, while the global system of private accumulation of wealth similarly defeats the possibility of genuine democracy.

But obedience also includes another dimension not sufficiently emphasized by Milgram. These gigantic institutions offer many rewards in terms of status, comfort, wealth, and power to those who toe the ideological line and willingly place themselves in the service of these institutions. The ideology of the national or corporate institutions is always couched in terms of some abstract good – whether "free trade," "universal prosperity," "promoting democracy," or "defending freedom" – with which those who invest their lives in it can identify. The ultimate consequences of their actions, whether bombing and destruction of civilians, economic sanctions starving a population to death, or support for torturers and murderers, can be rationalized in terms of the system, especially a system that rewards them so highly with wealth, status, and a measure of power.

Milgram terms this "counteranthropomorphism": the ability "of attributing an impersonal quality to forces that are basically human in origin and maintenance. Some people treat systems of human origin as if they existed above and beyond any human agent.... The human element behind the agencies and institutions is denied" (pp. 8-9). Therefore, people rationalize their complicity with evil by statements like the following: "I did not throw all these people out of work, the dictates of the free market required that they be laid off." "I am not responsible for the massive torture and murder in Guatemala, I am only a federal employee in a democratic system fighting Communism there as elsewhere." "I am not responsible for the starvation and disease of more than a million people in Iraq because of economic sanctions, our government has top secret information that we lack."

The ideology also tells us our acceptance of the system includes some greater abstract goal or good serving as the goal of the system that allows participants to ignore and rationalize the human consequences of their actions. "Most subjects in the experiment," Milgram writes, "see their behavior in a larger context that is benevolent and useful to society" (p. 9). Fragmented persons give over their ethical autonomy and agency to delusional, self-justifying sets of ideas.

Fragmented institutions themselves draw into them fragmented persons who are willing to deny their ethical intuitions of wholeness and the need for unity-in-diversity in order to reap the adolescent rewards of affluence, status, and ego-gratification. The quest for power and domination has been a fundamental aspect of much human behavior throughout the modern period. The results are evident in the domination of one nation over others, the domination of an ethnic or religious group over others, the domination of oppressive governments over citizens, the domination of whites over blacks, rich over poor, men over women.

This has been manifest in ideologies such as that of the Nazis or the myth of American goodness and superiority. It has caused tremendous suffering among oppressed peoples and shows few signs of abatement at the dawn of the twenty-first century. But it requires a mode of personal being deeply fragmented. As educator Paulo Freire points out in *Pedagogy of the Oppressed* (1974), the dominator requires a dominated for his, her, or their sense of self-worth (pp. 42 and 45). Fragmented institutions draw fragmented people to them with rich rewards.

Milgram writes that *"the problem of obedience, therefore, is not wholly psychological. The form and shape of society and the way it is developing have much to do with it."* The wholeness of human action in which people take responsibility for the consequences of their actions is destroyed: "Thus," he says, "there is fragmentation of the total human act; no one man decides to carry out the evil act and is confronted with its consequences. The person who assumes full responsibility for the act has evaporated. Perhaps this is the most common characteristic of socially organized evil in society" (p. 11).

Finally, the complement of those who participate in positions of authority within modern social and economic systems is the multitude of those who obey their authority. Personal wholeness is not the placing of oneself in obedience to a system, corporation, or nation-state, thereby giving up responsibility for one's life or one's actions. The dynamics of fragmentation for this kind of self and the previous one described are much the same. The following are among the recurring themes that Milgram derives from his interviews with ordinary United States servicemen who committed atrocities in Vietnam:

- Responsibility invariably shifts upward in the mind of the subordinate.
- The actions are almost always justified in terms of a set of constructive purposes, and come to be seen as noble in the light of

some high ideological goal.
• There is frequent modification of language, so that the acts do not, at the verbal level, come into direct conflict with the verbal moral concepts that are part of every person's upbringing.
• Individual values of *loyalty, duty,* and *discipline* derive from the technical needs of the hierarchy. They are experienced as highly personal moral imperatives by the individual, but at the organizational level they are simply the technical preconditions for the maintenance of the larger system. (pp. 186-187)

A key point to observe here is the interface between personal and institutional fragmentation. Fragmented institutions, organized for self-maintenance and justified with vague ideological goals, cultivate and perpetuate fragmented individuals who fulfill roles of authority or subordination within these institutions.

All six of these misdirected actualizations of the self are part of a common reaction to the general fragmentation of modernity. They each perpetuate and mirror that fragmentation. The self of power and domination makes a desperate grab for domination in the service of its own ego or the ideology to which it has enslaved itself. Unable to fulfill itself in an openness to being, in compassion, truth, or the spontaneous joy of wholeness, it substitutes domination and the feeling of superiority for the fullness of life (Freire, 1974, ch. 1). The self of obedience has given up entirely the quest for personal autonomy and freedom that form an essential part of wholeness and gives over its deepest humanity to blind faith in the "authorities" and blind obedience to their commands and to their ideology.

Fundamentalisms make a desperate grab for stability in a world of flux by denying the multiplicity of life and clinging to what they take to be stable and secure. Narrowing of focus to the details of daily tasks is another form of denial that cannot deal with the scope and complexity of life and finds its solace in smallness, pettiness, and trivial concerns. Instrumentalism denies any non-subjective grounding to values and clings to an atomism that it mendaciously takes to be revealed by modern science. We have seen Harris at the head of this chapter state that science reveals just the opposite of this sort of instrumentalist fragmentation.

Finally, ungrounded therapeutic subjectivism remains part of the same fragmentation of modernity to which the other versions of the self are reacting. It denies a non-subjective grounding to value. It ignores the sphere of public freedom requiring political engagement, commitment, and social action, and it constricts individual focus to a set of personal subjective concerns not likely to result in fulfillment, meaning, or a transformed human condition. Our task through this volume is to uncover possibilities of integration, wholeness, depth, openness to meaning, public accountability, and political commitment that can truly make the beginning of the third millennium an era of dawning for humanity. Let us turn to an initial sketch of our potential for wholeness that we will be developing throughout.

5. A Paradigm for Personal Unity-in-Diversity

Twentieth-century science has revealed our universe to be a continuously ascending scale of parts integrated within wholes that are in turn integrated within ever larger systems of parts and wholes from the microlevel to the level of the universe itself. Living systems are a part of this universal scale of parts within wholes. The human body, for example, functions as an extremely complex integration of dozens of systems and organs (liver, kidneys, spleen, heart, eyes, ears, and so on) each of which is a provisional and highly specialized unity in its own right. The awareness of living organisms involves an integration of multiple sensory data for the use of the organism as a whole, and organisms are integrated into species that are themselves natural wholes, the species flourishing within ecosystems that form an ascending series of wholes and parts within ever larger wholes.

At the human level, the mind processes and integrates an immense amount of internal and external data. Self-awareness and reason emerge as characteristics of the species. Human beings are able to investigate the patterns of nature, to see the relationships of wholes and parts and the laws by which these are integrated, and thereby generate knowledge. We are able to relate ourselves to the whole universe, or to the source and meaning of the whole universe, and therefore practice religion and philosophy. As the ancient philosophers so often put it, each of us is a tiny microcosm (a small whole) mirroring the macrocosm (the greater whole) of the larger universe.

The immense complexity and quantity of the data, ideas, perspectives, and thoughts processed by our minds can easily lead to relativism or skepticism as it did in some great philosophers, such as Friedrich Nietzsche: *es giebt keine Wahrheit,* there is no truth (1967, pp. 148-158). But the integration of wholes and parts, of unity and diversity on every level of existence that has been revealed by twentieth century science, shows that the criterion for truth is coherence: apparently contradictory perspectives must be understood in terms of the larger wholes of which they are a part. The integration of parts within the ever-ascending series of wholes in the universe reveals the conflicts and contradictions at lower levels of existence to be complementary from the point of view of their coherence within the larger wholes of which they are necessarily part (Harris, 1987).

The collective efforts of many scientists and thinkers of the twentieth century formulated this emergent paradigm for the universe. In the last century, science and many philosophers uncovered this dynamic principle of truth. Each individual mirrors this dynamic principle in his or her own life in that we are always processing information and ideas to which we are exposed (consciously and unconsciously) in order to find order and coherence within our world. The human mind seeks to overcome what psychologists have called "cognitive dissonance," to reconcile contradictions and make sense of the world. The human mind seeks wholeness.

Part of the complexity faced by human beings is the plethora of natural drives and instincts, often in conflict with one another, often appearing to tear us apart from within. Yet many ethical traditions of the world (from Lao Tzu to Buddha, Śankara, Aristotle, Thomas Aquinas, or Nietzsche) speak of the need for integration and harmony of the self in the face of this internal multiplicity. We endeavor to integrate the many demands and drives within ourselves while simultaneously facing the many demands, apparent contradictions, and imperatives from the community.

Yet each of these classical thinkers was concerned with community life as well: the linguistic, cultural, religious, and social communities that twentieth-century social science has revealed as inseparably linked to our development and characteristics as individuals. Each of them in differing ways saw the need to harmonize the demands of the community with the drive for integration and harmony within the individual. We are all inseparably linked to our communities, as we have seen, communities that form an ever ascending series of parts within greater wholes: the family, the neighborhood, the town or borough, the municipality, the province or state, the nation, the geographical region, the world.

Although the rights, interests, needs, and demands of our individual lives often seem in contradiction to the demands, interests, and needs of the community, the *telos* for wholeness inherent in our lives and in the human situation points to a need for integration. Personal autonomy and wholeness need to be integrated with the need for wholeness and harmony on every level of society up to the planetary level. Our integration must extend to the series of planetary life-communities with which we share our global ecosystem.

The apparent contradictions between the demands for integration and wholeness with society that most normal human beings feel arise for the most part because our ideas of self-fulfillment and self-satisfaction are the products of a fragmented social order. The fragmented nation-state system, the fragmented economic system pitting human beings against one another in a dog eat dog struggle for survival and ascendancy, and the fragmented culture of mastery and domination of nature and other human beings, leads each of us to envision self-fulfillment and self-satisfaction in an extremely atomistic and fragmented manner. But human beings are extremely malleable in their characteristics, as the history of world culture and religion has shown. Fulfillment and satisfaction may be found in many forms that our present fragmented and limited imagination does not entertain.

Yet we each also contain intimations of what a true integration of individual and community might mean and the personal fulfillment that could accompany this. In a subsequent chapter, we will look deeply into this issue under the heading of "human spirituality." Each normal person is capable of responding to the implications of a world peace that respects the diversity and richness of different races, cultures, and religions, a worldwide sustainable life preserving the planet for future generations, and a planetary economy of universal prosperity with social protections for each person with respect to accident, sickness, or old age (as specified in Article 25 of the U.N. *Universal Declaration of Human Rights*).

A healthy, non-fragmented self finds fulfillment, at least in part, through the joy and fulfillment of others. And this joy and fulfillment of others can only be maximized through authentic democracy on a planetary scale. A healthy, non-fragmented person demands a healthy, non-fragmented institutional matrix for the human community. The wholeness and unity within ourselves is also sustained and fulfilled precisely through our affirmation and integration with the diversity of our experience and the world around us. The two dimensions are inseparable, unity-in-diversity is the ethical and paradigmatic model for our personal lives and for life on planet Earth.

6. The Existential Roots of Personal Fragmentation

The normal human mind functions as a natural structural unity of consciousness. My subjectivity, experienced as a unity, confronts the multiplicity of the world as an "I." I am the subject of my experience. I am a single subjectivity that encounters the manifold of my experience throughout the course of my life. In his *Critique of Pure Reason*, Immanuel Kant was the first great thinker to articulate the dynamics of what he called "the transcendental unity of apperception" and the synthetic functioning of the human mind that integrates the multiplicity of experience into the unity of my experience. Descartes had been mistaken in his *Meditations* when he took the unity of the "I think" as a self-substance, a mental thing or reality on a par with physical things or what he called "extended substance."

Subject and object arise together in experience, or better, they are *a priori* conditions of experience. No subject exists without an object and no object without a subject, a principle that G. W. F. Hegel was to make the foundation of his world-historical dialectical system, a system that intimates the principle of unity-in-diversity discovered by twentieth-century science. The structure of human experience embodies the principle of unity-in-diversity.

But Kant's unity of apperception is not the self in the sense of ego-awareness of myself as a particular human being with particular characteristics. Habermas and Taylor, to name two of the philosophers who have gone deeply into this issue, indicate that the ego-self is a product of language, community, and social interaction, not an independent reality preexistent to its relationships. This self is deeply problematic and the source of many of our problems.

This structural unity of consciousness (the transcendental unity of apperception) confronts two vast dimensions of multiplicity: the ever-changing world around me and the multiplicity I experience in myself. Within myself I encounter an ever-changing stream of emotions, thoughts, feelings, images, intuitions, sensations, and experiences, as David Hume pointed out in *A Treatise of Human Nature*. I also experience a multiplicity of possible personality tendencies, a multiplicity of potentialities, possibilities, drives, needs, and wants.

This multiplicity inevitably means that I am in conflict with myself. I am torn apart in different directions. I could become different persons depending on the decisions I make or the wants and needs that I satisfy. Or better, I am a collection of different persons competing with one another for dominance and further actualization. I am confronted with numerous ideologies and ideas competing for my allegiance. Which ones I choose to follow will actualize some potentialities within me and I will be a different person accordingly. If I choose (or let my community choose for me) a neo-Nazi ideology, the potential for violence, hatred, and domination within me is thereby encouraged.

The realization that my ego-self is a product of language, community, and social interaction does not solve the dilemmas faced by the self. It gives me a greater bond to the community, but it does not resolve the problem of who I am or should be within this vast multiplicity of possibilities that I find within myself. At any particular point in time, I experience innumerable internal conflicts, possibilities, competing claims, impulses, or desires.

Therefore, the transcendental unity of consciousness is not sufficient for my unity as a person. If I am to be whole, it appears that my ego, my personal self, must be realized or created or developed from the multiplicity of often conflicting selves and potentialities within me and in response to the multiplicity and dynamism of the world around me. Nietzsche was one of the great philosophers describing this inner multiplicity and the need to be an artist of the self, for creation of an aesthetic and ethical unity from this seething multiplicity within and without.

But the matter is much more complex and difficult than this, for my consciousness is structured as subject to object, and I find it impossible to know myself directly and purely as subject. I can only objectify myself in one way or another: turn myself into an object or create a mental image of myself. But in doing this, I lose precisely what I would like to know: who am I? How can I be whole, fulfilled, and happy? What is this self that I believe to be there but can never be known directly? I can only create mental images of it, constructs, ideologies.

However, when I do this I know that my idea is merely a construct, objectifying (and hence falsifying) some aspects of the multiplicity within me and ignoring others. I know what I take myself to be is just a self-created image, perhaps wishful thinking, perhaps negative thinking, but always arbitrary – never, so to speak, the real thing. If I look at my situation honestly, all my experience appears to be filtered through this arbitrary construct that I call my ego-self. But this idea is frightening, so most often I semi-consciously cling to an imagined ego-self (an arbitrarily constructed self-image) as if it were a reality and the true recipient of experience (Martin, 1999).

This is a primary source of what the Existentialist movement often referred to as "existential anxiety." Our existential condition is being trapped, so to speak, in this subject-object bifurcation. We seem never to be able to find happiness or freedom or fulfillment because we are lost in a hall of mirrors. We continually penetrate, in Nietzsche's image, into caves behind caves, never finding the last cave, never finding a real self, never achieving self-knowledge. This reality that we seem to be is only apprehended as a shifting mirage from which we are ever cut off by the subject-object structure of consciousness.

We are divided and cut off from the world around us by this dualism of consciousness, and we are divided within by this same dualism. We can only apprehend ourselves in duality as an arbitrary image or object for our subjectivity. Our subjectivity itself cannot be directly apprehended. We feel forever lost, forever insubstantial, forever confused, forever filled with anxiety and dread as we face death, and life appears to slip through our fingers day by day. How do we develop a mature, integrated, fulfilled self, living happily on planet Earth, in the face of this irrevocable existential condition?

What is worse, we see that most people in our contemporary world are in a process of denial of their existential condition. This denial was described in various ways, for example, by Martin Heidegger in *Being and Time*, Jean-Paul Sartre in *Being and Nothingness*, and Gabriel Marcel in *Man Against Mass Society.* Contemporary human beings cannot cope with the ambiguities of their existential condition and cling to some small but secure identity or ideology such as those discussed above. They form a narrow ego-self at least in part through identification with family, race, class, nation, ethnic group, or religion.

But the cause and the inevitable consequence of this clinging to the smallness of the ego-self is fear – fear of death, fear of other nations, fear of "terrorists," fear of other religions, fear of change, fear of what is different, fear of diversity, fear of "the other," fear of the fullness and ecstasy of life itself. This pervasive fear that haunts the fragmented self only further ramifies that fragmentation and inhibits the ability to experience the unity-in-diversity of the world fully and meaningfully.

This leads to devastating social consequences for our already fragmented institutions. We must increase our military budget because of all the unknown and possible terrors hidden within the multiplicity of the world. We must make those other nations just like us so that they are no longer a threat to our "way of life." We must defend our "private property" and make sure no one else encroaches upon it. We must torture and murder the "subversives" in our wars of counter-insurgency. We must prevent change at all costs. We must maintain our religious identity as different from those heathens. We must hate the idolators as evil and a threat to the existence of everything decent and good. We must kill Communists, as we previously killed Indians, because their mere existence challenges our fragmented self-identity with its self-justifying ideology that must be protected at all costs. Ultimately, "the only good Indian is a dead Indian" is not fundamentally different from "the only good Commie is a dead Commie."

7. The Cosmic Dimension of Personal Unity-in-diversity

As we saw in Chapter One, human beings have emerged into this level of self-awareness, with these possibilities of self-objectification and objectification of the world only since the Axis Period of human history about 2500 years ago. Our era for the past 2500 years has been confused and obsessed with the apparent power placed in our hands by the power of objectification. We can understand and master nature. We can place ourselves over and against anything – from human groupings to the forces of nature – and struggle for conquest of what we oppose or dislike. We can oppose ourselves economically to the welfare of other human beings and accumulate for ourselves vast wealth and power. We can dehumanize other persons and turn them into Blacks or Jews or Commies fit only to be killed or enslaved.

And we are filled with fear of what will happen to our identity if those who are different "take over." We can create vast empires to extend our power and sameness over the Earth: the Greek, the Roman, the Holy Roman, the Portuguese, the Dutch, the French, the German, the Spanish, the British, or the American empire. Our fragmentation requires that we tear unity-in-diversity apart, with the result that we have neither.

We lack the ability to deal with "the whole human being" as Finch puts this at the head of this chapter. So we cling tenaciously to the smallness of the ego-self that fosters greed and the desire for domination. This serves as the easy way out of our confusing and debilitating existential situation. This also is ultimately self-destructive of the human project on planet Earth and the natural world that forms our planetary ecosystem. But in the face of our constricting and debilitating fears, even this fact fails to become a source of genuine existential transformation.

On a personal level human beings have repeatedly taken the easy way out, the self-destructive way of fragmentation, denying the challenge of unity-in-diversity and, with it, the depth and wholeness of life itself. Instead of struggling with the complexities and difficulties faced by the self, I can give up my quest to become an authentic, whole human being through giving my identity over to the nation-state, to the military of some power grouping, to the compulsion for wealth and power, to hatred of some other group, nation, or race, to the passionate oversimplifications of some ideology, to the trivial concerns of everyday life, to an amoral, instrumental self available for use by whatever power grouping wishes to exploit it, or to a religious ideology that claims a simple solution for our complex human condition has been sent by God.

The dawn of the third millennium is the beginning of a new era in the development of human maturity. We are at the end of the line as the quotation from Finch asserts above. We have exhausted the principles by which we have been living and are living today with the cumulative consequences of this fragmentation in the multiple global crises humankind is facing. But the next step is not some new ideology or proposal to return to some era of the past. The next step is realization of the real potential within us – the integrating of the unity and diversity that has been within us all along (Martin, 2002). We have not seen what is most fundamental because of the ethos of fragmentation that has dominated our lives. The fragmented systems of the modern world (economic, nation-state, the drive for scientific and technical mastery) have promoted fragmented selves in the citizens of the planet, since each of these systems flourishes and promotes itself precisely through the use of human fragmentation.

Each of these systems encourages the development of an ego, a narrow sense of identity that defines itself over and against some other, something it must negate to be itself. I am wealthy and successful, they are not. I need to protect my future and that of my company, regardless of the environmental and human consequences that do not directly affect me. I am of the white race, they are not. I am an American, they are not. I am of the true religion, they are not. The first step in overcoming what psychologist Lifton calls the "dangerous forms of fragmentation of the self" is to recognize and appreciate the richness of our "protean self." "Fragmentation," he says, "can be associated with different kinds of self-process, all of them precarious... The fragmented self is radically bereft of coherence and continuity, an extreme expression of dissociation" (1993, p. 202).

We have seen that Lifton's book, *The Protean Self – Human Resilience in an Age of Fragmentation* (1993), studies the fragmentation of our age and describes our human capability for a "protean self" of largeness, multiplicity, diversity, and creativity. He argues that this enlarged unity-in-diversity is inherent to the "social evolution of the self" in our time. We have moved through several levels of identification "from individual to family to social or ethnic group to nation" and can move today toward "species consciousness" without leaving the other levels behind.

Unity-in-diversity on any of these levels is its healthy, creative, and dynamic mode of existence. The family, for example, that forms a unity of loving relationships only flourishes as a true unity when it affirms the diversity and multiplicity of the persons within it. But as soon as the family is the limit of a person's identification, it becomes a fragment over and against larger wholes and again a destructive and fragmenting force in our lives. Lifton writes:

> This evolution of the self toward its own species can help it overcome dis-
> sociative tendencies. One moves toward becoming what the early Karl
> Marx called a "species-being," a fully human being. Once established, the
> species identification itself contributes to centering and grounding. In no
> way eliminated, prior identifications are, rather, brought into new alignment
> within a more inclusive sense of self. (p. 231)

The problem with fragmented versions of the self that do not allow of a universal dynamic of unity and diversity is the problem inherent in the structure of the human ego itself that tends to identify itself with the contents of its awareness and its desires. I am these experiences, this body, these social relationships and commitments, this nationality, these desires, hopes, and fears, and so on. We form attachments to these contents of consciousness (because we mistakenly think they are us) so that the ego-unity that we settle for is always a unity also defined in terms of the negation of someone else. I am not your body, those social relationships, those other nationalities, those desires, hopes, and so on. The unity of the ego thus understood is necessarily a fragment and necessarily excludes diversity.

Psychologist Steven Levine asserts that when this identification of the mind with its objects (inner and outer) is transcended, the result is a new wholeness and liberating sense of "spaciousness":

> Unable to differentiate between the object of awareness and awareness it-self, we think of all the content of mind as our own, as "me".... Aware-ness could be said to be like water. It takes on the shape of any vessel that contains it. If one mistakes this awareness for its various tempo-rary forms, life becomes a ponderous plodding from one moment of de-sire, from one object of the mind, to the next. Life becomes filled with urgency and the strategies of fear, instead of lightly experiencing all these forms, recognizing that water is water no matter what its form....
>
> But when the mind is closed around fear or desire, this encouragement to stay open allows a moment of clear seeing, an opportunity to experience the freedom with which we can live our lives.... As we begin to let go of identification with the mind, we discover that there are other means of un-covering the natural satisfactoriness of the mind's essential spaciousness.... Its expanse is so great that waves of energy wash through the body making any satisfaction we've ever had , even our profoundest sexual gratification, pale by comparison. The natural energy of the mind is released. Grasping has stilled long enough so that we experience the immensity and intensity of our deepest nature. (1982, pp. 41-47)

Some thinkers, like Richard Maurice Bucke, M.D. (1974), call this spaciousness of the mind "cosmic consciousness," a wholeness to the self so profound that it can live from an awareness of the unity permeating the great and wonderful multiplicity of the cosmos itself. This may be the ultimate unity-in-diversity for which the evolution of human consciousness is destined, but given our planetary crises at the dawn of the third millennium, the related "species consciousness" of which Lifton speaks should also be a primary concern.

This "species consciousness," a sense of the whole of the human reality in which the diversity of each member is affirmed, constitutes the source of authentic planetary democracy. The sense of the depth, unity, and sanctity of the cosmos that forms the ultimate source of human wholeness, will in all likelihood become an inseparable feature of species consciousness as healthy, planetary institutions become established.

Philosopher and psychologist Richard De Martino (1960) calls our limited ego-identification a "filter" because it imposes mental images and a false unity (the self-image) on the vast multiplicity of life. This fragmentation is "repressedness," the blocking of our true human potential. Yet, as with Lifton, "universal man" constitutes the wholeness within which diversity is included:

> To the degree to which I can rid myself of this filter and can experience my self as the universal man, that is, to the degree to which repressedness diminishes, I am in touch with the deepest sources within myself, and that means with all of humanity. If all repressedness has been lifted, there is no more unconscious as against conscious; there is direct immediate experience; inasmuch as I am not a stranger to myself, no one and nothing is a stranger to me. (p. 127)

The "ego" constitutes our ordinary, limited modes of self-identification, some of which are outlined above. The richness and fulfillment of unity-in-diversity is impossible for fragmented selves, selves also conditioned and encouraged by fragmented institutions. The ordinary ego is therefore constituted by fragmentation: it defines itself precisely by excluding others. Philosopher and spiritual teacher Ruben Habito (1993) speaks of the ego as our "woundedness." We are distorted and maimed persons incapable of the wholeness of unity-in-diversity that he associates with our "true self":

> The key to healing our woundedness on the manifold levels of existence, including the ecological, social, and personal, lies in overcoming this ego-centered consciousness that controls our attitudes and actions in everyday life. As we begin to see through this idealized and falsely conceived self with which we identify in opposition to the Other, we hear an invitation from within, to launch into a search for our true self that underlies this delusive ego. (p. 15)

What Habito calls the "ego" is the smallness of the self-identity grasped by self-aware beings in their effort to objectify themselves and gain closure within the dynamic and frightening worlds of inner and outer multiplicity and ceaseless change. This necessarily puts us in opposition to "the Other." Habito quotes philosopher and theologian Paul Tillich who asserts that human beings are "in a state of separation from the Ground of Being" (p. 75). Something about our deeper selves and the cosmos itself, beyond the ego of confrontation, domination, and separation, requires our reconciliation, something that is the source of true integration within the multiplicity of existence. Unity-and-multiplicity is the fundamental dynamic of our universe and of every ecosystem, as twentieth-century science has revealed. The question is how do we find this principle in ourselves to heal our fragmentation and overcome the separation and isolation of unredeemed multiplicity? How do we release what Levine calls "the natural energy of the mind"? These thinkers suggest that we need to go deeper than the self-conscious ego to participate in the same principle within us that forms the ground of all unity-in-diversity in the universe.

Tillich asserts that a human being needs to identify with a whole larger than his or her self. However, we have a tendency to identify with limited wholes to find closure from the anxiety of uncertain existence. He calls this identification "idolatry," the investing of one's life in a limited, finite reality (for example, the nation-state, wealth, or family) and therefore not relating to the "infinite" source of all meaning and personal wholeness. We are faced with a paradox. Our selves are finite and limited, and yet something about our human situation can be termed "infinite." There is something beyond all concrete identifiable finite realities that we must make our "ultimate concern" (1957, chs.1 and 2). Tillich calls this ultimate concern "faith" and finds that it transcends the multiplicity of our conscious and unconscious minds yet unites them all in "a personal center."

> Faith as the embracing and centered act of the personality is "ecstatic." It transcends both the drives of the non-rational unconscious and the structures of the rational conscious. It transcends them, but it does not destroy them. The ecstatic character of faith does not exclude its rational character although it is not identical with it, and it includes nonrational strivings without being identical with them. In the ecstasy of faith there is an awareness of truth and of ethical value; there are also past loves and hates, conflicts and reunions, individual and collective influences. "Ecstasy" means "standing outside oneself" – without ceasing to be oneself – with all the elements which are united in the personal center. (pp. 6-7)

Here is one way of expressing the mature unity-in-diversity that can relieve us of our unbearable fragmentation and transform the divisive nightmare that we have made of planet Earth. A true personal center is "ecstatic" in that it transcends the ego while integrating the multiplicity of forces that operate within our conscious and unconscious minds. The self not closed off in fragmentation, but open to the ultimate principle of wholeness within and without, is a self able to identify with larger and larger wholes.

A self is capable of compassion, of identification with others and with the natural world, as Fox puts it, because it operates dialectically out of the dynamic of "both-and" instead of out of the narrow egoistic "either-or" (1990, pp. 82-85). Only when we open up to the depths of being and the great spaciousness and freedom of the self can we truly embrace and identify with the multiplicity within us and without. (We will examine the question of religion and spirituality more deeply in subsequent chapters, but at this point we are concerned with outlining the wholeness in diversity of a healthy sense of selfhood.)

As Tillich and the other thinkers mentioned here insist, such largeness of self does not obviate our ethical sense of right and wrong, nor our sense of justice (1957, p. 6; Martin, 1997). Instead, it redeems and enlarges these fundamental human capacities, liberating them from dogma and fetishism, and transforming them into truly liberating capacities. A person works for justice because this work flows naturally from dynamic awareness of unity-in-diversity. Justice is no longer defined for me by the social or ethnic group, religious dogma, or the nation-state. And I am entirely liberated from the shallow notion of the instrumental and utilitarian self that justice is merely emotion, merely subjective, and therefore to be discounted. Only a truly whole self, beyond the fragmented ego, a self that De Martino calls the "universal man," can be just and realize justice in the world.

Fragmented selves nearly always define justice in their favor: justice is our way of doing it, justice is our economic and social ideas, justice is our notion of democracy, and so on. The emerging paradigm of unity-in-diversity, which is the next step in human social evolution and the process of maturing for human beings on this planet, is also the beginning of the era of authentic and dynamic justice. The quest for wholeness is, as Harris points out at the head of this chapter, "the groundspring of morality and the social order."

Only the unity of all human beings on Earth can create justice for each in their individuality and multiplicity, and for the natural world that embraces us. The paradigm of unity and diversity within the whole of the universe revealed by modern science does not exclude the imperative for justice. Nor, as we have seen, does it exclude the possibility of a "cosmic consciousness," a deep awareness of unity-in-diversity that transcends even the empirical generalizations of science.

In their book *The Conscious Universe – Part and whole in Modern Physical Theory* (1990), Menas Kafatos and Robert Nadeau synthesize the amazing revelations concerning the whole of the universe in relation to its parts that has been accomplished by contemporary science (see also Zukav, 1979; Siu, 1957). In relation to the question of consciousness and the role of the human mind in relation to the whole, they have this to say:

> Although the two experimentally confirmable non-localities may bring us to the horizon of knowledge where we confront the existence of the undivided whole, we cannot cross that horizon in terms of the content of consciousness. Yet the fact that we cannot disclose this undivided wholeness in our conscious constructions of this reality as parts does not mean that science invalidates the prospect that we can apprehend this wholeness on a level that is prior to conscious constructs. It merely means that science qua science cannot fully disclose or describe the whole....

The evidence for the existence of the ineffable and mysterious disclosed by modern physics is as near as the dance of particles that make up our bodies, and as far as the furthest regions of the cosmos. The results of the experiments testing Bell's theorem suggest that all the parts, or any manifestation of "being" in the vast cosmos, are seamlessly interconnected in the unity of "Being." Yet quantum physics also says that the ground of Being for all this being will never be completely subsumed by rational understanding. (pp. 179 and 180)

This "ground of being" at the root of the direct awareness, and not limited to a fragmented ego-identification, is the source of unity within the human being as within the whole of the universe. As Kafatos and Nadeau insist, this unity is not far away. It includes the "dance of particles that make up our bodies." It forms the source of that free awareness that Levine says breaks our identification with the fragments of existence and gives the mind a liberating "spaciousness." It forms the source of that "ecstatic standing outside oneself -- without ceasing to be oneself" described by Tillich. It forms the source of the "species consciousness" of Marx and Lifton.

Kafatos and Nadeau go on to assert that awareness of this wholeness at the root of existence must move in our lives from "theoretical reason" to "practical reason." It must become internalized in our everyday living and acting:

If theoretical reason in modern physics does eventually refashion the terms of constructing our symbolic universe to the extent that it impacts practical reason, then conceiving of a human being, as Einstein put it, as "part of the whole" is the leap of faith that would prove most critical. It is only in making this leap that we can begin, as he suggests, to free ourselves from the "optical illusions" of our present conception of self as a "part limited in space and time," and to widen "our circle of compassion to embrace all living creatures and the whole of nature in its beauty." Yet one cannot, of course, merely reason or argue oneself into an acceptance of this proposition. One must have the capacity, in our view, for what Einstein termed "cosmic religious feeling." (pp. 179, 180 & 182)

The authors affirm that Einstein himself, one of the primary sources of the revolution in science that has led to the insight that the multiplicity of existence is "seamlessly interconnected in the unity of Being," saw the deeper implications of the new scientific paradigm. If this revolution in science impacts our practical reason, then we can be freed from what Einstein calls the "optical illusion" of the self as "a part limited in space and time." As with our understanding of justice, "our circle of compassion" widens "to embrace all living creatures and the whole of nature." The uniqueness and integrity of the parts is loved, enhanced, and protected precisely because they are embraced within the unity of genuine wholeness.

The paradigm of unity-in-diversity revealed by the scientific breakthroughs of the twentieth century is not merely an intellectual construct or proposed model for human thought. It reflects the deepest core of the cosmos and of human existence. "Cosmic religious feeling," or "cosmic consciousness" is not a mere subjective state of those rare persons called mystics or saints. Cosmic consciousness is the unity of what Habito calls the "true self" as opposed to "the falsely conceived self with which we identify in opposition to the Other." The deep awareness of unity-in-diversity is our mature capability as human beings, overcoming our fragmentation and pointing to a truly transformed world at the dawn of the third millennium.

Chapter Three

Deep Nonviolence
The Dynamic Relationship of Compassion, Critical Theory, and Active Nonviolence

The reader may well object that a compassionate society is a utopian dream which has never existed anywhere on Earth. The author would, of course, agree, with the qualification that some individuals and some small groups have been highly compassionate. However, the instant recognition of the utopian character of a compassionate society is a sure sign of how far we are from actualizing such a society, which seems to be required if human existence is going to continue on this Earth very much longer.

But how are we going to change ourselves and our societies from compulsion to compassion?... As long as the status quo is believed to be given by God or by Nature, little or no progress can be expected.... Given the basic assumption that some sort of cognitive dissonance has to be aroused before there would be any inclination toward social change, the question should then be directed toward the methods of arousing such dissonance. At least four nonviolent methods come to mind which have been used throughout human history: research, education, legislation, and demonstration.

William Eckhardt

Distant thinkers, those who had a perspective of the center from the periphery, those who had to define themselves in the presence of an already established image of the human person and in the presence of uncivilized fellow humans, the newcomers, the ones who hope because they are always outside, these are the ones who have a clear mind for pondering reality. They have nothing to hide. How could they hide domination if they undergo it? How would their philosophy be an ideological ontology if their praxis is one of liberation from the center they are opposing? Philosophical intelligence is never so truthful, clean, and precise as when it starts from oppression and does not have to defend any privileges, because it has none.

Enrique Dussel

A transformed world as an expression of planetary maturity involves a dynamic holism of unity-in-diversity and must be understood as encompassing the social and spiritual dimensions of existence. Human maturity is a process of continuous increase in political freedom, justice, and spiritual awakening to the unity and diversity of the universe that expresses itself through us. These dimensions are dynamically interrelated, as we shall see further in this chapter.

We will reflect below upon the implications of the holistic transformation necessary in the ascent to planetary maturity. We must activate in ourselves a dynamic confluence of compassion, critical theory, and active nonviolence. Spiritual freedom requires a compassion born of deep silence. Political freedom requires the activation of a genuinely critical consciousness. And for both of these to be realized, human life must move from its present passive acceptance of all forms of violence into the active, transformative way of life that I call "active nonviolence."

In the above epigraph, Canadian peace researcher William Eckhardt affirms this same conclusion. A compassionate global society is what is "required if human existence is going to continue on this Earth very much longer." At the dawn of the twenty-first century, we are facing a limit situation where we are facing the limits of the Earth's ability to absorb our unremitting violence and immaturity. Our modern societies, like our selves, are permeated by what can be called "deep violence," a pervasive and substantial violence so fundamental to our way of life and so universal that it is often not even recognized as such. Yet we are at a turning point in human history where the future has become a matter of life and death.

In this chapter, I will try to clarify the nature, function, and extent of this violence so we can respond effectively through that depth of understanding that implies a transformation of our being toward deep nonviolence. The task is often one of great difficulty for a thinker from "the center," to quote Dussel in the above epigraph. The task is to think our world as far as possible from the point of view of its victims, from the bottom up, from the periphery of empire and privilege. Only so far as we are successful in doing this will our work as philosophers, thinkers, or human beings contribute to the process of human liberation. From the bottom up, things look very different than they do looking from the top down. From the bottom up, that is, from the perspective of the majority of humanity, our global economic, social, legal, enforcement, and communication systems appear as unremitting violence.

1. Deep Violence: Three Interrelated Forms of Violence

The idea of deep violence is meant to be a term encompassing a wide range of actions and relationships that we may think of as violent. The Oxford English Dictionary defines "violent" as "having some quality or qualities in such a degree as to produce a very marked or powerful effect (especially in the way of injury or discomfort); intense, vehement, very strong or severe." I will subdivide deep violence into three main categories, each of which covers a range of phenomena often thought of as violent, and consider each of them in turn: first, forms of overt physical violence, like war and militarism, terrorism, or violent crime. These, I argue, are primarily the overt manifestations of the deeper forms of institutional and spiritual violence.

Second, our planet is pervaded by forms of structural or institutional violence. In our era these are primarily associated with exploitative economic institutions, with their attendant commodity relationships and so-called free market forces, social phenomena of incredible violence that are treated in the dominant ideology as if they were natural forces independent of human control. Third, overt and institutional violence both produce and require forms of spiritual violence. In our era, the structurally violent institutions reproduce in each generation a false self and corresponding fictitious world of false social relationships, ideas, and forms of communication that form the basis of spiritual violence. For each of these forms of violence, the effect is "to produce a very marked or powerful effect (especially in the way of injury or discomfort); intense, vehement, very strong or severe."

Overt physical violence in the United States has been a major topic of attention for some years. Of the three forms of violence identified here, physical violence least requires elaborate elucidation, as it has been recognized and analyzed extensively by the mainstream media where family violence, random street violence, senseless acts of nihilistic violence, violence resulting from hatred, and organized criminal violence appear endemic. For example, the 19 June 1994 issue of the *Washington Post Magazine* features a well researched article by Peter Carlson on "The American Way of Murder" that details the astonishing homicidal violence of American culture and social reality. The article draws on the work of many experts.

In its homicide rate, according to criminologist Hugh D. Barlow, "the United States ranks first among Western and other industrialized nations and has done so for as long as the data have been available" (pp. 12-13). Criminologists today speak of the American "subculture of violence," much of it associated with the extensive poverty in the United States (p. 29). Violence in the United States, the author says, "has been studied and analyzed by an army of criminologists, sociologists, psychologists, historians, and distinguished panels of learned experts, who can explain everything about homicide except how to stop it" (p. 13). I suggest that addressing overt violence requires that we recognize and respond to the deeper levels of violence in our modern culture – structural and spiritual violence.

This same principle applies to the other dimension of overt violence in the United States: militarism. While this is a global phenomenon, requiring global solutions, the United States leads the world in militarism, spending some 400 billion U.S. dollars per year. The U.S. Department of State "Fact Sheet" for 6 February 2003, estimates the world military expenditures for 1999 at $852 billion, a figure that has been approximated annually for some years (see Sivard, 1996). This pervasive violence, institutionalized to an extraordinary degree, is rarely acknowledged as such by the same army of criminologists, sociologists, psychologists, historians, and experts who are so deeply concerned with the pervasive civil violence. These experts somehow fail to notice that the United States has been on a war footing since about 1940, never having demilitarized or abandoned its war economy or militarism since end of the Second World War (Johnson, 2004).

While social problems have mounted steadily since that time, and while education, health-care, and the infrastructure of the country have been neglected, many trillions of dollars have been invested in keeping the society militarized – in regular wars, "interventions," or "low intensity conflicts" abroad, and in inundating the population with military propaganda directed toward keeping them fearful of enemies in every corner of the world, pliable to wasting immense resources on war preparation and research, pliable to living with weapons of mass destruction, and amenable to regular foreign wars or "military conflicts." Such training and preparation for destroying people and property is violence pure and simple. Yet this form of overt violence is so deeply imbedded in U.S. and world society, so acceptable, and so promoted by the mass media and ruling powers, that it remains invisible to most, including, conveniently, the "army of experts" currently studying violence in the United States.

But overt violence is in many ways a symptom of a deeper form of violence, structural violence. Structural or institutional violence is a broad concept covering a range of social arrangements that serve to deprive one class or group of people of basic necessities of life while another group or class prospers from these social arrangements. Much is written on structural violence, for example, in the literature of liberation theology. This literature often combines a clear awareness of the unspeakable poverty and misery of the poor, primarily in the third-world, with a social analysis of the structural features of international capitalism that create this immense poverty and misery.

The immense overt violence of militarism is necessary to enforce the "order" of a world in which three fifths of humanity live in unspeakable poverty (Renner, 1996). Under these conditions, wars, arms transfers to dictatorial regimes, covert military operations, interventions, counter-insurgency warfare, and low-intensity conflicts designed to repress rebellion and revolutionary aspirations in desperate peoples become a necessity (Klare and Arnson, 1981; Herman, 1982). Massive overt violence on a planetary scale becomes imperative to maintain and enforce the globalized system of structural violence.

Brazilian theologian Dominique Barbé asserts with reference to the international debt that poor countries have been forced to incur to the wealthy lending institutions of first-world countries: "Yes! It is institutional violence. The cheap sale of raw materials, our natural wealth, has paid for the debt. We have enriched the countries of the First-world through financial groups operating in Brazil. This type of institutional violence kills millions of persons, many more than a world war" (1989, p. 167).

Close similarities exist between the notion of "institutional violence" and the concept of "exploitation." In *A General Theory of Exploitation and Class,* John Roemer argues that one class (S) can be said to be exploited by another class (S') whenever: "(1) There is a feasible alternative state in which coalition S would be better off than in its present situation; (2) Under this alternative, coalition S' would be worse off than at present; (3) Coalition S' is in relationship of dominance to S. This dominance enables it to prevent coalition S from realizing the alternative" (1989, pp. 194-195).

The international debt mentioned by Barbé as massive institutional violence responsible for the deaths of millions of persons serves as a case in point. Poor countries are trapped into their debt structure for all sorts of reasons, not the least being the structure of international capitalism and the hold financial institutions controlling this debt have over the fate of the debtor nations. Roemer's three conditions apply here as they do to all class societies where power and ideological control fall to the dominant class and the conditions under which at least some sectors of the subservient class suffers are not those people would voluntarily choose.

To be born anywhere in today's world is to be born into a situation of structural violence. To be born in a poor country like Nicaragua today (more than a decade after their Sandinista Revolution was destroyed by the United States supported Contra terrorists) is to be born into a system of violence so severe that a person's life-chances are severely diminished. Massive poverty, lack of health-care, lack of schooling, and malnutrition make Nicaragua a kind of prison for its citizens. To be born there for the majority is to lead a life (if one survives infancy) of poverty, suffering and misery, while the Nicaraguan government compliantly services its immense international debt by selling off the country and its resources to wealthy first-world corporations and allowing its people to work at near starvation wages while growing food for export to the comfortable middle class citizens of wealthy first-world countries (see Barry, 1987).

On the other hand, to be born in the comfortable classes within the United States or other first-world countries, and to consume the coffee, bananas, beef, clothing, or other products produced in Nicaragua or other third-world countries is to be caught within a similar system of pervasive structural violence, this time in the role of dominator, exploiter, and oppressor. For to wear the affordable clothing produced in third-world sweatshops, to consume the affordable coffee, bananas, beef, or lumber imported for our consumption, means precisely that our comfort and wealth are predicated on their poverty. If those working in labor-intensive coffee production for export were paid a decent, living wage, our coffee would cost many times what it does presently. First-world citizens could not afford coffee, bananas, beef, clothing, or any of the many other commodities produced for export in the third-world if it were not for the reason that their poverty is being exploited to make these commodities affordable to us while generating a substantial profit for the capital investors in this system (Chossoudovsky, 1998).

First-world comfort and wealth also buys complicity in this system. Every time we go to the supermarket or department store we take advantage of a structural violence in which our affluence is predicated on their poverty, misery, and death. Roemer's three conditions apply here as well. Just as third-world people would not voluntarily choose their nightmare lives but find their conditions structurally enforced by the dual power of the system of global capitalism in tandem with the militarized system of sovereign nation-states, so most first-world citizens would not likely choose to be agents of death for third-world children. Most mature, decent people would not voluntarily choose to be dominators and exploiters of third-world peoples. We are trapped in a condition of structural violence where we have no choice but to exploit others in order to live. We may work to change this system, but if we are to live – if we are to buy clothing, coffee, or bananas – we must participate in this horrific and deadly structural violence.

In our modern world of material abundance that has emerged out of the industrial and electronic revolutions, feasible alternatives are available to the scarcity of essential goods and services in which massive portions of humankind live out their lives. "Scarcity" means that people do not have enough of the basic necessities for living a decent life. This scarcity is institutionalized and is a fundamental aspect of global structural violence. Our global technological and industrial capability can produce an abundance of the basic necessities for every citizen on this planet. But the system will not do this as long private ownership exists of the means of production, distribution, and communication. This system will produce only what generates a profit for the owners, the already wealthy investors.

In the analysis of French philosopher Jean-Paul Sartre, scarcity under capitalism is not natural scarcity but artificial scarcity (1976, pp. 129-131). Those who lack the basic necessities (and also, in Sartre's terms, lack the basic life prospects that those of the dominant classes enjoy) endure "scarcity" (1968, pp. 91-100). Because the abundant necessities of life are the private property of the dominant class, and available only on a selective basis to those who increase the wealth of this class, deep structural violence exists at the heart of the global economic system, a violence protected by the law and enforced by the police and military.

The supermarkets are packed with food, yet the food is available only to those with money. We commonly hear that worldwide enough food is grown to feed every person on the planet, yet nearly a third of the population of the Earth goes to bed hungry each night. Most of this food grown is private property, available on the market only to consumers who can pay the market rate, a rate that in turn makes a private profit for the producers.

In many societies, we find an abundance of medical knowledge, physicians, and medical facilities, but these are available only to those with insurance or wealth. Inexpensive housing is easily constructed for a fraction of what many societies spend for armaments, yet two billion humans do not have adequate housing. Artificial scarcity is a product of the exploitative structures of society and the implicit threat of overt violence by the agents of the dominant classes who have the power to prevent those who lack basic necessities from procuring them or taking them. When some are deprived of the most basic needs for human life, such as food, shelter, clothing, or health-care, by the power and authority of law and police, violence is being done to those people.

Mexican thinker José Miranda underlines the violence of globalized economics by describing it as "that mechanism of violence which we call the market, whether the consumer market, the wage market, or both." Today, he writes, "99% of all exploitation is legal" (1974, p. 12). Exploitation in the sense defined above could not exist without violence. People are not going to voluntarily allow themselves to be exploited. According to Thomas Berry and Brian Swimme, "when we bargain over these issues of life and survival for monetary gain or some commercial advantage for a few individuals or a corporate enterprise," this is evidence of a "deep pathology" in our civilization (1992, p. 251). Pathological violence is ingrained in the basic structure of capitalist society.

As critical thinkers from Karl Marx to Jürgen Habermas have emphasized, the exploiting class within political democracies does not keep its dominance solely through the use of overt physical violence. Some capitalist societies, like those in twentieth-century El Salvador or Guatemala, have used overt massive physical violence to keep the property-owning class in power against a destitute majority (Chomsky, 1992, pp. 61-74; Porpora, 1990, ch. 7). However, by and large, in the major democracies, the structurally violent character of society is masked through ideology, and physical violence is held in reserve to be used only as far as the ideological legitimation of the society in the eyes of the population fails (Chomsky, 1989).

Barbé suggests that the power of ideology is such that it may even serve to seduce the poor in third-world countries: "There's a profound Marxist saying: 'The dominant ideas are the ideas of the dominating class.' Since the dominating class has everything at its fingertips, including its ideology and the means of communication, it passes its idols on to others, even to the poorest of peoples. However, reality reveals that these idols deceive" (1989, p. 169).

The ideology masking this system of exploitation is itself a form of violence, best understood under my third heading of "spiritual violence." The word "ideology," is used here not in the broad sense of a world-view that all persons assume in one form or another, but in the sense of a collective set of assumptions, distortions, and lies that the dominant class in a society uses to justify itself and the social arrangements over which it has significant influence.

"In reality," Miranda writes, "the accumulation of capital in a few hands, could not and cannot be achieved without…institutional violence," a violence aided by "ideologies, education, and communications media," which comprise "the violence of deception" (1974, pp. 12 and 14). For example, much of the world sees the United States backed holocausts in El Salvador and Guatemala during the second half of the twentieth century as examples of the unspeakable brutality with which imperialist powers maintain their hegemony over their "spheres of influence." Yet within the United States, this mass murder of a population by its ruling elite, trained, armed, and massively financed by the United States, is understood by the government, mainstream press, and much of the population as support for "fledgling democracies" (Chomsky, 1992, p. 72, see Shalom, 1993).

Ideological lies have violent consequences, and are themselves violence against the human spirit, as is any lie. On the basis of this insight Mahatma Gandhi took his stand on the truth and complete openness. Violence, like all oppression and exploitation, requires lies to conceal its true motives and situation. Alternatively, nonviolence, ideally having no ulterior motives but justice, peace, and freedom, has nothing to hide (1973, ch. 7).

Spiritual violence involves any assault against the integrity of persons, including oneself, that is not overtly physical. This is also deeply interconnected with structural violence and even overt violence. We are seeing the interconnectedness of all forms of violence and some of the ways spirituality is reflected in our actions and institutions. The violence of competitiveness, envy, fear, anger, hatred, and resentment is reflected in our economic, social, and political institutions as well as in our everyday relations with family, community, and the environment.

An account of spiritual violence will necessarily involve some of the dimensions of overt and structural violence we have been discussing. Most violence stems from the present immaturity of humanity and its institutions. As Chapter Two made clear, our planetary home is currently dominated by fractured institutions and fractured human beings who have not yet grown into their mature potential for unity-in-diversity on all levels of existence.

Our human selves and the institutions within which we live are mutually reinforcing and co-producing. Spiritual philosopher Jiddu Krishnamurti affirms that on the deepest level "society *is* ourselves, the world *is* ourselves, the world is not different from us.... We are aggressive, brutal, competitive, and we build a society which is equally competitive, brutal, and violent" (1972, p. 31). A verb form of the Latin root of the word "violence" (*violentia*) is *violare* meaning "to violate." Spiritual violence violates the deep silence of being and the relational self arising from this matrix. The result is a distorted and dehumanized human spirituality that in turn treats its fellows, and the environment of the Earth, with manifestations of its own violence: overt, institutional, and spiritual.

One way of expressing this sense of an assault on the integrity of persons is through the intuition expressed by Immanuel Kant in his second form of the categorical imperative: "Always treat every person as an end in themselves, never merely as a means" (1964, pp. 95-96). I believe most people have a basic intuition that treating people as a means, using them, instead of recognizing them as having what Kant calls "dignity" instead of "price," is legitimately understood as a form of spiritual violence. Therefore, as Kant affirms, lying, like verbal abuse or insult, attacks a person's dignity and demeans that person. Most commercial news and advertising falls within this category.

Similarly, the structural conditions under which the poor are forced to live also demeans and degrades them, for both are forms of *himsā or* spiritual violence. Gandhi insisted that any personal or systemic forms of degrading people meant assaulting their dignity as persons and more easily allowing those with power to treat them as a means (1972, p. 38) This is why Gandhi identified so deeply with the plight of the "untouchables" in India, giving them the special name of "children of God."

This violence expressed in the using of people, in the treating them as things, instead of as persons, is institutionalized in the global economic system of exploitation where people are treated as one commodity among others, whose labor power can be bought and sold on a market by those who wish to make a private profit from this arrangement, and where governments act to exploit other countries for the benefit of their own ruling classes. Similarly, the commercial marketplace uses the lie, in a multiplicity of forms of psychological seduction and deception, to manipulate people into buying its products, and to create in people artificial needs for the sole purpose of perpetuating and maximizing the profits of the owners. Finally, the ideology spewed forth by government and mass media in first-world countries, designed to cover-up and justify the global system of institutionalized violence, constitutes the "violence of deception."

Spiritual violence goes much deeper than the systematic deceits of commercialism and ideology: for the distortion and hurt we experience today is inseparable from a violation of our most basic selves in our relatedness and unity with the universe that constitutes our deepest way of being in the world and is our goal in the process of maturing. It includes the suffering of a human creature who is fragmented, isolated, and immature and the violence with which this creature treats others and its environment in thought, word, and deed. It includes the suffering of a human creature who has lost the wholeness of what Max Picard calls "silence":

> When language is no longer related to silence it loses its source of refresh-ment and renewal and therefore something of its substance.... In the modern world language...springs from noise and vanishes in noise....-that is what si-lence is today: the momentary breakdown of noise..... Nothing has changed the nature of man so much as the loss of silence. The invention of printing, technics, compulsory education – nothing has so altered man as this lack of relationship to silence.... Man who has lost silence has not merely lost one human quality, but his whole structure has been changed thereby. (1952, pp. 40 & 41)

With the "noise" of radio, television, telephone, compouter, and fax, our modern world in particular has helped disintegrate the human capacity for deep nonviolence. Our entire way of being human is being distorted by the loss of silence and wholeness in our lives.

2. Institutionalized Violence and the Fractured Human Self

Institutionalized violence pervades our world: a world where each year twenty million children die of starvation or starvation-related ailments, while countless billions of dollars are spent on war and armaments, including the weapons that may mean the extermination of the human race. Almost no sphere of human life in the modern world exists that is not pervaded by institutional violence. The prostitutes chained to their beds in Burma are victims of a system, just as are the six or eight year old children in South India forced to do construction work to survive, or the Central American women locked up daily and subjected to routine beatings in the clothing factories in the "free trade zones" of Honduras or El Salvador. And in the wealthy northern countries such as the United States, the clean comfortable homes, luxurious automobiles, and overabundant supermarkets are manifestations not only of colonial exploitation of the people whose dehumanized labor and appropriated resources make such excess possible but also of a systematic violence to the environment and the energy resources of the planet.

What implicit conception of being human, what kind of "self," what kind of maturity lies behind this dehumanization of human beings in routine economic interactions and the institutions that determine the form of these interactions? In Chapter Two, we examined some aspects of the fragmentation of the self characteristic of our modern world. Let us examine this fragmentation and its relation to violence within a larger and deeper context.

The "oppressor classes," according to Paulo Freire, are themselves dehumanized and brutalized by their oppression of others. Their consciousness revolves around a "to have" model of being human. They make themselves and others into objects and automatons, which is "the very negation of their ontological vocation to be more fully human" (1990, pp. 43-61). Under our present historical situation, the "self," for oppressors and oppressed, is constituted within the framework of international capitalism.

The modern world emerged in tandem with a series of philosophical conceptions of the self as an independent ego substance (such as that of René Descartes, 1596-1650) in which thoughts, feelings, and relationships only inhere as contingent phenomena passing over the surface of consciousness (see Martin, 1988a). In one of the early justifications for emerging capitalist philosophy by John Locke (1632-1704), this emerging conception of the self was linked to the notion of private property, a "natural" self, mixing its labor with its environment, and accruing to itself "naturally" accumulations of private property (1963; see Macpherson, 1971).

In their economic theories, the political economists of capitalism assumed this model of a human being as independent of its relationships and as "possessor" of "properties" external to its self. These economists of capitalism, writes economist Thorstein Veblen, see human beings as a passive "human material": "In all the received formulations of economic theory, at the hands of the English economists or those of the continent, the human material with which the inquiry is concerned is conceived in hedonistic terms; that is to say, in terms of a passive and substantially inert and immutably given human nature" (1919, p. 73). We often hear the claim that capitalism is the system best suited to selfish and egoistic human nature. In reality, capitalism is a system reflecting our adolescent immaturity.

The conception of a "substantially inert and immutably given human nature" promoted by the theorists of capitalism does violence to the integrity of the human self and reflects the spiritual violence in the lives of these theorists. The mature self involves a holistic, dynamic process of growth, a progressive realization of unity-in-diversity. Yet behind the dominant capitalist world system of the last five centuries, and behind the totalitarian pseudo-socialist states and fascist states that have arisen within it, lies the fragmented and nihilistic ego-self, relying on Cartesian, Lockean, and Newtonian assumptions. This self is understood, under the outmoded "Newtonian" set of assumptions, as an independent substance and as an automaton compulsively pursuing pleasure and avoiding pain while promoting its private interests (Macpherson, 1973, pp. 341-347). The idea of growing toward relational maturity is quite beyond those who would justify the idea that capitalism correctly reflects a fixed, self-centered, greedy, pleasure seeking human nature.

As philosopher Ludwig Wittgenstein's pervasive critique of our modern assumption of a human being as a privatized ego-self reveals, our most fundamental problem is not "private property" but that the notion of private ownership is built into the way our selves are socialized and constituted in the modern era (Martin, 1989, ch. 5-8). We believe we are "owners" of a private self, defined as a passive enduring reality, over and against others and the world, an external world "enforced upon" us, as Thorstein Veblen says, "by circumstances external and alien" to us (1919, p. 73). We relate to this external world in the modes of fear, aggression, and competitive promotion of our interests. Our potential for a mature, relational identity respecting the diversity of other human beings and the natural world is ignored or treated as a secondary phenomena resulting in these deep and resistant forms of spiritual violence that, as we have seen, are reciprocally interrelated with the structural and overt violence pervading modern civilization.

Linked with this distortion of our subjectivity is the ability of human beings to "objectify" the other, to turn them into things. This dehumanization of the other is fundamental to the violent institutions of our world. Freire writes, "The oppressor consciousness tends to transform everything surrounding it into an object of its domination. The Earth, property, production, the creations of men, men themselves, time – everything is reduced to the status of objects at its disposal" (1990, p. 44). And Sartre speaks of modern institutions as constituted by "seriality" in which people objectify themselves and others and live their lives without a sense of oneness or "fusion" with other subjectivities, but seeing themselves and other people as the "Other" (1976, pp. 357, 378 and 601-602).

The central importance of this ability of human consciousness to objectify and dehumanize other persons or groups is today also commonly recognized by peace researchers. Charles Hauss, for example, refers to a world-view characterized by the "image of the enemy." "At least, when conflict becomes intense, we see a world divided between 'us' and 'them'.... Once this dehumanizing process is allowed to take hold, people extend their differences all out of proportion....Our identities are bound up in what defines 'us' *as opposed to* 'them'" (1989, p. 207). And peace educator Betty Reardon relates personal and systemic violence to our ability to see persons as "other": "Otherness connotes,...in its negative form, hierarchies in human worth, the fundamental assumption that makes possible the dehumanization of the other sex, another race or class, citizens of another state, or adherents to another political philosophy" (1985, pp. 50-52 and 93).

Similarly, a sense of a distortion within our subjectivity and its reflection in human institutions has been expressed by many critical theorists since the time of Marx. In his *1844 Manuscripts*, Marx speaks of the consequences of the institutions of capitalism as the objectification and commodification of human beings: people understood, not as equally human and participating equally in being human but instead as objects and commodities to be used in the service of the process of accumulation, to be laid off and discharged when no longer profitable to the owners (1978, pp. 66-125).

The only way into a genuinely humanized future is a deep transformation of the institutionalized violence of this world-order (Wager, 1989, pp. 197-202; Nielsen, 1976-1977, pp. 516-532). This intimates a "postmodern" or "transmodern" world constituted entirely by global rebirth: transformed paradigms, institutions, and persons (Lula da Silva, 1993). Such a postmodern sensibility, which looks toward global transformation, "implies," internationalist thinker Richard Falk suggests, "the rediscovery of normative and spiritual ground upon which to find meaning in human existence" (1992, p. 7). Mature institutions will be a reflection of our spiritual maturity and vice versa.

What contemporary peace research and education is pointing to has been a subject of analysis and reflection within the Buddhist tradition for many centuries. The primary source of violence is to be found in the fractured, immature human self, the "ego" that objectifies itself and others (see De Martino, 1970, pp. 142-171). And today many scholars influenced by the Buddhist tradition recognize that this phenomenon of the objectification of other persons is intrinsic to the structure of the phenomenal ego. The large volume of literature from the Zen-Buddhist tradition that was first widely translated by D. T. Suzuki, to be appropriated and extended by many Western philosophers, has much to say to critical theorists and peace researchers concerning our global condition of institutionalized violence.

In this tradition, the ego is most often understood as *constituted* dualistically, that is, by objectifying itself as a permanent reality over and against what is "not self" (Jacobson, 1983, pp. 95-103). This makes the tendency to objectify or dehumanize others intrinsic to the untranscended ego-self. Without an encounter with that silence that can break open the limited self and transform it, there can be no real solution to the global nightmare in which we seem to be locked. As the American philosopher Nolan Pliny Jacobson writes: "The major source of retardation endangering the future planetary civilization about which so much has been written is not the autonomous nation whose wars have made our century infamous for all time. *The major obstacle is the kind of selfhood in which the terrors of the modern nation are rooted. It is the archaic legacy of a self-substance, mutually independent of all others, which supports the entire superstructure of Western nations"* (1982, p. 41). Growing toward maturity requires a deep transformation of this "legacy" of our adolescence.

The overt and structural dimensions of violence cannot be dealt with without including the spiritual. And spiritual disorder cannot be dealt with by the "I," the ego-substance, of our present spiritual condition. "If the 'I' negates disorder," Krishnamurti asserts, "that very I, which is separate, will create another form of disorder....that is, I see disorder in myself: anger, jealously, brutality, violence, suspicion, guilt.... The mind is totally aware of all this disorder. Can it completely negate it, put it away...? Now the negation of disorder is silence" (1972, pp. 106-107). Krishnamurti sees the (Cartesian) ego as the source of disorder and division within the self. By contrast, he speaks with great clarity of that silence in which all separateness is abandoned resulting in the nonviolence of that "unity in multiplicity" discussed in Chapter Two and spoken of in meditative traditions *throughout* human history.

Human beings are capable of a transforming freedom, Krishnamurti says, "but that freedom cannot come about if you divide the world as between the me, the thinker, the thoughts which are my own, and the rest of the world as totally disconnected from me" (1970, p. 100). This freedom involves a release from the acquisitive and self-promoting Cartesian ego that is the basis of modern social, political, and economic institutions. "A very serious person,..." Krishnamurti says, "is outside both the field of individuality and the structure of society, he is an entirely different human being" (1970, p. 91). The mature, nonviolent self is an entirely relational self, reflecting the relational character of the world we inhabit.

The universe is a process universe that is relational through and through, just as the self is a relational process and one with the matrix within which it is constituted. The traditional Buddhist notion of *anātta* or "no-self" is meant to convey just this, that the idea of a private self, prior to its relationships and interconnections is a pseudo-reality, a nothingness, and a source of perpetual misery, greed, unhappiness, and violence (Jacobson, 1983, pp. 147-169). A mature self reflects the relatedness, the unity-in-diversity, at the heart of reality.

In the epigraph to this chapter, Eckhardt asks "how are we going to change ourselves and our societies from compulsion to compassion?" The dualistic, fragmented ego is never free and is driven by unending compulsions such as fear, greed, hate, lust, and desire for security. These manifestations of a deep anxiety at the heart of our being (De Martino, 1960), dominate every aspect of society and make it inherently violent. Governmental and corporate propaganda promote and exacerbate these compulsions and reproduce this pseudoself in subsequent generations. Compassion can only arise to the extent that we are free of these compulsions. Jacobson identifies three factors in the domination of compulsion in human life:

> Unconscious motivational drives attach themselves to the self for three reasons: first, because the indeterminacy at the center of a person's being, the possibilities for unlimited and ultimate growth, can be felt as troublesome; second, because this substantial self is an infection spread from one generation to the next, without ever reaching conscious awareness; and, third, because a pseudoself once concealing the truth must be defended at all costs, lest anxiety over the indeterminacy of life may rise to dominance despite all that has been done to suppress it. (1983, p. 95)

When we have seen deeply into the bifurcated self and its violent manifestations, when we have become fully self-aware in terms of both

critical social understanding and self-understanding, then we will be able
to transform the endless cycle of fragmented institutions and fragmented
persons drawing humanity toward ultimate catastrophe. This is the deep
nonviolence of planetary maturity.

As some peace researchers have pointed out, our contemporary human
situation may look hopeless (Hauss, 1989, p. 215). But an unpredictable
factor works in the world that cannot be appropriated for use in rational
calculations of the future of humankind. Through it, we encounter the
possibility of a transcendence of the human ego and the institutions arising
from it with all their inherent partiality, dualism, and violence. Many
names exist for the experience and reality of the dimension that beckons us
toward transcendence. In the quotation above, Picard named it "silence,"
a pervasive dimension that continues to embrace our lives whether we are
aware of it or not.

Identifying the reality and possibility of genuine transcendence for
ourselves and humankind actuates a hope not limited to the current volumes
of horrifying "empirical evidence." This hope is currently expressed by
many persons across the globe in their concrete and practical responses
to overt institutional and spiritual violence. It provides a living response
to our global institutions that I believe is inherently transformative and
points to an "eschatological" factor that is our real basis for hope. We will
examine this eschatological factor in more detail in later chapters.

3. Planetary Maturity as Deep Nonviolence

Our modern era is characterized by violence, a pervasive disorder
that violates the wholes of which we are part as well as the self that should
be inseparable from these wholes. The sanctity of the self and the world
with which the self is primordially one is violated by the ego of fear, greed,
and competition. This is a deep violence reflecting quite deep distortions
in the human psyche and in our view of the world. *Deep nonviolence is
the only possible realistic response to the deep violence that encompasses
the overt, institutional, and spiritual aspects of our lives.* It involves a
transformation of life so that the overt, structural, and spiritual spheres are
all converted to nonviolence.

Love, compassion, and tolerance must be built into the very
foundations of our personal being, our societies, and our life on this planet.
These are the words of Tenzin Gyatso, the Fourteenth Dalai Lama, "love,
compassion and tolerance are necessities, not luxuries," he says, "without
them, humanity cannot survive" (1990, p. 3). Human maturity requires
nothing less. Without a world based on such a "deep nonviolence" arising
from a transformation of our very being-in-the-world, the pervasive

destruction of human beings and nature on this planet will continue until all that will be left is a wasteland.

Christian thinker Jacques Ellul affirms that a standpoint of violence can never result in a genuine transformation and liberation from our modern human condition. Violent deeds, like the fear and greed which generate them, and like the military conflicts which achieve nothing but the generation of ever greater hatred and dehumanization of those considered the "enemy," only perpetuate the inhuman and desperate condition in which we currently live. Deep nonviolence portends real change. This is the only path, Ellul writes, toward "a revolution in depth": "My study of politics and sociology have convinced me that violence is an altogether superficial thing; that is, it can produce apparent, superficial changes, rough facsimiles of change. But it never affects the roots of injustice – social structures, the bases of an economic system, the foundations of society. Violence is not the appropriate means for a revolution in depth" (1978, p. 118).

Our understanding of these issues, as well as our meditational and life practices, must transform us beyond the superficial patchwork remedies popularly touted to deal with the deep misery of the human condition in the modern era. Deep nonviolence aims at the "roots of injustice – social structures, the bases of an economic system, the foundations of society." Another way of expressing the holistic character of deep nonviolence is to think in terms of transforming ourselves toward what Falk calls "global citizens" who "seek an end to poverty, oppression, humiliation, and collective violence" (1993, p. 39). "Global citizenship," Falk says, is "premised on the biological and normative capacity of the human species to organize its collective life on the foundations of nonviolence, equity, and sustainability."

Such global citizenship reflects planetary maturity. The inseparability of nonviolence from all other concerns and relationships is here recognized. The response to the deep violence of our world is a deep nonviolence that involves a fundamental transformation of our selves with all that this implies. For Falk, this is to "combine local rootedness with planetary awareness, and the underlying belief that the security and sanctity of the human community rests, in the end, on embodying an ethos of nonviolence in political practices at all levels of social organization, from the family to the world" (1993, p. 50).

We saw Nolan Pliny Jacobson characterize the terror of modern nation-states as rooted in the kind of selfhood pervading our modern world and its institutions that he calls " the archaic legacy of a self-substance, mutually independent of all others." The Buddhist tradition calls this selfhood "ignorance" (*avidyā*), since it can and must be transcended in the direction of direct identification with the whole, including all other living beings. "Ignorance," Canadian philosopher Robert Carter writes, "and the resulting delusion of individualization or separation, come to be the source of suffering, which to the Buddhist is evil. Where there is not a trace of a sense of the whole, the result is alienation from the cosmos, the world, and eventually even from yourself" (1992, p. 161).

The penetration of silence into those definitional self-images that constitute the ego is not a matter of ascetic self-denial but the highest self-realization. "My 'identity,'" according to Christian thinker Thomas Merton, "is not to be sought in that *separation* from all that is, but in oneness.... This identity is not the denial of my own personal reality but its highest affirmation" (1967, p. 18). And philosopher Charles Hartshorne writes that our compulsive self-protection and concern for the future of this particular egoistic entity is not especially important, but instead, "...from the Buddhist-Whiteheadian point of view....the future that ultimately matters is not mine or yours, or even human, but cosmic and divine" (1967, pp. 109-110). For a Christian philosopher like Hartshorne, the future is ultimately "divine." For a Buddhist, the future is ultimately "cosmic": the mutual interpenetration of the one and the many, the simultaneous "fullness" and "emptiness" of a transformed existence (see Martin, 1989, ch. 9).

All this is implied in the Buddhist relation of "compassion" (*karunā*) as I am using it in the title for this chapter. Scholar of Buddhism Jeffrey Hopkins defines compassion as "the heartfelt wish that sentient beings be free from suffering and the causes of suffering" (2001, p. 157). The realized and authentic self that exists in deep relationship with the world and other persons is a self that realizes its ultimate identity and inseparability from the world and other persons, encompassing and redeeming the precious multiplicity of existence. The self of deep nonviolence is a mature self of compassionate action and freedom.

The ideological self-understanding of the modern world, operating through concepts such as "free enterprise," "promoting democracy," "combating terrorism," "fighting communism," "defending law and order," "encouraging development," and so on, presents a network of conceptual appearances that simultaneously justify and veil the massive system of institutionalized violence and domination, what Sartre calls the global "structure of scarcity." "To see the world through this [ideological] lens," philosopher Roberta Imboden writes, "is to see every aspect of society, every individual, through the structure of scarcity as if that structure were inevitable and therefore correct and moral" (1987, p. 82). To penetrate these appearances as part of the struggle for institutional and structural transformation toward authentic universal human liberation is the work of critical social theory. To transform the limited ego-self toward universal human liberation is the work of spiritual practice. It is clear that these two dimensions (subjective-personal and rational-critical) are inherently related.

4. The Inseparability of Compassion and Critical Theory

My analysis of structural violence and spiritual violence derives from the Marxist tradition and is often referred to as "critical theory," "critical social theory," or "critical social analysis." We must recognize that this intellectual and rational approach to liberation is a necessary aspect of the conversion to deep nonviolence. If the deep realization of compassion is mystical and arational (as distinguished from irrational), the wholeness of human liberation requires a critical, rational understanding as well. The rational and arational dimensions of a human being cannot be separated from one another without violating human wholeness. And just as Buddhism at its best understands this, so Marxism at its best also understands the wholeness of the human being, including the rational and arational dimensions. The human being must be made whole through a transformation and unification of the rational and arational aspects of our being.

A liberated, mature person has a deep critical understanding and a compassionate relationship with all sentient beings. Without this, no Buddhist in the modern world can be truly liberated, and no peace activist or critical social theorist can be truly effective. For even if members of both groups feel compassion for the victims of exploitation and oppression worldwide, their compassionate action will inevitably end up treating symptoms, instead of the roots, of the suffering. The charity of Mother Teresa in Calcutta or the activist concern for the homeless on the streets of New York City are non-revolutionary and self-defeating actions insofar as they are not joined with action to transform the global economic and nation-state systems, which are at the root of poverty and homelessness.

For truly transformative action is impossible without a deep understanding of the exploitative structures of capitalism and the need for a democratic socialism free from this violence, deception, and domination of the poor by the rich. By "critical theory" I mean precisely the awakened critical consciousness promulgated by the Marxist tradition from the time of Marx to the present. Human liberation is never exclusively "spiritual." Mature liberation can only be holistic: economic, social, cultural, and spiritual all at once. Critical theory is a necessary component of deep liberation and is indispensable if deep nonviolence is to be realized on our planet.

The breakthrough beyond the dualistic ego to the larger self realized through silence simultaneously brings us to true universality and true compassion. The universality implied in the concepts democracy, humanity, justice, freedom, or peace is used by the critical social thinker to point beyond ideological justifications for violence to a self-aware, rational society. The transformed self that must accompany the use of critical social theory is the source of true compassion. The result is a mature wholeness in which the activation of "compassion" (*karunā*) is not dependent on the contingent cultivation of those feelings of caring or concern that may or may not coincide with true universality. Critical social analysis reveals fundamental principles exposing overt, institutional, and spiritual violence. The breakthrough beyond the dualistic ego reveals a self whose compassion is not dependent on contingent feelings that tend to come and go for the dualistic ego. A new planetary maturity appears where compassion and critical understanding are inseparable, non-contingent aspects of human wholeness.

Many critical theorists and Marxist revolutionaries such as Karl Marx, Herbert Marcuse, Ernst Bloch, Walter Benjamin, Jean-Paul Sartre, and Jürgen Habermas were aware of this in one way or another. They saw that ultimate human liberation goes beyond the current structures of duality that constitute the self-encapsulated ego. A new dimension of being human shows up that Marcuse names the "oneness" of all human beings and Sartre calls the overcoming of seriality with its alienation of isolated individualism in the "fusion" of "mutual recognition and subjective unity" (1976, pp. 265-266 and 378-379).

As we will examine in subsequent chapters, these Marxist thinkers recognize the possibility of a mature fulfillment of our human condition in the emergence of a new kind of selfhood beyond the confines of the self-encapsulated ego. Yet one might say that the "eschatological" possibilities intimated by critical theorists find their experiential realization in philosophical Buddhism that has for 2600 years focused on the practical possibilities for transcendence of Jacobson's "culture-encapsulated self," an ego structure that is substantially a natural by-product of the institutions and ideologies of class societies (1982, pp. 46-48). Throughout its history, however, Buddhism has focused on personal transformation and individual liberation, leaving the institutions that reproduce the culture-encapsulated self mostly intact.

By contrast, the critical tradition has sought a transformation of our institutions: for the early Marx this involved a "universal class," which represented our "species-being" and truly human, instead of particularized, interests. For Buddhism, this universality is not found in any particular socially conditioned class but within each of us through transcendence of the ego in the encounter with silence. But Marx was correct in realizing that human beings will only be fundamentally changed through abolition of the institutional violence of repression expressed in all forms of class domination.

Neither the personal nor the structural can be omitted. Critical analysis and, ultimately, transformation of the structures of domination are necessary to create institutions that promote human transcendence and mutual identification. These in turn will produce individuals who directly realize, through universality and compassion, the seeds of a mature, truly liberated society.

To adapt the well-known Kantian maxim: *compassion without critical theory is blind; critical theory without compassion is empty.* Compassion without critical theory is blind because persons experiencing the suffering of others as their own suffering may still spend their life-energy treating the symptoms of human suffering and violence, not their institutional and structural roots. Yet critical theory without compassion is empty. The theoretical unveiling of the ideological self-justifications of society, revealing its structures of exploitation and violence, requires a direct identification with the suffering of the oppressed to be fully human and effective.

We have witnessed the practical operation of critical theory without compassion in the gulags of Soviet Marxist-Leninism, in the degradation of Eastern Europeans, and in the brutality of Chinese Red Guards. Critical theory gives compassion the intellectual tools to identify the real roots of social violence and domination and therefore the ability to take effective action. Compassion gives critical theory the living ability to treat all human beings as free subjectivities with individual dignity instead of as abstract categories of a social philosophy. Compassion and critical theory must both be rooted in a transformed self that has broken through the suffocating dualistic structures of the culture-encased ego.

In the service of the Biblical promise of human freedom, liberation theologians such as Gustavo Gutierrez (1973) and Juan Luis Segundo (1985) have appropriated as necessary tools the demystifying structural analyses of critical theory. Others, such as Imboden (1987), have developed the parallels between Jesus' eschatological teachings of the kingdom of God and the goals of critical theory: a truly free human subjectivity in mutual relationship with a liberating and non-repressive society. Yet the vital relevance of 2600 years of Buddhist analysis and practical experience in bringing human awareness to universality and compassion has not yet been fully recognized.

The eschatological hope inherent within the human situation is not dependent on the Biblical promises of the kingdom of God on Earth, however crucial these may be. The transforming silence that can bring the self beyond its egoistic cultural encapsulations to a oneness with the universe and all sentient beings fills the interstices of our world and makes itself available wherever the chatter and noise of our modern languages pause for breath. Planetary maturity involves an ever-deeper awareness of the fullness of reality.

5. Active Nonviolence

The living confluence of these realities reveals the real truth of active nonviolence, the third aspect of a holistic transformation to deep nonviolence. Active nonviolence is more than a teaching of direct action and more than a mass approach to oppression and injustice. Active nonviolence is the direct, living consequence of the dual realization of universality and compassion through transcendence of the ego. Nonviolence is here conceived as a way of characterizing the predominant orientation of a transformed self and society, not as a dogmatic moral absolute prohibiting the use of force in every conceivable situation. It is meaningful and effective nonviolence only when it takes its stand against all three forms of violence: overt, institutional, and spiritual.

The dynamics of nonviolence realized in this way are significantly reflected in the totalistic and living quality of Gandhi's nonviolence (see Richards, 1991). But the differences are also significant. Although Gandhi located the spiritual roots of his nonviolence in the teachings of karma yoga in the *Bhagavad Gītā* and in the Hindu belief that the deep soul of each person (*Ātman*) is God (*Brahman*), the nonviolence arising from a breakthrough to silence does not require appeal to any particular religious tradition, nor to an experience of "faith" in traditional senses of this word.

The links with Buddhism noted above are with those aspects of this tradition that are practical, pragmatic, and based on wisdom gained through personal experiences. There need be no appeals to faith or scripture and no metaphysical notions such as "God" or "soul." Nolan Pliny Jacobson has developed at length these qualities of Buddhism that place it, in many ways, closer to our scientific and critical methods than to the other world religions such as Judaism, Christianity, Islam, or Hinduism. The core traditions of Buddhism see life as a process characterized by radical openness to the future and to change. They understand spirituality through this same notion of "openness" in which human beings can experimentally, from their living experience, learn to grow beyond suffering, partiality, hatred, and violence (1983, ch. 6).

Yet the nonviolence toward which Buddhism points, involving

a transcendence of the ego with its inherent impulse for objectification of itself and others, carries the same holistic quality as that of Gandhi. For Gandhi, each human being is experienced as an expression of God, and this transfigured spiritual attitude transforms his social theory in the direction of conceptualizing and developing nonviolent institutions. As Ignatius Jesudasan, S.J. puts it, for Gandhi, "nonviolence was an indicator of inward freedom to which outward freedom, or political independence, would be in exact proportion" (1984, p. 117).

In the terminology of this chapter, the realization of silence in mind and heart leads beyond the ego and its dualisms to an experience of identification with all that is. The other and the self, while requiring infinite mutual respect for one another's otherness, become unique expressions of one, living reality. The inherent violence of dualism disappears, and compassion arises as a realization that the suffering of others is my suffering.

This idea of the identity of my suffering and that of others is not a mere subjective feeling in Buddhism, but instead the concrete human expression of the oneness of the silence that encompasses and informs our being. Perhaps we all share an intuition of this identity between ourselves and others, for the notion is sometimes expressed in the peace research literature as ideal or metaphor. As Reardon puts it, following Robert Lifton, "If you die, I die. If you survive, I survive, but also, and perhaps more basically, If you are debased, I am debased. If your identity is distorted, so is mine" (1985, p. 93). Yet in the experiential confluence of critical theory and compassion, these notions move beyond ideal to the reality of living nonviolence. Holistic nonviolence, experientially based and practically discovered in concrete human spirituality, addresses the problem of individual suffering and that of institutional violence. At root, they are one problem.

Although Gandhi attained only a truncated critical consciousness during his lifetime and never developed an advanced critical understanding of capitalism, the same sense of the relatedness of the issue of nonviolence to a deep transformation of the self is found in his thought. For Gandhi, nonviolence involved the whole of life and necessarily involved social, cultural, economic, and spiritual dimensions. Gandhi also insists that what he terms the "religious" and the political cannot be separated. Human life is one integral matrix of relationships, and spiritual nonviolence is inseparable from structural nonviolence and overt physical nonviolence.

As in Marx's idea of "praxis," theory and action, or thought and action are not to be separated for Gandhi. Neither are society, truth, and nonviolence. Just as the modern state, according to Gandhi, is "violence in a concentrated and organized form," so "capitalism" (as opposed to the capitalist), he says, must be destroyed, for "the entire social order has got to be reconstructed" (1972, pp. 120-132). Gandhi's name for the reconstructed social order is a "socialism" in which "truth and ahimsa must be incarnate" (1957, p. 3).

We need a nonviolent social order replacing our present structural violence in which "the few ride on the back of the millions" (1972, p. 115). "Socialism," Gandhi writes, "is a beautiful word and, so far as I am aware, in Socialism all the members of society are equal – none low, none high." But such a society will be established by those who have attained spiritual nonviolence: "Only truthful, nonviolent, and pure hearted Socialists," he says, "will be able to establish a Socialistic society" (1957, pp. 1-2). This is one way of describing planetary maturity.

Like Gandhi, representatives of contemporary as well as traditional Buddhism also often speak in terms of an integration of all dimensions of life in deep nonviolence. Ken Jones, for example, in *The Social Face of Buddhism*, speaks of the larger, transformative implications of what he calls "creative nonviolence":

> The philosophy of creative nonviolence recognizes that protester and adversary are caught up in the same historical web of socially supercharged bitterness and antagonism,...fear, ill will, acquisitiveness, and existential blindness. The so-called "method" of nonviolence by which the specific affliction is to be removed is therefore more important than the specific question at issue, for it seeks to help undercut the human roots from which afflictions arise again and again. It does this by seeking to bring into awareness of the adversary the suffering which arises from greed and domination, and also to share with him something of a higher level of consciousness through the experience of mutual respect, genuine communication and some recognition of ultimate common interest. (1989, p. 303)

Jones is describing concrete nonviolent action as a manifestation of a "higher level of consciousness" that it seeks to share with the adversary. This higher level of consciousness, this "compassion" in which the suffering of the adversary is my suffering, is fundamental to the living transformation I am calling deep nonviolence and planetary maturity. And this is inseparable from a critical theory in which the deep violence of our economic institutions is comprehended and responded to with effective, nonviolent direct action.

All these relationships, from family to community to world, involve the way our human self is understood and constituted. Deep nonviolence means a transformation that includes all levels of human life: nonviolent actions on the individual level are but a small part of it. In deep nonviolence, people promote the opposition to and withdrawal from the structural violence of capitalism, class society, and the disparities of wealth and poverty worldwide. Deep nonviolence perpetually delegitimates these violent institutions. Such a life perpetually struggles against the violence of exploitation and domination. It means a life free of the diminution and dehumanization of those of another gender, race, ethnicity, color, religion, or educational background. It means the coextension of unity and multiplicity.

Beyond this, deep nonviolence includes a life project freeing itself from doing violence to the planet and the life systems within which we are embedded. Our lives must orient to ecological sustainability and living harmoniously within the systems of air, water, earth, and fellow non-human creatures with which we are vitally interconnected. Finally, deep nonviolence means a self that is at peace (as opposed to war) with itself and others because it expresses a transformed self free of the ego-illusion that sets it in violent opposition to others and the environment. The self of deep nonviolence realizes its unity-in-multiplicity with the community of other beings. It does not need to define itself over and against the matrix of life systems within which it flourishes.

The self of deep nonviolence ultimately manifests what the Buddhists call "great compassion" (*mahākaruṇā*), for once the ego-illusion of separateness is substantially abandoned, the sufferings of others become my sufferings, and my actions become nonviolent in the deep sense that they are moving toward a dynamic in which they cause no further suffering to others. Yet far more than avoiding causing suffering to others (at a physical, structural, or spiritual level), deep nonviolence is manifested in a positive life energy that impartially works to alleviate the sufferings of others (again, since my "own" needs, interests, and desires are no longer given existential or metaphysical priority over others). Such a life is fully aware of the hidden structural and spiritual dimensions of violence whose transformation is imperative to accomplish genuine liberation from suffering.

Under this deep nonviolence of a self that has understood itself as formed within the matrix of its relationships, attitudes of physical violence toward others (the military and "self-defense" model) dissipate, the need to economically compete with, dehumanize, and exploit others (the capitalist model) loses all attraction, and the attitude of carelessness toward the environment and future generations (the "mastery of nature" model) becomes incomprehensible. For the root of these "external" forms of violence is a "self-violence": a self divided, bifurcated, and estranged, a distortion of the self of deep peace and nonviolence in which the unity of the one and the many is the source from which all thought and action flows. Transformative and redeeming action now arises from a truly critical insight into the institutionalized violence of society and the spiritual violence of the modern self.

And this is a crucial point. The self of deep nonviolence does not withdraw from transformative action into some corner of life where it attempts to do as little harm as possible. Such self-indulgent selfishness in the face of the massive suffering of others and our planet is an antithesis of deep nonviolence. Instead, such a self engages in action flowing from a dynamic of compassion in which it works to transform structural, spiritual, and overt violence in the direction of freedom, justice, truth, and deep nonviolence.

A world of deep nonviolence in which human beings and societies are largely free of overt, structural, and spiritual violence is the true destiny and meaning of our planetary life. The only realistic response to the deep violence of our modern era is a fundamental transformation of every aspect of our lives to deep nonviolence. The only realistic response to our present suicidal form of life is rapid growth toward planetary maturity.

Transformation of society through the giving up of wealth and power by the six percent who presently dominate the institutions of the world, whether representative of nations, classes, or multi-national corporations, must be part of a holistic transformation that includes the institutional and spiritual dimensions. The rich in our present world will obviously not voluntarily renounce wealth and power, and it may be that it will require collective actions of the masses of human beings to create global laws that place reasonable controls on wealth and power. But neither must mass action reproduce these patterns of violence and domination in the name of the many. It will require transformed institutions to make possible transformed people and vice versa.

Holistic transformation involving critical theory, compassion, and active nonviolence is the only way toward a just, free, and nonviolent global community that will be characteristic of our planetary maturity. Compassion is here our central term for the breakthrough beyond the fractured and divisive human ego to wholeness and world solidarity. Critical theory exposes the patterns of domination and exploitation that are veiled by the mass media and dominant ideology of class societies. It points to a redeeming, democratic socialism where the welfare of all is the fundamental premise of economic, social, and political life.

And active nonviolence expresses compassion and critical theory in a form of action that is itself transformative, and moves history forward in ways that do not generate further violence and domination. Human maturity is a process of realizing this wholeness. Five billion years of evolution on planet Earth and two million years of human development have given us these concrete possibilities.

We have seen Picard write that a human being "who has lost silence has not merely lost one human quality, but his whole structure is changed thereby." Alternatively, a person who has regained silence and become free from bondage to the culture-encapsulated ego is thereby redeemed, transformed, and opened up into our larger human reality. The depths of silence must permeate our institutions and our lives so that every human being on Earth is a necessary part of one human reality, and the "welfare of all" is reflected in every institution.

PART TWO

Spiritual Liberation

Chapter Four

Religious and Spiritual Maturity
in the Twentieth and Twenty-first Centuries

The majority of men in every generation, even those who, as it is described, devote themselves to thinking,...live and die under the impression that life is simply a matter of understanding more and more, and that if it were granted to them to live longer, that life would continue to be one long continuous growth in understanding. How many of them ever experience the maturity of discovering that there comes a critical moment where everything is reversed, after which the point becomes to understand more and more that there is something which cannot be understood.

Søren Kierkegaard

Our experience of the world involves us in a mystery which can be intelligible to us only as a mystery. The more we experience things in depth, the more we participate in a mystery intelligible to us only as such; and the more we understand our world to be an unknown world. Our true home is wilderness, even the world of every day.

Henry G. Bugbee

The publication of Nicholas Copernicus' *De Revolutionibus Orbium Coelestium* in 1543 has become a symbol for the revolution in human self-understanding that was created by the scientific revolution that began in the 16th century and has continued to the present. For many centuries prior to the sixteenth century, the dominant scientific view believed the Earth was the center of the universe, and that the heavenly bodies (the sun, moon, stars, and planets) moved in perfect circles around Earth. The drama of human life also took place at the center of the universe.

With the ascendency of Christianity after the conversion of the Emperor Constantine in the early fourth century, to many there appeared to be a perfect correlation between what the astronomers were telling us as the result of systematic empirical observations (the heavenly bodies can be daily observed in their movement around the Earth) and what the holy scriptures told us as the result of direct revelation from God. Just as observation placed us at the physical center of creation so scripture placed us at the spiritual center of creation. We alone, of all the world's creatures, were made in the image of

God and found ourselves at the center of a divine-human drama whose broad features were paradise, a fall from paradise, a journey of struggle within history, and the promise of a future redemption.

1. The Copernican Revolution in Religion

Copernicus' book *On The Revolution of Heavenly Bodies* initiated a process of change in our self-understanding as profound as any in world history, a process of change from whose implications we are still staggering. Copernicus fundamentally simplified the ancient astronomical system of Claudius Ptolemy with the alternative hypothesis that the sun, not the Earth, was the center of the universe. The Earth was merely one of the planets, spinning on its axis in orbit a great distance from the sun. In one revolutionary moment, we shifted from being the most significant object in the universe, stationary at its center, to being inconsequential and insignificant, spinning in a double movement, on an axis and in orbit, at the apparent periphery of universe.

Not long after this, Galileo Galilei looked through the first telescope (1609), discovering mountains on the moon (a moon long thought to be made of the perfect "fifth element," ether) and Johannes Kepler published his *Astronomia Nova,* mathematically demonstrating that the planets moved not in perfect "divine" circles but in ellipses around the sun. After these discoveries, with every advance in science human beings became geometrically smaller and more insignificant in relation to the scale of the universe, even to the present.

In the early 1920s, the American astronomer Edwin P. Hubble was investigating the "nebulae" or tiny fuzzy points of light that appeared randomly at great distance from the Earth in every direction that he pointed his telescope at Mt. Wilson Observatory in California. Suddenly it dawned on him that these tiny, fuzzy star-like lights were not star-like at all. They were "island universes," later to be called "galaxies." Untold numbers of galaxies, each encompassing a hundred billion stars like our galaxy, appearing to our telescopes as tiny points of light in the night sky. At that moment in the early twentieth century, the magnitude of our insignificance on the scale of the universe again sank dramatically, this time to virtually zero. Today's astronomy, observing a billion galaxies, each with a hundred billion or more stars, at nearly inconceivable distances from one another, gives us a universe that the human imagination cannot begin to fathom.

The implications of the Copernican Revolution for the naive religious frameworks prior to the sixteenth century are staggering. Religion attempted to resist the onslaughts of science, and often continues to do so to the present day. But the struggle frequently seemed futile for religion, for science is not only here to stay but represents a great maturing in human self-understanding, a great awakening as to the nature, limits, and conditions of human knowledge.

Western religion, in its first encounter with the emerging sciences of the Renaissance, found an option through turning away from cosmology and claiming dominion over the domain of the "soul" that had been part of its province all along. Emergent Protestantism and a Catholicism, still reacting to the scientific and religious rebellions of the sixteenth century, insisted that the invisible soul was not open to scientific investigation and that the real drama of sin and salvation took place within this domain. Yet even here, religion's spiritual domain of inwardness was threatened by the encroachments of science. Charles Darwin's *On the Origin of Species* was published in 1859, effecting a new kind of Copernican Revolution in human self-understanding by questioning the uniqueness of our humanity (traditionally thought to be different from the animals by being made in the image of God) and by placing us squarely in the evolutionary process, cousins to monkeys and distant relatives to earthworms. Had human consciousness itself evolved?

A few decades later, in the twentieth century, modern psychology developed out of the work of Sigmund Freud and others and religious motivations and ideas were easily now understood as expressions of unconscious drives or as expressions of unfulfilled childhood dreams of love and security in the arms of idealized parents. The result was the emergence of late modern secularism, scientism, and positivism, orientations claiming that human beings had outgrown the naive unscientific epistemologies of our religious past that attempted to "explain" the phenomena of nature and human life through appeal to spiritual "causes" or other superstitions, just as we have outgrown the naive metaphysical speculations of prescientific eras that were not clear about the relationship between the scientific grounds of human knowledge and what we may legitimately conclude about "reality."

In spite of the domination of twentieth-century thought by positivism and scientism, there exists an altogether different option for religion that has become available, maturing and flourishing in the twentieth century. Many of the great religious and spiritual thinkers of our time pursued this option. The twentieth century should be understood as the time of a transformation in the human comprehension of religion, just as it has also seen a transformation in our comprehension of nature through the development of ecology, and of the physical universe through relativity theory and quantum mechanics. Traditional religion grew to maturity, transformed and redeemed itself, in the same way as our understanding of the universe was transformed through science.

Religion in the twentieth century reappropriated its entire tradition on a new level, free of the conflict with science and open to an entirely new human maturity. Instead of opposing or ignoring the tremendous accomplishments of science, religion reexamined itself, and in doing so reexamined the human situation itself in the light of the revelations offered by science, in addition to those offered by traditional scriptures. The process of accomplishing this transformation in our understanding of religion, to which an immense amount of energy has been devoted throughout the twentieth century, is now bearing fruit.   What was parochial, limited, or naive in the original expressions of religion was slowly discarded throughout the century.   We now distinguish doctrine and dogma from living spirituality.

And what was profound, universal, and significant in religion is redeemed and understood on a higher level corresponding to the new maturity made possible by the Copernican Revolution and its consequences. Many thinkers see religion (and spirituality) as our basic mode of being in the world, instead of as a mere aspect or dimension of human life. For example, philosopher J. N. Findlay expresses this in one way in his essay "The Varieties of Religious Knowing":

> Religion is not therefore some alien graft upon our conscious human life, inspired perhaps by the terrifying or marvelous powers of circumambient nature, as many have surmised. It is rather a carrying to the limit of the basic aspirations of conscious life, its search for practical mastery, for deep understanding, for widely ranging vision, for spectacles that please by their harmonious, not-too-easy perspicuity of structure, for penetration of the inner life of others and for finding it deeply understandable and supportive of our own. Inevitably, we form an ideal of pure reason, as Kant styled it, in which all the basic aspirations of consciousness are carried to the limit, of a thought that covers all truths and all possibilities, of a power that can realize anything and everything, of a sympathetic entry that surmounts all personal difference and understands everyone in every situation, of a judgment that can assess the value and disvalue of anything and everything in the light of all facts and all fundamental goals. It is also a consciousness that understands the possibility of all deviations and corruptions, distortions and departures from what is good, and understands the many mitigations which render them well-nigh predictable and certainly forgivable. (1985, pp. 68-69)

This formulation attempts to express something universal about the human situation to which religion is responding. It links the emerging evolution of human consciousness with the development of a religious sensibility for the human species in general. The spirituality of our "inner life" mirrors our consciousness of the whole of the outer universe understood in terms of "all facts and fundamental goals." Religion in this sense reflects our highest human possibility. Other formulations may differ, but, within a broad spectrum of understanding, religion exhibits today a new maturity that cannot be ignored by anyone concerned to understand the human situation and to respond to the agonizing problems that humanity faces in the world today. Let us review some of the primary developments that made this new religious and spiritual maturity possible.

2. Seven Historical Developments Behind The New Religious Maturity

One of the first steps involved the development of modern historical and critical scholarship and its application to traditional religious scriptures. These methodologies investigated the Bible first but were soon extended to Eastern religious traditions as well, although the Western religions (Judaism, Christianity, and Islam) appear especially dependent on claims to historical truth. Scholars began to understand that the Bible, like the *Qur'an*, is a product of the social and cultural forces of its day, that its cosmology was the pre-scientific cosmology of the eras during which it was written, that its conception of the origin, scope, and history of the world involves the pre-Copernican assumptions of the peoples of the Near East where it was written, and that even its dating and authorship were not those that the religious traditions of reverence and veneration had supposed.

For example, the "Synoptic Theory" concerning the composition of the Gospels adduces evidence to the effect that none of the Gospels were written by those who knew Jesus directly. It deduces that Mark was likely a disciple of Peter who wrote his gospel after Peter was crucified in Rome about 65 CE. It believes that the author of Matthew is likely unknown and that Matthew and Luke (the traveling companion of St. Paul) had Mark's gospel as a source as well as the "Quelle" (a now lost collection of sayings of Jesus of the early church). It concludes that both these gospels were written about 80-85 CE, long after Jesus' death. Similarly, many scholars believe that the Gospel of John was probably written as late as 100-110 CE in Ephesus. Ephesus is the city made famous by Heraclitus, who earlier promulgated the notion of the "Logos" that John applied to Christ in the Prologue to his gospel (see Connick, 1974).

Similar examples apply to Judaism and Islam, the other two Western monotheistic religions apparently so heavily dependent on claims about historical events for their legitimacy. Are the Christian Gospels dependent on the traditional assumptions that the authors of the gospels knew Jesus, and that the events recorded about Jesus' life and teaching were eyewitness accounts? Was Christ literally resurrected from the dead? If he was not resurrected, St. Paul writes, "our faith is in vain." More broadly, what is the relation of the traditional claims about historical events to the spirituality and legitimacy of the traditions that bring these momentous claims to us in the present?

A second, related, realization of the modern world has also deeply affected the contemporary understanding of religion. Since Hegel and Darwin in the nineteenth century, and since the development of scientific cosmology in the twentieth, thinkers comprehend the historical or evolutionary character of all social and natural phenomena, including the universe itself (the latter currently within the framework of some version of the "big-bang theory"). All social, cultural, and religious forms are not only products of a limited historical period with inevitable assumptions and limitations, but these forms continually evolve and reappropriate the inherited tradition in new ways. We live in a process universe, and human history is itself a process containing no ahistorical truths or cultural expressions.

The original expressions of the great religions were history-bound, just as our relationship to them is history-bound and necessarily involves a different framework of understanding from the originals. Yet even our understanding is in the process of transformation historically and therefore may make no final claims to be an expression of ahistorical truth. Does this insight lead to complete relativism concerning the great traditional claims of religion concerning such matters as God, eternity, the soul, redemption, and the promised Kingdom? The historical character of all these concepts must also be assimilated into the new human maturity regarding religion and spirituality if this new understanding is to be possible.

Third, historical and critical scholarship, in conjunction with the understanding that the insights of religion must be appropriated within our historical framework, inevitably led religious thinkers like Rudolph Bultmann and Paul Tillich to undertake a process of "demythologization" of the Bible. This process involved not primarily removing cosmic and historical myths from worship and liturgy but instead understanding them in a new way as expressing the stories and symbols of the human relation to God and not as literal accounts of past events. For Tillich this process is essential to the vital core of the Biblical revelation. He names it the "Protestant Principle," which involves "divine judgment over man's religious life" as we struggle to free ourselves from "idolatry" (1957, p. 29). As long as we take as ultimate what is not genuinely ultimate, we are living with an idolatrous faith, not an authentic, centered, and upright faith.

Yet a great maturity-fear has seized people throughout today's world. Many people resist this process of developing mature faith in relation to the new understandings made possible through modern science and scholarship. The implications of the Copernican Revolution are too staggering. They require us to stand upon our two feet and grow in spirituality and understanding far beyond the simple and concrete world of literalist faith that existed for most people right up to the beginning of the modern period.

Some of our modern institutions reinforce this maturity-fear by keeping us, for example, from developing a mature politics and economics. The present system of commercial manipulation and mind control, and of the totalitarian control of most people throughout their working lives by their employers (the possessors of private capital) as well as by state "security" arrangements, keeps people in a state of numbness, immaturity, and childlike dependency. It deprives them of their right to grow toward becoming ever more fully human, with dire consequences for the kind of spirituality in which many modern people live their lives.

Yet many significant religious thinkers, like Bultmann and Tillich, who have seen the possibilities for growth provided by modern science and scholarship, assert that the core of traditional religion (and the core of revelation) is the great demand of God precisely that we grow to a maturity. The foundation of this maturity is the process of freeing ourselves from idolatry, a process that is fundamentally in harmony with the Copernican principle of a relational universe within which the literal, pictorial imagination must be given up for a more mature imagination swinging outward toward the depths of existence. Tillich writes:

> The radical criticism of the myth is due to the fact that the primitive mytho-logical consciousness resists the attempt to interpret the myth as myth. It is afraid of every act of demythologization. It believes that the broken myth is deprived of its truth and of its convincing power. Those who live in an unbroken mythological world feel safe and certain. They resist, often fanatically, any attempt to introduce an element of uncertainty by "break-ing the myth," namely, by making conscious its symbolic character.... The resistance against demythologization expresses itself in "literalism." The symbols and myths are understood in their immediate meaning.... The char-acter of the symbol to point beyond itself to something else is disregarded. Creation is taken as a magic act which happened once upon a time. The fall of Adam is localized on a special geographical point and attributed to a hu-man individual. The virgin birth of the Messiah is understood in biological terms, resurrection and ascension as physical events, the second coming of the Christ as a telluric, or cosmic, catastrophe. The presupposition of such literalism is that God is a being, acting in time and space, dwelling in a special place, affecting the course of events and being affected by them like any other being in the universe. Literalism deprives God of his ultimacy, and, religiously speaking, of his majesty. It draws him down to the level of

that which is not ultimate, the finite and conditional. In the last analysis it is not rational criticism of the myth which is decisive but the inner religious criticism. Faith, if it takes its symbols literally, becomes idolatrous! It calls something ultimate which is less than ultimate. (1957, pp. 51-52)

For Tillich, three Biblical principles reflect the "inner religious criticism" that is at the core of revelation: the theme of prophetic criticism, the first commandment prohibition of idolatry, and the cross of Christ. They all demand that human beings develop a mature, non-idolatrous faith. This demand applies to all religions. There exist elements in nearly all religions that point beyond literalism toward mature spirituality.

A central question for our future on this planet asks whether we can move beyond the naive cosmologies and literalist implications of traditional scriptures to a new vision of the life of faith or the religious vocation. For without creatively reaping the fruits of modern science and scholarship, we will never be able to move to a free, democratic, humane global society. Related to this is a second challenge to our spiritual maturity. Can we move beyond the exclusivist claims (also explicit or implicit in many scriptures) in the light of the twentieth century's discovery of the depth, profundity, and legitimacy of all the great world religions?

This question brings us to a fourth great development with respect to religion in the twentieth century: the comparative study of religion. With scholars acquiring expertise in languages of the world, translations give us a wealth of historical and exegetical knowledge that has allowed each great religion to rid itself of the myths and prejudices regarding its superiority. Each religion now commences to appreciate the depth and profundity of the others. From this twentieth-century accomplishment, interreligious dialogue has developed among all the great religions such as Judaism, Christianity, Islam, and the varieties of Hinduism and Buddhism. This dialogue deepens and enriches each tradition through its encounter with the others.

Works of great comparative scholars of religion appeared, such as Carl Jung, Marcia Eliade, Frithjof Schuon, and Joseph Campbell. These works open to people who have the privilege and leisure for education a spiritual wealth from every corner of the planet unimagined in previous centuries. Greater expertise in the translation and interpretation of the world's religions led to the realization that early historical eras held stereotypes and ethnocentric prejudices regarding the inferiority of the religions of others. Like naive doctrinal "truths," comparative scholars help expose naive claims regarding the superiority of the religion into which I happen to be born.

As Ninian Smart expresses our present situation: "The paradox is this:

on the one hand nothing seems more certain than faith or more compelling than religious experience. On the other hand, nothing seems less certain than any one particular belief system, for to any one system there are so many vital and serious alternatives" (1985, p. 76). As with the Copernican Revolution in science that moved human beings from the physical center to the periphery of the universe, the encounter of world religions helped move thinkers in each tradition from thinking of their particular religion as the center of God's concern and attention to the realization of the deeply ecumenical character of the experience of divine love and concern.

Fifth, there has been a significant degree of philosophical reflection concerning the nature and claims of religion. And some significant philosophical thinkers have focused on religion in the light of our modern situation, thinkers like Alfred North Whitehead in *The Making of Religion*, William James in *The Varieties of Religious Experience*, and Ludwig Wittgenstein in his "Lectures on Religious Belief" and "Notes on Frazer's *Golden Bough*." Wittgenstein provides a careful philosophical articulation of the differences between the inner logic of religious belief and other kinds of belief, such as scientific and factual belief.

He shows that the logic of religious belief places a significance, a weight, upon what were traditionally thought to be religious "facts" that no rational person, even centuries ago, would place upon them. For this reason, the logic of religious beliefs is different. The religious focus on particular historical events taken to be factual has an entirely different significance from scientific fact. He finds the innermost logic of religious beliefs linked to responsiveness, to our ability to respond fully to the great events of creation, salvation, life, and death, and to our ability to hinge the entire meaning and significance of our lives on our religious beliefs as these are focused on particular historical events.

He points out that we are moving here in a dimension entirely different from that of science, with its verifiable facts, statistical probabilities, systematic doubt, and theoretical models (1972). Wittgenstein took religion seriously, and his thought is indicative of a great deal of serious philosophical thought now accomplished and is still continuing with respect to religion and its differences from science (Martin, 1988). Religion is not dying out as some early advocates of a narrowly conceived "scientific world view" had predicted. Instead, philosophers of religion reinterpret and reappropriate all the world's major traditions in the light of twentieth and twenty-first-century intellectual and spiritual maturity.

Sixth, a movement emerged from comparative scholarship and the flood of literature on "inter-religious dialogue" concerned to formulate a universal theology of religion. Such an attempt goes beyond systematic comparison and dialogue to an attempt to formulate the presuppositions of a universal theology, the presuppositions of religion and spirituality themselves. These endeavors to formulate such a universal theology often attempt to express or point to the ultimate groundless-ground of the human spirit. They understand religion not as one compartment of human existence (a sense of the sacred over against the profane of life) but as the highest expression of that existence. They attempt to express that which gives rise to any and all spiritual orientations, whether or not these are identified with traditional religions and even whether or not these identify themselves with being "religious," such as evolutionary humanism or many forms of socialism.

The revolution initiated by Copernicus leads us past a calling-into-question of the entire religious orientation, manifested in modern secularism, positivism, and critiques of religion, to a renewed appreciation of religion and spirituality at a higher, more universal, and more self-critical level than could have been previously imagined. As Smart asserts, the heritage of the Enlightenment itself, properly understood, is not opposed to our new religious maturity: "Thus there is a sort of solidarity, in a strange new way, between a plural religious world and the heritage of the Enlightenment. For the free and scientific society is critical and imaginative, and the life of religion can offer a transcendent place of criticism and a path to liberating the imagination. But such criticism needs not only the transcendent reference point but also the nourishment of spiritual values through that kind of religious knowledge which still remains to us" (1985, p. 86).

A universal theology of religions presupposes the unity of the human race in relation to the ultimate ground of existence, however this ultimate is experienced or expressed. As such, it does not renounce the scientific, scholarly, and self-critical fruits of the Copernican Revolution but requires them, for mature spirituality requires them. Tillich writes: "The history of religions in its essential nature does not exist alongside the history of culture. The sacred does not lie beside the secular, but in its depths. The sacred is the creative ground and at the same time a critical judgment of the secular. But the religious can be this only if it is at the same time a judgment on itself, a judgment which must use the secular as a tool of one's own religious self-criticism" (1991, p. 41).

The attempts to articulate a universal theology of religions closely interrelate with the other aspects of the twentieth-century reappropriation of religion and spirituality. They assimilate the legacy of the Copernican Revolution that we have been discussing: the rise of modern historical scholarship and consciousness, the process of demythologization, the comparative study of religion, and the philosophical examination of religious beliefs (see Swidler, 1987).

This is true also of the final and seventh development of the twentieth century that has involved the widespread study of "mysticism" as possibly the universal core of all religion, beginning with such early works as Rudolph Otto's *Mysticism East and West*, to William James' *The Varieties of Religious Experience*, Richard Bucke's *Cosmic Consciousness*, Evelyn Underhill's *Mysticism*, Walter Stace's *Mysticism and Philosophy*, and F. C. Happold's *Mysticism – A Study and an Anthology*, and continuing in a host of more recent works, some of which I will discuss in Chapter Five.

Functioning, in part, as a phenomenology of mystical religious experience, together with an account of the core features of such experiences, these studies often point out that mystical experiences or forms of awareness are surprisingly similar in every century and in every religious tradition. What are termed "mystical experiences" sometimes happen outside of any religious tradition to so-called non-religious people. They are often life-transforming and illuminating, and they resist being forced into the Procrustean bed of traditional dogmatic religious doctrines of nearly any sort. It may be that the study of mysticism from the variety of the world's great traditions leads to a deepening and transformation in the way mysticism and religion are understood.

This maturing of our understanding also underlies the attempts to formulate a universal theology of religions and supports our sense of the urgency of social, political, and economic change if human beings are to survive and flourish on this planet. Could it be that mystical spirituality is a fundamental key to our ability to deal adequately with the global crisis confronting modern humanity? Could it be the key to our ability to realize a new unity and common ethical spirit to the human race, and to transform ourselves away from greed, possessiveness, and mutual alienation to interrelatedness, compassion, and solidarity among all peoples? In many places within this book, I attempt to communicate something of this idea.

Similarly, in her study of the thought and spirituality of Pierre Teilhard de Chardin called *Towards a New Mysticism*, Ursula King stresses this connection:

> Besides the current Western interest in the mystical heritage of the world religions there exists another, quite different area of dynamic growth where religious insights are applied to the transformation of the social order. The message of spiritual freedom is related to the liberation of man from external structures of oppression, whether expressed in the liberation theology of South America or in socialist reinterpretations of Buddhism in South Asia. In a way, the greatest religious problem today is how to be both a mystic and a militant, as Adam Curle has expressed it; in other words, how to combine

the search for an expansion of inner awareness with effective social action, and how to find one's true identity in the synthesis of both. (1980, p. 228)

The widespread study of mysticism, of which King's book is an expression, complements the widespread practice of mysticism from all world traditions, including Zen Buddhism. Zen Buddhism transferred widely from Japan to the United States and Europe during the last half of the twentieth century. It focuses on the awakening of a transformed spirituality without any dogmas or doctrines whatsoever. Zen's influence was tremendous, not only directly, through the creation of monasteries, meditation centers, and zendos everywhere, but also indirectly, through allowing people in other religions to distinguish a core of spirituality in their own particular traditions, the possibility of an awakening that is independent of dogmas, doctrines, or beliefs about historical events. We will discuss mysticism more deeply in Chapters Five, Six, and Ten, but for the present I wish to point out the great impact that the study and practice of mysticism have had on contemporary understanding of religion.

We are confronted, therefore, with a plethora of twentieth century developments. All these developments take religion and/or spirituality quite seriously. They also militate for a transformation in our understanding of religion that has tremendous significance for the possibilities of human liberation. As we have seen in earlier chapters, human liberation means a new planetary maturity. It means spiritual liberation in the form of a spirituality of justice and compassion, and political and economic liberation in the form of a democratic socialist world community.

If twentieth-century developments in religion and spirituality are leading to a new universal theology and spirituality, then we approach, more than we may have imagined, planetary unity and political and economic liberation. The Copernican Revolution in science not only served to bring about a great step forward in human maturity with respect to understanding the nature of human knowledge and the universe. It also helped transform religion from its immature forms and confronts it with the possibility of effecting its unique Copernican Revolution. Religion must shift away from a naive dependence on ancient cosmologies and factual claims to a new appropriation of its spiritual and ecstatic core, to a new relationship with the depths and source of existence itself.

This Copernican Revolution in religion is, I believe, an essential element in the present struggle to form a global democratic society, for global democratic socialism is the political and economic expression of love (see Perry, 1998). True democratic socialism expresses a society in which human beings and their welfare are the end and goal of all institutions, and not the means for the enrichment of the few at the expense of the many. The Copernican Revolution in religion shows us the possibility of "unheard of" social and personal transformation and points up the ground of a truly revolutionary unity of the human race. It creates the possibility of moving to a global spirituality that may well transform our conception of what it means to be human, our relationship with one another, and our relationship with the precious Earth and the astonishing universe of which we are an integral part.

This spiritual transformation is essential if we are to realize a sustainable and ecologically sound world of peace, justice, and freedom. A wide variety of thinkers today express the obstacles, as well as the possibilities, for such a transformation. Brian Swimme and Thomas Berry express these in one way in their book *The Universe Story – From the Primordial Flaring Forth to the Ecozoic Era, A Celebration of the Unfolding of the Cosmos*. These authors recognize that we are today confronted with truly revolutionary possibilities. They call the new age that we will face in the twenty-first century the "Ecozoic":

> Yet the tendency to minimize the difficulties before us is the greatest ob-
> struction to the radical change in human consciousness, a change at the
> order of magnitude required for entry into the creative phase of the Ecozoic.
> This change requires something of a different order but equivalent to a new
> religious tradition. Our new sense of the universe is itself a type of revela-
> tory experience. Presently we are moving beyond any religious expression
> so far known to the human into a meta-religious age, that seems to be a new
> comprehensive context for all religions. (1992, p. 255)

The Ecozoic era will involve a new era in human consciousness, a new participation in the universe that bears directly on the wonderful possibilities for religious understanding and awakening that have emerged through the scholarly examination of religion throughout the twentieth century. It requires a new mysticism, a new appropriation of the transformative possibilities available to us all through the mystical traditions of the world. Through mystical participation we can rediscover what Swimme and Berry call "a bonded relationship with the more comprehensive unity of the universe itself" (1992, p. 264). We discover that "our individual being apart from the wider community of being is emptiness. Our individual self finds its most complete realization within our family self, our community self, our species self, our Earthly self, and eventually our universe self" (1992, p. 268).

A compassionate world system of justice and decency, which will necessarily take the form of a planetary society based on love and compassion (and therefore democratic socialism) will require the deep realization of our "species-being" or "species-self" as this was intuited by Karl Marx. As with the survival of the ecostructure of our precious planet, such a world system will require nothing less than a transformation of consciousness, the emergence of a new religious dimension to life.

3. Misguided Reactions to the Copernican Revolution

At least three fundamental reactions to the legacy of the Copernican Revolution deny the general orientation I am developing here. The first, already mentioned, involves scientism, secular scientific humanism, and positivism. This first reaction claims that the Copernican Revolution leads our understanding of the nature and grounds of human knowledge to the point where we can disentangle metaphysical and religious world views that do not conform to the nature of knowledge. "Reality" is the totality of facts and their theoretical framework revealed by science. Representatives of this orientation often claim that there exists only one thing available to guide us: the facts, and their grounding in scientific, theoretic models. I believe that the poverty of this orientation will continue to become clearer throughout this book. Positivism and scientism deny the unspeakable depths of existence that confront the awakening human spirit at every turn.

These orientations insist on reducing the universe to a one-dimensional world that is a construct of our faculty of instrumental rationality alone, to the exclusion of the entire range of other human cognitive and spiritual faculties. This amounts to a narrow and truncated view of human life and its possibilities. It evokes in its followers a kind of living death, a one-dimensional existence that fails to see the depths of the universe that confront us on every side. The more human beings live fully through the use of the entire range of their cognitive and spiritual faculties, the more the unspeakable depth and mystery of the universe becomes a part of everyday life, as Kierkegaard and Bugbee indicate in the headings to this chapter.

Religious fundamentalism is the second misguided reaction to the Copernican Revolution. Unlike scientism and positivism, it does manifest insights into the need for human spirituality, to which it clings tenaciously. It embraces insights such as the fundamentally religious framework of human life itself, the need for serious commitment to the point of conversion, and the need for an awareness of "grace" or the unconditional "giveness" of God.

Yet fundamentalism mistakenly believes we are faced with a choice between faithfulness to God and faithfulness to the scholarly and scientific legacy of the Copernican Revolution. It revolts against the apparent relativism implied by Copernicus' shifting the Earth (and human beings) away from the center of things, a shift leading to the apparent scientific understanding that no privileged position exists anywhere from which to view the world or the human situation. Fundamentalism insists on the centrality of God. But as a consequence fundamentalism centers also on humanity, since human beings for it are the sole focus of the drama of redemption.

Fundamentalism fears the relativism and uncertainty of modernity and consequently defies modernity through its irrational clinging to arbitrarily grasped absolutes. In this way it cuts itself off, not only from modernity, but from any true participation in the solutions, transformations, and possible redemption of humanity as a whole made possible by the legacy of Copernicus. It cannot participate in mutual understanding among peoples, for it insists that its understanding is the absolute truth.

It cannot participate in mutual harmony and solidarity among peoples, for its insistence on absolute truth always implies ethnocentrism, the superiority of our revelation, our tradition, or our nation over others. And it cannot participate in the transformation implied by the possibility of a universal existential faith or spirituality because it confuses its experience of the existential dimension of faith with the claim to an absolute, literal revelation. Fundamentalism, therefore, misunderstands not only the nature of modernity but also the nature of faith.

Faith cannot exclude openness, radical openness to what may be given, without limiting itself to an appropriation and narrowing of what is already given into a dogmatic and closed form. In contrast to this understanding of faith, "we could describe faith," Raimundo Panikkar writes, "as *existential openness toward transcendence* or, if this seems too loaded, more simply as *existential openness.* This openness implies a bottomless capacity to be filled without closing. Were it to close, it would cease to be faith" (1991, p. 56). The Copernican Revolution makes such openness possible.

Perhaps we can say it makes this "more mature" faith possible, a faith so radical that it opens even to a deep understanding of other religious expressions. "A Christian will never fully understand Hinduism," Panikkar asserts, "if he is not, in one way or another, converted to Hinduism. Nor will a Hindu ever fully understand Christianity unless he, in one way or another, becomes a Christian" (1991, p. 53). By rejecting the legacy of the Copernican Revolution, fundamentalism cuts itself off from the deepening, transforming effects of these new possibilities for human growth, awareness and openness, including the depths of faith itself.

In addition to scientism, positivism, and fundamentalism, the late twentieth century confronts us with an apparently opposite reaction to the legacy of Copernicus. The nexus of relativism, skepticism, and nihilism is the third misguided reaction to that transformation in our understanding of the human situation symbolized by Copernicus. How are we to comprehend this wave of relativism, skepticism, and nihilism that has swept over the modern world, especially in the industrialized countries of the first-world? For in breaking the pre-Copernican naivete of traditional religious and metaphysical world views, modern science and scholarship have thrown many people into the vortex of infinite doubt. Is there presently any truth at all in human life?

Friedrich Nietzsche was one of the first great thinkers to identify this apparent consequence of modernity. He announced "the nihilistic consequences of contemporary natural science" (1967, p. 8), that "all science...has at present the object of dissuading man from his former respect for himself, as if this had been nothing but a piece of bizarre conceit" (1969, pp. 155-156). We find ourselves not liberated through the scientific project of modernity, but instead in a situation in which all our traditional values and ideals appear as empty and devalue themselves, leaving us without any values at all, a life without meaning or purpose. Truth, even the value of truth, appears called into question.

"Since Copernicus," Nietzsche writes, "man seems to have got himself on an inclined plane - now he is slipping faster and faster away from the center into – what? into nothingness? into a '*penetrating* sense of his nothingness'?" (1969, p. 155) Nietzsche expresses this consequence of the Copernican Revolution in the powerful symbol of the "death of God" announced by a "madman" in his famous section 125 of *The Gay Science.* God is dead, he says, and *we have killed him* through our scientific drive for truth at any price. Existence no longer has any discernible meaning and value, it no longer has the center provided by traditional religion and morality. Nietzsche's madman expresses the relativistic and nihilistic consequences of this event: "Is there still any up or down? Are we not straying as through an infinite nothing? Do we not feel the breath of empty space? Has it not become colder? Is not night continually closing in on us? Do we not need to light lanterns in the morning?" (1974, p. 181)

Nietzsche announced the "death of God" in *The Gay Science,* first published in the year 1882, a formula that he also expressed in his slogan *es gibt keine Wahrheit,* there is no truth. And the tide of nihilism he predicted has occurred, and does not show many signs of abatement. It has moved through different expressions and permeated even the philosophy of science through popular interpretations of the work of such thinkers as Thomas Kuhn (1970) and Paul Feyerabend (1975). As Herbert Marcuse has argued in *One Dimensional Man* (1966), such relativism plays right into the hands of the ideology of positivism promoted by the dominant powers to preserve their system of domination and exploitation. For if there is no truth, then all that is left to us are the immediate "facts" of this particular set of institutions (see Edwards, 1996). The "ideal of freedom" now appears as no argument against universal surveillance by governments. For "security arrangements" and militarism, we are told, are based on facts, not ideals.

This system, these laws, these social, political, and economic arrangements, arbitrary and "untrue" as they may be, are self-evidently the way things are. Like positivism, which argues that no alternatives exist to the domination of what factually is the case, nihilism limply concedes that no alternatives exist, for we discover no non-arbitrary values on which to base a vision of alternatives or a viable critique of the present system. Nietzsche's own thought attempted to creatively use nihilism to create new values. But the tide of nihilism he diagnosed has carried us into the contemporary relativism and skepticism of much "post-modern" thought. This pervasive form of thought claims that all "grand narratives" are dead and that all of life is a series of "texts" open to various readings, always variable, never stable in their meanings, always open to new rereadings in a morass of interpretations upon interpretations. Since the greatness of the "grand visions" is gone forever, we are left with the pettiness, smallness, and fragmentation of multiple interpretations (see Eagleton, 1996).

Lanterns lit in the morning are extinguished by evening when darkness penetrates everything. And every new lantern lit will reveal a new landscape, a new "reality," without grounding, without stability, without any meaning to the word "truth." In terms of my account of religious maturity above, this reaction to the Copernican Revolution also represents a failure to grow into the possibilities offered by modern science and scholarship (despite its often scholarly pretensions). It also reflects the immaturity of our political and economic institutions that cultivate an immature attitude, claiming that the "realistic" person clings to no universal values and operates only from personal self-interest.

Like fundamentalism, scientism, and positivism, much relativism is a product of the implicit nihilism produced by global capitalism. Fundamentalism deeply reacts to what it perceives as the rootlessness and relativism of modernity. But its reaction is "otherworldly," in the worst sense of this term, the sense in which Marx understood religion as the opium of the masses that promised people surrogate rewards and an otherworldly dignity within a system that exploited and dehumanized them. However, a predatory system that systematically distorts and manipulates truthfulness also leads to widespread relativism.

As Liberation Theology has so deeply understood, the larger movement of Christianity does contain within its broad spectrum of spiritualities a clear possibility of rejecting the institutions of the modern world in favor of a transformative process within this world, directed toward preparing the kingdom of God on Earth. But within much of the fundamentalist framework, its otherworldly orientation makes it in reality deeply conservative, accepting the nightmare of capitalism and the institution of the nation-state as the inevitable framework within which "sinful" human life on Earth must be lived. "Thus men will lie on their backs," Henry David Thoreau exclaims, "talking about the fall of man, and never make an effort to get up" (1962, p. 359).

Yet in similar ways, not only positivism and scientism, but relativism and postmodernism are also deeply conservative. Positivism and scientism best fit the framework of twentieth-century capitalism since they tend to deny the legitimacy of values (as opposed to the "facts") as representing anything beyond subjective human attitudes. Values as mere subjective attitudes of people are, therefore, no basis on which to critique the framework of society, its nation-state system and dominant economic system. As early as the 1950s, thinkers like Erich Kahler elaborated the "monstrous" effects of a modern mass society that has forfeited the depth and significance of human life through its repudiation of value:

> Radio, television, movies, omnipresent advertising, mass slogans, the functional lingoes of business and the professions, have all produced and fostered those stereotypes of public opinion upon which a collective thrives. The modern state too, be it democratic or totalitarian, must be regarded as an accomplished collective. Through the vast scope of its tasks it has become overwhelmingly bureaucratic, a monstrous, rationalized and systematized organization. (1967, p. 10)

Since no genuine ethical principles exist, the representatives of this framework feel free to manipulate these mere subjective attitudes for their own ends. Propaganda, advertising, and social engineering are the stock and trade of positivism and scientism, and people who hold these views are often highly rewarded by the society. Engineers, scientists, academics, and researchers are lavishly rewarded with status and money for doing the bidding of the big corporations, the state apparatus, or the weapons-development facilities. The incentives to adapt our thought and actions to the orientation of scientism or positivism are immense.

Something similar is true of postmodern relativism. Some of its representatives rebel, some "deconstruct," some put up a multitude of tiny intellectual "resistances" to the obvious absurdities of the status quo. However, since their ultimate root is a relativism that can find no values by which to oppose the dominant institutional framework of the modern world, postmodernists content themselves with publishing their tiny "resistances" in the form of books and articles, and in the process gaining tenure, security, promotions, and pay raises within the system they claim to be resisting. Yet unlike the fundamentalist religious denial of modernity, much postmodernism, with its strange conservative bedfellows positivism and scientism, manifests a deep misunderstanding of the implications of modern science and scholarship, a misunderstanding also coincidentally in their interest as academic or corporate elites participating in the wealth and power of the exploiting classes within a global system of immense squalor and misery.

Another determinant factor exists within all these basically conservative reactions to modernity. In each case, we also often find a deep maturity-fear, an unwillingness to stand upright and open ourselves to our possibilities for spiritual, religious, and institutional growth and transformation, an unpreparedness to respond to the demands and the opportunities inherent in our human situation and our current historical epoch. For the first time in human history, we stand on the cusp of transformative possibilities that can lift the world from its current nightmare into a genuinely practical and operative utopia. We stand at the cusp of planetary maturity.

Dropping our false relationship to ourselves and the world would mean that we would lose nothing except our compulsive greed, fear, and impulse to dominate other people and nature. And we would gain an openness to the unspeakable depths and riches of life inherent in our situation and easily available to those whose lives are established in simplicity, availability, and compassion. The world's great religions, as with the doctrine-free spirituality of Zen, need not be taken in a dogmatic metaphysical way as "grand narratives" claiming a final truth about the world. Nor, properly understood, are they in the slightest conflict with science (as opposed to scientism). And the dreams of a "religious" form of society so dear to fundamentalism would be immediately realizable, although in a non-dogmatic and deeply open manner.

To "demythologize" the great religions, to see symbols as symbols, and to open ourselves to the simplicity of the present moment so well understood in Zen, leads to an encounter with the "depths" of existence, unknown to most of postmodernism, and to a liberation from the loss of value and meaning characteristic of nihilism and much of the modern world. Scientism, fundamentalism, and relativism, as with human beings in general, remain "entangled," as Wittgenstein tells us, "all unknowing in the net of language" (1978, p. 462). Only those who can encounter the unspeakable mystery beyond language can escape scientism, fundamentalism, or postmodern relativism.

Religious maturity involves the willingness to let go of the compulsive ego with its need to be in "control" through basing its decisions on a narrow technocratic rationality and to encounter, as Kierkegaard and Bugbee affirm in the quotations at the head of this chapter, that moment in which everything is reversed, in which spiritual growth consists in a journey ever deeper into the unspeakable depths of existence, into the sacred "wilderness" of the world.

Yet as with positivism and fundamentalism, the challenge of a new maturity that is staring us right in the face at the dawn of the twenty-first century is something only a few postmoderns have been willing to face. Maturity is, after all, as Thoreau tells us in "Life Without Principle" (1967), primarily the dropping of the illusions of youth and a seeing ever more clearly into the depths of our human situation, which is what life is all about. Only if we contract into a dullness solidified through fear, habit, routine, and the pressure of corporate propaganda, can maturity be thought as "conservative."

The practices of the corporate brainwashing system are no accident. The system promotes the cult of mindless youth – wolfing down pizza, zooming around in shiny automobiles, oogling the opposite sex, staring at moronic movies, and indulging in fine (but "casual") clothing, toiletries, and a host of other corporate-generated trash. And no accident exists in the images directed toward the older, more well-off, generation of a "good life" of possessions and luxury that was aptly characterized by poet Lawrence Ferlingheti as "imbecile illusions of happiness" (1958, p. 9). Immaturity in the population is essential to the capitalist system, as well as to the nation-state system.

Corporate and government propagandists intuit quite well that for these intertwined systems to continue, the population must be kept in a condition of adolescence, focusing their energy on football contests, action movies, sensationalist news stories, or virtually meaningless political campaigns. It is easy to distract an adolescent population from paying attention to inhuman corporate or national imperialist practices in the third-world or from recognizing social and economic institutions that would create a decent society for everyone.

It may be that the threat of destruction to our planetary ecosystem or the present continuing exposure of "capitalist freedom" for the sham that it is will force the need for this new maturity upon us. But it will be up to us to change the structures that resist change, precisely because immaturity is deeply institutionalized within the ethos of capitalism and the nation-state. Contemporary institutions include the restriction of people's consciousness to a narrow technocratic rationality, as well as conditioning for blind obedience to the authorities. Although today's empire defines "maturity" as loyalty to these values of the system, this can now be understood as a deep immaturity, if not a form of madness. In the light of what we now know about ourselves and our history, in the light of the suicidal crises that confront us in the twenty-first century, and in the light of the seven wonderful developments of twentieth century thought outlined above, we can now understand the enlargement of our consciousness that constitutes authentic maturity.

Religion has radically evolved since the first nearly incomprehensible practices of the shamans scattered within the depths of caverns in the "Age of Magic," fifteen to forty thousand years ago. Today, mature religion appropriates the advances of human knowledge and understanding that have accumulated from the distant past through the twentieth century. It expresses the highest aspirations of the human spirit. In *Beyond the Chains of Illusion*, Erich Fromm summarizes this advance:

> We consider people to be "religious" because they say they believe in God. Is there any difficulty in *saying* this? Is there any reality in it, except that the words are uttered? Obviously I am speaking here about an experience which should constitute the reality behind the words. What is this experience? It is one of recognizing oneself as part of humanity, of living according to a set of values in which the full experience of love, justice, truth, is the dominant goal of life to which everything else is subordinated; it means a constant striving to develop one's powers of life and reason to a point at which a new harmony with the world is attained; it means striving for humility, to see one's identity with all beings, and to give up the illusion of a separate, indestructible ego....
>
> The evolution of religion is closely interwoven with the development of man's self-awareness and individuation. It seems that with the development of self-awareness, man developed also the experience of his aloneness and separateness from others.... Yet at one point in history, very recently indeed, less than four thousand years ago, man made a decisive turn.... He recognized that he could solve his problem only by moving forward, by developing fully his reason and his love, by becoming fully human and thus finding a new harmony with man and nature, feeling again at home in the world. (1962, pp. 156-158)

Without a conscientious appropriation of the twentieth-century breakthroughs in scholarship reviewed in this chapter, religion and spirituality might not be fully understood as a glorious and fundamental expression of our being-in-the-world. We made a decisive turn four thousand years ago, and we are making another decisive turn at the dawn of the twenty-first century.

Chapter Five

Mysticism and Spirituality

What man most passionately wants is his living wholeness and his living unison, not his own isolate salvation of his "soul": Man wants his physical fulfilment first and foremost, since now, once and once only, he is in the flesh and potent. For man, the vast marvel is to be alive. For man, as for flower and beast and bird, the supreme triumph is to be most vividly, most perfectly alive. Whatever the unborn and the dead may know, they cannot know the beauty, the marvel of being alive in the flesh. The dead may look after the afterwards. But the magnificent here and now of life in the flesh is ours, and ours alone, and ours only for a time. We ought to dance with rapture that we should be alive and in the flesh, and part of the living, incarnate cosmos.

D. H. Lawrence

One may be struck clean by sunlight over a patch of lawn, by clouds running free before the wind, by the massive presence of rock. What untold hosts of voices there are which call upon one and summon him to reawakening. He remembers, and is himself once again, moving cleanly on his way. Some measure of simplicity again informs the steps he takes; he becomes content to be himself and finds fragrance in the air. He may eat his food in peace. He does not wish to obviate tomorrow's work. He is willing to consider: not to suppose a case, but take the case that is. He becomes patient. Things invite him to adequate himself to their infinity. The passage of time is now not robbery or show; it is the meaning of the present ever completing itself. It is enough to participate in this, to be at home in the unknown.

Philosophy is not a making of a home for the mind out of reality. It is more like learning to leave things be: restoration in the wilderness, here and now.

Henry G. Bugbee

A mystic apprehends what cannot be fully expressed in language. Scholar of world religions Huston Smith reminds us that "the word 'mystic' derives from the Greek root *mu*, meaning silent or mute – *muo* = 'I shut my mouth' – and by derivation unutterable" (1977, p.110). One reason for the great interest in mysticism since the early twentieth century is that its representatives throughout history and throughout all cultures of the world have spoken of an awareness or "knowledge" to which humans have access independently of language, reasoning, empirical evidence, or science. They claim an access to what is "unutterable." Scholars find a phenomenon that may be independent of culture and history intriguing. Many mystics developed a language of "apophaticism." Many developed a "negative theology" that cuts off, through the use of paradox, negation, or negative metaphors (such as "darkness," "emptiness," "silence," "desert," "abyss," or "nothingness") our impulse to fit what they are saying into our ordinary categories of reasoning, evidence, or knowledge (Sells, 1994). We are faced with an apparently universal phenomenon claiming to see "ultimate truth" beyond language, knowledge, or culture. And some mystics claim that awareness of this "ultimate truth" is our true human destiny.

The literature of mysticism tells us over and over that we must give up our exclusive reliance on language and the cognitive intellect if we are to awaken to the transforming silence variously called the "Godhead" "Brahman," "Tao," "Eyn Sof," the "Absolute," "Dharmakāya," or "Truth." We must learn not daily accumulation of more knowledge but "daily loss," daily attentiveness to "emptiness" (*śūnyatā*), daily living with "non-acting action" (*wu wei*) so that we may move "beyond name and form." As Huburt Benoit affirms, "all perception on the profound plane is without form. On the contrary perception on the surface plane is formal" (1959, p. 73).

1. The Contemporary Study of Mysticism

The several interrelated developments in the twentieth-century study of religion discussed in Chapter Four serve significantly as part of this process of negation, of daily loss, or the giving-up of our desire to grasp and possess spiritual awakening through the linguistic and conceptual forms in which this is expressed in traditional religions. We must understand the study of religion in the twentieth century as involving this process of giving-up aspects of the traditional religious orientation that we thought we possessed and could appropriate unproblematically for our lives.

In the nineteenth century, Søren Kierkegaard and Friedrich Nietzsche rebelled against such comfortable bourgeois religious assumptions, demanding instead a "fear and trembling" before the unknowable Infinite, on the one hand, or standing before the abyss of the "death of God," on the other. At the dawn of the twenty-first century, as Chapter Four demonstrated, we are in a position to understand their rebellion in the light of twentieth-century scholarship that can bring us to the point of an entirely new understanding of religion and spirituality. This new understanding frees us from dogmatic metaphysics, neurosis, blind belief, and immaturity.

We examined the development of historical and critical scholarship that required a giving-up of the traditional assumptions about the nature and composition of religious scriptures. Concomitantly, the development of historical consciousness required the giving-up of assumptions about the ahistorical and immutable character of the world's scriptures. These developments led to a process of "demythologization" that involved giving-up our claims to a literal reading of scripture in favor of an understanding of its symbolic character. This symbolic character, Paul Tillich points out, opens us to the sacred "depths" of existence (1987, p. 49). Demythologizing strips away the illusions generated by religion, culture, or science, preparing us to encounter the unsayable.

The comparative study of religions had similar consequences. It requires people of all religions to give up the assumed superiority of their religious views and become open to a process of growth that can deepen their understanding of their particular religions. Philosophical reflection on the nature of religion and its claims, as in the work of Ludwig Wittgenstein, helped people give up their naive assimilation of the logic of religious beliefs to the logical of factual and scientific beliefs. We now recognize that something entirely different is going in connection with religion. We now recognize the universality of the sacred and the possibility of our participation in a radically different dimension from that in which science moves.

We saw the movement toward formulating a universal theology of religions requiring a critical judgment on science as well as expressions of the sacred, a process of negation toward the parochial and naive traditional assumptions about both. Finally, the study of mysticism itself, as this is expressed in a large body of literature from every culture and every age, confronts claims that the sacred dimension is ineffable. We find mystics everywhere developing an apophatic language of negation in the attempt point to, or express indirectly, the inexpressible.

We must give up a host of traditional false assumptions about religion and recognize a depth aspect to all religion, often obscured by the naive presuppositions of traditional religion. We realize that religion itself, when its beliefs and practices are "unbroken," as Tillich terms it, remains deeply problematic. Religion unnegated by scholarship, historical awareness, comparative insight, philosophical analysis, and "mystical unsaying" may well serve to obscure the sacred and even inhibit the transformation of our lives that was supposed to be at the heart of religion all along.

The developments of the twentieth-century study of religion involved a tremendous giving-up of our traditional assumptions, and opened up concomitantly wonderful possibilities for a new religious maturity, a process very much in accord with the age-old demands of mysticism. Scholarship regarding religion brought us through a series of negative learning processes, some of which appear to point beyond knowledge to the unutterable. Scholarship revealed that the sources of religion cannot be knowledge in the scientific and scholarly sense, yet they are "given" to all peoples and in every century. We confront once more intimations of what is simultaneously unutterable and universal.

However, this process of appropriating the negative wisdom of twentieth-century scholarship only occurs if we willingly go beyond the objectivating attitude inherent in the scholarly stance and enter the domain of direct realization of the ineffable. Scholarly knowledge provides valuable materials for reflection in all the above areas of the modern study of religion. But because mysticism deals with an unutterable dimension, we understand that what is fundamental about our human situation goes beyond such knowledge. We must move not into emotionalism or irrationalism, but to a fuller realization of intelligence born of a comprehension of the limits of knowledge. Indian-born sage Jiddu Krishnamurti provides one expression of this larger understanding of intelligence:

> There's no knowledge of the inner, only of the outer.... The skill of intelligence is to put knowledge in its right place. Without knowledge it's not possible to live in this technological and almost mechanical civilization but it will not transform the human being and his society.... The study and the understanding of the movement of our own mind and heart give birth to this intelligence. You are the content of your consciousness; in knowing yourself you will know the universe. This knowing is beyond the word for the word is not the thing. The freedom from the known, every minute, is the essence of intelligence. It's this intelligence that is in operation in the universe if you leave it alone. You are destroying the sacredness of order through the ignorance of yourself. This ignorance is not banished by the studies others have made about you or themselves. You yourself have to study the content of your own consciousness. The studies the others have made of themselves, and so of you, are the descriptions but not the described. The word is not the thing.... Negating without resistance this content of consciousness is the beauty and compassion of intelligence. (1982, pp. 81-82)

Even study of those who have realized mystical awakening will not lead to that transformation within ourselves. Such transformation will only come through "study of ourselves" that can "put knowledge in its right place" and lead to an awareness that is the "essence of intelligence," an awareness that involves "freedom from the known, every minute."

Scholars debate significant issues concerning mysticism, but the debate necessarily remains at the level of objectivating knowledge and cannot in itself lead to spiritual transformation. Even progress in the resolution of these issues will not lead us to the depths of life that are beyond objectivating knowledge. Yet the overview (in this and the previous chapter) of the central issues debated within the scholarly literature of mysticism points in the direction of what is beyond scholarly knowledge.

"This also means," Richard Jones asserts, "that the philosophical examination of mysticism is not merely an academic matter of interest only to professional philosophers. The...examination of possible mystical belief-claims and value-claims becomes of value to all who are examining their own lives" (1993, p.15). Such examination may "create a space" through "a process of negation" that points toward a deeper, non-cognitive intelligence. Krishnamurti calls this "negating without resistance the content of consciousness," so that we come upon that transformed spirituality he calls "the beauty and compassion of intelligence."

Different scholars of mysticism attempt to identify the fundamental characteristics of mystical awareness as expressed the world over by mystics themselves. There are innumerable reports in world literature of human beings having direct experiential awareness of what they often take to be "ultimate reality." They describe an awareness often characterized by absolute oneness, beyond the duality of subject and object, by a sense of timelessness, being caught up into eternity, by a sense of sacredness, that this "reality" is God or the Absolute, and, by a sense of utter joy, bliss, and peace.

William James, in his classic study of religious experiences, identifies four basic characteristics of mystical experience. First, "ineffability." It "defies expression, that no adequate report of its contents can be given in words." Second, "noetic quality." It involves "states of insight into the depths of truth unplumbed by the discursive intellect." Third, "transiency." "Mystical states cannot be sustained for long." Fourth, "passivity." Something comes to the mystic who "feels as if his own will were in abeyance" (1958, pp. 292-293). Other scholars have added to or modified this description in an attempt to capture the universal characteristics implicit in this astonishing literature of testimony.

F. C. Happold expands the set of characteristics to seven, the first four of which repeat the list of James: ineffability, noetic quality, transiency, and passivity. Happold adds three additional characteristics. The fifth is "consciousness of the Oneness of everything" in which "all feelings of duality and multiplicity are obliterated." Sixth, mystics report a "sense of timelessness" that is "an entirely different dimension from clock time," for "the mystic feels himself to be in a dimension in which time is not." The seventh characteristic to which mystics attest is "the conviction that the familiar phenomenal *ego* is not the real I, that this phenomenal self is "not the true self." Instead, the true self is, like the Hindu Âtman, "immortal, constant, and unchanging, and is not bound by space-time" (1975, pp. 45-48).

Smith presents a set of four characteristics that correspond fairly well with those of James and Happold. His first is "ineffability," second, "unexpected unity" or "at-one-ment," third, joy that is "not fortuitous" but intrinsic to the experience of unity, and, fourth, a noetic quality that is a kind of "seeing" or "knowing" (1977, pp. 111-112). We begin to witness an astonishing agreement among scholars regarding the basic characteristics of "mystical experience."

The seven characteristics listed by philosopher Walter Stace repeat some of the above or expand on other aspects of mystical experiences stressed by mystics and described by James, Happold, and Smith. Under what Stace calls "introvertive mystical experiences" he lists, first, "the Unitary Consciousness; the One, the Void; pure consciousness." Second, mystical experience is "nonspatial, nontemporal." Third, there is a "sense of objectivity or reality," apparently similar to the "noetic quality" mentioned by the others. Fourth, mystics express feelings of "blessedness, peace, etc." Fifth, we find a "feeling of the holy, sacred, or divine." Stace's sixth characteristic is "paradoxicality." When considered from the point of view of ordinary logic, description of the mystical experience will almost invariably require the use of paradoxical language. Finally, the experience is "alleged by mystics to be ineffable" (1960a, pp.131-132).

These authors give extensive quotations from the literature of world mysticism to illustrate these characteristics and show that, as James puts it, "the world of our present consciousness is only one out of many worlds of consciousness that exist" (1958, p. 391). From such studies we begin to understand that an "experience" (or related set of experiences) occurs that defies ordinary description. These experiences go beyond the subject-object dualism assumed by language, claiming that this dualism is transcended in a unity that is also a kind of "knowing." *"Phenomenologically,"* Nelson Pike writes, "the undifferentiated unity lacks subject-object structure and... this is one of the defining features of this experience type" (1992, p. 211).

As Ken Wilber describes it, "there remains in one's awareness no bottom – that is to say, no sense of any inner subjectivity confronting any world of outer objectivity" (1993, p. 262). It is not as if the mystic as an individual has experienced some wonderful spiritual reality or God. Instead, in a host of testimonies, the mystic as experiencer appears to be gone. There no longer exists a subjectivity experiencing anything. There literally is only "the One." Yet in the subsequent testimony of the mystic, this One is taken to be "reality," more real than the world revealed through the subject-object duality.

As Jones explains, even the word "experience" applied to mysticism can be problematic if this word connotes the subject-object duality of ordinary awareness. "Since the term 'experience' suggests a subject distinct from other objects which experiences an object," he writes, "when in fact no such duality is present, mystics often resist referring to the culmination of the path to a depth mystical experience as an experience at all" (1993, p. 3). This feature of mysticism, its transcendence of the subject-object duality, is a primary factor in giving rise to the "paradoxicality" that Stace refers to above. We saw Krishnamurti affirm that this awareness is beyond the known, "unconditioned." When Krishnamurti once said that the unknown is encountered without an experiencer or self, someone asked him if he was saying that a person cannot "experience" reality. Krishnamurti replied "to experience implies that there must be an experiencer, and the experiencer is the essence of all conditioning" (1977, p. 127).

Yet mystics tell us this "beyond the known" has a "noetic" quality giving the certainty of a "higher" form of knowing. It appears as a knowing without a knower. Carmody and Carmody define mysticism as "direct experience of ultimate reality," yet in some fundamental way this is an experience that is not an experience (1996, p.10). Scholars often describe the experience as "transient," occupying a specific brief time, yet paradoxically involving simultaneous awareness of reality entirely outside of time and space. Evelyn Underhill calls it "conscious union with a living Absolute," yet this is not "consciousness" in any ordinary sense of the term (1961, p.73).

Sidney Spencer concludes that the "experience" is "always felt to be an awakening to truth and reality" that makes our ordinary perception of the world "blindness, ignorance, illusion." Yet how, he asks, can scientific and scholarly knowledge involving careful and hard-won evidence be "blindness, ignorance, and illusion?" (1963, p.331). And if "truth" and "reality" refer to what is tested, corroborated, and experientially confirmed, how can something utterly beyond language in which there is no duality of subject and object be called "truth" or "reality?" This paradox is fundamental. As Raimundo Panikkar puts it, "if beings are real, God cannot be real; if things exist, God has no existence, and so on. Thinking that addresses God, then, transcends all categories that help the human being to maneuver in this world" (1989, p.146).

In addition to these difficulties, the testimony of most mystics clothes itself in the language of the religious traditions to which they belong, such as Christian, Islamic, Hindu, or Buddhist. This means that systematic comparison of their testimony raises the issue of comparability among these traditions. These scholarly difficulties (the paradoxical aspects of mysticism, along with its ineffability, variability of interpretive expression, and the ultimacy of its claims to truth) make the writings of the world's mystics intriguing to many thinkers. But these difficulties also help generate several controversies that are debated in the contemporary literature.

I will discuss six of these controversies briefly. The last two relate directly to my purposes in this book. My purpose is not to give an exhaustive account of mysticism but to articulate a twenty-first century understanding of spiritual and social transformation and a corresponding vision of planetary maturity. I will present a brief overview of some central scholarly issues regarding mysticism and place them within the context of a twenty-first century spirituality.

2. Six Issues in the Study of Mysticism

The first issue asks whether we discover a single core "mystical experience" to which this wide-ranging world literature gives testimony or whether we discover a vast multitude of differing religious experiences with only apparent similarities? Books like *The Varieties of Religious Experience* by James, for example, bring together a vast variety of non-ordinary experiences. Does this variety refute the assumption of a central mystical experience shared by mystics worldwide in every century and in every culture? It is possible to deny the assumption of a central mystical experience in favor of an irreducible variety of religious experiences. It is also possible to overlook differences among this variety in the enthusiasm for discovering the core mystical experience everywhere. Finally, it is possible to affirm a wide difference among experiences with a few of them sharing the common characteristics identified by many scholars as features of the core experience. Ninian Smart, for example, affirms that there occurs a variety and a core experience:

> One way into the question is to consider whether there is a single sort of mystical experience, clothed differently so to speak by the differences of cultural and creedal interpretation. On this view there is an essential similarity between the experiences of the Sufi, the Hindu yogi, the Buddhist contemplative, the Christian mystic, the Taoist sage, and so on. If so, then how do we account for the very different things they say? Well, it is because their hindsight view of their experience, and their preconditioning too, have helped to color and embroider their accounts of what happened. But we can detect from a core of similar things said about the experience itself that it is alike. There is naturally a host of questions and methodological problems which arise wormlike out of this can. Personally, however, I am favorable to the likeness of mystical experience thesis, and favorable to the thesis of the diversity of types of religious experience. (1985, p. 81)

A second issue addresses the question of the extent to which the testimony of the mystics is necessarily an "interpretation" of their "experience" or whether the mystics often resorted to a kind of pure phenomenological language to describe what happened. There are many epistemological as well as descriptive issues here, given the above-cited general characteristics of mysticism, including its paradoxicality and apparent ineffability. This issue often leads toward the huge project of disentangling a topology of mystical experiences and identifying the core characteristics of each. Pike, for example, discusses some of the complexities of this in his book *Mystic Union – An Essay in the Phenomenology of Mysticism* (1992).

Related to this task is a third and broader epistemological issue between those that Jones calls "constructivists" and those he terms "nonconstructivists" (1993, pp. 8-15). Constructivists tend to hold the post-Kantian assumption that there can be no direct, unmediated awareness. They believe with Kant that all experience has a conceptual element. Therefore, the core experience of unity or union that many mystics describe must be a product of some constructivist elements such as concepts or beliefs. John Tabor's book *Transformative Philosophy* (1983) provides an example of this approach. Tabor argues that the transformations described by Johann Gottlieb Fichte, Martin Heidegger, and the Hindu sage Śankara presuppose the replacing of one constructivist framework (involving, for example, the subject-object duality and the empirical ego) with another framework (which is non-dual, an absolute instead of empirical self, and so on). My review of Tabor's book (1986) shows that, as plausible as this thesis may sound, it is in direct contradiction to the claims of many mystics themselves.

Nonconstructivists, on the other hand, argue "that the depth-mystical experience is a contentless awareness.... Nonconstructivists also leave open the possibility of a realism grounded in an awareness unshaped by our concepts" (Jones, 1993, pp. 8-9). Such an awareness appears to violate the Kantian claim that all experience is mediated. For Kant, such mediation provides the possibility of having any experience at all. Yet there are respected philosophers, such as William P. Alston in *Perceiving God: The Epistemology of Religious Experience,* who challenge this Kantian principle (1991, pp.37-38). Krishnamurti, quoted above, also attests to nonconstructivist awareness.

A fourth issue is the place of theism in the testimony of the mystics. The majority of mystics in the Western religions (Judaism, Christianity, and Islam) understand even their non-dual experiences as union with the personal biblical God with whom they (as individuals) are not identical. And some theistically oriented scholars of mysticism such as Pike, or Alston in *Perceiving God,* disagree with those sharing Stace's perspective that the "introvertive" mystical experience is that of an "undifferentiated unity," which only is then "interpreted" by mystics in terms of their belief in a personal theistic God.

Part of the issue here is what, if anything, the core mystical experience tells us about "ultimate reality." Eastern mystics often appear to speak in terms of a metaphysical monism instead of a personal God (a monism that tends to denigrate the empirical world to the status of *māyā, samsāra*, or illusion). Are they giving a more accurate interpretation of "reality" than Western mystics who assume a personal God who created the concrete, finite world in which we live? Pike argues that we cannot so conclude:

> This would be to say that *phenomenologically* the undifferentiated unity lacks subject-object structure and that this is one of the defining features of this experience type. But, of course, this is not to say that the undifferentiated unity (or the description of the undifferentiated unity) implies metaphysical monism, that is, implies that there is, *in reality,* no distinction between subject and object. The latter implication would only hold if we could make no distinction, in principle, between appearance and reality. (1992, p. 211)

If the mystic takes the ordinary world to be appearance in some way, after having encountered the overwhelmingly convincing reality revealed in the mystical "experience," scholars need not follow uncritically. For what appears to some mystics to be reality (in this case undifferentiated unity) may itself only be an appearance, for example, of the mode of union of a distinct personal God with a human being who is metaphysically distinct from God.

In other words, if we assume for the moment, as S. Abhayananda does in his *History of Mysticism – The Unchanging Testament,* that we can speak sensibly of mysticism as providing an "intimate knowledge.... through contemplation...which directly reveals the Truth, the ultimate, the final Truth of all existence," the question arises as to whether this final Truth is the theistic personal God of the West or an impersonal "pantheistic" One of the East. Abhayananda sees a "unanimity of agreement between them all" (1996, p.1).

Yet is theistic mysticism superior to, and of a type distinct from, impersonal Eastern mysticism as some have claimed, for example, R. C. Zaehner in *Mysticism, Sacred and Profane* (1978)? Or does the mysticism more characteristic of the Orient have a better conception of the Absolute? Alternatively, the situation may be more complex than this disjunction would assume, for when we go deeper into the literature of mysticism we find apparently pantheistic, monistic mystical claims in the West (Plotinus, Meister Eckhart, Nicholas of Cusa, Giordano Bruno), and we find apparently personalistic theistic expressions in the East (for example,

Bhakti Hinduism or Pure Land Buddhism).

Many authors see no essential differences. Carmody and Carmody, for example, agree with Abhayananda when they assert that "the two halves of the mystical whole of the world religions, the Eastern and the Western, take up positions close to those of mirror images. Most of the primary concerns of the East appear in the profiles of the Western mystics, though in different proportions, and vice versa" (1996, p. 304).

The fifth and sixth scholarly issues interrelate and concern us most within the scope of this book. On these I will take a position and sketch out some of the reasons for my position. My purpose, again, is not to write a treatise on these scholarly issues in mysticism, but to articulate a coherent framework that brings together the social-political and spiritual traditions and shows the possibility of a real and effective response to our global crises in terms of a deep transformation of society as well as human consciousness.

The fifth issue expressed in one way concerns the quality of "transiency" listed by James and Happold. Is the mystical awareness most fundamentally about the fairly rare "introvertive" experiences of nonsensuous unity that are reported as a portion of the mystical literature, or is mysticism about something much more common and available? The "introvertive" mystics themselves report that these rare experiences transform their lives and their attitude toward ordinary empirical consciousness as well. They also claim they have seen something about reality that applies universally and all the time, something that stays with them after the experience of unity has ended. If this is so, perhaps scholarly focus on these rare experiences is misguided.

Other mystics claim to experience a unity-in-diversity all the time in their everyday lives. Is there something about our everyday background experience, something universally present and for the most part ignored, that may be the key to our spiritual transformation? If we are trying to learn from mysticism, is it misguided to set up these rare experiences of undifferentiated unity as the central paradigms for study?

Stace influenced many scholars when he made these rare experiences the paradigm for study and reflection in connection with mysticism and religion. Others, however, such as Krishnamurti, or Japanese philosopher Nishida Kitaro, articulate a transforming spirituality that explicitly repudiates the focus on rare "mystical experiences" as ignoring what is staring us in the face in our everyday lives. The issue, in part, involves how we wish to use the word "mystical." However, Kitaro repudiates this word altogether:

Religion is often called mystical. But when I speak of religion, I do not refer to a special kind of consciousness. "There is no mysterious power in the true Dharma" – the mystical has no use at all in our practical lives. Were religion some special consciousness of privileged persons it would merely be idle matter of idle men. "The true Way cannot exist apart even for an instant; what can do so is not the true Way." Again, "When we run, we are on the true Way; when we stumble and fall, we are still on it." Religion is not apart from common experience. (1987, p. 115)

Kitaro quotes passages from the Zen tradition to justify his repudiation of "mysticism" as the heart of religion. Yet the anthologies prepared by Stace (1960b) and Happold (1975) quote similar passages from the Zen tradition as illustrative of mysticism. Stace and Happold cite such passages as the testimony of people who have had a "mystical experience" characterized by such qualities as awareness of the nonsensuous unity of all things, timelessness, paradoxicality, and ineffability. This may be partly merely a matter of semantics. Below, I will suggest a framework for coming to terms with this issue.

The sixth issue debated in the literature of mysticism is closely linked to the fifth. Stace defines his study of mysticism around a fundamental distinction between "introvertive mysticism," which we have described above, and what he calls "extrovertive mysticism." In Stace's listing of the common characteristics of these mystical experiences, the latter differs only in the first two of the seven characteristics listed above. First, instead of a "unitary consciousness as 'the One' or 'the Void,'" the extrovertive mystic does not lose awareness of the ordinary world of multiplicity. He or she experiences "the Unifying Vision – all things are One" simultaneously with awareness of the world's diversity. Secondly, instead of having an experience wholly "nonspatial, nontemporal," the extrovertive mystic experiences "the more concrete apprehension of the One as an inner subjectivity, or life, in all things" (1960a, p.131). In his introduction to *The Teachings of the Mystics,* Stace summarizes the relation between these two:

> There appear to be two main distinguishable types of mystical experience, both of which may be found in all the higher cultures. One may be called extrovertive mystical experience, the other introvertive mystical experience. Both are apprehensions of the One, but they reach it in different ways. The extrovertive way looks outward and through the physical senses into the external world and finds the One there. The introvertive way turns inward, introspectively, and finds the One at the bottom of the self, at the bottom of the human personality. The latter far outweighs the former in importance both in the history of mysticism and in the history of human thought generally. The introvertive way is the major strand in the history of mysticism, the extrovertive way a minor strand. I shall only briefly refer to extrovertive mysticism and then

pass on, and shall take introvertive mysticism as the main subject of this book. (1960b, p.15)

The literature Stace refers to is striking and compelling. Abhayananda, for example, describes it in the following way:

> These assertions by the great mystics of the world were not made as mere philosophical speculations; they were based on experience – an experience so convincing, so real, that all those to whom it has occurred testify unanimously that it is the unmistakable realization of the ultimate Truth of existence. In this experience, called *samādhi* by the Hindus, *nirvāna* by the Buddhists, *fanā'* by the Muslims, and "the mystic union" by Christians, the consciousness of the individual suddenly becomes the consciousness of the entire vast universe. All previous sense of duality is swallowed up in an awareness of indivisible unity. (1996, p. 2)

Yet a striking similarity exists in those characteristics of the "extrovertive" and "introvertive" experiences described by Stace. I believe there are hidden philosophical and ontological assumptions in Stace's way of categorizing the literature of mysticism. Why should such priority be allocated to the "introvertive" experience? As Jones comments, "while some ordering of mystical experiences is inevitable, there is nothing inherent in the experiences themselves that requires a particular order" (1993, p. 4). Perhaps it is a mistake to dismiss extrovertive mysticism as far less significant in the history of human thought.

Camody and Camody, for example, find that the distinction is not as basic as Stace suggests:

> This does not mean that the mystic lost all sense of separation from ultimate reality or was so united with ultimate reality as to feel dissolved into it. Some mystics have spoken this way, claiming that all difference vanished; but other mystics have not spoken this way, have not claimed that they became ultimate reality or that they lost all partiality or uniqueness.... Rather, we are saying that the core of the experience, what the mystics stresses when describing the moment, is a vivid presence of ultimate reality (however named) that makes any intermediary transparent and secondary. (1996, pp. 11-12)

The core insight is the same in both cases. Yet we will see thinkers and mystics like Pierre Teilhard de Chardin, Krishnamurti, and Kitaro emphasize exactly the reverse of Stace's distinction. For them, it is not the case that the "extrovertive mystic" intuits the beginnings of an experience that will eventually deepen into an "introvertive" experience, as Stace assumes. The extrovertive mystic is not at the tentative beginnings of the awareness of a deeper "reality" beyond the everyday world. On the contrary, perhaps an awareness available to all normal persons as part of the background of everyday experience infuses the extrovertive mystic's experience. The issue here relates to the fifth issue discussed above: whether rare religious and "mystical" experiences are the key to human spiritual transformation or the key is something absolutely common and available in our ordinary experience.

With the twentieth-century scientific revolutions in our understanding of the universe, one significant theme that repeatedly emerges is "cosmogenesis" or emergent evolution, a theme I introduced in Chapter One. Science today understands that everything evolves, including the universe as a whole. Life on earth is only one dimension of the cosmic evolutionary process. And the new scientific paradigm, discussed in Chapter Two, includes within its understanding of evolution awareness of the dynamic interdependence of the parts and the wholeness of the universe within this process.

In the light of what we now know scientifically about the universe, contemporary philosopher Errol E. Harris, in books such as *Cosmos and Anthropos* (1991), *Cosmos and Theos* (1992) and *Apocalypse and Paradigm* (2000b), details the astonishing convergence of all the sciences in the twentieth-century paradigm-shift that understands the inseparability of parts from the whole within the universe. Many thinkers and scientists now see the evolutionary process as a *telos*, a goal-directed cosmogenesis, giving birth to ever-greater constellations of wholeness and new emergent qualities. Harris writes:

> If the implications of this scientific revolution and the new paradigm it introduces are taken seriously, holism should be the dominating concept in all our thinking. In considering the diverse problems and crises that have arisen out of practices inspired by the [older] Newtonian paradigm, it is now essential to think globally. Atomism, individualism, separatism, and reductionism have become obsolete, are no longer tolerable, and must be given up.... In short, explanation must be teleological, for the proper import of teleology is the domination and direction of the part by the whole. Further, the parts discovered are to be treated as provisional wholes in their own right, participant in and contributory to more complex and more highly integrated wholes. Such holistic thinking would make an incisive and far reaching difference to both theory and practice in every field of human interest and activity. (2000b, p.90)

The holism pervading our universe as understood by contemporary science gives rise to an evolutionary process continually intensifying the complexity and convergence of unity and diversity. Human intellectual maturity involves thinking more and more holistically and globally. Human spiritual maturity intuits the wholeness behind the process of cosmogenesis, a wholeness that does not obliterate diversity but articulates it as inseparable from the evolving, ascending scale of unities comprising the universe as understood by science.

In the light of what we scientifically know about our universe, the "introvertive" mystical experiences appear as something of a backward pointer. Perhaps they represent a regression into a primal one that is the matrix of the evolving universe but not its evolutionary vanguard, its "consequent" nature, as philosopher Alfred North Whitehead might express it. The extrovertive orientation, on the other hand, involves an awareness of the common, evolving ground on which we stand, where the multiplicity is becoming integrated with a higher emergent unity entirely different from the introvertive sinking backwards.

Jewish philosopher Eric Gutkind stresses this idea in his essay "Neo-Mysticism" in his book *The Body of God* (1969). He advances a distinction between "reductive mysticism," which retreats to a primal unity or uniformity "behind all things," and "integrative mysticism." Integrative mysticism does not give up the separate reality of the world's multiplicity, but within this awareness "everything is integrated into a higher unity" (1969, p.80). Similarly, Ursula King's book *Towards a New Mysticism* studies the cosmogenesis of Teilhard de Chardin and its relationship to human spirituality. King distinguishes Teilhard's "new mysticism" from what she calls "traditional mysticism." With Gutkind, King sees "integrative" mysticism as the more advanced form of human awareness. King writes:

> Usually, mysticism is taken to refer to extraordinary states of contemplation, inner visions, trances, stages of illumination, and so on. In this sense, it means an experience of inwardness without correlating it to outwardness, to mans' external world and the multiple concerns of society. Thus, traditional mysticism is, par excellence, an individual quest which has often been in tension with official religious institutions. Teilhard, however, does not restrict mysticism to contemplative states or extraordinary experiences of the individual alone, but gives it a more comprehensive meaning. Even when talking about mysticism primarily in relation to the individual, he links it to a continuum of progressively more centered experiences, ranging from pantheistic and monistic to theistic forms. But mysticism stands also for the goal of *all* spiritual life. It then refers to the most powerful and activating center of human spirituality which can only be achieved through correlating and integrating mans' outer activities with his inner life. (1980, pp.194-195)

King asserts that Teilhard understands the higher form of mysticism as integrative, instead of reductive, moving toward a unity integrating our outer activities in the everyday world with our spiritual lives. In terms of cosmogenesis, the process of evolution creates this integration of unity with diversity on ever more complete levels, and human beings are an advanced stage in this process. And just as Gutkind focuses on the social consequences of mysticism, so does Teilhard. The most fundamental issue for these thinkers is not the supposed "purity" of the introvertive mystical experience versus that of the integrative experience. Instead, the issue is the degree of unity in awareness and the ability to effectively integrate into that unity the multiplicity of existence in daily life. The many forms of human fragmentation, examined in Chapter Two above, impede our natural growth and destiny as human beings. They fail to integrate unity with diversity.

The undifferentiated "introvertive" experience is "oneness" and "self-transcendence." But ample testimony exists that oneness and self-transcendence animate "extrovertive" or "integrative" experiences as well, while the latter do not simultaneously obliterate the rich diversity of existence. Thinkers like Kitaro, Krishnamurti, Gutkind and Teilhard de Chardin show us that comprehension of mysticism moves away from the personal quest of the mystical recluse for a union beyond the world. Today, we are in a position to reap the rich harvest of the testimonies of mystics throughout the ages.

Some thinkers also realize the transformative social and spiritual implications of mysticism understood as our common possibility, the possibility of a breakthrough in awareness available to all normal human beings. In *The Reflexive Universe: Evolution of Consciousness* (1976), Arthur M. Young links this expansion of human consciousness to "the evolutionary force" in "all life": "We should view the evolutionary force in man, and in all life, as the promise of self-transcendence. It is not a compulsive force like gravity, if indeed it is a force at all, but it induces internal transformation" (1976, p. 245). These are fundamental considerations with respect to our contemporary global crises, for they link the scientific and scholarly achievements of our modern world with its spiritual possibilities.

Nevertheless, in the insight that the real significance of the mysticism is not about any rare paranormal experiences or occasional states of rapture, the most fundamental factors are not scientific reflections concerning cosmogenesis. The real significance of this insight is the spiritual transformation available here and now at the ground on which we stand. And there exists no final argument to convince persons of this, except through ourselves awakening into direct integrative awareness.

If "reality" is to be encountered anywhere, including a reality that is non-dual, timeless, and free of fear and violence, it must be encountered in the everyday world of the present, in what Young calls "the eternal now of consciousness" (1976, p. 28). As the work of Wittgenstein has made clear, metaphysical dualisms are a thing of the past (see Martin, 1989, chs. 4-9). Only one world exists, one reality, although it may have "transcendent" and "immanent" aspects. Our spiritual problems about how to live in this world will not be addressed though arguments concerning some other worlds, be they heavens, hells, or "undifferentiated Oneness."

What is it about our experience of this world that leads to a revolutionary transformation of our being-in-this-world? This is the question that the study of religion and the study of mysticism in the twentieth and twenty-first centuries must address. Science points to a universe characterized by cosmogenesis, but intellectual comprehension of cosmogenesis alone will not transform us. Yet such comprehension is extremely important, for science emphatically does not reveal the godless world of secularism.

Such a conclusion would be mere scientism, a turning of the limits of empirical knowledge into a dogma, a refusal to look deeply at what is right in front of us. It would also involve a clinging to an outmoded Newtonian scientific paradigm. With quantum physics, all Newtonian "materialism" becomes a thing of the past. And the alternative is not traditional "idealism," but a concrete, dynamic process of emergent unity-in-diversity.

David Krieger examines some implications of our contemporary situation in *The New Universalism: Foundations for a Global Theology*. In commenting on the "global theology" of Tillich, he writes:

> These questions should make us more sensitive to the scope and significance of Tillich's new formulation of the problematic of theology. For if there is in fact no *neutral* position, if thinking has always already taken a *stand*, then Secularism can no longer naively identify itself with an allegedly universal and impartial reason. It must acknowledge that its own principle is grounded in revelation. "The sacred," says Tillich, has not been "fully absorbed by the secular." That is to say, it reappears within Secularism as soon as Secularism develops its own claim to universality. Within the realm of the secular, therefore, an absolute dimension distinguishes itself from the relative and conditioned – as its "creative ground." This "ground" is the "God" of Secularism, in whatever way it is there understood and whatever name it is given. "The sacred does not lie beside the secular," as Tillich says above, "but it is its depths." (1991, p. 41)

No neutral ground exits. Secularism is a blind faith like any other fundamentalism that has taken a stand and claimed that its partial perspective is universal and rational. At the dawn of the twenty-first century we are beginning to realize this deception. We confront the possibility, and the demand, to discover the sacred within the relative and conditioned. We must squarely face the demand to realize the transformative social implications of this discovery, and to transform the implicitly demonic, techno-nightmare that secularism has forced upon the world.

Apart from any discussion of mysticism, therefore, there are twentieth-century religious thinkers who find the source of all religion in the often unrecognized background of everyday life. We have seen that Paul Tillich is one such thinker. He understands that the process of demythologizing traditional religious symbols allows those symbols to more effectively open up depths and dimensions of reality in our everyday lives that otherwise might be closed to us (1957, pp. 42-43). Another such thinker is Karl Rahner in his book, *Foundations of Christian Faith*:

> This unthematic and ever-present experience, this knowledge of God which we always have even when we are thinking of and concerned with anything but God, is the permanent ground from out of which that thematic knowledge of God emerges which we have in explicitly religious activity and in philosophical reflection. It is not in these latter that we discover God just as we discover a particular object of our experience within the world. Rather, both in this explicitly religious activity directed to God in prayer and in metaphysical reflection we are only making explicit for ourselves what we already know implicitly about ourselves in the depths of our personal self-realization. Hence we know our subjective freedom, our transcendence and infinite openness of the spirit even where and when we do not make them thematic at all. (1985, pp.53-54)

Whether this is put in explicitly Christian terms as the "knowledge of God," as Rahner does, or in the Buddhist terms of Kitaro as the "true Dharma" from which "we cannot exist apart even for an instant," we find a growing recognition that the depths of existence are not discovered in some other world but confront us at every moment of our lives in this world. As philosopher Henry LeRoy Finch expresses this: "the greatest beyond we can imagine is too close to be said! If we will 'let go' of the world then something entirely new will be revealed" (1977, p. 123).

As with Finch, a universal philosophy of religion will formulate this insight independently of any religious tradition. For example J. N. Findlay, writes:

> The supreme object of religion is, in my view, universal in the sense that it is active in everything and in every conscious person, and is not separately individual; but it is individual in the sense that it is concrete and active in individuals, and is not a mere abstract or side of their being. It corresponds most closely to the Logos of Saint John's Gospel which is the light that lighteth everyone that cometh into the world, or to the Holy Ghost, which, the Creed says, spake by the prophets. I am sure we all understand and know this unique sort of categorical status. (1985, p. 73)

In terms of a universal theology of religions, all religions respond
in one way or another to this factor that is "active in everything and in
every conscious person." J. M. Cohen and J. F. Phipps in their book *The
Common Experience* (1979) generalize this factor deriving from their
study of mysticism in the world's religions as our "common experience."
We saw that the characteristics of what Stace terms the "extrovertive"
mystical experience are nearly identical to those of the "introvertive"
experience. This means that Nirvana, or awareness of Christ as the *Logos*,
need not involve denial of the world through an "introvertive" turning
away. The unsayable sacred dimension is universally available through
encountering the depths of this concrete world of the here and now:

> The mystical path is not mysterious. It is not the private path of monks and
> yogins. It is open to all and has been liberally signposted by writers famil-
> iar with its various stages, men and women who have used the language of
> their own traditions – Christian, Buddhist, Sufi, Hindu, Taoist, Platonic or
> Jewish – to describe experiences which are not easily reduced to words, but
> which are sufficiently clear for anyone to understand who has a practical in-
> terest in exploring this universal path. The signposts are visible. There are
> even detailed maps of the terrain, which stretches from the bordering hills
> whence a preliminary vista may be obtained, as though a break in the mist,
> to the sunlit plains of enlightenment and beyond them to that paradoxical
> sea where being and non-being, selfhood and unity are one, to Nirvāna or
> the heavenly state at the end of the journey. (Cohen and Phipps, 1979, p.9)

How might the mystical path become our "common experience"?
How might society be reorganized to allow people to appropriate the
depths of their experience and be transformed to the point where hatred,
conflict, greed, exploitation, violence, and war are unthinkable? A
society fostering human growth and spiritual maturity would certainly
be nothing like our present society of greed, institutionalized violence,
and competitive conflict. We now understand that fragmented societies
perpetuate themselves from generation to generation through vast systems
of propaganda and brainwashing in support of their consumerist and
capitalist wasteland.

What I am calling "integrative mysticism" is the subject of Matthew
Fox's book *The Coming of the Cosmic Christ*. Fox writes:

> Once the churches have knelt and begged forgiveness, they must rise rapidly
> and begin contributing to the renaissance that the planet so desperately needs.
> They must lead with revitalized worship and with a revitalized commitment
> to a *deep ecumenism* flowing from a morality of reverence for all creation that
> in turn is born of a mystical awakening about the awe, wonder, and "radical
> amazement" (Rabbi Abraham Heschel's phrase) that our existence is all about.

Wendell Berry wisely declares, "Perhaps the great disaster of human history is one that happened to or within religion: that is, the conceptual division between the holy and the world, the excerpting of the Creator from the creation." Mysticism is the cure to this religious dualism, yet mysticism has been ignored in most Protestant, Roman Catholic, and Jewish theological training and leadership.... This book is about the sacred and our response to it: reverence. The sacred what? The sacred everything. The sacred creation: stars, galaxies, whales, soil, water, trees, humans, thoughts, bodies, images. The holy omnipresence of the divine in all things. The Western term for this image of God present in all things is "the Cosmic Christ." (1988, pp. 6-8)

What could we do differently? What must we do differently if we are to survive on this planet? We must grow to a living experience of the unity-in-diversity of all things. We must attain a planetary maturity that experiences all things as sacred and in deep relationship to one another. We must become integrative and extrovertive mystics who do not repudiate science but draw the profound connections between the contemporary scientific paradigm of evolutionary and emergent wholeness and a living spirituality of wholeness. We must discover a "deep ecumenism" that draws upon what is profound and creative in all the world's religious traditions. We must appropriate the astonishing results of contemporary scholarship concerning religion and spirituality to the processes of growth and transformation.

3. The Possibility of Spiritual and Social Awakening at Twenty-First Century Dawn

The study of religion in the twentieth century and the study of mysticism in particular brings us to the recognition that there are possibilities for spiritual transformation available to us that have been completely overlooked or denied by the cultures of positivism, relativism, and fundamentalism. At the same time, from the last decades of the twentieth century to the present, we understand the magnitude of our global ecological and human crises, outlined in Chapter One. The severity and interdependence of these crises places us under extreme temporal limitations. We must avail ourselves of our spiritual possibilities immediately. For we also begin to realize, as Japanese philosopher Keiji Nishitani puts it, that human beings must transform themselves through realization of what he calls our "Buddha nature" (as the next great step in evolution) or simply die (1982, p. 55).

The Copernican Revolution fostered radically opposite consequences. On the one hand, it engendered the scientific explosion of knowledge about the universe that transformed our lives through successive technological revolutions, continuing through the present and showing no signs of abatement. On the other hand, it led to a great negation of traditional Western assumptions about the nature and limitations of knowledge. Traditional religion, like most traditional Western philosophy, identified the God of the Bible with "Being" sought by the great metaphysical thinkers from the Greeks down through the Romans to the Christian Medieval thinkers.

This "Being," as Nietzsche points out in the Third Essay of the *Genealogy of Morals* (1969), was the dualistic negation of our concrete world of change, multiplicity, and death. It was assumed that the truths of revelation could be articulated and translated into the truths about a finite creation metaphysically opposed to "Infinite Being." But the Copernican Revolution called into question the naive literal interpretations of revelation as well as the unlimited power of reason to comprehend ultimate reality under the heading of metaphysical "Being," the opposite of "becoming." Experimental knowledge about the phenomenal, observational world exploded at the same time that our assumed knowledge about ultimate reality was called into question.

In this sense, the great modern philosophers who have shown the limitations of knowledge also express the legacy of Copernicus. David Hume in the eighteenth century developed a skepticism so pervasive that it challenged even our assumptions about the laws of causality and the substantial nature of the human self. Immanuel Kant in the same era called into question the power of the human mind to know anything about ultimate reality. For Kant, only the empirical- phenomenal realm was now the object of scientific knowledge and the "noumenal realm" or "reality in itself" was utterly unknowable.

In the nineteenth century, we have seen, Nietzsche and Kierkegaard continued this critical tradition of winnowing our minds from false pretensions to absolute knowledge and exposing the abyss that appears to open up when the limitations of our situation begin to dawn on us. In the twentieth century, Heidegger and Wittgenstein have continued this process of seeing ever more clearly the radical limits of human knowledge. For Heidegger the traditional quest of religion and philosophy in the West, the tradition of "onto-theo-logy" (the quest for Being and God), has been brought to an end in his own thought, which, in a fundamental way, is also the end of philosophy itself.

At this juncture, for Heidegger, we are faced with the opening up of a new "meditative thinking" in which the traditional philosophical quest for knowledge of the ultimate is replaced by an openness, a waiting, a listening without presuppositions or assumptions about what might be encountered. Our orientation to existence becomes "poetic," not as personal attitudes but as modes of openness in tune with the depths of the universe (1971, chs 1 and 4). This new openness takes us beyond conditioning to the depth dimension of everyday existence.

For Wittgenstein, a careful investigation of language and meaning, sense and reference, leads to a seeing clearly of the limits of language itself and the impossibility of metaphysics. Language, a collection of patterns of response within everyday situations, is unable to express "ultimate reality," these words themselves now understood as "nonsensical" (see Martin 1989, chs. 5-9). Here again we face the end of traditional philosophy and the ending of all human pretensions to knowledge of anything that might be termed Being or Reality beyond what is presupposed by science. As a result, Wittgenstein awakens to something unsayable, and, at the same time, "glorious" (1968, p. 159).

On the other hand, the idea that philosophy articulates the metaphysical presuppositions of science (and therefore clarifies for us the "reality" of the observable universe) is a perfectly legitimate use of the word "reality" as long as we understand the limits of this type of knowledge. It does not denigrate reason to recognize that reason and language do not exhaust the limits of awareness. Awareness beyond reason and language is not "irrational" but, as Krishnamurti insists, a manifestation of a deeper "intelligence."

The legacy of Copernicus involves the explosion of scientific knowledge on the one hand and the radical negation of knowledge of God, Being, or ultimate reality, on the other hand. As with the scholarly study of religion in the twentieth century, it represents a significant process of negation, a seeing ever more clearly our human limits and limitations. Here, in some ways, we begin to come upon what the traditions of mysticism pointed to all along.

Our conscious minds, our reason, our language, or belief systems cannot by themselves bring us to "ultimate realities." Not seeing our limitations in these dimensions, mystics tell us, is often a basic source of our problem. For metaphysics and religious belief systems keep us trapped within language. We need to realize a fundamentally new way of being-in-the-world that is not irrational but, at the very least, a-rational, free of self-conscious mind, instrumental reason, the interference of language, and all arbitrary belief systems.

And this new way of being is available every minute. We just have to wake up and begin to live from this deeper immediacy, prior to ordinary knowledge and language. The "paradoxical" language of the mystics attempts to effect this awakening. We need a self that is no self, an experience that is no experience, a knowing that is no knowing, a way of speaking that perpetually undercuts its own assertions and points beyond all language. Yet once this awareness begins to dawn (we are told repeatedly in the literature of mysticism), we know it as utterly simple and self-evident. And we are amazed that we did not see it all along.

This quality of mysticism, we have seen, accounts for the difficult issues discussed in twentieth-century scholarship of mysticism. Is there a single universal "experience" worldwide or a variety of different experiences? Is the mystic's language of assertions like "unity," "union," "void," "emptiness," "bliss," or "being" a purely descriptive one or is it already interpretive? Is a pure, non-constructivist "experience" possible, as many mystics seem to claim, or is all experience necessarily conditioned?

Do the mystics encounter a personal God or an impersonal Absolute? Are we discussing quite rare human experiences of another dimension or something in the background of our everyday experience? Which are more significant and revealing, "introvertive" or "extrovertive" mystical experiences? Scholarship can only go so far. Knowledge and language, as significant as they are, remain limited. The legacy of Copernicus has made this quite clear to us.

The history of modern philosophy, the twentieth-century study of religion, and the study of mysticism itself all appear to agree on the radical limits of human knowledge beyond the scientific. Philosophy and scholarship point to these limits, but they cannot bring us to spiritual transformation. For that, we need an entirely different path beyond the conscious self, instrumental reason, ordinary language, and our traditional belief systems. And we are ready for it. Becoming clear about the limits is an essential first step. Science in the twentieth century has taken a immense step forward in recognizing the fundamental dynamic of the universe as an emergent process of ever greater unity-in-diversity. But intellectual understanding alone is insufficient for spiritual transformation.

Our situation at the dawn of the twenty-first century is that we must take the next step into fundamental transformation, or we will destroy ourselves and our planet. We must move beyond dependence on science, knowledge, and language to a living-in-oneness with the overwhelming immediacy prior to language and reason that encompasses our lives from the beginning. This immediacy is its own fulfillment and reason for being. It opens us to a dimension that can be called the "absolute present" in which the temporal present as a mere instant between past and future is overcome (see Martin, 1991).

Instrumental, technocratic rationality, trapped in the temporal present (correlative to the perspectival ego), condemns itself to compulsively appropriating a private, secure future for its isolated self. Its compulsive struggle defines itself over and against a host of fears and insecurities appearing within the temporal structure into which it is locked. It must invest for future wealth and power, while simultaneously possessing a gun or a military organization for self-defense in the dangerous temporal world that is all it perceives.

It must build more bombs, devise ever more sophisticated security systems, increase surveillance against terrorism, control and monitor the population, dominate, and engineer nature. It must continue to do this even after the pending ecological collapse of nature on this planet has become evident. It must continue to do this even in the face of growing worldwide poverty, misery, and social disintegration. For the compulsions of the isolated and insecure ego are built into the foundations of technocratic rationality.

Not that the integrated consciousness does not or cannot plan for the future. Instead, awareness of the depths of the present moment and the unsayable oneness that encompasses our lives breaks the compulsive hold of the insecure ego and makes rational planning for the future something for the first time free, compassionate, and intelligent. Not that the temporal dimensions of past, present, and future are lost in an hypnotic disappearance into a present unconcerned with the "real" world. The eternal present of direct awareness does not obliterate temporality.

Instead, in spiritual awakening we encounter a tremendous freedom with respect to the temporal dimensions, once the insecure and self-obsessed ego is seen as an illusion. For the isolated ego only sees the future in terms of self-defense, security through wealth and power, and control of threatening forces (including, therefore, the poor). Its illusory isolation dictates this compulsive orientation. This compulsive unfreedom forces it to miss the fullness of life and the depths of meaning and fulfillment encompassing our lives in the non-temporal present, a present always available as the background and depth of all human experience. In this present, we experience the unity-in-diversity of integrative mysticism.

The life lived in the simplicity of openness to the present beyond the compulsive ego for the first time clearly discerns the future (so far as this is possible) in the light of past experience and carefully plans for that future with freedom, flexibility, and openness. And it is also a life that desires to plan in conjunction with others, a life deeply concerned, for the first time, with the future of others. Progressively freed from the selfishness of the ego and the illusory threats and insecurities that the ego compulsively projects onto the future, the awakened person understands that planning can and must be done cooperatively for our common future, reasonable security, and the prosperity of everyone.

Progressively freed from the selfishness of the ego, the awakened person begins to identify compassionately and lovingly with others. As love for others and involvement with others develops, the fullness and meaning of life further flows into present awareness. We realize that our common social and economic life must be one of careful, non-instrumental but ethically rational planning and concern for the welfare of everyone, as well as for the precious planet on which we dwell. This is planetary maturity, as well as the realization of freedom and fulfillment on our precious planet.

Without this spiritual transformation, we have seen in Chapter Three, a socialist revolution beyond capitalism will avail us quite little. Yet spiritual transformation is not a necessary antecedent for a socialist society, for this society is, at the same time, the prerequisite for widespread spiritual transformation. Institutional transformation and spiritual transformation must be concomitant and simultaneous. Those "apolitical" explorers of spirituality who claim that spiritual change must happen first often appear deeply hypocritical. They bemoan the spiritual benightedness of their fellow human beings while retaining the comfort, privilege, and leisure of the global system of exploitation and domination from which they benefit. However, the spiritual awakening they advocate will not happen under this present system of institutionalized fragmentation and division.

In the chapters below, I will fully explore why planetary democratic socialism (committed to production for human needs and focused on the common good of all human beings considered as ends-in-themselves) is precisely the political form of love and compassion. On the deepest level, socialism has little to do with government ownership of the means of production. It alone provides space for the development of authentic human spirituality, something only fully accomplished when the goals of political and economic organization are human beings as well as harmony with our planetary environment (and not private profit). Only socialism on a planetary scale, in conjunction with truly democratic world government, fosters the freedom that provides every human being with the opportunity for authentic spirituality.

A decent society, based on human and planetary needs and the opportunity for human fulfillment, might easily provide non-denominational meditation centers everywhere. Parks, retreat centers, and quiet spaces might easily be available if society were planned for human welfare, even within large cities. Materials from the world's religions could be easily accessible in libraries, through computers, or within non-denominational meditation centers. The beauty of nature and our place within it could be expressed everywhere, in a variety of forms. Culture, theater, the arts, film, books, and other publications could be open to the simplicity and beauty of our life on earth and free of their present imperative to manipulate people in the interest of private profit.

In any truly human and humane society, plenty of space exists for spiritual and religious growth and exploration. Such growth is essential to being human, and a sane society would see that the opportunity for spiritual growth and exploration is available to every citizen as part of the heritage of being human. Needless to say, such growth cannot be legislated but requires creation of an environment to which people freely have access.

The economic and commercial domination of human life would cease, and the business of producing goods and services for all would slip into the background, managed with the participation of all, but managed, like the taking of showers or the brushing of teeth, almost unconsciously. For the production of such necessities is only tangential to the meaning and purpose of life that is connected, if anything, with the development of human potentialities for growth. Henry David Thoreau expresses this point in his essay "Life Without Principle":

> Those things which now most engage the attention of men, as politics and the daily routine, are, it is true, vital functions of human society, but should be unconsciously performed, like the corresponding functions of the physical body. They are *infra*-human, a kind of vegetation.... Thus our life is not altogether a forgetting, but also, alas! to a great extent, a remembering, of that which we should never have been conscious of, certainly not in our waking hours. Why should we not meet, not always as dyspeptics, to tell our bad dreams, but sometimes as eupeptics, to congratulate each other on the every-glorious morning? I do not make an exorbitant demand, surely. (1967, pp.372-73)

Such are conditions in a society where there is true freedom of religion and spirituality. In today's world, where people suffer massive political and commercial manipulation and domination, there is no true freedom. And such a "practical utopia" is easily within our reach. It requires giving-up what we never possessed in the first place: our grasping, fearful, maniacal, yet arrogant egos, that are transcended through the process of spiritual awakening and maturity. And we see, as we do in the quotation from Bugbee at the head of this chapter, that the multiplicity of tasks that comprise our everyday lives find their meaning and redemption in the perpetual "reawakening" embracing our lives.

The true spirituality and mysticism permeating our ordinary lives manifests itself in ways such as this. In moments of awakening to our true situation, we discover ever again our authentic vocation as wayfarers on an astonishing and immense journey of cosmogenesis, of intellectual and spiritual discovery and openness. As the quotation from Lawrence at the beginning of this chapter affirms, we discover a fullness of life flowing into our everyday awareness, which is what we have been dreaming about all along.

What is significant is this sacred life "in the flesh," within this holy cosmos. Krishnamurti affirms the simplicity of this revolutionary awakening: "Live, live in this world. This world is so marvelously beautiful. It is our world, our earth to live upon, but we do not live, we are narrow, we are separate,...we are frightened human beings.... We do not know what it means to live in that ecstatic, blissful sense" (1973, p. 14).

Planetary maturity is just such an adventure in perpetual growth, wonder, and spontaneous joy in living. We discover ever again a life of simplicity and joy in which democratic socialism, the sharing with others in mutual work for our own welfare and the common good, becomes as simple and self-evident as the ecstatic unity-in-diversity of life itself.

Chapter Six

Stages of Human Development
Toward Ethical and Spiritual Maturity:
A Critical Dialogue with Habermas,
Kohlberg, Carter, and Fowler

Marx said... "Philosophers have only interpreted the world differently. What matters is to change it." From the standpoint of "X," one would have to add, "Yes, one must change the world, but one has to go beyond philosophy as well as a change of the world. What matters is that man himself becomes different! But that means that man must discover values that can become efficient motives of his actions. At issue is not only the changing of the world and certainly not only the various interpretations of the world, but rather the question, 'How can man become so profoundly transformed that the values that he has hitherto recognized only ideologically, become compelling motives for his personality and his action?'"

Erich Fromm

Personality is the only truly creative and prophetic element in moral life; it coins new values. But it suffers for doing so. Creative personality defends the first-hand, pure, virginal character of moral thought and conscience against the constant resistance of the hard-set collective thought and conscience, the spirit of the times, public opinion, etc. In doing so the creative personality may feel itself a part of a spiritual whole and be neither solitary, nor self-assertive.... A person is connected with a communal spiritual whole through his own free conscience and not through social compulsion and authority. The ethics of creativeness is always prophetic, directed towards the future; it originates from the individual and not from a collective unity, but it is social in import.

Nicolas Berdyaev

The work of twentieth-century science gives us a universe characterized by a series of ascending wholes in which the parts are integrated in ever more complex and intricate ways. And twentieth-century study of spirituality shows the way to a direct realization of wholeness through integrative mysticism. In all branches of knowledge, we are in the midst of a paradigm-shift that lifts us out of our egoistic fragmentation toward a redemption of human life and the precious natural environment on this planet.

Similarly, the twentieth century witnessed tremendous advances in our understanding of the process of human growth and maturity as a movement toward spiritual awareness, moral autonomy, and wholeness.

In this chapter, we examine some of what contemporary philosophy and social science say about human growth toward maturity. The above quotation from Erich Fromm accurately describes the demand for transformation inherent in our situation. And the quotation form Nicholas Berdyaev gives an excellent brief description of planetary maturity. Transformative compassion, ethical maturity, and the assent to personal and planetary wholeness constitute our great human hope.

1. Stages in Human Development

The pioneering work of such thinkers as Jean Piaget, Lawrence Kohlberg, Eric Erickson, James Fowler, and Jürgen Habermas articulates and extends the Kantian critical insight into the structural presuppositions of our capability for perception, conception, and experience in general. This orientation is broadly epistemological, leading to an understanding that the growing human being synthesizes the coherence and meaning of her or his world in differing ways through stages of infancy, childhood, adolescence, early adulthood, and so on. The process of growth does not end with early adulthood, however.

As these and other thinkers demonstrate, the process of conceptual, moral, and spiritual integration continues into adulthood and throughout life. It continues toward an ever deeper awareness and ever more encompassing understanding of what Fowler calls "the ultimate environment" within which life is lived. This "ultimate environment," we will see, involves the wholeness of life within our holistic cosmos. Growth toward maturity aims at a unity-in-diversity similar to that experienced by integrative mysticism.

In the eighteenth century, Immanuel Kant initiated a revolution in the way we understand human knowledge and cognition, a revolution that continued through the twentieth century. He understood that knowledge is not derivable directly from our perceptions of the world. For the organizing ability of the human mind and human senses contributed to the form of the world we encounter. Kant called these organizing principles the *a priori* or presuppositional conditions of experience and knowledge. The world we encounter is a product of the content of our perceptions, on one hand, and conditioned by the forms provided by our *a priori* capacities of knowing and perceiving, on the other. The Kantian revolution continued developing through the twentieth century in the work of such thinkers as Ludwig Wittgenstein, Martin Heidegger, Edmund Husserl, and Emmanuel Levinas, further clarifying the nature and limits of human knowledge

In the eighteenth century, Kant understood the presuppositional or *a priori* conditions of experience and knowing as atemporal. He assumed *a priori* structures for understanding and perceiving as identical in all normal human beings and atemporal across the centuries. His work was transposed in the twentieth-century thought of Wittgenstein and others toward a richer understanding of the *a priori* aspects of meaning. Generally speaking, for Wittgenstein, meaning is *a priori* and prior to questions of truth.

Meaning (language) must be there, already fully in operation, before we can begin to discuss questions of truth and falsehood, in other words, before we begin to discuss *a posteriori* facts and theories. Language provides the *a priori* forms of possible expression. However, Wittgenstein understands meaning (the entire linguistic world within which human beings live their lives) as inextricably linked to concrete meaning situations within everyday life in such a way that what serves as *a priori* or presuppositional in one linguistic context may function in an *a posteriori* way in another context (see Martin, 1989, ch. 8).

Because of this fluidity, these *a priori* aspects of meaning appear differently from the atemporal Kantian model. Fundamental changes in the way human beings think and organize their experience become possible. They become dynamic possibilities for evolving new and unheard of "forms of life" as we move into the future (Martin, 1989, pp. 246-256). There exists no frozen, unchangeable "human nature." At the same time, thinkers like Habermas, Kohlberg, Robert E. Carter, and Fowler use this insight into the possibility of evolving or changing sets of *a priori* conditions by which we synthesize our experience to understand not only the quite different world inhabited by children at different stages of growth, but the presupposed world views of those from differing cultures and traditions. Yet the basic assumptions by which we synthesize our experience are stable and discernible as a pattern of growth toward ever greater maturity.

As with the work of Heidegger in *Being and Time*, Wittgenstein and the above-mentioned developmentally-oriented thinkers temporalized Kant's understanding of the *a priori* conditions for possible experience. The possibility of evolution in the presuppositions of cognition helps us understand the variety of ways that human beings comprehend the world and the dynamic, changing, and often developing nature of these patterns of comprehension. Yet in addition to showing the epistemic conditions of human experience as temporal and subject to change and possible development, these thinkers helped to clarify the synthesizing aspects of knowing and awareness in terms of levels of generality and universality.

In the light of their work, we discover different levels and overlapping dimensions of *a priori* conditions of experience. Human life is dynamic and extremely complex. As Wittgenstein (1972) suggests, some of these levels are more removed from the possibility of change or empirical investigation than others. The most general background of our knowing, thinking, and practical decision-making in Wittgenstein's thought is what phenomenologists term the "lifeworld" (*Lebenswelt*) (Gier, 1981). Similarly, Habermas claims that the presuppositions of communicative rationality in the "lifeworld" are quasi-transcendental. Although they must not be "hypostatized," they are relatively open to empirical investigation (1998, pp. 42-46; 1992, pp. 115-148). Beginning with the highest levels of *a priori* conditions of meaning , such as Wittgenstein's "forms of life" or Habermas' "lifeworld," we find historical, cultural, or personal structural frameworks for organizing experience at decreasing levels of generality.

These levels may interpenetrate with one another and dynamically evolve, making impossible the development of any rigidly hierarchical, static model for levels of meaning and generality. All these thinkers wish to understand how we know and how we synthesize our experience. Twentieth-century thought taught us that we do not construct experience with purely formal, atemporal Kantian categories. We use imagination, reason, intuition, and emotion in relation to our inherited "forms of life" as well as the communicative presuppositions of language. All these bear on how we construct our self, others, the world, and what Fowler calls the "ultimate environment." For Fowler, self, others, and world interact and hermeneutically resynthesize these constructions in the light of experience and growth (1981, p.98). "In any holistic approach to the human construction of meaning," Fowler writes, "account must be given of the relations of reasoning to imagination, of moral judgment making to symbolic representation, ecstatic intuition to logical deduction" (1981, p. 99).

In terms of the growth and development of children, the situation is more exact. The work of Piaget and his followers empirically describes more specified cognitive levels through which children at different stages of development synthesize their experience. We derive an approximation of the trajectory of human growth from studying their work. We understand the crucial principle that human beings can and do grow through specific stages of cognitive, moral, and spiritual development. Logically implicit in this model is the insight that some forms of adulthood express greater cognitive, ethical, and spiritual maturity than others.

We see that these stages are fairly linear (in that in the normal course of development each stages builds and enlarges the cognitive basis of the previous stages). We find that the process is broadly universal across varying cultures (Kolhberg, 1984). Finally, we perceive that these stages have an end point comprehensible as a fulfillment of the moral quest and a criterion for understanding the ethical life (Kohlberg, 1984; Carter, 1992;

Fowler, 1981). All this means that these thinkers profoundly disagree with the post-modern relativists who hold that all narratives are equal and no criteria (grand narratives) exist for distinguishing "truer" or more valuable narratives from those less so (Carter, 1992, ch. 6). Some "philosophies" or perspectives on life and the world are more mature than others.

Twentieth-century philosophy and social science developed beyond providing insight into the stages of growth through which we move as children. These thinkers also outlined for us the *telos* of this growth toward understanding the way a mature human being cognitively, ethically, and spiritually synthesizes his or her world. Thinkers like Habermas, Kohlberg, Carter, and Fowler attempt to theoretically comprehend this highest stage of human maturity.

2. Jürgen Habermas

The theorists of moral development, such as Piaget, Kohlberg, and Fowler, examine human development from childhood into adulthood by studying the changing sets of *a priori* principles by which we cognize our world as we grow. Just as adult human cognition may evolve historically, so in the life of each individual the forms by which we synthesize our experience and cognize a meaningful world also evolve. This evolution of cognition includes a concomitant evolution in ethical maturity. Habermas follows the basic patterns of this development offered by Kohlberg and others, but he sees the *a priori* criteria for a full human maturity as presupposed by all natural human languages. These criteria must be presupposed if meaningful communication is going to occur at all.

For Habermas, the developmental model derived by the theorists of moral development parallels the development of communicative competence, lending additional empirical confirmation to his theory of discourse ethics. Habermas' "universal pragmatics" develops the universal, formal developmental characteristics of communicative competence from the earliest stages of incomplete communicative interaction to the highest stages of communication resulting in what he terms "discourse" (1998, pp. 21-103). The progressive development of interactive competence brings a person ever closer to the capability for, and realization of, discourse and, therefore, ethical maturity.

Discourse directed toward mutual understanding recognizes the assumptions, imbedded in the lifeworld (or most general linguistic horizon within which life is lived), of "intelligibility, truth, normative rightness, and authenticity" (1998, pp. 77-92). These assumptions or presuppositions make communication possible, since language itself derives from utterances directed toward mutual understanding. We discover here some of the material necessary for a broadly conceived criterion for human development. Ethical values are not relative, as skeptics claim, but arise from the fundamental presuppositions of language.

Speech-acts locate speaker and hearer within a common reality that includes, first, the speaker's "internal nature." Implicit in speech directed toward mutual understanding is the expectation of truthfulness and authenticity regarding our thoughts, needs, and wants. Second, speakers are located within "external nature" in terms of which are statements are expected to express factual truth. A lie would never work effectively if it were not for this implicit expectation of truthfulness. Finally, our common reality includes a social or "interpersonal" reality in terms of which our statements should express normative rightness (1998, pp. 77-92). If a conflict arises, a listener may challenge a speaker with respect to the validity of any of these claims embodied implicitly or explicitly in every speech act. Building on this foundation, Habermas argues that the highest stage of moral development finds expression in the universal ethics of speech that begins with, and goes beyond, Kohlberg's initial six stages of moral development.

Habermas summarizes Kohlberg's six stages as follows: The preconventional level of young children includes two stages. The earliest stage is "the punishment and obedience orientation" where "the physical consequences of action determine its goodness or badness." Stage two, also preconventional, follows "the instrumental relativist orientation" where "right action consists of that which instrumentally satisfies one's own needs and occasionally the needs of others." The conventional level includes stages three and four. Stage three is "the impersonal concordance or 'good boy-nice girl' orientation" where "there is much conformity to stereotypical images of what is majority or 'natural' behavior." Stage four is conventional as well. It follows "the 'law and order' orientation" where "right behavior consists in doing one's duty, showing respect for authority, and maintaining the given social order for its own sake" (1979, pp. 77-81).

The "postconventional, autonomous, or principled level" includes stages five and six. Stage five exhibits "the social-contract legalistic orientation" where "right action tends to be defined in terms of general individual rights, and standards which have been critically examined and agreed upon by the whole society." Stage-six involves "the universal ethical principle orientation," where "right is defined by the decision of conscience in accord with self-chosen ethical principles appealing to logical comprehensiveness, universality, and consistency" (1979, pp.79-80; 1991, pp. 116-194).

Habermas argues that this developmental process can be characterized by a development of the formal characteristics of "(a) reflexivity, (b) abstraction and differentiation, and (c) generalization" (1979, p.87). He argues that this development is also integral to the development of communicative competence. Therefore, in general, "someone who possesses interactive competence at a particular state will develop a moral consciousness at the same stage" (1979, p. 91). This progressively realized communicative competence moves through Kohlberg's stage-six to a seventh stage that Habermas calls "a universal ethics of speech."

Kohlberg's stage-six exemplifies the Kantian ethics of the categorical imperative where "each individual is supposed to test monologically the generalizability of the norm in question." Kant had argued that our ethical reasoning power identifies a morally correct action by asking whether the proposed action could be made into a universal law, applicable to all. This is qualitatively different from a universal ethics of speech where norms are justified not monologically but through a "communally followed *procedure* of redeeming normative validity claims discursively" (1979, p. 90). For Habermas, ethical legitimacy is not determined subjectively (internally) by asking whether a proposed action can be universalized. Instead, reason enters into discussion with others seeking consensus about what we wish to recognize as universal ethical principles.

There is a second way in which the universal ethics of speech differs qualitatively from Kohlberg's stage-six understood as the Kantian ethics of the categorical imperative. For Kant, the command to follow the moral law identified through universalizing a proposed action was always sharply distinguished from a person's needs, wants, or desires ("inclinations"). A person had to do what is right "regardless" of his or her inclinations. And since Kant linked satisfaction of inclinations with happiness, moral action never pursued happiness, only moral "duty" (1964, pp. 64-69).

For Habermas, speech ethics do not automatically find the validity of actions in the internal legislation of universal laws based on practical reason in contradiction to the "inclinations" that are considered given and in some sense "natural." For Kant, because we must do what is right (as universalized through the categorical imperative) "regardless" of inclinations, morality never created happiness, but the "worthiness to be happy." The procedural denial of a person's needs and desires (inclinations) places a person in the stance that moral action can never be directed to that person's own happiness. For Kant, all actions directed toward personal happiness involve the non-moral satisfaction of inclinations (1964, pp. 83-84).

The universal ethics of speech, articulated by Habermas, supplies a higher stage of moral development that serves as a criterion and fulfillment of the developmental process. It provides the possibility, in contradistinction to Kant's monological view, of reconciling "worthiness with happiness" (1979, p. 94). For when ethics becomes discursive and all normative validity claims become subject to discussion and debate with a view to a possible communicatively arrived-at consensus, then even "need interpretations are no longer assumed as given, but are drawn into the discursive formation of the will." Morality is no longer "then split up into legitimate and illegitimate components, duties, and inclinations. Internal nature is rendered communicatively fluid and transparent to the extent that needs can...be kept articulable" (1979, p. 93).

Habermas' stage-seven goes beyond Kohlberg's stage-six in a third way. The process of growth through Kohlberg's stage-six involved a process of growth in autonomy, or "a field-*in*dependent style of perception and thought." Kant also emphasizes this autonomy as central to our ability for acting on practical reason and doing what is right regardless of our inclinations. A person can only act independently of inclinations this way, Kant says, if he or she is acting under a moral law he or she has autonomously legislated (1964, pp. 98-100).

For Habermas, the development of autonomy remains a necessary condition for the universal ethics of speech. However, Kant's field-independent style of cognition must now be ethically fulfilled in an autonomy that assumes a "field-dependent" style. Such a field-dependent style means the normative claims of others and my own internal needs are opened to a discourse allowing for the possibility of a communicatively realized consensus. "Naturally," he writes, "this flow of communication requires sensitivity, breaking down barriers, dependency – in short, a cognitive style marked as field-dependent" (1979, pp.93-94).

With the realization of a universal ethics of speech, "internal nature is thereby moved into a utopian perspective." Habermas suggests that through stage-seven forms of communication people open up the possibility of becoming transformed and of creating a transformed community. In such a community, so-called private needs and interests are reformulated through discourse toward a collective will in which moral existence is no longer separated from the satisfaction of fundamental human needs (1979, pp. 93-94). Planetary maturity is precisely this level of growth where we no longer encounter an inseparable barrier between my private needs and interests and the common good of humanity.

This process operates, for Habermas, on the social and historical level as well. We are born into a social context, and individual autonomy arises from the process of socialization and is not prior to our social interdependence (as philosophers of capitalism, such as Hobbes, Locke, or Mill, would have us assume). And this social matrix, informed by language, already contains what one scholar of Habermas' work calls "immanent normativity." In other words, language already places us within a moral framework that exerts a "normative pull" on our interactions with others (Vetlesen, 1997, pp. 9-10).

This immanent normativity at the heart of language provides the basic moral principles that can be derived from Habermas' discursive version of Kant's "formula of universalization": that "all affected can accept the consequences and the side effects its general observance can be anticipated to have for everyone's interests" (1990, p. 65). Habermas argues that this principle is derived from the presuppositions of all discourse implicit in the linguistically mediated lifeworld that informs human life. The possibility of communication, we have seen, presupposes relationships guided by the four fundamental validity claims inherent in the nature of meaning: intelligibility, truth, truthfulness, and normative rightness (1990, p. 58). Every speech act implicitly assumes all of these, and assumes the right of the hearer to challenge any of them, even when the emphasis of the speaker is on one or the other of these validity claims.

In the light of this, every strategic, manipulative, or dominating use of language appears parasitic on the universal presuppositions of communication at the heart of language. Communicative rationality is prior to the instrumental rationality that is institutionalized, for example, within the capitalist system. Technical language strategically oriented to the pursuit of profit for its own sake, or to the manipulation of others through advertising directed toward the pursuit of profit, must be challenged for its validity on the basis of truth, authenticity, or normative rightness.

Such language appears unredeemable on these grounds, and the institutions that promote it find their "legitimacy" called into question and come under pressure to evolve in the direction of ever more communicative rationality (Habermas, 1975; 1979, pp. 178-205). Institutions and societies follow an evolutionary model similar to that applicable to individuals. The presuppositions of communication operate regardless of whether communication is personal or institutionalized. Implicit in language are normative criteria essential to a critical theory of society in the neo-Marxist tradition, criteria that exert a "normative pull" toward ever greater freedom, equality, and communicative, normatively structured rationality. In other words, implicit in language (and therefore human reason) is a *telos* toward a free, democratic, socialist society. In this way, Habermas claims to empirically justify Marx's assumption that a socially rational society is not only possible but immanent within the *telos* of history (Pusey, 1993, ch. 2).

Habermas therefore develops a parallelism between the ontogenetic and phylogenetic spheres of human life. In the ontogenetic sphere, the moral development of the individual develops normatively into an ever greater linguistic competence and achieves an ever growing individual moral autonomy as well as social solidarity. A person moves toward a form of autonomy that finally becomes capable of a genuine field-dependence where sensitivity and openness to others can give rise to that new level of transformative communication. Habermas calls this "discursive will formation."

On the phylogenetic level, the evolution of human societies is guided by the same presuppositions of discourse at the heart of all possible communication (all natural languages). The "normative pull" of these presuppositions draws human societies toward forms of social organization ever more fully based on communicative rationality. Such societies ever more completely recognize the parasitic and secondary role of instrumental, strategic, or technological forms of rationality.

For this reason, Habermas' perspective is extremely important for a theory of social transformation. It shows rationally and morally assessable forms of social organization can exist. And it illuminates the criteria at the heart of language by which human beings can move toward the practical utopia of free democratic socialism. His work shows that such a practical utopia is not a fantasy of unbridled human imagination but, instead, an extrapolation from the empirically describable processes of human development toward full maturity. Such a practical utopia is also an extrapolation from the processes of historical development, delineated by critical theorists since the time of Marx, toward a rational, just, and free world society.

Yet, we will see, there exists more to the story of human cognitive, moral, and spiritual development than can be encompassed within the naturalist and empiricist assumptions made by Habermas. His strength is simultaneously his weakness in terms of providing a philosophy adequate to the human situation. His focus on rationality (in a non-metaphysical way) opens the development of rationality to empirical corroboration and provides a substantial contribution to our comprehension of the human situation and its possibilities for transformation.

Habermas' stage-seven of moral development describes an important mode of human spirituality. It suggests that social-political revolution cannot be extricated from moral-spiritual transformation. The institutions created within a society of planetary maturity will be ones that foster communicative rationality and the ethics of discourse. A mature society will promote equality, freedom, justice, and the dignity of all citizens of the planet, just as our present institutions tend to foster the opposite of these. His philosophy shows that capitalism cannot be the basis of any society that aspires to a genuinely moral foundation. Its patterns of economic domination, its cultivation of private greed and egoistic competition, and its institutionalized patterns of propaganda and conceptual manipulation (advertising and "public relations") inhibit and even destroy moral maturity and the possibility of moving toward rational, truly democratic social structures (1979, pp. 130-177).

Habermas' weakness lies in his not having described the limits of human language and the possible encounter with the deep unspeakable mysteries that encompass our lives at every turn. Any deeply transformed individual, like any deeply transformed society, participates in the cosmos in ways that transcend the level of communicative rationality, necessary as this is. They participate on the non-cognitive level where these deep, unspeakable mysteries stand revealed. Precisely here, as we have seen, Wittgenstein's understanding of language makes an essential contribution.

A fundamental part of our moral and spiritual immaturity, and our confusion, Wittgenstein emphasizes, is that we are "entangled all unknowing in the net of language" (1978, p. 462). This entanglement does not allow us to see the limits of language and encounter the unsayable "absolute experiences" that, in fundamental ways, make valuation as well as the human situation clear. The limits of language do not confront us primarily through the mystery of the origins of language, which Habermas attempts to comprehend through an intrinsic social responsiveness (appropriated from the social pragmatism of George Herbert Mead (1992, pp. 149-204)). They confront us in everyday experience insofar as we are awake to the overwhelming immediacy of things, prior to linguistic mediation, that cannot be gotten into language.

For Wittgenstein, the primary significance of the development of communicative competence (if this can be said to include a detached comprehension of the ways in which language itself works) is the transformative encounter with this immediacy. Here the possibilities for moral-spiritual maturity and social transformation acquire new and exciting practical- utopian possibilities. Yet as I have made clear in *From Nietzsche to Wittgenstein* (1989), Wittgenstein does not develop this side of his philosophy explicitly. He tenaciously follows his resolution from his early *Tractatus* period to say only what can be said and pass over the rest in silence (1974, pp. 71-74). (Nor, as we saw in Chapter Five, does spiritual awakening to the immediacy of unity-in-diversity, prior to language, require a Wittgensteinian philosophical framework. There are many routes to this awakening.)

More and more, Wittgenstein's later philosophy delineated the limits of language and left the possibility of awakening to the immediacy "beyond" these limits to the reader. To find an explication of this aspect of moral and spiritual development to which Wittgenstein and others are pointing, we must look beyond Habermas to such thinkers as Carter, Fowler, and Kohlberg himself. Kohlberg (1984) developed a more encompassing "stage-seven" to serve as a ground and justification for the first six stages. His stage-seven provides a larger axiological context from which to make sense of the development of justice reasoning as identified in the earlier stages. Let us examine these more explicit accounts of spiritual transformation as the highest stage of human maturity.

3. Kohlberg and Carter in Relation to Habermas

Kohlberg calls his stage-seven a "soft stage" because it includes the formation of a broad background in terms of which the mature adult continues to grow after the attainment of postconventional justice reasoning. He summarizes this stage in the following way:

> A Stage 7 response to ethical and religious problems is based on constructing a sense of identity or unity with being, with life, or with God.... To answer questions Why be moral? Why be just in a universe filled with injustice, suffering, and death? requires one to move beyond the domain of justice and derive replies from the meaning found in metaethical, metaphysical, and re-ligious epistemologies.... Unlike the analytic and dualistic development of justice reasoning (i.e., reasoning based on the differentiation of self and oth-er, subject and object), ethical and religious soft stage development culmi-nates in a synthetic, nondualistic sense of participation in, and identity with, a cosmic order. The self is understood as a component of this order, and its meaning is understood as being contingent upon participation in this order.
>
> From a cosmic perspective, such as the one just described, post con-ventional principles of justice and care are perceived within what might be broadly termed a natural law framework. From such a framework, moral principles are not seen as arbitrary human inventions; rather, they are seen as principles of justice that are in harmony with broader laws regulating the evolution of human nature and the cosmic order. (1984, pp. 249-250)

In *The Psychology of Moral Development: The Nature and Validity of Moral Stages* (1984, pp. 375-386), Kohlberg addresses what he calls Habermas' "seventh hard stage of moral reasoning" and contrasts this with his own "soft" stage-seven. It is "soft" because it includes a "non-dual sense of participation" in the cosmos and serves as an ultimate answer to the question "Why be moral?" However, my above exegesis of Habermas' stage-seven indicates that Habermas' work implies more than simply a seventh "hard" stage, but includes something of what Kolhberg means by his own "soft" stage-seven, since implicit in Habermas' account is an encompassing vision of a transformed individual or society that I characterized as "practical utopian." In spite of this, we will examine below in what ways Habermas' stage-seven involves a very limited account of fully mature morality.

The need for a stage-seven, as Kohlberg and Carter point out, revolves around the question "Why be moral?" Does the empirical description of the six stages of moral development provide us with what "is" as opposed to what ought to be? Kohlberg's calls his "soft" stage-seven an "ethics" as opposed to the "morality" of the "hard" earlier six stages. It includes elements of "faith," of "religion," and of "intuition" in the individual's attempt to grapple with the ultimate meaning of life and the cosmos (Carter, 1992, pp. 49-53). From the vantage point of this encompassing sense of life, we understand the stages of moral development as valuational instead of merely descriptive. As Carter puts the matter:

> How do you "establish" your norm, your "ought"? I think the answer is that you select, from the plethora of descriptions of which you are aware, those that you take to be "better," or "conducive of more positive value," or more "morally adequate," or that make most sense. You try to *support* your choices, as best you can, by telling the "whole story," or by providing an account of your *horizon of understanding* and not just a small part of that horizontal perspective. Whether you are a utilitarian or a formalist, a Christian or a Buddhist, you are only able to explain the decision you have taken when you describe to another the entire broad context that encompasses the collection of value-positions you hold. If pressed, you must present your outlook on the world as fully as you can, including a description of your *way of life* as a valuing, feeling, acting, and aspiring human being. And this is not merely to provide an intellectual account of your beliefs and your claims to knowledge. R.M. Hare's description of this procedure is worth attending to: "If pressed to justify a decision completely, we have to give a complete specification of the way of life of which it is a part...if the inquirer still goes on asking 'But why *should* I live like that?' then there is no further answer to give him, because we have already, *ex hypothesi*, said everything that could be included in a further answer." (1992, pp. 48-49)

Here we move beyond the narrow sense of "reasoning" that applies the first six stages of human moral development. We reach a point of human maturity inclusive of not only a broad sense of rationality but also affective, intuitional, and religious-responsive aspects of our being. These dimensions of a person integrate with reason in a new wholeness that includes justice and care, fairness and love, affirmation of unity and diversity. We cannot separate this personal integration from the process of becoming integrated with the cosmic wholeness of things. A mature person experiences an ever deepening sense of oneness "with the broader laws regulating the evolution of nature and the cosmic order."

On this level, separating the "is" from the "ought" is difficult. The lived meaningfulness of life provides the "ought." The feeling of each person needing to protect his or her "own" skin and promote his or her "own" interests gives way to the sense of harmony with others. At this point, the promotion of the legitimate interests of others becomes inseparable from the experience of self-fulfillment.

In the passage above, Kohlberg compares that sense of "ought" to "what might be broadly termed a natural law framework." We act from a solidarity with others and with all life because this solidarity is at once the way things are in our deepest understandings of the universe and the way they ought to be. We cannot find a set of reasons to justify this nexus of wisdom and compassion to a skeptic. Only moral-spiritual-religious growth, or an awakening, makes this solidarity clear. Moral argumentation will not suffice (including Habermas' communicative rationality), and plainly not any appeal to evidence or "the facts."

Habermas might reject this account of ethical-spiritual human maturity as irrelevant to questions of moral theory, since we have moved beyond the realm of what the social sciences generally consider to be rationally confirmable. In a statement about the serious limitations of philosophy and moral theory with respect to dealing with the agonizing and complex global problems of the later twentieth century, Habermas concludes with a quote from Max Horkheimer: "What is needed to get beyond the utopian character of Kant's idea of a perfect constitution of humankind, is a materialist theory of society" (1991, p. 211).

Here "utopian" appears as a synonym for an idealism that goes beyond what is empirically and scientifically practical. For Habermas, who has retained a "naturalism" or "materialism" that Wittgenstein would consider metaphysical in character, human beings do not have access to any depths beyond the naturalistic world articulated by the social and natural sciences. Reason clarifies the world through empirical study, on the one hand, and through "the transcendental mode of justification" on the other. The latter, which forms the rational basis for his theory of communicative action, involves "a type of argument that draws attention to the inescapability of the general presuppositions that *always already* underlie the communicative practice of everyday life" (1991, p. 130).

In the light of this, the above descriptions of a mature "sense of the cosmos" confuse, for Habermas, what can be rationally articulated (questions of justice) from the pretheoretical evaluative feelings that persons inherit from their social and cultural traditions. Such evaluative feelings provide them with commitments concerning the good life, the *summum bonum*, what is ultimately valuable, and so on. Habermas argues that intellectual maturity introduces a "hypothetical attitude" that distances persons from their conventional social world and its values.

This maturity initiates the process of rational justification that must leave the good life to varying cultural traditions or individual preferences. "Moral questions" must be distinguished from "evaluative questions" that "are accessible to rational discussion only *within* the horizon of a concrete historical form of life or an individual life style" (1991, pp. 164-65 and 178). The source of conceptions of the *summum bonum* appears to have been reduced to cultural traditions. Habermas repudiates the possibility of a non-cognitive opening to the cosmos through a spiritual maturity that intuits an ultimate meaning or truth about life.

His justification for the "ought" dimension of the stages of moral development appears, therefore, correspondingly truncated. The "normative pull" referred to above appears to exert itself through the fact that the presuppositions of the possibility of communication include truth, truthfulness, and normative rightness. For any time we enter into discussion, the fact of communication alone demands that I be willing to justify myself with respect to these criteria. To refuse to do so is to violate the presuppositions of my speech and therefore to be caught up in "a performative contradiction" (1991, pp. 129-130).

But the fact that I may daily involve myself in performative contradictions hardly appears a compelling answer to the question "Why should I be moral?" A person might well respond, "So what if I contradict myself? I wish to pursue my selfish interests at the expense of others nevertheless." Although the descriptions of stage-seven by Kohlberg and Carter do not provide arguments adequate to convince a skeptic concerning why a person should be moral, they do appeal to a fullness of experience and understanding available through growth that prove utterly compelling for those who encounter it. By contrast, there appears no way to conceive of the threat of a performative contradiction as compelling in this way.

Habermas' own stage-seven, we have seen, shows hints of a more encompassing vision of human life than his account of the limits of reason would appear to admit. He points to a simultaneous transformation of human "internal nature" and social institutions in the direction of a practical utopia. But Habermas' assumptions do not allow him to draw upon a moral, spiritual, and religious oneness with the cosmos (or with God) as a source of ultimate value or a source of compassionate energy directed toward transforming the world. He discusses ethical philosophies of "sympathy and compassion" in a way that appears to miss the cosmic sources of compassion that I am emphasizing in this book.

He associates philosophies of compassion (or "empathy" or

"solidarity") with "the well-being of associated members of a community who intersubjectively share the same lifeworld." He appears to view compassion narrowly as feelings of solidarity by which individuals wish to "protect the well-being of the community" to which they belong (1991, p. 200). He contrasts such philosophies with those of "justice" that refer to individual rights and "the subjective freedom of inalienable individuality." Both types of ethical philosophy, he argues, "have one and the same root: the specific vulnerability of the human species, which individuates itself through sociation" (1991, p. 200).

For Habermas, the respect for individuality required for justice moralities and the compassion and social solidarity required for common good moralities arise from the same process by which human autonomy grows out of social interdependence and requires social solidarity for its maintenance. Because of this, he asserts that his communicative ethics encompasses both kinds of traditional moral theory: "Every morality revolves around equality of respect, solidarity, and the common good. Fundamental ideas like these can be reduced to the relations of symmetry and reciprocity presupposed in communicative action" (1991, p. 201).

Two features in particular should be noted here. First, Habermas does not posit a situation of potential solidarity with all other human beings (or, needless to say, with all sentient beings), but instead sees solidarity as arising from social life in a community whose members "subjectively share the same lifeworld." Therefore, the human potential for compassionate solidarity appears excessively reduced in a way that denies the experience of many persons who claim awareness of a universal human solidarity. He denies the claims to universal human solidarity, discussed in Chapter Two above, made by Robert J. Lifton, Karl Marx, Errol E. Harris, Ruben Habito and others. He also apparently denies the solidarity implicit in the "cosmic consciousness" of Mahatma Gandhi, for example, or that of Albert Einstein or Albert Schweitzer.

Secondly, to suggest that Habermas' discourse ethics includes and assumes what has traditionally been meant by an ethics of solidarity and compassion is to reduce a mountain of compassion to a mole hill of the "sociality" of speech acts. If any philosophy relies on an abstract social-scientific rationality incapable of inspiring greater compassionate energy than awareness of dangers of falling into a logically trivial "performative contradiction," this one does (Hendley, 1996). Our conclusion can only be that Habermas' naturalistic metaphysical assumptions have not allowed him to experience sources of compassion beyond those implied in communicative action. He misunderstands the meaning and possibilities of compassionate solidarity and our human situation.

The vision expressed in this book, on the other hand, certainly does not affirm some equally groundless set of non-naturalistic metaphysical assumptions. Habermasian "naturalism" is not confirmed by the new scientific paradigm emerging from twentieth century science. In Chapter Two we examined the more holistic perspective that encompasses today's revolutionary science. In Chapter Five, we examined the powerful testimony for direct, non-cognitive awakening prior to knowledge and language. This chapter examines social scientific work on moral maturity in relation to Habermas' communicative rationality. Our human situation encompasses all of these dimensions, and a coherent philosophy of liberation must show their interdependency and integration.

In distinction to Habermas' naturalism, Carter's description of his (and Kolhberg's) stage-seven ethics emphasizes that it has gone beyond the rationalistic, justice orientation of stage-six (or Habermas' stage-seven discourse ethics): "It is clear that the post-stage-six stage or stages move us beyond reasoning to agapistic loving, to selfless empathy, and to acts of supererogation...or the doing of actions that are clearly beyond the call of duty, e.g., sacrificing yourself for the sake of others" (Carter, 1992, p.62). Stage-seven insight is realized through growth and awareness. A person understands that there exist aspects of awareness that go beyond reasoning and include "experiences which may be intrinsically valuable," some of which may be intuitive, non-verbal, or affective (1992, p.67). Since I have discussed the issues of "mysticism" and non-verbal experiences of "oneness" more fully in the previous chapter, for the present I wish to focus on this conception of moral maturity and its relation to a possible critical theory.

Carter argues that the first six stages in Kohlberg's model of development are self-sufficient but that stage-seven "serves as the ideal ground out of which justice reasoning arises." Justice reasoning is not lost but "transformed in the light of the cumulative experience of genuine caring and identification" (1992, p. 64). "Without something like a whole story, you are not as fully aware a human being as you might be, nor are you as fully ethical, as fully matured, and so on" (1992, p. 60). Ultimately, our sense of morality and the moral "ought" finds grounding in those "intrinsically valuable experiences" that provide life with meaning:

> One such source of the intrinsically valuable experience is morality. The moral life is rationally required, and conceivably grounded in our nature and in the nature of the cosmos. Yet there is far more to life, meaning, and value than morality. Meaning arises from loving interaction with others, with the world's animates and inanimates, and through identification of yourself with the entire cosmos, of which you now feel yourself to be an inextricable part. Meaning in life arises out of acts of self-realization, self-

expression, the appreciation of beauty, intellectual achievement, and even good food and a congenial environment. (1992, p. 67)

On this level, a person's individual life, and the individuality of all other creatures, appears inseparable from the whole. Each person or thing expresses the whole and we experience our identity with others to the point of being willing to sacrifice ourselves to relieve their suffering or heal their wounds. Mother Teresa in India, for example, is often used as an example of a person whose entire being was dedicated to others, without self regard. Stage-seven ethics, as elucidated by Carter and Kohlberg, gives us the possibility of a deep compassionate solidarity at the heart of ethics that Habermasian rationalism cannot maintain. This is a solidarity, we will see, essential to a full conception of ethical-spiritual maturity.

4. Critique of Carter's Situation Ethics

Carter describes praxis of a stage-seven ethics as a situation ethics. Unlike the requirements of a stage-six justice morality, a person at stage-seven does not treat everyone the same according to a requirement of universality. She or he responds concretely to each situation with perceptiveness and a caring not blind to individual differences. This unique responsiveness may even at times conflict with the abstract requirements of justice (although in the name of a higher good that encompasses justice) (1992, p. 64).

Similarly, moral education ought to aim for this goal, Carter says, developing the individual's "fundamental characteristics of human conscious activity – knowing, feeling, and willing...harmoniously integrated into a self that is morally responsive" (1992, p. 65). Yet if this morally responsive individual may at times act at variance with the requirements of justice, as Carter claims, then we must ask how the moral appropriateness of such a person's actions is to be assessed. The phrase "morally responsive" appears unclear within the context of this "situation ethics." Are there no universal standards at all here that might help us discern whether a course of action is truly morally responsive? Would the action of a stage-seven person be entirely unintelligible to a stage-six justice-oriented person? Is the right action within each unique situation intuited spontaneously?

In the light of these questions, perhaps we should characterize this situation ethics as involving an integrated morally responsive self that not only takes individual uniqueness into consideration but raises universalistic justice reasoning to a higher level in which the individual and the universal are more deeply understood in their relationships and interconnections. One of these interconnections between the individual and universal is often termed "the connection between the personal and the political." Here, we cannot disentangle the personal dimension from institutions and structures that give the personal situation universalistic implications. Do the situation ethics of a person in Carter's stage-seven take into account the connections between the personal (the ethical) and the political (the institutional or structural) aspects of a situation?

In considering stage-seven situation ethics as Carter describes it, we must consider the formal parameters of the situation to which such a person is "morally responsive." How are the concrete situations in which we find ourselves to be characterized? Are these situations always transparently self-evident? Do these situations ever bear on the institutions within which we participate? If I spontaneously help a homeless person, does my ethical responsibility extend to asking why the person is homeless, what institutions are responsible for the phenomena of homelessness, and whether I am a participant or beneficiary of these institutions?

If such institutions exist, then helping the homeless person may be morally tainted, for I am at the same time a participant in (and perhaps beneficiary of) the causes of their and others's homelessness. It would seem that I have not adequately taken account of, nor responded to, the concrete situation of helping the homeless person. Carter's account of stage-seven ethics provides few hints of any such ethical responsibility, nor do most of the sources he quotes. It appears on his account that a person even at the highest stage of moral-spiritual development would have no clue as to the institutional causes of the suffering with which she or he identifies. Or, if such a person did have a clue, she or he would apparently feel no obligation to transform these institutions.

There appears to be a deep unconscious assumption in the thought of Kohlberg and Carter that the personal and the political are two different dimensions of human life and that the latter does not bear substantially on our ethical-spiritual lives. Their description and examples of highest-stage persons span different historical eras, as perhaps they should, ranging from the Buddha, to Christ, to Marcus Aurelius, to Albert Schweitzer. It appears irrelevant whether the moral education described by Carter goes on in ancient slave society, the deeply oppressive regions within medieval feudal society, in the first or third-worlds under modern global capitalism, or in twentieth-century fascist societies.

The situation ethics faced in these societies apparently involves identification with victims and willingness to act on their behalf without consideration of the institutions that create these victims. Apparently, there would be no ethical obligation, depending on the situation, to act to make political or structural changes. Moral education for Carter appears to have few political implications, and he gives no hint in this account of stage-seven ethics that in some situations my highest obligation might be to take political action to transform institutions.

Each Chapter in Carter's well-written book is introduced with personal experiences or reflections apparently intended to illustrate the central theme of the chapter. The chapter on "Kohlberg's Stage-seven" that we have been discussing is introduced with a description of the sensitive and caring way he was treated in a visit to Japan by his host (a recently retired chief executive officer of a Japanese automobile manufacturing company) and his host's family. They had discussed at great length what would be the most special gift for him, and after putting him up in the family-owned apartment building in Tokyo until his guest apartment was ready and serving "a magnificently prepared and graciously served meal," they revealed what they had finally realized would be the best gift for him, to use their time and experience to help him shop for family and friends back home:

> The next morning the family car was waiting for me shortly after nine a.m. Both mother and daughter had decided to come, and as experienced shoppers they showed me a day that left me both exhausted and exhilarated. It included both whirlwind shopping and a leisurely and secluded lunch. They had been able to put themselves in my shoes, not only saving me time and frustration but turning the full day of shopping into one of intense pleasure and cultural exploration. Of the gifts they might have given, this was the least flashy and ostentatious but clearly among the most important and genuine of the many acts of hospitality I enjoyed while in Japan. It came from the heart, and was an everyday example of *kokoro*: acting from one's heart and mind out of concern for the other person, and with no thought of gain or personal reward. (1992, pp. 44-45)

Kokoro, for Carter, illustrates the spontaneity, selflessness, and situation ethics of stage-seven, and this example perhaps shows that substantial wealth is not an impediment to ethical maturity. Yet we cannot help wondering if these Japanese hosts who put themselves in Carter's shoes were also able to put themselves in the shoes of the workers who swept the floors and cleaned the bathrooms of their automobile manufacturing company.

We wonder if it matters in the ethical lives of this family that the automobile is an utterly unsustainable commodity that spews millions of tons of carbon dioxide into the Earth's atmosphere yearly, a major cause of global warming, and that the highways built for it are destroying ecosystems and slaughtering animals at devastating rate worldwide. We wonder whether a person gets to be the chief executive officer of an automobile manufacturing company through a life of ethical maturity and numerous acts of supererrogation. We wonder if the third-world people living in the abject poverty systematically exploited by Japanese companies (as by U.S. companies, including automobile manufacturers) have the opportunity to develop the kind of refinement and cultural graciousness described in this vignette. We wonder if this family ever reflects on the morality of substantial concentrations of private wealth in the face of the one and one half billion people worldwide who are living in what the U.N. calls "absolute poverty," who literally have nothing.

We wonder, finally, if this family has ever reflected on the possibility that their wealth involves them in massive structural or institutionalized violence, which might mean that, for all their moral sensitivity, they are participants in a global structural violence that is destroying millions of lives daily. In Carter's description of stage-seven, these questions would appear irrelevant. The ethical would appear to be a dimension entirely separated from political, institutional, and structural analysis. A situation ethics that addresses the institutionalized systems within which a person makes moral decisions does not seem to be part of the equation.

In terms of a stage-seven ethics applied to contemporary citizens in our world (persons who have apparently realized "solidarity" and oneness with all creatures in their ethical lives), what moral obligations do they (and we) have? What kind of ethical actions or principles would (and should) be manifested in their lives? In their situation ethics, do they find themselves in a structural situation in which they are part of a first-world exploiting class benefitting from the misery and despair of untold millions in the third-world?

Do they look at the labels on the clothes they wear, on the products that make their lives so comfortable, or at the places where their food is grown, and ever take the trouble to find out the disturbing truth about the conditions under which these products are produced? Does it occur to them that accidents of birth have placed them in a position to realize their potential as human beings in ways that are institutionally denied to the vast majority of human beings? Does institutional analysis and awareness enter into their situational analysis? Or does their cosmic consciousness with its "figure-ground" awareness at the ultimate (universal) level lack the sophistication to discern a lesser figure-ground situation in which the oppressed suffer because of background institutions from which first-world people benefit and in which each of us is deeply implicated?

Plainly, ethically mature persons would need to take these aspects of our "situation" into account, and evidently something quite important is missing in this regard from the Kohlberg-Carter account of ethical maturity. Perhaps the bourgeois nature of Carter's conception is pointedly suggested in the above quotation where we are told that part of the meaning of life can include experiences of "good food." This certainly may be true under some circumstances. But in a world where one and one half billion citizens live in an "absolute poverty" within which they have never experienced anything remotely implied by this reference to "good food," we wonder why ethical questions are not themselves raised by such a reference within this particular world situation at the cusp of the twenty-first century.

5. James Fowler and Stages of Faith

Fowler has done extensive empirical study on the "stages of faith" or religious development similar to the work of Kohlberg on the stages of moral development. His findings parallel Kohlberg's stages of moral development fairly closely and culminate in a stage-six that has many similarities with stage-seven ethical development as described by Kohlberg and Carter. Carter's account of stage-seven quotes from Fowler on several occasions. Yet Fowler's description of the highest stage of faith or religious development includes references to political implications of people having encountered the "depth of reality" that are lacking in the Kohlberg and Carter accounts.

At the highest stage, we have seen, the self-preservationist and self-centered apprehension of universal justice is overcome in a compassionate identification of the self with others. As the quotation from Berdyaev at the head of this chapter expresses this, the "creative personality" of a mature person develops moral autonomy and the ability to resist conformity with public opinion and social pressure precisely to the extent that he or she is in harmony with the "spiritual whole." And this connection with the whole makes the "ethics of creativeness" prophetic, future oriented, and deeply political in nature. A mature person's "social solidarity" is not conformist but fundamentally critical of the status quo and prophetically directed toward a transformed future.

In Fowler's stage five, we still encounter a conservative or status quo tendency transcended in those who become an "activist incarnation... of the imperatives of absolute love and justice of which stage-five has partial apprehensions." Therefore "universalizers are often experienced as subversive of the structures (including religious structures) by which we sustain our individual and corporate survival, security and significance" (1981, pp.199-201). On the other hand:

> Stage 5 remains paradoxical or divided...because the self is caught between these universalizing apprehensions and the need to preserve its own being and well-being. Or because it is deeply invested in maintaining the ambiguous order of a socioeconomic system, the alternatives to which seem more unjust or destructive than it is.... Stage 6...persons....have become incarnators and actualizers of the spirit of an inclusive and fulfilled human community. They are "contagious" in the sense that they create zones of liberation from the social, political, economic and ideological shackles we place and

endure on human futurity....[which include] the criteria of inclusiveness of community, of radical commitment to justice and love and of selfless passion for a transformed world, a world made over not in *their* images, but in accordance with an intentionality both divine and transcendent." (1981, pp. 200-201).

Stage-five persons have matured to the point where they are epistemically open to the "universalizing apprehensions" for which the mature human organism is suited and toward which it ontogenetically grows. They see that the partial identifications and loyalties of family, group, community, nation, race, sex, or class, and wealth (or to a God limited by any of these partialities) are merely functions of stages of growth that were epistemically flawed identifications if taken as ultimate. Since societies as they currently exist are institutionally structured to promote these immature loyalties (for example "patriotism" to the nation-state), as person's authentically mature, they will become more and more subversive.

A maturing person will become ever more critical of the status quo with its unjust, violent, and exploitative institutions and the moral and religious compromises people make to live within these institutions. Fowler refers to Martin Luther King, Jr.'s "Letter from a Birmingham Jail" as an example of the "subversive" quality of stage-six engagement. This letter is not directed to the racist oppressors but to those moderate, liberal religious leaders who compromised with an unjust status quo. Even though Fowler elucidates other meanings of this "subversive" quality of stage-six persons, one dimension of it identifies the ethical with the political and presupposes institutional or structural analysis as part of our "situation ethics":

> Here I refer to what has been called the "subversive" impact of their visions and leadership. Even as they oppose the more blatantly unjust or unredeemed structures of the social, political, or religious world, these figures call into question the compromise arrangements in our common life that have acquired the sanction of conventionalized understandings of justice.... In these persons of Universalizing faith these qualities of redemptive subversiveness and relevant irrelevance derive from visions they see and to which they have committed their total beings. These are not abstract visions, generated like utopias out of some capacity for transcendent imagination. Rather, they are visions born out of radical acts of identification with persons and circumstances where the futurity of being is being crushed, blocked, or exploited....
>
> In such situations of concrete oppression, difficulty or evil, persons see clearly the forces that destroy life as it should be. In the direct experience of the negation of one's personhood or in one's identification with the negations experienced by others, visions are born of what life is meant to be. In such circumstances the promise of fulfillment, which is the birthright of each mother's child and the hope of each human community, cries out in affront at the persons and conditions which negate it. The visions that form

and inform Universalizing faith arise out of and speak to situations such as these. (1981, pp.202-204)

Politics and ethics are perhaps separable only for stage five persons who are still clinging to the primacy of their self-interest in spite of their "universalizing apprehensions" that suggest the identity of the personal and the political. They may well be "deeply invested" (literally and figuratively) in a morally ambiguous "socioeconomic system," not only because the alternatives seem "more unjust or destructive than it is," but because their self-centered perspective makes them want to believe that no less just alternatives exist. They want to believe that they can live ethically justifiable lives while ignoring the political and institutional structures in which they are imbedded.

They have not apprehended fully the "practical utopia" of a fulfilled human community so perceptively described by Fowler in these passages, a vision not arising from the idle imagination but from the concrete moral-political world that we confront daily. If it is wrong for peoples's personhood to be crushed under foot, whether by military dictators, economic exploitation, racism, or poverty, then the vision of a global human community promoting respect for personhood and universal justice arises directly from this insight. Our present institutions, from corporate capitalism to the autonomous nation-state, promote all of these evils. Whether or not this community has ever existed historically is irrelevant. Fowler calls this the "futurity of being," the birthright of every human being is that "promise of fulfillment" today, as in the past, denied to the majority of the world's citizens.

As with Habermas, who asserts the inseparability of the ethical and the political, Fowler also understands their inseparability. In Carter's account, on the other hand, even though it quotes several times from Fowler's chapter on stage-six faith, the "subversive" quality of Fowler's religiously developed person is interpreted as subversive of the highest ideals of persons at lesser stages of development. The chapter is silent on the radical political implications of ethical-spiritual maturity.

Fowler's description does not emphasize a "situation ethics" focusing on the concrete uniqueness of the situation, sometimes at the expense of abstract justice, as Carter suggests. He emphasizes an "activist incarnation" of the identity of the universal and the particular. Fowler comprehends a living unity-in-diversity that sees through our "social, political, economic and ideological shackles" and explodes the pretense that we can quietly participate in unjust and dehumanizing institutions while claiming to be morally concerned individuals in our private lives.

6. The Inseparability of the Ethical and Political

The conception of ethical maturity we have extrapolated from the thought of Habermas, Kohlberg, Carter, and perhaps even Fowler, remains truncated. For their conception of moral development, even into a stage-seven spirituality informed by compassion, remains a partial, bourgeois conception of spiritual and ethical maturity. It lacks the truly transformative dimension, which is a necessary aspect of the fullness of moral development at least partially evinced, we will see below, in the thought of Marx.

Bourgeois spirituality is primarily inward and "private," the inner counterpart to the "private property" that dominates its external world. This morality claims to provide a meaning to life, a faith, a religious inner peace, and perhaps the ability to make a difference in personal, "private" moral relations with family and friends. In rare instances it may lead to a life of service to the poor or unfortunate. But beyond these possibilities it has little effect on the institutions and structures of the world, and allows the world go its own way "in peace." These inner "private" qualities are essential to bourgeois spirituality, since this spirituality must not disturb its own outer commitments to economic security, competitive advancement, success, and comfort in a world dominated by monetary and exchange values.

In other words, bourgeois notions of spiritual maturity are implicated in the process of veiling and justifying our moral complicity in the external system of exploitation and domination. These notions naively assume that maturity develops as a private affair of individuals. They assume that the social institutions encompassing our lives do not defeat real growth. They ignore the huge organizations devoted to private accumulation of wealth that generate a numbed and merciless attitude in the new generations that are acculturated into this system.

The notions of spiritual and ethical maturity become merely additional ideological tenets in the system of ideas serving to protect and perpetuate a way of life that is the antithesis of ethical maturity. For unless that spirituality itself is directed toward transformative change of this horrific system, it remains merely personalistic and bourgeois. In the face of these realities (which in one way or another have been the realities of nearly every society historically), speaking of a spiritual maturity that is not also a politically prophetic and transformative maturity has little meaning.

Those who are truly compassionate must have developed a critical, transformative consciousness characterized by insight into the systems and structures that violate, block, and deny the possibility of moral maturity for new generations and create immense suffering in the world. Human maturity involves wholeness, and development toward it cannot fully disentangle intellectual development from intuitive, affective, and communicative development. Spiritual maturity without transformative critical consciousness is a truncated and maimed maturity. Compassionate solidarity without critical insight into the structural and institutional causes of suffering is an impotent and limited solidarity, ideologically veiling its own immoral complicity in the systems largely responsible for that suffering.

Although the descriptions of ethical maturity given by Kohlberg, Carter, and Fowler are often insightful and important, they remain an inadequate account of ethical-spiritual maturity. Their thought remains mired in the bourgeois dogma separating private morality from supposedly "public" politics. Despite their claims that they have taken into account Carol Gilligan's criticisms of the gender bias inherent in Kohlberg's original study of the stages of moral development (Carter, 1992, pp. 46-47), they have not yet fully discovered the insight promoted by many feminist thinkers that "the personal is political."

This puts their account far behind the insights developed by critical theorists or philosophers of liberation worldwide who realize that ethical maturity is inseparable from a critical-transformative insight into worldwide structures of domination and dehumanization. Political transformation is inseparable from spiritual transformation, at least if a person is concerned with human beings as opposed to a persons's private, personal spirituality (the bourgeois "private property" version of human maturity). This was a fundamental axiom in the thought of Marx. In his study of *Marx's Concept of Man*, psychologist and philosopher Erich Fromm links Marx's thought with the Biblical prophets and with much of the spiritual philosophical thought of the Western tradition:

> This means that mans' spiritual aims are inseparably connected with the transformation of society; politics is basically not a realm that can be divorced from that of moral values and of man's self-realization.... No doubt the prophetic Messianic tradition influenced him indirectly through the thought of the enlightenment philosophers and especially through the thought stemming from Spinoza, Goethe, Hegel. What is common to prophetic, thirteenth-century Christian thought, eighteenth-century enlightenment, and nineteenth-century socialism, is the idea that State (society) and spiritual values cannot be divorced from each other; that politics and moral values are indivisible. (1992, pp. 65-66).

We also saw that Habermas, whose thought is evolutionary instead of transformative, has insight into the inseparability of morals from politics:

> There are indications that developed social systems already accept, or are on the point of accepting, certain international imperatives of life – namely, the elimination or war as a legitimate means of settling conflicts, and the removal of mass poverty and disparities in economic development. Even where these systems do not at present offer adequate motives for the solution of such global problems, one thing is nevertheless already clear: a solution of these problems is hardly possible without the application throughout life of those universalist norms which were hitherto required only in the private sphere. Someone still tied to the old categories might call this the 'moralization' of politics. But this kind of idea ought not to be dismissed – simply on those grounds – as naive enthusiasm. (in 1995, p. 5).

As German theologian Johann-Baptist Metz asks with reference to our contemporary world: *"Is not moral action becoming a factor in world politics?* To put it another way, are not economics and politics becoming part of morality in a new way?"* (1995, p. 24) I should add (with Fromm and Marx) that the integration of moral and political action may be experiencing a renewal, but such action is not new. Instead, it draws upon a philosophical and religious tradition that goes back to the Biblical prophets. Our reflections on planetary maturity show that critical consciousness (economics and politics) and compassionate solidarity (morality and spirituality) necessarily interpenetrate in any understanding of cognitive, ethical, and spiritual maturity.

7. Maturity and Transformative Praxis

Ethical-spiritual maturity involves a direct awareness of the holistic depths of existence to the point of experiencing a compassionate identification on a planetary scale of the suffering of others as our suffering. It simultaneously includes a critical awareness of the institutional and structural causes of most human suffering. The radically democratic implications of compassionate identification are conjoined with a critical awareness of the spiritual and social factors that produce human suffering.

Yet it is also important to keep reminding ourselves what we have seen from the work of Errol Harris and others about how much of the unity-in-diversity of our universe is knowable and describable. Twentieth-century science revealed the structure of the universe as an ascending series of parts inseparable from wholes evolving toward ever more complex forms of wholeness and integration. We grow significantly in the direction of compassion, solidarity, and critical consciousness through intellectual comprehension of the unity-in-diversity revealed by twentieth-century science. However, the kind of ethical and spiritual solidarity in which the suffering of others is literally my suffering requires a non-cognitive, direct appropriation of these insights. It requires a direct awakening beyond the private, bourgeois ego that objectifies and commodifies its surroundings.

A liberated awareness does not intuit an "is" to which an ought is added, nor an "ought" of some ideal kind. Yet awareness of the depths connected with our "ultimate environment" (Berdyaev's "spiritual whole") infuses life with a sense of ethical and spiritual demand. Demand for what? Just as Kant's categorical imperative is a purely formal principle, all versions of which express a general imperative such as "Always do what is right (morally and spiritually) regardless of your inclinations!" so the demand inherent in ethical-spiritual maturity cannot be reduced to a specification of exactly what the right is. We might express it as a "purely formal" demand to act in solidarity with others, with sentient beings, with planet Earth, and with the cosmos. The concrete actions required to fulfill this demand, however, vary from situation to situation.

In this respect Carter is correct that we are faced with a "situation ethics" in which what is right cannot be assessed independently of the concrete situation. The "ultimate environment" (which appears to make speech possible from an unsayable level, itself the origin of speech (Picard, 1952, pp. 24-30)) comes to us in awareness as an "ought" that cannot be identified with any particular "is" within the world as we encounter it. Nor can it be identified with the world as a whole as we conceptualize it factually or scientifically.

Ethical maturity combines the demand for action often associated with the Western ethical tradition with awareness of the unsayable "ultimate environment" associated with the Eastern tradition. Although Wittgenstein's thought lacked insight into the structural-critical aspect of ethical awareness, his "Lecture on Ethics" (which does exhibit an inclusive understanding of ethics as encompassing the dominant forms of awareness East and West) expresses the mystery of this imperative (Martin, 1997, pp. 79-92). For Wittgenstein, a deep wonder "*that* the world exists" and the experience of feeling "absolutely safe" intimate an ultimate environment in which we are faced with an unspecified "absolute" ethical demand encompassing our lives.

We face a concrete demand as a formal requirement that has no specific content, although in concrete situations it often becomes "evident" what fosters equality, freedom, dignity, or justice and what does not. This awareness is not a structural component of our human situation as some of these thinkers might suggest, nor is it (*qua* unsayable awareness) entirely identifiable with the presuppositions of language as Habermas urges (although language does have the presuppositions and the *telos* he attributes to it). Instead, we experience the absolutely unsayable imperative that informs the ultimate environment beyond language and thought. In traditional religious language, it has often been experienced as a "call," or a "demand," from God.

For Kant, the absolute imperative to act morally, regardless of our desire for happiness, inevitably leads our thought to God (England, 1968, pp. 169-184). He attempts to articulate the force of this imperative by distinguishing the "absolute" demand that we experience from those impulses, desires, hopes and fears that arise from either our natural biological lives, our private subjective lives, or the imperatives inculcated in us by society. He sums up all of these "contingent" factors as "inclinations." He recognizes inclinations as a main source of human action, but biological, subjective, and social sources of action leave us in a world prior to morality (1964, pp. 61-88).

In terms of the present chapter, inclinations may leave us in a bourgeois world of inner privacy, prior to the public and universal demand that human beings act morally, and that we grow to planetary maturity. But for Kant, practical reason provides an alternative to the biological, subjective, and social sources of action. This alternative is available to us in the simple "good will" to do what is right, regardless of our inclinations. With this good will, reason can discern the form of moral action (the categorical imperative) and act from the absolute commands of morality, not from inclinations.

On the other hand, we have seen Habermas make the excellent practical-utopian point that our inclinations (and "need interpretations") must be taken up into discourse with an eye to a possible "discursive will formation" that may transform our ethical lives. In the light of this, he repudiates Kant's distinction between duty and inclinations as representing an inner, "monological" version of the categorical imperative that needs to be publicly universalized in the form of a social discourse ethics directed toward reaching consensus. Instead of privately legislating the moral law for myself as an inwardly formed universal law, I should enter into a "communally followed *procedure* of redeeming normative validity claims discursively."

Habermas' point is well taken on one level, yet he appears to miss a central feature of Kant's distinction between duty and inclinations at another level. He misses Kant's awareness of the absolute force of the moral imperative. Kant attempts to clarify the apparently inexpressible, unconditional imperative normal human beings feel (that does not have its source in biology, subjectivity, or society) to act in terms of what is right. We saw that Habermas' explanation of moral life fails to account for this ethical demand. This demand exists in the background of all human awareness. We only need attend to it, and it becomes a real force in our lives.

This "inner voice" takes the form of an apparently contentless awareness and a demand that does not come to us from any identifiable source in the scientifically describable natural world. Nor does it derive from an intellectual understanding of the scientifically revealed principle of unity-in-diversity. This sense of a demand often gives us the feeling that we are not presently doing something we should be doing. We sense this not only in terms of our everyday ethical lives, but in terms of our entire way of life. It calls us in the direction of the fulfilled, transformed life and society that I have characterized as "practical utopia." We should be transforming our broken and fragmented world, not settling down to live peacefully within it.

In this respect, Habermas' purely formal ethics of justice needs filling-in with the content of a practical utopia informed by love and compassion and premised on the direct awareness of the simultaneity of unity and diversity. The ethically mature human being has moved beyond subjectivity and so-called objectivity to awareness of the non-dual, groundless-ground that includes our "ultimate environment." The "maturity fear" exhibited by positivism, scientism, and relativism, discussed in Chapter Four, attempts to distract people from this "voice," to divert attention to indulgence of my private bourgeois interests and inclinations. But the demand is there. It cannot be demonstrated empirically. It can only be experienced existentially through a process of growth toward planetary maturity.

Human spirituality (ethics, faith, "inwardness"), in some respects requires, paradoxically, the "swinging outward" of a human being (Gutkind, 1969). Our cognitive-structural development through the stages of intellectual, moral, and religious growth resembles developing a "receiver" that opens out into the ultimate environment, into the depths and heart of existence. Yet this analogy with a receiver is limited.

First, the reception requires an active openness on our part that exists at the heart of genuine attention. The "receiver" is not automatic, nor is it passive. Secondly, the structural integration and development necessary for this awareness does not serve to set *a priori* limits on experience in this respect. It does not result in a distinction between the knowable phenomenal world and an unknowable noumenal world for the reason that this awareness is not a form of knowledge, nor "experience" in the ordinary sense of the word.

A cognitive-spiritual development is necessary to make this possible, just as the proper construction of a radio-receiver is necessary to make reception possible. But here the analogy ends, for the *a priori* structure of the radio receiver not only makes possible but also conditions the content of the reception. A radio receiver cannot, for example, pick up visual images. However, in terms of ordinary language or ordinary knowledge, awareness of the "ultimate environment" does not have a cognitive content. Instead, an unsayable unity and solidarity accompanies our every experience of diversity and particularity.

As Wittgenstein might express this, we confront here the "inherited background" against which anything I might say has a meaning (1972, p. 15). The imperative to act in terms of what is "right" is a result of this "swinging outward." All adult humans possess this capability for swinging outward in the sense of a receptive openness to the depths of their situation, and nearly all do this to some extent, whether they are consciously aware of it or not. This responsiveness to the depths of our situation does not arise from biology, subjectivity, or society but takes the form of something "heard," a call or voice that does not specify a concrete content to the action demanded (Bugbee, 1961, pp. 76-77 and 158-159).

It is important to recognize here that the realization of spiritual maturity can take the form of a transforming "breakthrough" experience, especially when there has been sufficient preparatory growth in a person. Because of this, although adulthood is usually presupposed for the possible onset of "cosmic consciousness" (as Richard Bucke's study of "cosmic consciousness" attempts to show (1974, pp. 51-68)), an unusual event, or a sudden moment of attention may be necessary to activate the "receiver." But "breakthrough" is theoretically possible at any time from the late teen years on as an awakening to the depth dimensions of the cosmos, to the depths of what surrounds us (and is within us) at every moment of our lives. There exists an absolute ethical demand inherent in this awakening.

Such awakenings have a transforming effect and open up a way of living that cannot easily be forced into the kind of chronological mold suggested by Kohlberg, Carter, and Fowler. The closed, private, self-conscious ego is broken open in a "swinging outward" that the individual immediately recognizes as our natural and fulfilled mode of awareness. We no longer act from the isolated me over and against a threatening universe, but, instead, I (and all other individuals) live as a necessary, integral expression of the wonder, wholeness, and mystery of the cosmos.

The false ego of fear and anxiety finds its entire self-awareness and understanding transformed by "swinging outward," through opening up awareness to what was there all the time. The "inner voice" of conscience identified by Kant as coming from a source neither biological, nor subjective, nor social, becomes part of a holistic, living immediacy. This immediacy supersedes what is usually called the "ethical" to a sense of "cosmic consciousness" and the fullness of a transformed existence. This living immediacy includes the absolute ethical demand in compassion and solidarity. Each person or situation appears absolutely unique and valuable. For, in each, the sacred whole is expressed. Ethical and spiritual maturity directly intuits unity-in-diversity.

The contentless content of this awareness informs a human life ever more deeply the more a person attends to it. A society whose institutions do not make this possible or likely for the majority of the population is a failed society; it cannot be considered democratic, nor free, nor moral. Here the profoundly important issue of the separation of state and religion must be seen as a false polarization. The state must never support any particular form of religion nor any religious dogmas, nor the institutionalization of religious powers, but a free and democratic state must provide the conditions necessary for ethical and spiritual maturity in its population.

Such a practical utopia (a world society of ethically-spiritually mature persons) forms not only the general *telos* of history (which complements, but goes beyond, the Habermasian *telos* of a communicatively discursive society). It also arises from the transformative ("eschatological") demand inherent in realized human awareness. Reflection on our present societies in the industrialized first-world helps make clear the content of this transformative demand. Structurally and procedurally, any decent society must make such spirituality possible for every normal citizen. Whatever institutions block such possibilities are subject to transformative critique and action. We will examine this "eschatological" demand more fully in Chapter Ten.

As we have seen, a mature practical utopianism must be able to show in general terms why present institutions actively militate against the utopian condition understood as normative for mature persons. It must be able to expose the hidden meaning of present institutions, veiled and legitimated by the ideology spewed forth by government, business, military, and mass media. This propaganda legitimates exploitation of those who have little or nothing by those who possess massive concentrations of wealth as well as the imperial domination of powerful nations (the first-world) over weaker nations (the rest of the world).

The descriptions given by Kohlberg, Carter, and Fowler, in this respect, mislead and make inappropriate characterizations of the higher stages of human maturity. A person may see, in Fowler's language, "the absoluteness of the particular" and understand the universality inherent in the particular symbols and events that the great religions have appropriated as revelatory of the unconditioned (God, Being, or Emptiness). But such a person remains a naive and immature utopian insofar has he or she cannot give a concrete account of the systematic blockage of this understanding in the masses of people through the operation of specific institutions.

These thinkers express some insight into the oppressive and

inadequate role of present institutions. However, in contemporary terms, they remain to some extent victims of the anti-communist propaganda of their societies that is directed precisely at preventing the population from seriously examining alternatives to the system of private greed and immaturity. Their writings, while potentially liberating, ultimately lose their liberating promise and become unwitting apologists for the status quo. Fowler, for example, follows H. Richard Niebuhr by speaking of our spiritual situation as one in which "the reality of God – transcendent and ever exceeding our grasp – exerts transforming and redeeming tension on the structures of our common life and faith." (204)

The ultimate environment (call it God, Being, or Emptiness) puts a genuine "tension" on the institutions that make up our common life. That tension, in part, involves the *nisus* within us for maturity, which places the spiritual search of human beings in direct conflict with the immature and limiting institutions of the society. We encounter a tension between the "call" of the ultimate environment and the institutions of our society precisely because those institutions do not cultivate or enhance human growth toward awareness of the ultimate. But to say this, as Fowler does, is to say quite little. A rich tradition of critical analysis of our capitalist and imperialist social institutions is available to anyone willing to make the effort to understand why these institutions block human growth and spirituality. Fowler, Kolhberg, and Carter do not draw significantly on this tradition.

For example, Carter urges us to be concerned for the environment, for he sees the relation between the harmony with which the spiritually realized person is integrated with the ultimate environment and the insight of ecology that all things are interdependent and interrelated (1992, pp. 162-163). Yet his call for concern for the environment totally fails in the face of the massive institutions of exploitative capitalism that are destroying the ability of the Earth to sustain life. His call, in the name of a high degree of human spiritual maturity, misleads those who crave spiritual maturity into thinking that their only option is the hopeless stance of being concerned about the environment without a penetrating critical analysis into why capitalism in most of its forms is incompatible with a sustainable environment.

To be concerned about the environment without enough maturity to see that production for exploitation, domination, and private profit spells suicide for the planetary environment is to be part of the problem instead of the solution. For this stance perpetuates the illusion that the environment can be preserved under a global capitalist system, which is quite naive if not willfully destructive and immature. Even active environmentalists like Thomas Berry (1990) or Anne Rowthorn (1989), who call for a spiritual reconnection with the Earth and the deep spirituality of human life, fail to offer a truly critical-structural analysis of the incompatibility of capitalism with a sustainable environment.

Similarly to refer to the political values of democracy, equality, freedom, and justice as elements of the present system that need to be enhanced and preserved is disingenuous in the light of the rich heritage of thought from the critical tradition demonstrating in what ways the ideology of democracy (and the maintenance of "formal" instead of "substantive" democracy) veils and legitimates a system of massive domination of the poor by the rich within the wealthy countries and worldwide.

The values of democracy, equality, freedom, and justice are necessary for any institutions that would promote human maturity, but not in the sham form that currently serves as a justification for the utterly undemocratic status quo. Evolutionary development of these elements within the present system is close to impossible, for they are incompatible with the structural features and fundamental assumptions of the system itself. Political liberalism is naive and dangerous. Substantial transformation of the system is the only viable option. Only some form of mature socialism on a planetary scale will foster genuine democracy, equality, freedom, and justice.

The implications of the higher stages of spiritual maturity are not "liberal" but "radical." "Radical" means to go to the heart, the "root" (*radix*) of something. Authentic human life and our relation with the ultimate environment are utterly incompatible with present society and its dominant institutions. And if we grow mature enough to contrast the fullness of life with the present system that denies and blocks the fullness of life, then we must work to transform that system.

If this maturity eventuates in a conception of practical utopia, then it must present an analysis that shows in what ways the present system blocks and destroys the fullness of life as well as life itself. We think of the countless victims of this system in Afghanistan, Argentina, Brazil, Cambodia, Chile, Columbia, East Timor, El Salvador, Guatemala, Haiti, India, Indonesia, Iraq, Laos, Nicaragua, Palestine, Peru, Vietnam, and elsewhere. The list ultimately includes most of the world, including the exploited classes within the imperial powers (Blum, 2000).

Some of our best thinkers and representatives of an adequately developed human maturity, such as Helen Caldicott, Noam Chomsky, Ramsey Clark, Richard DeMartino, David Edwards, Eric Fromm, David Korton, Herbert Marcuse, Robert Muller, E.F. Schumacher, Vandana Siva, Cornel West, or Howard Zinn, have attempted to do just this. Their analysis often shows the incompatibility of capitalism and its institutions with enhancement of spiritual maturity and the fullness of life. Their critique includes suggestions for concrete sensible alternatives to the present system. Their critique, therefore, fosters radical, not reformist, action. They make clear that the problem with the present system is its fundamental premises. The system cannot be reformed without changing these premises themselves.

Transformative praxis does not mean violence. Praxis means action devoted to creating a world system based on human well-being as its first principle. It understands that "well being" begins with creating a social-economic structure that supplies every human being with the basic necessities of life and progresses from there to providing every human being with the opportunity to grow intellectually, emotionally, ethically, and spiritually. I will make specific economic recommendations for such a transformed world in Chapter Eleven.

The *telos* inherent in the stages of human ethical-spiritual development mirrors the dialectical *telos* inherent in human historical development. Both are practical utopian. Our potential as persons, like our historical potential as human beings, portends genuine fulfillment. And transformative praxis flows from a human maturity that understands that social-economic critical theory and spiritual compassion are equally necessary for human liberation.

Karl Marx and Gautama Buddha together symbolize true human maturity. Neither is sufficient alone. The creation of the practical utopia of global, democratic, socialist world government in the twenty-first century is neither an idle dream, nor an empty ideal. We confront the next major step in the development of human maturity. We discover this as the most practical and realistic of alternatives. Either we overcome our maturity fear, and take the steps that lead to real growth, or we will perish from the Earth.

PART THREE

Economic and Social Liberation

Chapter Seven

An Ethical and Spiritual Foundation for Socialist Theory:
Marx, Habermas, Kant, Levinas, and Krishnamurti

"Philosophy means the love of truth, not love of words, not love of ideas, not love of speculations, but the love of truth. And that means you have to find out for yourself where reality is and that reality cannot become truth. You cannot go through reality to come to truth. You must understand the limitations of reality, which is the whole process of thought.

Jiddu Krishnamurti

This problem of man takes precedence over that of society or of culture, and here man is to be considered, not in his inner spiritual life, not as an abstract spiritual being, but as an integral being, as a being social and cosmic, ... Only a form of Socialism, which unites personality and the communal principle, can satisfy Christianity.... But the true and final renaissance will probably begin in the world only after the elementary, everyday problems of human existence are solved for all peoples and nations, after bitter human need and the economic slavery of man have been finally conquered. Only then may we expect a new and more powerful revelation of the Holy Spirit in the world.

Nicolas Berdyaev

In examining the highest stages of moral and spiritual growth according to several contemporary psychologists and philosophers, we found the ethical dimension of human life also expresses the principle of unity-in-diversity as a foundational aspect of human maturity. Ethical maturity dovetails with the spiritual maturity of integrative mysticism in this respect. Throughout earlier chapters, I have identified "democratic socialism" institutionalized within a planetary political system as the social, political, and economic system corresponding to a natural growth of human beings from planetary adolescence to planetary maturity. If we are to survive much longer on this planet, we must grow up ethically and spiritually as well as socially and economically.

Today the dominant ideology in the United States and its imperial allies still maintains that only capitalism allows people the freedom to realize their moral potential and that socialism in the Marxist tradition can only give us a "godless communism" that is utterly amoral or a "scientific socialism" that engineers people as if they were mere things. As might be expected, this is nearly the exact opposite of the truth and the deeper aspect of this matter. Contemporary scholarship with respect to religion and mysticism has revealed our wonderful human potential for spiritual transformation. And contemporary scholarship with respect to the stages of human growth has revealed planetary maturity as the natural goal of the growth process.

In a similar way, contemporary scholarship in the Marxist tradition of critical theory has revealed a depth and moral sensitivity to Karl Marx's work and subsequent neo-Marxist socialist theory ignored by the anti-communist ideology of the mass media. The foundation for democratic socialism is a vibrant ethical and spiritual maturity within society made impossible by capitalism and the nation-state system. In Chapters Eight and Nine, I will investigate the history and "maturing" of Critical Social Theory at some length in conjunction with a systematic critique of capitalism. Democratic socialism, we will see, represents the principle of unity-in-diversity as this applies to social and economic life.

1. Defining Socialism

There is a moral-spiritual foundation for socialism already implicit in the works of Marx that can be articulated more fully using the works of Jügen Habermas, Immanuel Kant, Emmanuel Levinas, and Jiddu Krishnamurti. We saw that democratic socialism means a society where economic, social, and political institutions are premised on the inherent value and dignity of each person as well as on a sustainable harmony with the other creatures and delicately balanced ecosystems of our planetary home. This means that all economic, political, or social institutions that exploit, dehumanize, or dominate human beings have been abolished from the Earth. Such a system is a function of planetary maturity.

Democratic socialism is not definable in terms of any one, particular system. In his book *A Future for Socialism* (1994), John Roemer describes seven different versions of market socialism alone. In a broad sense, it is true that the means of production, transportation, and communication can no longer be in the hands of huge private monopolies, planning in secret (outside of democratic control and accountability) not for the common good but for further accumulation of private wealth. For this reason, Bernard Crick in *Socialism* (1987) says that socialism includes "both an empirical theory and a moral doctrine" (p. 79). The moral doctrine requires authentic democracy in human society and emphasizes "the mutual dependence of the values 'liberty, equality, and fraternity'." The empirical theory shows that these values are realized through cooperation and economic conditions leading to substantial economic equality. It shows how "the relationship to the ownership and control of the means of production" is the key to defeating or promoting these values (p. 79).

A similar principle holds for Michael Luntley, in his book *The Meaning of Socialism*:

> Socialism is not a moral theory which offers a particular version of the good life, instead it is a theory about how the good life is possible. It is, in short, a theory about the conditions necessary for creating a society in which our lives are shaped by moral values – we defer to the authority of the good – rather than a society in which our moral traditions have been erased by forces inimical to the moral life. And part of this theory about the conditions necessary for the good life provides the leading critical aspect of socialism. That part is the claim that it is capitalism which has been largely responsible for the destructions of the conditions necessary for the good life. (1990, p. 15)

Distinctive values about the good life arise, we saw in Chapter Six, with growth in human maturity. These distinctive values revolve around the principle of unity-in-diversity. In human social life, this means, as Crick asserts, "liberty, equality, and fraternity." Liberty maximizes freedom for all persons, something only possible if there is roughly equal wealth. Similarly, equality cannot mean merely formal political equality leaving untouched vast differences in power and life- potential due to economic inequality. Finally, fraternity (human brotherhood and sisterhood) means cooperation, mutual understanding, peace within and between communities, and compassion for others.

It is crucial to realize that socialism is not an attempt to impose upon people a particular conception of the good life. Socialism most fundamentally provides a *framework* that makes it possible for people to realize their conceptions of the good life. Naturally, mature people will reject some ideas (for example, war to achieve political ends, exploitation of others, male domination of women, and so on) as unworthy of a good life. But mature people also affirm liberty. Liberty means the right to live life as one sees fit as long as this does not interfere with the liberty of others to pursue the good life as they envision it. Any form of class society organizes society for the benefit of the few and makes impossible pursuit of the good life for most of the exploited.

Luntley's definition of socialism conforms to these ideas. Normal, mature human beings value democracy. They value liberty, equality, and community. Human beings have accumulated five centuries of empirical evidence that these ethical principles are destroyed by capitalism. Alternatively, such values are enhanced whenever people work cooperatively together to promote "liberty and justice for all." If planetary society moved in the direction of authentic democracy, Luntley argues, the good life would emerge of its own accord. It would not be imposed by government. The role of government is to make possible the pursuit of the good life for everyone. This means genuine democracy and a significant degree of social-economic equality, precisely what most contemporary governments do not provide.

This principle is also affirmed by John Dewey, who argues that the realization of democracy in human life is identical with the progressive realization of socialism. Before democracy is a political or economic system, however, Dewey argues that it is a moral ideal. "Democracy," he writes, "is a social, that is to say ethical conception, and upon its ethical significance is based its significance as governmental. Democracy is a form of government only because it is a form of moral and spiritual association" (1993, p. 59). As Jerome Nathanson put it, for Dewey, democracy is neither a political, social, nor economic concern, but instead "a moral ideal, a statement of the relations that *should* prevail among human beings. It is the hypothesis, if not the belief, that if man creates the proper institutions, then his better possibilities will actualize themselves" (1951, p. 83).

The social values of liberty, equality, and community, Dewey maintained, are all inhibited or destroyed by capitalism in which industrial organization, the production of economic necessities for human life, and the lion's share of the wealth produced through this system, are all controlled by what he termed a "plutocracy," a small group of individuals who possess massive concentrations of private wealth (1993, pp. 148-149). "Industrial organization must be made a *social* function," he says. In other words, just as democratic political life involves people working together to maximize the possibility of everyone actualizing their potential for the fullness of life, so economic organization of society must do the same. Hence, to bring the "democratic community" forward toward completion, we need a "socialized economy" in which economic life is brought under social control (1993, pp. 148-152).

For Dewey, the ideal of democracy, implicit in human intelligence and experience, is a planetary ideal. Human experience involves us in a perpetual growth toward planetary maturity. Democracy is "equivalent to the breaking down of the barriers of class, race, and national territory which kept men from perceiving the full import of their activity" (1993, pp. 110-111). It involves seeing "the secondary and provisional character of national sovereignty" and emphasizing the superior value of the democratic ideal in which "the fuller, freer, and more fruitful association and intercourse of all human beings with one another must be instilled as a working disposition of mind" (1993, p. 120).

There can be no authentic democracy as long as the world is divided into fragments: nation-states, economic classes, racial or ethnic divisions, or male domination of women. For all these thinkers, the good life of freedom, equality, and community among human beings cannot be realized without democratic socialism. A variety of specific political and economic arrangements may promote this maturity and are, therefore, of secondary concern. The criterion of democratic socialism states that specific arrangements must be premised on the unique value of each human being and the need to maximize his or her life potential as a human being within a context of liberty, equality, and community.

For this to happen, human beings as planetary citizens must democratically and cooperatively plan their political and economic arrangements with these goals in mind. Democratic socialism emerges as the simple and logical consequence of mature human values. Yet in a fragmented global society that is founded on the very opposite of these values (division, exploitation, and domination), they become truly revolutionary. For Mortimer J. Adler, mature human thought requires democratic world government and socialism, for the values of liberty, equality, and community are necessarily universal. In *Haves Without Have Nots. Essays for the 21ˢᵗ Century on Democracy and Socialism,* he stresses the revolutionary character of planetary maturity:

> "All" – when what is meant is *all without exception* – is the most radical and, perhaps, also the most revolutionary term in the lexicon of political thought. It may have been used in the past, but it was never seriously meant to include every individual member of the human race, not just the members of one's own class, or even one's fellow countrymen, but every human being everywhere on Earth. That we are now for the first time in history beginning to mean all without exception when we say "all" is another indication of the newness of the emerging ideal of the best society, the institutions of which will benefit all men everywhere, by providing them with the conditions they need to lead good human lives. (1991, p. 90).

2. The Dignity of Persons in Marx

Many scholarly commentators on Marx today are addressing the issue of morality in relation to his thought. For while Marx never developed an explicit ethical theory, his writings from early to late are well known for their apparently implicit sense of human dignity and corresponding moral outrage at what he calls the "exploitation," "theft," or "alienation" wrought by capitalism. For example, José Miranda writes that "according to Marx...the motives for making the revolution are perceived by the moral conscience of human beings" (p. 17). Similarly, Robert C. Tucker writes, "for him the ethical starting point was the dignity of the individual.... Respect for their dignity as persons was the proper basis of morality" (1970, p. 38). These remarks coming from such scholars can be startling in the light of Marx's many attacks on "bourgeois morality" as an ideological veil arising from the productive relationships dominant in capitalist society.

Commentators struggled to come to terms with the implicit moral views of Marx with respect to how these might bear on the development of a socialist and/or communist ethical theory. George G. Brenkert, for example, argues that Marx's perspective encompasses ordinary morality from a larger perspective, and his attack on ordinary ethics and morality must be understood in the light of his attempt to integrate science and daily life (1983, pp. 55-81). Similarly, R.G. Peffer builds his book *Marxism, Morality, and Social Justice* around several basic theses, first, that Marx's concepts of "alienation" and "exploitation" can be analyzed in terms of more basic moral principles such as the values of freedom, community, and self-realization. Second, Marx assumes a principle of equality or egalitarian distribution of goods, including the good of freedom. Finally, Peffer writes, "if these values and principles can be analyzed in terms of some even more fundamental notion, it is...that of human dignity and the good of self-respect – notions with a distinctly "deontological" [Kantian] ring" (1990, pp. 35-36).

I will attempt to use the thought of Habermas, Kant, and Levinas to articulate these ethical views, especially the fourth and perhaps most fundamental of Peffer's theses: Marx's (and our) intuitive sense of human dignity and its implications for a viable socialist ethical theory. In doing so, I will argue that there are strengths and weaknesses in these thinkers that require our drawing on insights from each of them, as well as from Marx, in our account of a socialist ethical theory. I will also develop the relationship between spiritual awakening and socialism using the thought of Krishnamurti as a touchstone. Ultimately, I hope to make clear why socialism is the "political-economic form of love."

Marx expressed his vision of a fulfilled ethical and social relationship among human beings in his *Comments on James Mill's 'Elemens D'Economie Politique'*. Even though the language here is that of the early Marx (1843-44), the ethical assumptions behind the language remained with him throughout his career.

> We are to such an extent estranged from man's essential nature that the direct language of this essential nature seems to us a violation of human dignity, whereas the estranged language of material values seems to be the well-justified assertion of human dignity that is self-confident and conscious of itself....Let us suppose we had carried out production as human beings.

Each of us would have...*affirmed* himself and the other person. I would have been for you the mediator between you and the species, and therefore would become recognized and felt by you yourself as a completion of your own essential nature and as a necessary part of yourself, and consequently would know myself to be confirmed both in your thought and your love.... In the individual expression of my life I would have directly created your expression of your life, and therefore in my individual activity I would have directly confirmed and realized my true nature, my human nature, my communal nature. (in Hewitt, 1995, p. 52)

Marx here does not deny human dignity but asserts that capitalism's linking of material values (such as production for private profit) with human dignity is a sign of estrangement from our true dignity. The dignity and fulfillment he describes arise from a mutual affirmation of self and other within a rational social matrix that allows human dignity to become manifest and human fulfillment to occur. And this recognition of human dignity within a rational social order is so profound, according to Marx, that it can be described as a relationship of "love." This moral and spiritual aspect of Marx's thought serves as an inspiration for many thinkers in the Marxist tradition to continue to elaborate the true ethical foundations of democratic socialism.

Marx's projection of specific economic arrangements through which human beings might realize universal dignity and freedom for all are of secondary importance. The specific projections in his writings are sketchy and speculative. Marx may have thought in terms of exclusive state ownership of the means of production, transportation, and communication and, from his vantage point in history, this perhaps made perfect sense. But all this is secondary to the need for human beings to realize social, political, and economic arrangements premised on human dignity, instead of private appropriation of socially produced wealth. The consequence of a truly human order predicated on liberty, equality, and community for all would be "love."

3. Habermas and Socialism

Habermas is among the thinkers who argue that the ethical dimension of human existence necessitates a rational, democratic socialist society as the only truly moral form of social organization for human beings. We encountered his thought in Chapter Six within the context of stages of human growth toward planetary maturity. Here I will review the basic ideas of his work as a possible foundation for an ethically-based socialist theory. I will then examine ways the thought of German thinker Kant, French philosopher Levinas, and Indian spiritual thinker Krishnamurti can more fully articulate the foundations of socialist theory. In this process we are elucidating in ever more depth the claim I have made throughout this book that democratic socialism is the political-economic form of planetary maturity.

Habermas agrees with Marx concerning the social nature of the self. We are born into a social context, and individual autonomy arises from the process of socialization and is not prior to our social interdependence (as philosophers of capitalism, such as Thomas Hobbes, John Locke, or John Stuart Mill, would have us assume). Yet, for Habermas, the social matrix, informed by language, already contains what we identified in Chapter Six as "immanent normativity"; language already places us within a moral framework that exerts a "normative pull" on our interactions with others.

This immanent normativity at the heart of language gives us the basic moral principles that can be derived from Habermas' discursive version of Kant's "formula of universalization": that "all affected can accept the consequences and the side effects its general observance can be anticipated to have for everyone's interests." Habermas argues that this principle is derived from the presuppositions of all discourse implicit in the linguistically-mediated lifeworld that informs human life.

As we have seen, for Habermas, the possibility of communication presupposes relationships guided by the four fundamental validity-claims inherent in the nature of meaning: intelligibility, truth, truthfulness, and normative rightness. Every speech act implicitly assumes all of these, and assumes the right of the hearer to challenge any of them, even when the emphasis is on one or the other of these validity-claims. In the light of this, every strategic, manipulative, or dominating use of language can be seen as parasitic on the universal ethics of communication at the heart of language.

Communicative rationality is prior to the instrumental rationality that is embodied in the capitalist system. Implicit in language are normative criteria essential to a critical theory of society in the neo-Marxist tradition, criteria that exert a "normative pull" toward ever greater freedom, equality, and communicative, normatively-structured rationality, in other words, toward democratic socialist society. In this way, Habermas claims to empirically justify Marx's assumption that a socially rational and truly free society is not only possible but immanent within the *telos* of history.

Yet as we also saw in Chapter Six, some Habermas scholars have indicated that Habermas' discourse ethics has difficulty with the question that so concerned Kant: "why should I be moral?" (Hendley, 1996, pp. 515-516). Habermas' central idea may be expressed in terms of an immanent normativity inherent in the lifeworld that exerts a "pull" on me to live ethically. Alternatively, this is expressed as the idea that I am faced with a "performative contradiction" if I use language strategically and manipulatively. In either case, Habermas does not appear to have an adequate answer to those who question why a person should be concerned with realizing the ideal speech situation of a truly discursive ethics in one's relations with others. Neither a "normative pull" nor the threat of a "performative contradiction" gives me an unconditional obligation to be moral.

Habermas claims that immoral behavior such as deceiving or manipulating people for my own interests violates the foundations or presuppositions of communication that always implicitly assert truth, truthfulness, and normative rightness. Since this is the case, to use language strategically in the service of my own interests by manipulating or deceiving people is to commit a performative contradiction. By acting deceptively, I am contradicting the basis on which my speech acts are possible. But critics point out that recognition of this does not give me an "absolute obligation" to be moral (to do what is right regardless of my inclinations) that Kant insisted was the foundation of all genuine morality.

Habermas does not identify any unconditional imperative that provides, as Kant would express it, an absolute duty to be moral regardless of my inclinations or how I happen to feel. In Chapter Six, I attempted to explicate Kant's sense of an "absolute obligation" to do what is right, regardless of inclination. I also attempted to show a related sense of "absolute obligation" informing the life of a person of planetary maturity. In Habermas' thought, this transformative and revolutionary obligation is missing. We apparently must wait patiently for our personal moral evolution and for the moral evolution of humanity before attaining true moral maturity and eventual democratic socialism.

Here the thought of Kant remains primary as addressing our sense of absolute moral obligation. Similarly, the thought of Levinas (like the liberation philosophy of Enrique Dussel, whom Levinas influenced) addresses an aspect that is missing in Habermas. Levinas' presentation does not use the social-scientific discourse of Habermas, but the language of phenomenology, for phenomenology through its method of *epoché* would seem able to indicate primordial relationships not open to theoretical discourse (1985, pp. 31-33; see 1969, pp. 175-183). In the thought of Kant and Levinas, we again encounter the sense of absolute obligation that also informs the writings of Marx.

4. Kant: the Absolute Obligation for a Transformed Society

Habermas believes he has freed himself from metaphysics when in fact he has only adopted naturalistic metaphysical assumptions that apparently limit his openness to the depths of existence. To drop naturalistic metaphysical assumptions does not mean to adopt non-naturalistic assumptions. It can mean opening to the unspeakable depths of existence in an ecstatic awareness that does not need to ontologize them in the form of linguistic dogmas. Both Kant and Levinas are open the depths of existence in different ways. Kant is open to the absolute obligation that flows into our lives from the foundations of the universe. Levinas is open to the dimension of infinity that breaks into our awareness in moments of recognition of the other as Other. These two forms of openness are closely related.

In a famous passage of the *Critique of Practical Reason*, Kant writes:

> Two things fill the mind with ever new and increasing admiration and awe, the oftener and more steadily we reflect on them: the starry heavens above me and the moral law within me. I do not merely conjecture them and seek them as though obscured in darkness or in the transcendent region beyond my horizon: I see them before me, and I associate them directly with the consciousness of my own existence. The former begins at the place I occupy in the external world of sense, and it broadens the connection in which I stand to an unbounded magnitude of worlds beyond worlds and systems of systems and into the limitless times of their periodic motion, their beginning and continuance. The latter begins at my invisible self, my personality, and exhibits me in a world which has true infinity but which is comprehensible only to the understanding – a world with which I recognize myself as existing in a universal and necessary...connection, and thereby also in connection with all those visible worlds. (1956, p. 166)

Kant's awareness opens him to a form of cosmic consciousness and to his "necessary connection" to the foundations of existence through his sense of absolute moral obligation ("the moral law within"). As soon as we open in awe and wonder to depths of existence such as these, we may encounter again the ethical and transformative demand at the heart of our being. Kant built the entire edifice of philosophy around this immense awareness that he called "the categorical imperative." This absolute obligation includes the imperative to create a mature and fulfilled human society on planet Earth.

In Chapter Three I introduced Kant's categorical imperative to indicate our understanding that social arrangements must be founded on our sense of the infinite dignity of persons, persons understood as "ends-in-themselves." In Chapter Six, we saw in what way Habermas' use of the categorical imperative ignores this aspect of it as an absolute moral demand upon our actions. I summarized this demand in the formula "always do what is right regardless of your inclinations."

This formula does not merely apply to personal moral decisions. It includes our duty to transform society toward one predicated on the dignity of each and every individual. In doing this, each of us must ask what our social obligations are regardless of our desire for comfort, wealth, social respect, reputation, or privilege. Our social duty is to create a world where every person has the opportunity for a decent, fulfilling, and meaningful life. As we saw above, the meaning of "socialism" denotes organizing society to make this possible for the first time in human history.

Such a society cannot be one in which people are used as means to the end of private accumulation of wealth. It cannot be a society predicated on any form of exploitation or domination, since all such arrangements treat people as a means, in Kant's language, and dehumanize them. It cannot be a world where powerful nations dominate or exploit weaker nations. Ultimately, as Kant's *Perpetual Peace* (1987) argues, the rule of law under a "republican constitution" guaranteeing the freedom and equality of all (p. 12) is required for the entire planet Earth.

Harry van der Linden has done a great service in his book *Kantian Ethics and Socialism* (1988) toward overcoming the dogma that Kant's ethics are primarily personal and allow moral individuals to ignore social action. He shows at great length in what ways our moral duty is most fundamentally a social duty, for Kant. And he shows at great length that we can prescind from Kant's own historically bound statements (about commercialism, and so on) to conclude that the overwhelming force of Kant's ethics advocates democratic socialism.

Kant formulates the categorical imperative in a variety of ways in the *Groundwork of the Metaphysic of Morals* (1964), claiming that each formula expresses the same ethical demand. In every case it is "universal law" at stake, as the first formula makes clear: "*Act only on that maxim through which you can at the same time will that it should become a universal law*" (p. 88). Human beings are co-legislators in a process of bringing all of human life under universal laws that conform to the demand that all human beings be treated as "end-in-themselves," never used, exploited, or dominated as a means to someone else's personal ends.

In the *Groundwork*, Kant also formulates the categorical imperative in terms of "the Kingdom of Ends." He writes:

> I understand by a 'kingdom' a systematic union of different rational beings under common laws.... If we abstract from the personal differences between rational beings, and also from all the content of their private ends – to conceive a whole of all ends in systematic conjunction...we shall be able to conceive a kingdom of ends which is possible in accordance with the above principles.
>
> For rational beings all stand under the *law* that each of them should treat himself and all others, *never merely as a means*, but always *at the same time as an end in himself*.... Thus morality consists in the relation of all action to the making of laws whereby alone a kingdom of ends is possible. (1964, pp. 100-101)

A "systematic union of rational beings under common laws" is good government, for Kant. Our ultimate social-moral duty is to live under such a government. The influence of such government will transform our moral behavior in the direction of greater moral perfection. In Chapter Three, I stressed the interrelation between human ethical and spiritual awareness and the kind of institutions under which we live. Kant affirms the same point.

Kant expresses our moral obligation as working for "the happiness of others." This action does not stem from the impulse toward our personal happiness but our "worthiness to be happy" (our moral worthiness) (1964, pp. 61-64). The kingdom of ends is the goal of a free society composed of morally-developed individuals all of whom work for the happiness of others. For Kant, the good (the general happiness of people) cannot be dictated to society.

What is dictated by the moral law is republican government maximizing the freedom and equality of all and the social duty to work for realization of the kingdom of ends. This conforms to the definition of socialism offered in Section One above. As Luntley expresses this, "socialism is not a moral theory which offers a particular version of the good life, instead it is a theory about how the good life is possible. It is, in short, a theory about the conditions necessary for creating a society in which our lives are shaped by moral values." For Kant, good government does not impose a conception of the good life, but makes possible its realization through the free action of citizens.

Kant was never subject to the naive anarchist idea that government itself is the problem. The problem of injustice in human life is due in large measure to social institutions that defeat the realization of the kingdom of ends because they are not predicated on what is truly universal (human beings as ends-in-themselves). We saw in the quotation from Adler above that what is truly universal is the most radical of concepts. But this most self-evident of principles has never been realized in history. As long as legal systems embody class privilege or exploitation, as long as some nation-states can dominate others, then we are in violation of our social duty to create a "kingdom of ends" upon Earth.

The key to fulfilling our duty to realize the kingdom of ends is to create good government over all the Earth. If constitutions and legal systems conform to moral principles (expressed in truly universal laws predicated on the dignity of each within the social matrix of the kingdom of ends), then human life will also be morally transformed. In *Perpetual Peace*, Kant speaks of the relationship to good government to the population:

> This relationship not only gives a moral veneer...to the whole but actually facilitates the development of the moral disposition to a direct respect for

the law by placing a barrier against the outbreak of unlawful inclinations. Each person believes that he himself would hold the concept of law sacred and faithfully follow it provided he were sure that he could expect the same from others, and the government does in part assure him of this.... Since even respect for the concept of right (which man cannot absolutely refuse to respect) solemnly sanctions the theory that he has the capacity of conforming to it, everyone sees that he, for his part, must act according to it, however others may act. (1987, p. 41)

Governments that base laws and institutions on pragmatic concerns or "political realism" are not legitimate, for Kant, for they are not attempting to realize the "pure concept" of republican government (maximizing the freedom and equality of all) that is an ideal of human reason. As van der Linden points out, as human beings mature to the point where a moral society begins to emerge, government will not disappear but "it will lose its repressive character" (1988, p. 9). Good government, as I argue in Chapters Ten through Twelve, is a key, not an impediment, to human liberation.

Yet whatever moral condition we have achieved at present, Kant argues in this quoted passage, our social moral duty remains the same. We have an absolute obligation to work for the realization of the kingdom of ends, "however others may act." For Kant, we are born into a framework of *a priori* moral obligation that is inherently social, laying upon us absolute social duties to transform our world in the direction of the kingdom of ends. A *telos* toward this goal is also embodied in human language, as Habermas asserts. Kant adds to our understanding of this *telos* the direct moral obligation to socially transform our present fragmented and unjust world-order.

5. Levinas, Habermas, and Marx

Agreeing with Marx, Kant, and Habermas, Levinas affirms that I am born into a world in which I already encounter other persons. My subjectivity is not prior to my encounter with others, but is initially "for another" and does not exist in itself prior to my ethical relationships (1985, p. 96). This inwardness at the heart of the ethical is utterly unique in a way that transcends all the totalities of knowledge such that the uniqueness of the Other, and the ethical relationship with the Other, can be said to open to "infinity" (1985, p. 80; see 1969, pp 171 & 207). "Knowledge," he says, "does not put us in communion with the truly other" (1985, p. 60).

The ethical relationship is therefore prior to being and knowledge and could never be fully understood through the theoretically oriented social scientific discourse used by Habermas. Only a "meta-phenomenological" description begins to elicit this dimension of human existence. In the "face of the other," we experience a direct relationship with another human being that is the source of our absolute ethical obligation. Levinas says that in this relationship we encounter "infinity" because the experience goes beyond anything we "know" about the Other or any conception we have of the reality or "being" of the Other.

For Levinas, the Other confronts me as "a face" that is "uncontainable." "The humanity of man – is a rupture of being" and leads beyond knowledge (1985, p. 87). "The signification of the face makes it escape from being," he says, "as a correlate of a knowing." Yet in the human face I experience a primordial absolute imperative: "Thou shalt not kill." "There is a commandment in the appearance of the face," Levinas writes, "as if a master spoke to me." This relation is "presupposed," he says, in all human relationships (1985, p. 89).

The Other as vulnerable, as open to the possibility of my violence, confronts me as a freedom, an infinite Otherness that grasps my freedom with this unconditional commandment. Even with those I have never met, I can encounter the vulnerability of the widow, the orphan, and the stranger reflected in their faces as Other and find myself under absolute obligation with a "total responsibility" concerning their plight (1985, p. 99). As with Kant, who took the "humanity dwelling within each person" to be a source of infinite dignity that was the foundation of my moral responsibility to others, Levinas points out that we encounter in persons an "infinite" of absolute Otherness that claims our responsibility prior to language and rationality (1969, pp. 41-43).

The thoughts of Habermas and Levinas can be understood as complementary, instead of antagonistic. Both see the moral dimension as inherently social, as inhering in language or in the face of the Other, respectively. Yet Levinas articulates for us Marx's deep sense of the unconditional dignity and potential freedom of human beings, and the need to found a social and economic order on that dignity. For as we have seen in the passage from Marx quoted above, our unconditional dignity arises only in ethical relationship. On the other hand, Habermas articulates the normative presuppositions of language itself that point toward a truly rational social and economic order. Both agree that the ethical relation is manifested in authentic conversation.

For Levinas, authentic discourse does not attempt to thematize and encompass the Other within a knowledge framework, but requires "pure 'disclosure'," "to 'let him be'." *"We call justice,"* he says, *"this face to face approach, in conversation"* (1969, p. 71). Yet Habermas is correct that there can be no just economic or social order without institutional structures that appropriate our accumulated theoretical and technical knowledge in the service of the equality and freedom at the heart of communicative rationality. Both dimensions are at work in authentic conversation, the absolute ethical claim of the Other upon me and the rational communicative demand for equality and freedom.

However, neither Habermas nor Levinas are truly transformative thinkers. While Levinas may help articulate the sense of the dignity and value of human beings implicit in Marx's thought and Habermas may help articulate Marx's understanding that human existence must be grounded in a rational social and economic order, neither of them expresses Marx's transformative insight that capitalism cannot be reformed in the direction of non-exploitation and non-dehumanization of persons. For, as Marx says several times in Volume One of *Capital,* this is its essence (1990, pp. 716 & 723-724).

A truly transformative perspective requires that capitalist society, like all forms of non-democratic class society, be abolished, completely dismantled. In its place, we must create a new global society founded on entirely different principles such as the dignity, freedom, and equality of all persons. These principles must institutionalize democratic supervision of the means of production, a production directed toward human fulfillment and human needs, not the accumulation of private profit.

Therefore, the attempt to articulate an ethical basis for socialist theory must appropriate the insights of Levinas and Habermas but move beyond their limitations. It is not only because of its Hegelian element, which has been emphasized by some Marxist traditions, that Marx's thought is transformative. The "contradictions" within capitalism are also ethical contradictions. For example, the contradiction between the cooperative social effort required by the modern forces of production and the private appropriation of the wealth deriving from that production. This private appropriation of socially-produced wealth is immoral. Capitalism must be abolished for the simple ethical reason that exploitation and dehumanization of persons should not exist.

Moral outrage permeates Marx's writings, early to late. Volume One of *Capital* overflows with statements morally condemning both the system of capitalism in general and the specific crimes occurring during Marx's day. "Capital," he says, "is dead labour which, vampire-like, lives only by sucking living labour" (1990, p. 342). "Capital's need for valorization...is made up of generations of stunted, short-lived and rapidly replaced human beings" (1990, p. 380). It is a "perpetual slavery of the working people" (1990, p. 386) or "systematic robbery of what is necessary for life" (1990, p. 553). He speaks of "that monstrosity, the disposable working population held in reserve, in misery, for the changing requirements of capitalist exploitation" (1990, p. 618).

Capitalism constitutes "a hierarchically organized system of exploitation and oppression" (1990, p. 695) "Capitalist production," he says, "thereby reproduces and perpetuates the conditions under which the worker is exploited" (1990, p. 723) and "property turns out to be the right, on the part of the capitalist, to appropriate the unpaid labour of others or its product" (1990, p. 730). "The working population," he says, "therefore produces the accumulation of capital and the means by which it is itself made relatively superfluous" (1990, p. 783). The moral outrage expressed in these and many similar statements is transformative precisely because it affirms the dignity and humanity of persons. It recognizes that capitalism in principle violates our humanity. It must, therefore, be entirely changed in favor of what he calls "a higher form of society, a society in which the full and free development of every individual forms the ruling principle" (739).

In contrast to Marx, the work of Levinas, while providing an absolute imperative to act with respect to the oppressed, does not provide a systematic critical insight into the structural or institutional conditions of violence and exploitation at the heart of capitalism. His thought is not transformative in the sense that there is a moral imperative to replace the present system with democratic socialism. The absolute moral obligation for justice, peace, and freedom so well expressed in his thought remains bourgeois in the sense that it does not call for institutional transformation.

Neither is Habermas' thought truly transformative. Habermas does provide systematic critical insight into the today's exploitative institutions. However, his philosophy merely describes an evolutionary model. The instrumentally rationalized system of modern capitalism, he argues, with its supporting mechanism of the state bureaucracy, has become "uncoupled" from the lifeworld that is the locus of critical communicative rationality. This situation does not call for transformation but for an emphasis on speech and communication (which is perhaps why so many comfortable, bourgeois academics prefer Habermas to Marx). As we saw, for Habermas the communicative presuppositions of the lifeworld merely exert a "normative pull" on history and do not contain any clear ethical imperative for transformative, revolutionary action.

Yet there is a another theme in Levinas and Habermas that might be developed for its radical potential in ways that could resonate with Marx's critical understanding of the ethical imperative for transformation. This theme involves the notion of what I have been calling "practical utopia." Marx himself can be termed a practical utopian in that a society founded on the principle of "the free and full development of every individual" has probably never existed. Nevertheless, he shows that such a society is entirely realizable within the presently developed capability of the forces of production.

Marx did not repudiate the goals of the so-called "utopian socialists" who envisioned a just, free, and classless society. He wished to make socialism "scientific" by identifying the real causes of class exploitation and the possibilities for their overthrow. "Scientific socialism," had superseded the utopians, Marx wrote in 1871, *"not because the working class had given up the end aimed at by these utopians, but because they had found the real means to realize them"* (in Miranda, 1986, p. 149).

The practical utopian element for Habermas arises insofar as language includes a normative *telos* toward "discursive will formation," a *telos* that is not idealist, he claims, since it is open to empirical verification. Discursive will formation occurs through the "universal ethics of speech" in which human beings work together to build a consensus where even "need interpretations are no longer assumed as given." The pseudo, egoistic needs, currently cultivated by the propaganda of capitalist consumerism will be abandoned and transformed through new and fundamentally different discursively formed need interpretations.

Human beings will no longer interpret their needs in terms of egoistic self-promotion at the expense of others, for authentic communication regarding their needs will lead beyond these adolescent ideas to more mature need interpretations such as the need for community, reciprocity, meaning, and wholeness that characterize stage-seven morality. "Internal nature is thereby moved into a utopian perspective...," he writes, and "naturally this flow of communication requires sensitivity, breaking down barriers, dependency – in short a cognitive style marked as field-dependent" (1979, pp. 93-94).

As with Marx, Habermas points toward a human condition transformed in the direction of a realized communal and social nature, which ultimately can be called "utopian." Yet however necessary the dimension of communicative rationality may be, it is not sufficient, for it lacks the unconditional imperative of an absolute and inviolable human dignity expressed in Levinas' thought. Levinas calls his own perspective "utopian," and here non-idealist spirituality must enter socialist thought and abolish the outmoded metaphysical distinction between materialism and idealism.

In our present condition, Levinas says "the humanity of the human – the true life – is absent." For we remain bogged down in the ontological attitude that reduces the infinite mystery and depths of existence to knowledge and ontological categories. But the historical emergence of subjectivity and inwardness, which is inseparable from absolute responsibility for the Other, means that ontological categories are exploded, "undone," in the possibilities opened up by the "'fathomless' and utopian depths of 'interiority'" (1985, pp. 100 & 116).

Human life shifts here as well into a utopian perspective. Only when the founding principle of a society is the ethical relationship with each person as infinitely Other, as having an absolute moral and social claim upon me, can there be a truly transformed society. Spirituality in this sense would need to be an integral component within the practical, communal utopia envisioned by Marx, and hence of a viable socialist ethics.

The ethics of socialism (in its most fundamental form that we are addressing here, bracketing for the moment the mystical and eschatological dimensions of human existence) must be articulated around the twin poles of the rationality of a universal ethics of speech and the infinite, unconditional ethical claim experienced in the face of the Other. The first encompasses the dimension of rationality fundamental to human life and the progressive realization of a free society. The latter points to the dimension of ultimate mystery within which human life and the universe are embedded and our sense of absolute dignity of the human being that cannot be entirely encompassed by theoretical terms.

But an ethics of socialism must also be at once critical, transformative, and practical utopian as these are expressed in Marx's writings. For the Marxist insight that capitalism as we know it is utterly incompatible with reason and human dignity, and cannot be reformed but only transformed, must remain at the heart of a viable socialist ethics. Any system that treats human beings as commodities whose labor is bought and sold for purposes of exploitation must be abolished. This must be replaced by a universal economic system founded not only on our absolute moral dignity but on discursively interpreted human needs, human vulnerability, and the norms of equality and interdependence inherent in our communal nature. Such are the ethical values at the heart of a viable socialist theory.

6. Socialism as the Political-economic Form of Love and the Work of Krishnamurti

Socialism as the political-economic form of love is fundamental to the categorical imperative of ethical life for human beings. We are not simply commanded to do what is right regardless of our inclinations by treating every person as an end-in-themselves, as Kant says (although this demand in itself leads to socialism (see Van Der Linden, 1988)). We are commanded by the logic inherent in our linguistic situation itself to engage in honest and open discourse with other persons in a process of discursive will formation, as Habermas argues (and this demand also leads to socialism, as we have seen).

We also saw an imperative to live our lives differently that is inherent in our situation. We should be doing something that we are currently failing to do. When we begin to intuit something of our "ultimate environment," the ground or matrix of our lives in relation to the question "why be moral?" begins to become clear. And the meaning of this "being moral," as this is understood from the earlier stages of moral development, takes on an entirely new quality. In stage-seven of moral-spiritual growth, we encounter a moral imperative not intimated in stage-six reasoning with respect to justice and fairness.

In the previous chapter we saw that Kohlberg, Carter, and Fowler all point to a higher order awareness arising with full human maturity that goes beyond anything that can be empirically or phenomenologically described. The infinite dignity of persons as Other, elucidated by Levinas, and the communal, dialogical framework within which others are understood in a relationship of equality and parity with one's self, articulated by Habermas, must now be encompassed within the groundless existential ground of the human situation itself. We have seen Kolhberg describe his highest stage of moral development as follows:

> To answer questions Why be moral? Why be just in a universe filled with injustice, suffering, and death? requires one to move beyond the domain of justice and derive replies from the meaning found in metaethical, meta-physical, and religious epistemologies.... Unlike the analytic and dualistic development of justice reasoning (i.e., reasoning based on the differentia-tion of self and other, subject and object), ethical and religious soft stage development culminates in a synthetic, nondualistic sense of participation in, and identity with, a cosmic order. The self is understood as a component of this order, and its meaning is understood as being contingent upon par-ticipation in this order. (1984, pp 249-250)

Kohlberg suggests that we understand a stage-seven of human development as moving beyond "dualistic" reasoning to a non-dual sense of "identity" with the cosmic order. And we saw Carter suggest a possible stage-eight where even "identity with the cosmic order" is transcended in an unspeakable immediacy of wholeness, beyond thought, and beyond language.

Of the many spiritual masters in our day pointing to this wholeness as the goal and fulfillment of our human potentiality, Krishnamurti is one of the most eloquent and penetrating. His spontaneous genius for spiritual awakening permeated his talks and writings over much of the twentieth century. Krishnamurti's many discourses again and again return to the dulling effect that mental habits, routines, and linguistic patterns have on our immediate awareness in the present. The "flame" of real attention takes us beyond dualistic mental habits that are always "condemning, judging, forming opinions, and concluding." We encounter a degree of alertness beyond duality to wholeness:

> The deeper the mind penetrates its own thought processes, the more clearly it understands that all forms of thinking are conditioned; therefore the mind is spontaneously very still – which does not mean that it is asleep. On the contrary, the mind is then extraordinarily alert, no longer being drugged...by the repetition of words, or shaped by discipline. This state of silent alertness is also part of awareness; and if you go into it still more deeply you will find that there is no division between the person who is aware and the object of which he is aware. (1989, p. 203)

Krishnamurti sees that human intelligence itself is linked with this capability for complete attention. This insight accounts for the mystery of why so many apparently "highly intelligent" persons, in the conventional sense of these words, can willingly be academic mandarins, government bureaucrats, corporate executives, or weapons researchers. Their deepest human capacity for intelligence experiences distortion through fear, ambition, tradition, and conformity. The dead hand of the past, whether in our personal linguistic and mental habits, or in social institutions, exacerbates the frightened and anxiety-ridden ego to deal with its fears through striving for success within the framework of a "rotten society."

> Do you know what intelligence is? It is the capacity, surely, to think freely, without fear, without a formula, so that you begin to discover for yourself what is real, what is true; but if you are frightened you will never be intelligent.... Life is really very beautiful, it is not this ugly thing that we have made of it; and you can appreciate its richness, its depth, its extraordinary loveliness only when you revolt against everything – against organized religion, against tradition, against the present rotten society – so that you as a human being find out for yourself what is true....
>
> Do you know what this means – what an extraordinary thing it would be to create an atmosphere in which there is no fear? And we must create it, because we see that the world is caught up in endless wars; it is guided by politicians who are always seeking power; it is a world of lawyers, policemen and soldiers, of ambitious men and women all wanting position and all fighting each other to get it.... You are encouraged to fit into the framework of this disastrous society. (1989, pp. 3-4)

Krishnamurti expresses awareness of the beauty and richness of life repeatedly throughout his career. The greater the "flame of attention," the more we encounter the depths and mystery of life with unfettered sensitive intelligence, the more we encounter beauty, wholeness, inner freedom, and love. A genuine education, he says, would provide a framework for activating precisely this kind of intelligence. We activate an intelligence "in constant revolt" against the dead hand of the past as this dulls our sensitivity and capability for perception in personal and social terms.

Practical utopia is not merely a romantic dream, but expresses our most immediate and realistic human possibility through becoming aware of our habitual dullness with its attendant fears, anxieties, and blind ambitions. A genuine education is an education for perpetual transformation, an ever-renewed awakening of attention and sensitivity to the beauty, wholeness, love, and freedom that are the fullness of human life.

> Now, is it the function of education merely to help you to conform to the pattern of this rotten social order, or is it to give you freedom – complete freedom to grow and create a different society, a new world? We want to have this freedom, not in the future, but now, otherwise we may all be destroyed. We must create immediately an atmosphere for freedom so that you can live and find out for yourselves what is true, so that you can become intelligent, so that you are able to face the world and understand it, not just conform to it, so that inwardly, deeply, psychologically you are in constant revolt; because it is only those who are in constant revolt that discover what is true, not the man who conforms, who follows some tradition. It is only when you are constantly inquiring, constantly observing, constantly learn-ing, that you find truth, God, or love; and you cannot inquire, observe, learn, you cannot be deeply aware, if you are afraid. So the function of education, surely, is to eradicate, inwardly as well as outwardly, this fear that destroys human thought, human relationship and love. (1989, pp. 4-5)

Krishnamurti frequently reflects on the dulling effect that the "momentum" or "dead hand of the past" has on society. He critiques our social institutions in a way that is fundamentally compatible with the thought of Marx and democratic socialism. All of society involves this momentum of the past. And even future socialist societies would be quite different from hitherto-existing socialist societies. For past socialist societies largely lost the perpetual spirit of revolt against the brutalities of the existing order promoted by genuine education and intelligence.

Nevertheless, the thought of Marx, like the thought of contemporary socialists such as José Miranda or Enrique Dussel, does contain this spirit of perpetual renewal that draws on the deepest potentialities of the human spirit. Socialism as the political-economic form of love is qualitatively different from socialism as state and party domination over the lives and aspirations of citizens. Within the socialist vision is the potential for planetary maturity.

We have seen, on the other hand, that accumulations of capital are the result of the productive lives of innumerable persons long dead, exploited in the past, whose surplus labor lives in the present to oppress others. Dead labor, as Marx puts it, oppressing living labor. And insofar as workers do not revolt against their present oppression and exploitation by big capital they are building the oppressive apparatus that will crush the lives of future generations. The momentum of the past cannot be broken through an evolution of this system.

As Marx repeatedly pointed out, the life of this system is the isolated ego in competition for profit and "success" in alienated struggle with all other isolated individuals. Meanwhile, whatever moral dimension the system represents is formulated in terms of an abstract citizen-self (outside the realm of private capital or "civil" society) possessing human rights, political freedoms, voting rights, and so on. As long as these domains are radically divided (our rights as abstract political citizens from our concrete daily lives), the primary domain of capital and greed will forever dominate and manipulate the abstract realm of "rights" and human dignity. In Marx's terms, "formal democracy" will never become "substantive democracy."

The transformation of awareness must break the momentum of the past in a new immediacy that brings wholeness, peace, and an end to anxiety-ridden striving, not only for persons, but for societies. A true social transformation must bring an end to the momentum of capital in the form of dead labor over living labor with its legalized exploitative relationships and social organizations (such as most national governments) devoted to preserving and promoting the momentum of the past into the future. Just as on the personal level striving and discipline to reform the past will only bind the individual more effectively under the momentum of his or her past, so attempts at progressive reform of the global capitalist system will only bind groups and societies more tightly to this system.

We free ourselves from the momentum of the past by a break-through, a discovery, for which there can be no formula, no dogma, no pre-existing, foolproof pattern ahead of time. To propose such a pattern is still to remain within the momentum of the past. This is the truth of many utopian visions and the answer to those who dismiss utopian thinking because it offers no formula to go from here to there. Any such formula already preserves the momentum of the oppressive past, which does not mean we cannot learn from the past. Transformative newness reflects precisely a break-through in social and personal awareness. It means reestablishing society on the integrity of the whole and the inviolability of the person, free from exploitation, manipulation, and dehumanization. To merely change the institutional structures of society, for Krishnamurti, is to remain within the framework of society, of the dead hand of the past:

> So there is a vast difference between the action of creative revolution, and the action of revolt or mutiny within society. As long as you are concerned with

mere reform, with decorating the bars and walls of the prison, you are not creative. Reformation always needs further reform, it only brings more misery, more destruction. Whereas, the mind that understands this whole structure of acquisitiveness, of greed, of ambition and breaks away from it – such a mind is in constant revolution. It is an expansive, a creative mind; therefore, like a stone thrown into a pool of still water, its action produces waves, and those waves will form a different civilization altogether. (1989, pp. 155-156)

Here we encounter once again the interface between spiritual and social transformation as well as the apparent paradox faced by any transformative praxis. For only spiritually transformed persons create a new society, and yet spiritually transformed persons will only appear through new educational and social structures. There is a reciprocal relationship, an intimate dialectic, between institutions and human consciousness. Krishnamurti, however, does not fully see this paradox and remains an advocate of spiritual transformation as the mainspring for a practical utopia. He recognizes only the "vicious circle" of historical revolution succeeding revolution without ever emerging into a society premised on true freedom, beauty, love, and intelligence:

Now, how is one to break through this vicious circle? Mind you, it is obvious that reformation is necessary; but is reformation possible without bringing about still further confusion? This seems to me to be one of the fundamental issues with which any thoughtful person must be concerned.... I think there is a way of life in which there is not this process of reformation breeding further misery, and that way may be called religious. The truly religious person is not concerned with reform, he is not concerned with merely producing a change in the social order; on the contrary he is seeking what is true, and that very search has a transforming effect on society...

To find out what is truth there must be great love and a deep awareness of man's relationship to all things.... The search for truth is true religion, and the man who is seeking truth is the only religious man. Such a man, because of his love, is outside of society, and his action upon society is therefore entirely different from that of the man who is in society and concerned with its reformation. The reformer can never create a new culture. What is necessary is the search of the truly religious man, for this very search brings about its own culture and it is our only hope. You see, the search for truth gives an explosive creativeness to the mind, which is true revolution, because in this search the mind is uncontaminated by the edicts and sanctions of society. Being free of all that, the religious man is able to find out what is true; and it is the discovery of what is true from moment to moment that creates a new culture. (1989, pp. 240-241)

Religion is here deontologized, a demythologized seeing-into-the-depths-of-reality. This lends insight into the transformative spirituality of planetary maturity. The depths of existence were also recognized in pre-Copernican ages but often only in an ontologized and mythologized form that undercut the critical force of these depths. Marx was largely right about the general function of religion in legitimating this-worldly oppressive economic and social forms. But religion purified through the twin fires of social criticism and deepened awareness becomes a force for social transformation.

Truth-seeking religion recognizes the transformative possibilities inherent in a demythologized human situation and acts to negate what is false in the dominant institutions. It makes clear the reciprocal interdependence of individual awareness and institutional arrangements. Post-Copernican purified religion becomes the matrix through which capitalism and the nation-state are delegitimized and deontologized. Such non-dogmatic, awakened religion or directly realized spirituality is a factor in the creation of a new civilization beyond the conflictive pseudo-realities of the past, free of the momentum of the past. (For a related, integrated vision see *After Capitalism* by Dada Maheshvaranda, 2003.)

To premise society on the living truth and the inviolability of persons will require a gestalt switch, a reversal of our egoistic and fractured mode of awareness to the transformative awareness of the inseparability of the whole and the part. It will not come about through an evolution of existing institutions in which the weight of domination perpetually grows (not diminishes) as the system flourishes economically and the oppressive accumulations of the past dominate, distort, and mythologize the thinking of the present. Transformative praxis, as Dominique Barbé puts it, must be informed by "grace," and the resulting organizational structures of authority must be informed by "grace."

The living truth must enter into our lives through the flame of attention and the realization of deep intelligence. With this, transformative praxis moves to genuine newness informed by the inseparability of the whole and the part and to a new integrity and simplicity in living. Just as there is no scientifically describable path to the spiritual transformation of individual persons, precisely because it is a break-through to genuine newness free of the past, so there is no path to genuine social transformation. There is no formula to move from here to there, for all such formulas preserve the momentum of the past.

Krishnamurti's "method of negation" for individual persons applies to societies as well. To be deeply aware of one's dullness, stupidity, and insensitivity is to become free of them. Similarly, to see clearly the exploitative nature of capitalism is to move beyond it instantly. A person does not need a blueprint for a socialist society to repudiate greed, exploitation, and undemocratic power-relations. To see the human and spiritual consequences of the so-called "free" market is to see that unemployment, homelessness, broken families, crime, race hatred, homophobia, destruction of the environment, militarism, war, and dehumanizing labor exploitation do not occur as incidentals that the system works to overcome but are intrinsic to the system.

Spiritual awakening is inseparable from social awakening. Spiritual enlightenment and social enlightenment are inseparable halves of human awakening, of liberation. The heir of the Western enlightenment is reason: not absolute reason, in this case, expressing the structure of being, but critical reason exposing the patterns of deception and exploitation on which societies are founded. And the birth-child of the critical study of religion in conjunction with "the flame of attention" is spiritual awakening. To realize either one without the other is to be half awake. To realize neither is to be lost in the nightmare of ego and capital, two complementary sides of the limitless misery of planet Earth.

7. Compassionate Planetary Socialism

It should be clear that "compassionate planetary socialism" does not provide another blueprint for a better organization of society. It indicates a transformed world free of the oppressive momentum of the past. Compassion is not sentimentality or pity, which is the most the egoistic orientation can generate. "I am so sorry you are suffering when, indeed, I have the good fortune not to be suffering." Compassion is solidarity, oneness, in which your suffering is my suffering and your joy is my joy. We are all one, as Krishnamurti never tires of asserting.

We are one in our entrapment within the mental and social structures of the past, and we are one in sharing the primal awareness of wholeness, harmony, and love. There is no path from the former to the latter, no evolution or progress, only break-through, the dropping of the false through seeing it clearly with full attention. Attention to one's mental processes, Krishnamurti says, is simultaneously attention to society:

> If you don't know how your mind reacts, if your mind is not aware of its own activities, you will never find out what society is. You may read books on sociology, study social sciences, but if you don't know how your own mind works you cannot actually understand what society is, because your mind is part of society; it *is* society.... Your mind is humanity, and when you perceive this, you will have immense compassion. Out of this understanding comes great love; and then you will know, when you see lovely things, what beauty is. (1989, pp. 83 & 86)

Social scientific critical analysis of ideology and the study of the causal conditions of oppression are vital to the quest for human liberation. But in the final analysis, authentic transformation cannot be entirely organized or engineered. There is no clearly definable path to social transformation, just as there is no path to spiritual transformation. Historical analysis of the causes of present day institutions will in itself not break the momentum of these institutions. These institutions not only control the laws, the politicians, and the military, but condition new generations in the same ideological framework that carries the momentum forward.

On the other hand, as Part Four of this book will make clear, we can very easily comprehend the kind of the global institutional framework that makes possible human liberation. And this global framework by no means requires state ownership of all means of production. We cannot organize society to engineer the realization of our higher possibilities, but we can organize to allow their emergence. These are two very different ideas. A rational, common sense framework promoting liberty, equality, and fraternity will make human liberation possible. Both morality in human life and higher stages of maturity are impossible for most without an institutional framework conducive to their realization. Such a framework will not produce unconditioned awareness. It will make it possible.

There is no absolute line between the conditioned mind and unconditioned awareness. In one sense, we may draw such a line, as Krishnamurti attempts to do repeatedly in his effort to emphasize the falsity of believing that a quest through time can result in a spiritual break-through. The ego is connected with the surface sense of time that ignores the depths of the present, so the setting of a goal for spiritual evolution (through time) only reinforces that ego. The seeing of the falsity of the conditioned mind is an immediate ending of that bondage. There is no path to freedom. Freedom itself is the only path. So in this sense a line can be drawn.

On the other hand, the unconditioned is the pure primal awareness that is always present, permeating our lives. There is only one reality and one world. The pure primary awareness breaks through continually in moments of silence, simplicity, or wonder. We only have to recall ourselves to a few seconds of quietness, or become still in the encounter with beauty, or allow authentic compassion to flow into our hearts, or step aside in moments of quiet reflection and meditation. Zen mind is always there, as Zen Master Eihei Dogen (1997) insists.

We need only awaken to the fullness of it. If this were not the case, we would have no idea of what Krishnamurti is saying or what they are talking about in Zen. We would be incapable of genuine compassion, of a deep encounter with beauty, or of astonishment, wonder, or awe at the sublime. The fact that these moments occur means that the primal awareness is always "knocking," so to speak, always asking to become manifest and fulfill our lives.

There is no path that the dualistic mind can devise to encounter primal awareness, since dualistic mind itself blocks primal awareness. In *Zen and the Art of Archery,* Eugen Herrigel bursts out at his Zen Master who had been urging him to be "purposeless" in holding the bow and arrow, drawing the bow, and releasing the arrow: "How can I become purposeless on purpose?" (1971, pp. 51-52). However, the moments of awakening that punctuate our lives can be cultivated. Just as an institutional framework can be created that does not inhibit our highest human possibilities.

Some modes of attention, some kinds of activity, make these moments more likely than others. There is the persistent intuition that the moments of revelation that punctuate our lives could be the dominant mode of awareness. These moments of revelation give us the possibility of authentic social action directed to ending the falsity of the institutionalized past and making possible the emergence of the genuinely new.

Personal awakening is possible, we have seen, because of the encompassing wholeness that makes possible moments of insight, compassion, awe, illumination, beauty, or oneness. Yet the wholeness that encompasses human life can also activate awakening on the social level of our species being. Transformed institutions will transform the persons participating in them. Socially whole institutions make possible moments of communal joy, celebration, unity, freedom, participatory democracy, solidarity, authentic communication, non-idolatrous worship, and love. We speak of the unity of humankind, the unity of planet Earth, or the unity of nature, not realizing how these dimensions permeate our lives and societies and make possible direct experience of these unities.

We fail to notice what little joy, celebration, unity, freedom, democracy, solidarity, communication, worship, or love we can experience within the framework of capitalist society and the nation-state system. These aspects of authentic social wholeness diametrically oppose the perverted unity of fascism, which is fragmentation: a regression into fear and hatred and merely the projection of a collective egoism, not freedom from the ego. Only compassionate socialism expresses planetary maturity.

Compassionate socialism already exists, in a sense, as the primal awareness, we need only to negate the false so that it may spontaneously emerge. As Henry Leroy Finch expressed this in relation to Wittgenstein's thought: "We are in the total presence of the unsayable, and...the greatest beyond we can imagine is too close to be said! If we will 'let go' of the world then something entirely new will be revealed. A new 'turning point' is very close" (1977, p. 123).

We must not ontologize or systematize this notion of "various levels" that encompass us (which I am using here as a mere pointer), for doing so will return us to the trap of attempting to objectify and engineer truth and the attempt to totally grasp reality through language. Speaking of the "effective reality" of various levels is meant as a pointer to aspects of our experience, not as an ontological determination of the nameless. What we can analyze and historically illuminate are the systems of language, causality, and ego that dominate our lives.

From the point of view of the totalizing drive, or the related drive for egoistic domination of life and the world through language, all so-called "utopian" thinking will be dismissed as unrealistic and hopelessly idealistic. But "realism" is precisely what is defined by the egoistic drive to domination and explanation, and whatever is outside its possible sphere of control, "whatever" is outside language, is automatically discounted as subjective illusion. These insights derive not only from spiritual thinker Krishnamurti, but from philosopher of language Ludwig Wittgenstein. Finch writes:

> Wittgenstein speaks for an age free from the obsessions with *causality, explanation, domination,* and *control* which characterize our age. He looks to a time when, instead of building ever greater and more grandiose edifices for the expansion of the human ego (collective or individual), we will search for a new directness and purity of thought and action. (1977, p. 251)

We are told it does not "work." This is why we must see that the totalizing-egoistic drive to domination through engineering, organizing, and manipulating life and the world is the opposite of an authentically practical and sane "realism." For the egoistic drive to domination does not "work." It does not create beauty, freedom, goodness, or peace. It "works" to create wealth, power, and a moral callousness for the few, and misery for the many. We need only look clearly at our world created over the last four centuries of the modern era, since Copernicus. It is a world of war, conquest, pillage, militarism, exploitation, chaos, misery, starvation, hatred, conflict, and unredeemed struggle. This world has not "worked," and its institutions are not legitimate.

To speak of a "sinful" or corrupt "human nature" is to ignore the moral and spiritual possibilities present in all of us and to justify the wealth and privilege of the few at the expense of the many. It is to blaspheme the sacred wholeness of our lives that is intimated by any normal adult willing to pay real attention to his or her experience. It should be clear that something is seriously wrong with the way we are living. To speak of a "fallen" human nature is to mistake the *result* of our egoistic mode of relating to life for the *cause* of our misery.

Human beings are "evil" only to the extent that we are lost within an orientation of egoistic struggle and domination and see no limits to language, which in our era is the expression of this struggle. We allow no "silence," "emptiness," or pure "flame of attention" to enter our compulsive, fear-driven lives. We allow no redeeming "grace" to enter our lives from which to see the pitiful limitations of this orientation. But the sacred wholeness encompasses us nevertheless, and we have but to drop our drive for domination to experience it and to experience the social transformation that arises from it.

I want to emphasize once again that I am not speaking here about any form of irrationalism. Rationality is vital and essential, and this has been worked out in great detail by such thinkers as Habermas. The traditional Platonic *eros* for the fullness of being, of which reason is an essential component, is fundamental to the human project. But the impulse to reason, to understand, and communicate must lead to a wisdom that sees the place and limits of reason. At present the defenders of reason see themselves as holding the dike against the potential flood of unreason in the form of hatred, nationalism, religious fundamentalism, racism, sexism, capitalism, and so on.

But these irrational passions are the obverse of a reason impotent to bring wholeness to our fragmented human situation. If reason were to recognize its own limits and we were to move beyond reason in the service of egoism to an era in which we were in proper relationship to the unsayable depths and wholeness of our being-in-the-world, then reason would find its fulfillment in practical planning in relation to these depths. The problem is not reason, but, as Finch expresses this, our "obsessions with *causality, explanation, domination,* and *control.*" Dropping the egoistic desire to control and manipulate our destiny would make a "purity of thought and action" possible for the first time. Something of this possibility is also uncovered in Kant's *Critique of Judgment* (1951) where reason finds a fulfillment in the encounter with what is deeper than ordinary reason, the experience of beauty and the sublime.

Krishnamurti sees the principle that liberation for individual persons requires going beyond the illusory individual self to the nameless meditative self in which the duality of self and other is abandoned. And he sees the principle that human beings are fundamentally one reality that is discovered when the individual self of greed, division, competition, and conflict is abandoned. Yet his advice for social transformation does not flow from his insight into these principles. Instead, he insists that individuals transformed through abandonment of the illusory self will have a "ripple effect" on society that will lead to a new world civilization. He ignores the institutional effects on the masses of individuals that are far more than sufficient to neutralize any effect transformed individuals might have on society.

Typical of thinkers who have not studied critical theory, he has little insight into the exploitative and dehumanizing effect of institutions themselves, although he sees clearly that they are "rotten." He focuses on the unawakened consciousness of individuals caught in the illusory self. He ignores the possibility that the ever-living oneness of our universal human reality can itself become present in large numbers of people. As we reviewed in Chapter One, some eras in history have seen fundamental and spontaneous transformations of consciousness: from the magical to the mythological, from the mythological to the philosophical, from the Medieval to the Renaissance. Our age offers the promise of another fundamental transformation, a "millennium dawn."

Just as Krishnamurti's method of negation can function for individuals through a seeing of what is false leading to abandonment of the false and an instantaneous realization of the nameless truth beyond language, so a social method of negation can lead to abandonment of false competitive, conflictual, and greedy social organization and the instantaneous realization of what Marx called our species being, a being we have seen him describe as one of mutual recognition and love. This is the only way that the momentum of the past can be abandoned and a freedom beyond the past realized on an institutional scale.

Institutions (material conditions) don't merely arise from human consciousness, as Marx correctly insisted. They also condition human consciousness. However, like individual consciousness, they can be spontaneously transformed if what is false in them is recognized as illegitimate and abandoned. Planetary maturity recognizes the illegitimacy of all that is fragmentary, divisive, and ego-driven. Its wholeness flows forth in compassion and in "purity of thought and action." The dropping of the false, Krishnamurti says, leads immediately to compassion and love, born of wholeness. The same is true of human institutions. Our reason and our compassion understand that democratic socialism is the political-economic form of love.

Chapter Eight
The Maturing of Critical Theory

*The question whether objective truth can be attributed to human thinking is not a question of theory but is a **practical** question. Man must prove the truth, that is, the reality and power, the this-sidedness of his thinking in practice. The dispute over the reality or non-reality of thinking which is isolated from practice is a purely **scholastic** question.... The philosophers have only **interpreted** the world, in various ways; the point, however, is to **change** it.*

Karl Marx

*The main thing is that utopian conscience-and-knowledge, through the pain it suffers in facts, grows wise, yet does not grow to full wisdom. It is **rectified** – but never **refuted** by the mere power of that which, at any particular time, **is**. On the contrary it confutes and judges the existent if it is failing, and failing inhumanly; indeed, first and foremost it provides the **standard** to measure such facticity precisely as departure from the Right; and above all to measure it immanently: that is, by ideas which have resounded and informed from time immemorial before such a departure, and which are still displayed and proposed in the face of it.*

Ernst Bloch

" Critical Social Theory," as I am using the term, links with the independent development of Marxist theory since the time of Marx, free of the "dogmatic" Marxism that was often promoted in the Soviet Union or Eastern Europe. The phrase "critical theory" apparently originated with Max Horkheimer's 1937 essay "Traditional and Critical Theory" in the tradition originating with the Frankfort Institute for Social Research in Germany in the early decades of the twentieth century. But the use of the term extended beyond the work of the Frankfort Institute to the point where it now often includes "Western Marxism" in general, and assumes the work of such well-known neo-Marxist thinkers such as Theodore Adorno, Walter Benjamin, Ernst Bloch, Erich Fromm, Antonio Gramsci, Jürgen Habermas, Max Horkheimer, Karl Korsch, Georg Lukacs, Herbert Marcuse, Wilhelm Reich, and Jean-Paul Sartre.

1. The Goals of Critical Social Theory

Since critical theory studies society in the light of its potentialities for freedom and human liberation (even in the light of its "utopian" possibilities as Herbert Marcuse affirms (1992, p. 10)), I would like to use the term to include all philosophers of human liberation, even those from religious traditions, such as Dominique Barbé (1987), Enrique Dussel (1990), Gustavo Gutierrez (1973), Franz Hinkelammert (1986), or José Miranda (1986), who understand that no human social revolution occurs without a new appropriation of religion in the form of an awakened human spirituality. Thinkers such as these include in their neo-Marxist critical social analysis the issue of a transformed human spirituality and awareness of the depths of existence.

Critical theory involves the philosophical and social-scientific study of society in the light of certain values, those of human liberation, with which even Plato was concerned in his theoretical construction of a just and redeemed state in the *Republic*. In the words of Marcuse, "The utopian element was long the only progressive element in philosophy, as in the construction of the best state and the highest pleasure, of perfect happiness and perpetual peace. Critical theory preserves obstinacy as a genuine quality of philosophical thought.... [and focuses on] freedom and happiness in the social relations of men" (1992, pp. 10-11). As Marx eloquently put it in the quotation at the head of this chapter, the goal is not merely to interpret the world, but to change it in the direction of its highest potentialities.

What is the basic characteristic of our age at the dawn of the third millennium? Is it that we have "settled down" in the botched and broken world of pain, suffering, injustice, greed, and hatred? The utopian light that flows from the great religions, that radiates from the great ethical teachings of the world, that scintillates from literature, art, and philosophy throughout the ages is ignored as "unrealistic," and is denigrated as "metaphysics" or "fantasy" (see Bloch, 1986). The most fundamental possibilities of human life, in many ways immediately available for realization, are ignored by "practical" and "realistic" people and their fragmented institutions. Yet we all know such "realistic" people and their institutions are flushing human history down the toilet of impending planetary disaster. Within this very "dark time" of history, a living critical theory can function as a beacon of light and hope.

Some recent "postmodern" thinkers criticized the Marxist tradition for claiming that it has discovered the eternal, metaphysical truth about the human situation. They attack what they call "Marxism" for its claims to discern the innermost dialectic of history, the "necessary" movement of history toward a classless society, the ultimate nature of human beings as material-social beings, or the ultimate dynamic of society as the "totality" of social relations. However, neither Marx, nor any other truly critical thinker, need be read as requiring grand historical narratives or metaphysical absolutes.

Such thinkers can be read, instead, in Wittgensteinian fashion, as emphasizing certain ways of speaking with an eye toward human liberation. We each have our intuitions and experiences of oppression and liberation that generate some metaphors useful in delineating the patterns of society. We also have the "tool box" of past thinkers to help us articulate these and find ways to move toward liberation. Marx provided many valuable tools, as did Aristotle, Nicholas Berdyaev, Ernst Bloch, John Dewey, Enrique Dussel, Antonio Gramsci, Jürgen Habermas, G. W. F. Hegel, Martin Heidegger, Immanuel Kant, Jiddu Krishnamutri, Emmanuel Levinas, Herbert Marcuse, Friedrich Nietzsche, Plato, Ludwig Wittgenstein, and many others.

That some themes are emphasized by Marx, and some metaphors preferred, does not make his work in the social-scientific study of capitalism either relativistic subjectivism or metaphysical dogmatic "nonsense." No human being can lay claim to absolute truth, but together the work of many thinkers can lend insight into the phenomena under consideration. No metaphysical absolutes are necessary for critical theory. Critical theory studies, social-scientifically, structural oppression within class societies with a view to the possibility of freedom and fulfillment in this world, on planet Earth. Social phenomena may be more fluid and less certain than those of the natural world, but systems of oppression can be elucidated just as can any other social or cultural realities. As with any other body of knowledge, we are historically developing a growing insight into these phenomena.

In terms of the ethical dimension behind the pursuit of such knowledge, and the ethical application and motivation within the knowing activity, our situation is different. In previous chapters we have seen that the ethical-spiritual dimension on the deepest level is not one in which progressive accumulation of knowledge and understanding is possible. Such a thing as growth and development of ethical-spiritual awakening occurs for individuals. People can grow in their rational ability for communicative discourse and understanding. And they may grow in their unmediated awareness of the living unspeakable wholeness that embraces our lives at every moment.

But growth here takes the form of a progressive openness to what ultimately comes "as a gift." If critical social theory arguably involves a domain of knowledge, spiritual awareness ultimately does not, and people can never be "taught" ethical-spiritual maturity in the way that they can be taught mathematics or biology. As we saw in Chapter Seven, you cannot engineer ethical awareness, spiritual openness, inner attention, nor cosmic consciousness. However, historically we can create social conditions in which most people have the opportunity for the maximum growth of their ethical-spiritual potential. This is what critical theory at its best understands. We have seen that the ethical and the critical dimensions are both necessary to a viable critical theory. Its motivation is precisely to create the conditions that make human liberation possible.

Concrete phenomena exist that can be scientifically understood. When I eat food, scientists tell me how it nourishes my body. If I shoot someone with a gun, scientists tell me how the bullet causes the death of the victim. If I hire someone for my business, scientists can tell me how I accumulate wealth through exploiting that person's labor. Of course scientists can be corrupted, for scientific knowledge can be used to create weapons or to exploit people, to provide medical treatment or to use medical knowledge for the profit and domination of its providers.

Knowledge becomes self-destructive for human beings in their deepest humanity unless used for human equality, justice, freedom, and dignity, unless used ethically. Economists, historians, philosophers, and educators can be brainwashed just as effectively as electricians or plumbers. They can be brainwashed to have little or no human conscience, or if they have a conscience, to apply it within an entirely misconceived conceptual framework that misplaces the causes of the evils rampant in the world. These are no reasons to abandon morality or science, but reasons to understand and embrace both ever more tenaciously.

Neither is the fact that the world is immensely complicated reason to abandon our commitment to both morality and science. The basic unwholesome alternatives, we have seen, are nihilistic relativism, blind, irrational fundamentalism, or dishonest positivism. The absolute mystery that we face with respect to existence and human life is not encountered authentically if we allow ourselves to collapse into nihilism. For the more deeply we encounter the mystery, the more deeply we understand that existence and human life are something momentous, something vastly important, even if we cannot express quite what is that significance.

The courageous engagement within morality and science (a commitment to truth and to the human project itself) should be a reflection of this sense of the significance of existence, as it was for Marx. The complexity of the world cannot be allowed to paralyze us, even at the dawn of the twenty-first century in the face of a nexus of global crises. Not to act, but to allow things to drift along their present course, will spell suicide for human beings and quite possibly for most life on our planet. We are forced to act on our best and deepest understanding of morality and science, even if many details within the complexity of the world remain opaque to us.

Within the economic, historical, political, cultural, and social dimensions of knowledge, the world has not become less complex but more so. Yet this vast complexity, often encountered as overwhelming by each new student entering college, can be clarified through a conscientious search for fundamental principles. Even with the added difficulties of this task introduced through postmodern relativism, some concrete principles emerge if we repeatedly ask ourselves, "What are the most fundamental issues? Which facts are the most basic? What is most basic to my being born as a human being? How can I encounter the living truth of my situation as a human being?" Or, as Kant expressed the most fundamental questions: "What may I know? How should I act? What may I hope?"

Struggle with these basic questions is no longer a philosophical luxury but has become an historical necessity. We have entered the period of the limit conditions of existence on this planet. We can no longer afford the luxury of sinking into nihilism, nor of perpetual search through the vast and beautiful wilderness of human knowledge. We must search for the most fundamental principles, discover them as best we can, and act on them, in time to turn around the historical movement of human beings on this planet toward ever more barbaric forms of truncated existence leading toward possible extinction.

I contend that the means for doing this are available if we muster the courage for action. These means come from many sources, ancient and modern, but some of the most fundamental principles were provided by the work of Marx and his followers through the development of what today is called "critical social theory." Critical theory, we saw in Chapter Three, is a necessary component of planetary maturity.

2. Defining "Critical Social Theory"

Critical theory involves, first of all, "theory." It concerns achieving a scientific, historical, and cultural understanding of human existence. "Theory" is a fundamental term of the sciences, a term that in large measure indicates the drive toward understanding the world. But critical theory is also "critical," and this in at least three fundamental senses. First, its understanding does not pretend to some Olympian neutrality standing above the misery and suffering of human existence. The vast misery and suffering that encompasses the lives of most people on the planet, today and throughout history, bears directly on myself in my efforts to be authentically human (see Taylor, 1991). These efforts are inseparable from the quest to social-scientifically understand human existence. My sense of the significance of human life is outraged by the world of death and misery that our institutions have created and continue to create. The drive of critical theory toward understanding revolves around a compassionate involvement with human existence.

Secondly, "critical" means that understanding focuses on penetrating the appearances of our economic, social, political, and cultural existence with the goal of human liberation. All science rests on some form of distinction between "appearance" and "reality." My compassionate involvement with human existence leads me to apply this distinction to economic, political, social, and cultural forms, as well as to nature. How can we critically penetrate the appearances generated by these forms with the goal of creating a world free of unnecessary suffering, misery, and death? In present society, the system of world-wide suffering is legitimated by the false consciousness of the majority of people, a false consciousness promoted by those who control the means of mass communication and the dissemination of the legitimating ideology (see Brueggemann, 1988).

This ideology veils the arbitrary and unjust power relations of modern industrial societies beneath legitimating propagandistic slogans speaking of free enterprise, human rights, democracy, equality, security, or the desire for peace. Yet as philosophers David Ingram and Julia Simon-Ingram declare:

> To understand the 'truth' implicit in their 'false' consciousness of capital-ism's contradictions requires a deeper philosophical reflection on the total-ity of society itself. Above all, it involves reflecting on the very cultural ide-als that legitimate existing domination in order to determine their potential for realization given existing levels of technological development. Once enlightened about their real interests and the prospects for satisfying them, people will be freed from the compulsion of social habits based on false consciousness. (1992, p. xxix)

Philosophy, as critical theoretical reflection on the social appearance and ideological justifications of the existing order, is crucial to any process of liberation. Marx continually distinguished the way things appear in our social-economic lives from the essential relations of production themselves, the real relations behind the appearances. The relations generate appearances that obscure the true relationships: "These imaginary expressions are, nevertheless, from the relations of production themselves," Marx writes in *Capital*. "They are categories for the forms of appearance of essential relations. That in their appearance things are often presented in an inverted way is something fairly familiar in every science, apart from political economy" (1990, p. 677). Scientists routinely make distinctions of this form and look for the reality behind the appearances. Yet for many mainstream academics, this is not typically done within the fields of political science, sociology, philosophy, or economics, within which (consciously or unconsciously) an ideology is generated: directed to obscuring and justifying the exploitative basis of capitalist society.

Third, critical theory is "critical," as we saw, in that it advocates action to transform the world. Our knowledge is not neutral but must be used compassionately to promote human liberation (see Holland and Henriot, 1993). The point of a critical theory, in the famous eleventh thesis of Marx quoted above, involves not merely understanding the world but changing it in the direction of a rational, free community of persons who collectively promote one another's happiness and self-realization. In Habermasian terms, critical theory transforms society in the direction of "the democratic formation of a common identity under conditions of perfect freedom and reciprocity" (1992, p. xxxi).

Finally, critical social theory involves an attempt on the part of human beings to become "self-conscious" actors and producers within the framework of social life on planet Earth. Capitalism exhibits a form of life that treats social phenomena (the so-called laws of production, exchange, and consumption) as if they were laws of nature. Most people within this system are genuinely unconscious of what is happening around them economically, socially, and politically. The attempt to place the imperative for socialism (already recognized by the "utopian socialists") on a "scientific" basis includes this effort to become more fully self-aware social subjects. Roslyn Wallach Bologh underlines this fundamental aspect of Marx's thought:

> Marx formulates history from within a form of life characterized by the possibility of self-conscious community.... He reads history in terms of repressed community (capitalism) versus natural community (pre-capitalism) and self-conscious community (post-capitalism).... This is how I interpret Marx's concept of socialism – a self-consciously social mode of (re)production, (comm)unity as a historical accomplishment not conceived as external to the members and their activity. (1979, pp. 237 and 239)

In Chapter Seven, we saw Krishnamurti underline our lack of attention to the workings of our minds, leading to ego-directed greed, fear, and compulsive behavior. We also saw that social change likewise requires a deeper level of awareness. The propaganda-advertising system under capitalism works to prevent this (see Smith, 2003b, ch. 3). Bologh understands Marx's vision of a "self-conscious community," a community designing institutions to serve human beings and their highest possibilities. Capitalism is the "repressed" community that actively works to repress our highest possibilities, for realization of these possibilities would mean the end of the ruling class and its complement, the nation-state (see Marcuse, 1962). "Socialism" does not necessarily mean state ownership of the means of production. Its deepest meaning involves a society eliminating the obstacles to our higher human possibilities (capitalism and the nation-state) and acting to create institutions that encourage these possibilities.

The origins of each of these aspects of critical theory are found in the works of Marx, who understood the inseparability of social scientific understanding and normative considerations. Critical theory builds on the Marxist project and extends it to contemporary social developments. It begins with Marx's thought, not dogmatically, but critically transforms that thought in the quest for liberation. Critical theorist Max Horkheimer writes that "the Marxist categories of class, exploitation, surplus value, profit, pauperization, and breakdown are elements in a conceptual whole, and the meaning of this whole is to be sought not in the preservation of contemporary society but in its transformation into the right kind of society" (1995, p. 218).

Critical theory is a form of political action. It does not operate under the lie of "objective, detached, apolitical" social science. It seeks, through the exposure of patterns of domination and exploitation and their ideological cover-up, to inspire others to political action. Philosopher David Held affirms that for critical theory "the purpose...is to analyze and expose the hiatus between the actual and the possible, between the existing order of contradictions and a potential future state. Theory must be oriented, in short, to the development of consciousness and the promotion of active political involvement" (1980, p. 22).

Therefore, to be "critical," means at once something scientific (to penetrate the appearances), something broadly normative (to direct our knowledge to the causes of human suffering and the possibilities implicit in the historical present) and, finally, something proactive (to use our knowledge to effect political action directed toward human liberation). Yet many versions of critical theory exist, although they all perhaps could be said to perceive the oppressive nature of the capitalist system and direct thought and action toward socialism of one form or another. The crucial point is not which version of critical theory a person holds, but that one's life embraces the quest for critical understanding coupled with normative action. In spite of our basic reaction to patterns of exploitation, dehumanization, and domination that are revealed as the ideological veil is lifted, critical theory has yet to fully philosophically elaborate the ethical-spiritual standards behind its critique of capitalism. I hope this book contributes to this project (see Pusey, 1993, p. 34).

The methods and insights developed by Marx provide many of the tools necessary to begin forging a critical understanding in relation to our contemporary global situation. We must appropriate what is valuable in his legacy, as with any other great thinker, and creatively apply it to our current historical situation. And perhaps the most important thing Marx provided was "critical theory" itself, as defined above, as a way of being in the world, synthesizing the moral and the scientific dimensions of our lives. This approach to life makes possible our being authentically human through involvement with the compassionate transformation of our world in the direction of equality, justice, freedom, and dignity.

As Douglas Kellner expresses this, commenting on the thought of Marcuse, "critical theory is to define the highest human potentialities and to criticize society in terms of whether it furthers the development and realization of these potentialities, or their constriction and repression. The ultimate goal and fundamental interest of critical theory is a free and happy humanity in a rational society. What is at stake is the liberation of human beings and the development of their potentialities" (1984, p. 122).

The situation with respect to the variety of critical theories developed during and after Marx's lifetime parallels the situation with respect to Kant and his interpreters. Most thinkers recognize Kant as a great turning point in the history of thought. His insight that there must be perceptual and conceptual presuppositions for the very possibility of experience stimulated a vast revolution in thought and engendered new ways of understanding ourselves and our human situation. Yet many of Kant's interpreters repudiate his specific account of these perceptual and conceptual presuppositions and have posed several differing accounts of what makes human experience possible. Nevertheless, his world-historical insight that something must be presupposed if we are to account for any possible experience remains fundamental to reflecting on our human situation, even when the details of his specific account have been called into question.

The case is similar with Marx. He labored for many years to develop what he and Friedrich Engels called a "scientific socialism." This socialism did not repudiate the goals of the "utopian" socialists who preceded Marx. Marx recognizes the greatness of these thinkers who attempted to conceive of human life within its proper moral framework of justice, equality, and freedom. Yet "scientific socialism" has superseded the utopians, Marx writes, "not because the working class had given up the end aimed at by these utopians, but because they had found the real means to realize them" (Miranda, 1986, p. 149). The "real means" to realize the goal of equality, justice, and freedom involves historical and scientific analysis of the concrete conditions of human life under capitalism, just as the real means to develop air travel involves concrete study of aerodynamics, strength of materials, propulsion, and so on. As Engels wrote in 1880:

> The earlier socialism certainly criticized the existing capitalist mode of production and its consequences. But it could not explain this mode of production, and, therefore, could not get the mastery of it. It could only simply reject it as evil. The more violently it denounced the exploitation for the working class, which is inseparable from capitalism, the less able was it clearly to show in what this exploitation consists and how it arises. But for this it was necessary, on the one hand, to present the capitalist mode of production in its historical interconnection and its necessity for a specific historical period, and therefore also the necessity of its doom; and, on the other, to lay bare its essential character which was still hidden. (Miranda, 1986, 148)

Marx created the social-scientific project of critical economic and historical analysis of the capitalist mode of production in order to expose the exploitation hidden beneath its appearances, just as Kant had created the philosophical project of searching for the presuppositions of any possible experience. These projects were more difficult than the genius of Marx or Kant imagined, yet both retain tremendous significance for understanding the human situation to this day. The transformative project of "scientific socialism" created by Marx has not in the slightest been "disproved by history" or by "mistakes in Marx's specific analyses" of history or economics. Moral outrage at the brutal, inhuman world in which we live is insufficient, Marx and Engels argued, to create a better world.

The goal of utopian socialism is correct, but it was missing scientific understanding of the means. As Maximilien Rubel and Margaret Manale express this:

> At the center of his writing was an ethical force: the postulate that human society or social humanity should ultimately result from technological progress, that man's barbaric prehistory would be superseded by an era of human self-realization. It was not because he fortuitously reread Hegel's Logic that Marx predicted the inevitable fall of an economic system based on profit and the simultaneous construction of a classless, stateless, and moneyless society, but because he was filled with the hopes and dreams of a Saint-Simon, a Robert Owen, a Fourier. (1976, p. xi)

Yet we have seen that Marx underestimated the complexity of capitalism and the difficulty of giving a complete account of the mechanisms of this system.

Nevertheless, we need careful social-scientific, economic and historical analyses that will pinpoint how exploitation and dehumanization occur, how they are foundational to the capitalist system itself, and how we might create a new system with economic, political, and cultural relationships that truly foster justice, equality, freedom, and dignity. As with Kant, Marx provides human beings with a vast step forward in that self-understanding that is a necessary ingredient in the realization of human freedom. As Richard J. Bernstein says of the tradition of critical theory since Marx, "what I take to be most central in this tradition is the way it attempts to at once recover and defend the critical moment or impulse required for any adequate social and political theorizing" (1978, p. 174).

As with Kant, the profundity and value of Marx's revolutionary creation of "scientific socialism" does not depend on the truth or falsity of this or that specific claim made by Marx. His methodological and systematic approach to understanding the capitalist system lays the groundwork for an adequate social and political theory and for the realization of a world system whose foundational economic, political, and cultural principles foster genuine human freedom and dignity.

Several "Marxisms" or "critical theories" have appeared, some even before Marx's death in 1883. Others did not appear in print until well into the twentieth century. Some of these Marxisms exhibit a clear misreading of Marx's writings; others, like those of Lenin and Stalin, were versions of Marxism adapted to the specific historical requirements of revolution and power struggles within individual countries and within the system of nation-states. Still others developed based on the intellectual impact of Freud's understanding of the unconscious. Others developed through a creative engagement with changing circumstances such as the growing power of ideology over the human mind as the capitalists consolidated control over the mass media and developed new forms of mass media (such as television and film) that made their grip over human thought ever more powerful and insidious.

It should be clear from our situation of global crisis at the dawn of the twenty-first century, that our task transcends petty partisan politics of all sorts, whether bourgeois or Marxist, to focus on what Marx and others can contribute to our concrete, scientific understanding the impending doom that we face on this planet. For the more we understand the world system that has evolved over the past five centuries, the more it becomes clear that unless we make fundamental changes in our economic, political, cultural, and spiritual relations to one another, and in the system that perpetuates these relations, there will no longer be a viable planet for our children to inherit. Some significant theoretical issues do confront critical social theorists, and I do not want to minimize this fact. But the maturing of critical theory must mean that we unite in the effort to realize a democratic socialist world society, instead of spending our energy in secondary squabbles.

My purpose here is not to provide an account of the final, correct interpretation of Marx. This would contradict the scientific, experimental, and investigative nature of Marx's work to assume that he intended to create a final system of truths. As Rubel and Manale put it, "Every interpretation of Marx's intellectual achievements which lays claim to the discovery of a new system of thought or philosophy necessarily amounts to a fundamental perversion of his actual intentions" (1976, p. x). Nor is my purpose here to defend a certain school of critical theory, say that of Horkheimer, Adorno, Marcuse, or Habermas. Marx, attempted to be at once as socially scientific as possible (and faithful to the truth of the human condition) and to be the great defender of human freedom and dignity.

A truly critical insight requires social science and the pursuit of truth in that we must develop the ability to see beneath the ideological surface of society (and the limited reality of its political freedoms) to the exploitative and coercive relations beneath. A critical insight also invites us to investigate institutional arrangements that truly foster human freedom and dignity. But a truly critical insight also involves a creative use of these truths, in relation to a person's particular society and position in history, in the service of human liberation. Human liberation, we have seen, can only mean a simultaneous transformation of consciousness and institutions.

Therefore, a second insight is required, as we saw, and the two together serve to make all truly critical insight transformative. For a critical thinker sees the moral principle that human beings are ends-in-themselves, and that a global society must be created (through the actions of free human beings as the agents of history) based on human equality, freedom, and dignity. This insight complements the "scientific" understanding that sees beneath of ideology of contemporary society to the mechanisms of exploitation and dehumanization that in effect (despite the political advances of bourgeois society vis-à-vis most earlier societies) deny human equality, freedom, and dignity. We must move forward rapidly to a self-conscious mode of social existence: spiritually, ethically, and scientifically.

3. Marx on Reform versus Revolution

Political democracy reflects a crucial development on the way toward a truly human society. But it remains merely abstract and formal within a system that dominates the lives of all with the imperatives of capital (and destroys the lives of the masses of exploited and unemployed in the third-world because of these same imperatives). True democracy, however, cannot exist unless the material conditions for democracy develop to the point where people no longer need be dominated by the struggle for physical survival.

Once this point is reached (with the advent of computers and automation this point has already been technologically reached for the entire planet), human beings must inaugurate a "higher form of society" that will finally allow the principles of democracy to come to fruition. Capitalism must be abolished if a transition to authentic democracy is to occur. In Volume One of *Capital,* Marx writes of the capitalist:

> He is fanatically intent on the valorization of value expand itself; consequently he ruthlessly forces the human race to produce for production's sake. In this way he spurs the development of society's productive forces, and the creation of those material conditions of production which alone can form the real basis of a higher form of society, a society in which the full and free development of every individual forms the ruling principle. (1990, p. 739)

Modern political democracies under capitalism consist of a number of living contradictions. One such contradiction involves the fact that people have political freedom, usually through a constitutionally guaranteed and institutionalized set of political rights, but do not have economic freedom. Instead, they are subjected to "blind market forces," economic exploitation, and social domination throughout their lives. At the center of their lives, in which they socially cooperate in order to earn their living, people are debased and dehumanized. In their "free" time, when they are resting to return to work, they are politically free (although constrained in such a way that there can be no effective change to this system through the mechanisms provided by the system, such as voting).

In "On the Jewish Question," Marx wrote: *"Political* emancipation certainly represents a great progress. It is not the final form of human emancipation, but it is the final form of human emancipation within the prevailing social order. It goes without saying, that we are speaking here of real, practical emancipation" (1978, p. 35). But a step forward is not fulfillment. No fulfillment is possible until the "ruling principle" of social, economic, and political organization becomes the "full and free development of every individual." This represents a level of human existence presently negated by the capitalist mode of production that drives at the accumulation of surplus value, not at the free development of every human being. The 1879 "Circular Letter" from Marx and Engels argues against movements within the Socialist Party that would make the movement reformist rather than revolutionary:

> The programme is not to be *given up* but only *postponed* – for an indefinite

period. One accepts it, though not really for oneself and one's own lifetime but posthumously, as an heirloom to be handed down to one's children and grandchildren. In the meantime one devotes one's "whole strength and energy" to all sorts of trifles and the patching up of the capitalist order of society so as to produce at least the appearance of something happening without at the same time scaring the bourgeoisie. (Miranda, 1986, pp. 274-5).

Here we see the basic distinction between critical theory and merely liberal thought. Liberal thought does not have an insight into the dynamics of exploitation at the heart of all capitalist relationships. It dreams of progress within the disconnected series of surface appearances and insights into specific abuses, and, while its moral consciousness may lead it to address these abuses (through campaign reform, environmental laws, and so on); it holds the naive hope that the system can be reformed or evolved through incremental changes. Marx held that incremental progress could be made, but only within the limits set by the system itself. But to move from the partial, class-based realization of human freedom in political democracies to the flowering of human freedom in authentic democracy required a society founded on entirely different assumptions. In his Inaugural Address of the International Working Men's Association of 1864 Marx writes:

This struggle about the legal restriction of the hours of labour raged and more fiercely since, apart from frightened avarice, it told indeed upon the great contest between the blind rule of the supply and demand laws which from the political economy of the middle class, and social production controlled by social foresight, which forms the political economy of the working class. Hence the Ten Hours Bill was not only a great practical success; it was the victory of a principle; it was the first time that in broad daylight the political economy of the middle class succumbed to the political economy of the working class. (1978, p. 517)

We see once more that limited progress within capitalist society is possible. Any decent law limiting the negative effects of "the blind rule of the supply and demand laws" serves as an example of "the political economy of the working class" based on "social foresight," on intelligent planning directed toward the welfare of human beings having equality and dignity. This principle of social foresight reflects an essential feature of human freedom in which human beings as agents of history fashion the conditions of their existence. By contrast, the essential feature of the political economy of the middle class (of capitalism) reflects the denial of freedom: "the blind supply and demand laws" in which even human beings are commodified as "labor" to be purchased or laid off in the service of profit as the laws of supply and demand dictate.

The capitalist system is predicated on these supply and demand laws, on the social relation between owner and worker in which the owner may exploit the worker for profit and lay off the worker when no more profit is to be made. When human beings serve these deterministic laws of unfreedom, their ability to live lives predicated on equality, freedom, and dignity is severely compromised (even, we will see, if they are making decent wages). Some progress can be made within this framework, but never a full realization of freedom. We have seen Marx say that "political emancipation...is the last form of human emancipation *within* the prevailing system." Only a transformation of the "system" (from capitalism to a system based on "social foresight") can lead to "general human emancipation."

Marx did not predict (at least in his mature works of the 1850s and beyond) the increasing pauperization of the working class leading to a revolution founded on their desperation and hunger. For he said that wages might rise and were in no sense at the heart of the matter. Instead, he predicted the increasing disproportion between the power of capital (as it grows into ever vaster concentrations) and the power of the workers whom capital exploits (Miranda, 1986, pp. 6-11). This has in fact happened, so that in our day some trans-national corporations control assets greater than some nation-states, and in our day entire governments are controlled or blackmailed by these corporations as they threaten to move elsewhere in the world with their vast resources if legal conditions are not provided to their satisfaction.

We have discussed the devastation wrought in the world today by the power and greed of these corporations. But the fact of their being powerful and greedy does not reflect the heart of the need for transformation. For the use of these adjectives might make it seem as if there could exist concentrations of private wealth that were not powerful and greedy, or at least not greedy. Two points need to be made here.

First, corporations under capitalism are institutions, not persons, devoted to the accumulation of private profit. As such, "greed" factors into the system. Any corporation not successful in the systematic drive for profit will lose investors, and ultimately fail (or be rescued by the tax-payers in the form of a government bail-out, through public give-aways for the sake of private accumulation). "By showing that greed presupposes money," Bologh writes, "Marx shows greed to be an historical as opposed to a natural phenomenon. This is not to say that greed is unnatural or deviant, but that its possibility derives not from an ahistorical human nature but from an historical, social development" (1979, p. 76).

Second, under the capitalist system, even if we could imagine a "non-greedy" corporation (say one that wanted only a "modest" return on its investments), we could not have a non-exploitative corporation. The only way of getting any return on investments involves the exploitation of resources, human labor power, and monopolization of markets. Therefore, the need for power, domination, and exploitation of nature and persons factors into the system. For labor, this means workers only live if they agree to produce a profit for the owners by working a portion of the day for free. The system prevents corporations from contributing to the common good in any meaningful sense. Even a "modest" return on investments means externalizing environmental and other costs to the society that bears the ultimate costs of supporting this system.

This relation cannot evolve into a truly self-aware and beneficent system without abolishing the relation itself. That most modern societies are built on this relation of exploitation of human beings by other human beings disintegrates human relationships, fosters crime, destroys communities, encourages dishonesty and hypocrisy, exacerbates scape-goating through racism, and so on. It prevents human beings from forming communities in which people cooperate to the mutual benefit of all members of the community. The subtle spirit of competition, rather than cooperation for the good of all, is insinuated into citizens from birth.

Only institutional transformation can establish a society based on the mutual dignity, respect, and community of all its citizens. Only a socialist society, in which the power of exploitation is legally abolished (and abolished on moral grounds that such forms of veiled "slavery" are wrong), realizes justice and equality for all, not only in name but in substance. Institutional transformation does not mean "violent overthrow" or social chaos, as we have seen. It means most fundamentally creating a new planetary human system based on the moral dimension of human equality, freedom, and dignity, something that has never yet fully existed in history. These goals are not "pious ideals" but our deepest human reality that will only emerge with the founding of a rational, free world society.

4. Marx's "Materialism" and Morality

Marx was a "materialist" in a special sense of this word, one in the last analysis compatible with both ethics and religion (properly understood). Some schools of Marxism and some schools of anti-Marxism have misread him in this respect. Marx continually repudiates the sense of the word "materialism" that suggests physical indulgence, concern only with filling the belly and with sensuous pleasures in life, or concern for the physical as opposed to the "spiritual" or "cultural" dimensions of life.

He also repudiates the traditional metaphysical materialism

originating with philosophers like Democritus or Epicurus with their assertion that "only matter exists" and no "non-physical entities" exist. This tradition culminates in the modern metaphysical materialists of the eighteenth and nineteenth centuries, some of whom even claimed to be followers of Marx. Even though he often contrasts his materialism to the "lofty idealism of the bourgeois political economy" (Miranda, 1986, p.4), Marx is not in a struggle over metaphysical world views. In some respects, Marx anticipates Wittgenstein in that he is struggling out of metaphysics and attempting to deal with the concrete world of the everyday.

In *Marx Against the Marxists*, José Miranda accomplishes significant work toward illuminating what Marx meant by "materialism" and demonstrating its compatibility with ethics and religion, properly understood.   The central motive for a socialist revolution does not involve hunger alone, according to Marx, nor a growing immiseration of the working classes. He argues that the lot of the working classes may improve through unionization, labor laws, or even a voluntary increase in wages from employers. The central motive of the revolution is ethical: the continued existence of a system of exploitation. Although capitalism contains internal contradictions that militate against its continued existence (and in our day government acts so as to mitigate the crises and effects of these contradictions), "the real, solid motive for revolution," Miranda says, is that for Marx "capitalism is unjust and that communism is the realization of justice" (1986, p. 18).

Private ownership of the planet, for Marx, appears as absurd as it was for the American Indians. Chief Seattle represents the American Indian view when he wrote to President Pierce in 1854 observing that the white man was destroying the land, the waters, and the beauty of the Earth in pursuit of profit: "How can you buy or sell the sky, the warmth of the land? The idea is strange to us.... The white man....treats his mother, the Earth, and his brother, the sky, as things to be bought, plundered, sold like sheep or bright beads. His appetite will devour the Earth and leave behind only a desert" (Fahey and Armstrong, 1992, pp. 153-154).

Similarly, Marx writes:

> From the standpoint of a higher economic form of society, private owner-
> ship of the globe by single individuals will appear quite as absurd as private
> ownership of one man by another. Even a whole society, a nation, or even
> all simultaneously existing societies taken together are not the owners of the
> globe. They are only its possessors...and...must hand it down to succeeding
> generations in an improved condition. (Miranda, 1986, p.18)

For Marx, private ownership is like the institution of slavery in more than one way. First, the fact of its existence is no justification, since the justification for human social arrangements must be a moral one. In *Capital,* Marx writes:

> The same justification would then apply also to slavery, since for the slaveowner who has paid cash for his slaves, the product of their labour simply represents the interest on the capital invested in their purchase. To derive a justification for the existence of ground-rent from its purchase and sale is nothing more than justifying its existence by its existence. (1991, p. 762)

The argument against slavery rests on moral grounds such as the dignity, freedom, and equality of all human beings. The fact of an existing institution of slavery accepted by society, the fact that people have purchased other human beings and used them for a return on their investments, presents no argument for slavery. Similarly, the fact that private corporations have purchased much of the Earth, and used the resources of the Earth for a return on their investments, gives no argument for private ownership. We can see here how thoroughly Marx repudiates positivism. Social arrangements require moral justifications, and so does our treatment of nature and other creatures. Marx presupposes here that owning other human beings in slavery is morally outrageous, and that the argument for the abolition of private ownership of the Earth (and the capitalist system in general) is that it too is morally outrageous.

The core of the morally outrageous nature of capitalism lies in the fact that it too is a "system of slavery" or exploitation of human beings by other human beings. The worker is paid a wage for working so many hours. Yet a value equivalent to the worker's wages is produced by the worker after only a portion of the hours he or she is required to work, say five hours out of an eight hour day. The rest of the value the worker produces during the day becomes profit for the employer. The worker must, as a condition of keeping a job, work part of the day for free to increase the capital of the owner in the form of profit.

In the *Critique of the Gotha Programme* (1875) Marx writes:

> It was made clear that the wage worker has permission to work for his own subsistence, *to live*, only in so far as he works for certain time gratis for the capitalist (and hence also for the latter's consumers of surplus value).... that, consequently, the system of wage labour is a system of slavery,...whether the worker receives better or worse payment. (1978, p. 535)

The moral comparison of capitalism to traditional slavery appears frequently in all periods of Marx's writings, early to late.

Note that Marx finds it irrelevant whether the worker is well paid or ill paid for the work. Even well paid workers remain in a relation of exploitation in which the owners are making a profit from the labor of others. As Miranda sums up this issue, for Marx:

> Capitalism consists in the fact that the proletariat are not permitted to labor to maintain themselves – to live, in other words – unless they agree to labor for nothing a certain number of hours during the day in order to enrich the capitalist. Since the capitalists are owners of the means of labor, they are the ones who give or refuse permission to labor.... It does not matter here whether the means of production were acquired properly or improperly (though in fact they were acquired improperly). What is certain is that I am not permitted to produce the necessaries I need to live unless I agree to work gratis for the enrichment of the wealthy. Now this is in fact slavery, and the fact that I am well fed does not change the situation one bit. (1986, p. 27)

We confront here the principle motive for institutional transformation according to Marx. He repudiates positivism, for capitalists and materialists. The fact that a certain system exists and we have done it this way for generations involves no justification. If internal contradictions within capitalism (or "laws of history," discoverable by science) portend its demise, these also simply reflect more facts and advance no justification for transformative action on the part of human beings. Marx soundly rejects such gross utilitarianism.

Human beings should relate to one another as moral agents, as ends-in-themselves, and not use one another as objects or commodities. Like slavery, capitalism does just this (treats persons as commodities), and despite the idealistic rhetoric through which it functions within a political system claiming that "all persons are created equal," it is in effect another system of slavery. We saw above that political emancipation, for Marx, was a great step forward. But for the slave to have the right to vote (while the legislature is in fact controlled by big money and power and his thought processes are controlled by those who own the means of communication) does not change his condition of slavery one iota.

The most fundamental contradiction within capitalism, for Marx, does not serve as a deterministic mechanism moving the world ineluctably toward socialism. The central contradiction is a moral one. Human beings are ends-in-themselves, free subjects, and should exist in a society that is organized around this principle. Yet capitalism, which espouses this principle in its democratic- political rhetoric, reflects a system that treats human beings as commodities who are used by capital for the production of profit for the owners. The human community does not yet manifest self-consciousness in the sense required by planetary maturity. Full awareness of the principle of unity-in-diversity that is the basis of nature and human life would transform the world socially, politically, and economically.

This moral contradiction at the heart of capitalism serves as the source of Marx's repeated evaluative remarks about the "commodification," "dehumanization," "alienation," and "exploitation" of human beings under this system. This contradiction will not be worked out through "iron laws of history" but through the free action of human beings in history to create a society for the first time based on human beings as ends-in-themselves. Our human potential cannot be predicated on the good of some particular class of persons in control of the system of exploitation and dehumanization of the rest. As Miranda asserts, the motive for the revolution is a moral one.

"Materialism," for Marx, means critical social theory that examines the concrete, historically conditioned, social relations of human beings as objectively and scientifically as possible. This materialism does not conflict in the least with the expanded definition of "critical theory" given in the first sections of this chapter. As Bologh explains: "Nature, for Marx, is always a particular nature understood as such in relation to a particular subject. Nature is not nature in the abstract external to social relations or production" (1979, p. 90). The point of the analysis includes human liberation, and some forms of spirituality and religion are necessary for full human liberation. Since a society must be founded on liberating principles, on human beings as ends-in-themselves, reform of capitalism is not possible and transformation is our only option.

"Morality," for Marx, is the motivation at the heart of critical social theory: human liberation in the form of a global society premised, or founded, on freedom, dignity, equality, and justice for all persons. For Marx, there is no positivistic, value-neutral "natural world" with "economic and social laws" to which human beings must conform, like it or not. In the quote at the head of this chapter Marx says "man must prove the truth, that is, the reality and power, the this-sidedness of his thinking in practice." We live within a vast human community on planet Earth. Through self-conscious, critical activity informed by ethical principles, we can rapidly transform our world toward a practical utopia.

Ernst Bloch, at the head of this chapter, asserts this same idea. Our human "conscience....first and foremost...provides the *standard* to measure such facticity precisely as departure from the Right." The world of "facts" is judged according to whether it is a "departure from the Right." This alone will lead toward a society of planetary maturity, of unity-in-diversity. Critical social theory, since the time of Marx, has been maturing, theoretically and practically.

Many in this movement today understand the inseparability of the ethical dimension and the theoretical dimension within a self-conscious *praxis* of liberation. In Chapter Seven, we saw Michael Luntley define socialism as "a theory about how the good life is possible. It is, in short, a theory about the conditions necessary for creating a society in which our lives are shaped by moral values." The Marxist tradition informed by ethical understanding, deep compassion, and careful theoretical reasoning forms another necessary component in the process of human liberation. Not only is critical theory in the process of maturing, but critical theory is fundamental to the development of planetary maturity for human beings.

Chapter Nine

The Nightmare of Monopoly Capitalism
and the Dream of Democratic Socialism

*All the greatest and most important problems of life are fundamentally insoluble....
They can never be solved, but only outgrown. This "outgrowing" proved on
further investigation to require a new level of consciousness. Some higher or
wider interest appeared on the patient's horizon, and through this broadening
of his or her outlook the insoluble problem lost its urgency. It was not solved
logically in its own terms but faded when confronted with a new and stronger life
urge.*

Carl Gustav Jung

*To speak of all those things, however, is to dream, in the good sense of the word:
that is, to believe in the existence of a poetic and utopian function in every human
being. To concretize these dreams, to render them viable, already means engaging
in politics – and in politics on a grand scale, in the most fundamental sense. It is
remarkable that in one sense the true curve of affairs is as follows. For economics
to be human, it must be related to politics; that is, it must rest on intelligent political
choices, which are abandoned neither to the whim of the marketplace nor to the
stifling rigor of planning. But in its turn, politics must be attached to mysticism;
that is, to people's capacity to dream of a new world. Mental representations of
justice and fraternity, implicit moral codes, are indispensable to the functioning
of societies.*

Dominique Barbé

*Nicaragua, journal entry, 16 May 1996. The level of poverty that we have seen
here defies the imagination and leaves one sick inside. We visited a woman in San
José de Bocay two days ago with nine children, no husband, and no shoes on her
feet. She works a small plot back in the rugged hills and lives in a dirt floor open
air shack on the back side of town. A tiny, illiterate, hard working human being
who lives from day to day, from hand to mouth, who owns nothing, not even an
aspirin to lessen the pain of her daily struggle to survive.*

*Today we traveled into the countryside to meet Mercedes' mother.
Mercedes is one of the many young people in this area befriended and helped by
Gary, who lives in Nicaragua and is serving as our guide. Today happens to be
Mercedes' birthday. She was so excited that Gary and his friends (we) were going
with her to visit her mother that two days ago she walked the two hours walk out
into the country to tell her mother we were coming.*

The poor do not have birthdays here. There are no records and no one remembers or notices them. The only reason Mercedes has one is that several years ago, when she was a young girl about 12, Gary asked her to pick a day and remember it every year. She is now 18 and is proud to be a person who has a real birthday. Her pride at having a real birthday, I imagine, may be because it is a clue to her that, despite all evidence to the contrary, she has dignity as a human being.

Mercedes' mother lives in a dirt floor shack about one half mile from the nearest dirt road and about two hours walk from Bocay. There is nothing in the house: one stool and two make shift benches. An adobe oven, openings for doors, ramshackle boards and ragged plastic sheeting for walls. Electricity or any kind of appliances are undreamed of here. Her only kitchen tool is an old machete. There are a few odd cups and dishes. No food, no cupboards, no sink, not even an outhouse - nothing. Excretion is done out in the bushes beyond the perimeters of the clearing. Toilet paper is leaves from these same bushes.

They carry water in plastic buckets 300 yards from a stream in a nearby gully. The food they prepared for us and the Kool Aid they served us were all from what we had brought as gifts. No other food was visible anywhere. There were a couple of pigs and a few chickens running freely around the house. All the other shacks dotting this area are basically the same. This is the way most people in the countryside live in Nicaragua.

Such poverty, found everywhere we have stayed in Nicaragua - in Jinotepe, Managua, Bocay, and now in the countryside – is a crime against humanity. It cries out for socialism and is a blight on the existence of all the rich. By "rich" I do not mean only the big corporations raping the natural resources of Nicaragua and exploiting their poverty for cheap labor. They are only the obvious ones. Rather, I mean 60% of the people in the first world, by "rich" I mean you and I, ordinary middle class people whose self-satisfied ignorance of their misery is an integral part of our crimes against humanity.

The very existence of such human misery as is found in the so called "third" and "fourth" worlds is a moral blight on our existence. Anyone who supports capitalism and so called "free enterprise" is wittingly or unwittingly complicit in the slow torture and death of these hundreds of millions of people who have nothing and are valued at nothing by the capitalist system.

Glen T. Martin

The capitalism that devastated the lives of countless millions of people in the industrialized countries of the West from the seventeenth to early twentieth centuries is not the "advanced" capitalism that currently dominates the global economy. This "advanced" capitalism is perpetuating the nightmare of human and ecological devastation that has been going on for the past five centuries, but for the first time in history it has attained domination over the entire globe. Therefore, "advanced" capitalism can be described in terms of its monopolistic control over the planet and its future.

1. Systematic Monopolization of Economic, Political, Ideological, and Military Power

Economist Samir Amin has identified five features or "monopolies" that characterize today's capitalism, whose financial, commercial and productive markets now have a global reach: (1) a monopoly over technology, chiefly through military research, (2) monetary control of worldwide financial markets, unprecedented in world history, (3) monopolistic access to the planet's natural resources, (4) media and communication monopolies that have led to the "erosion of democratic practices in the West," and (5) monopolies over weapons of mass destruction (meaning, I would add, that the capitalist class in control of nation-states is now holding the planet itself hostage to its rapacious practices) (1997, pp. 4-5).

"Advanced" capitalism is not only the neoliberal economic doctrine that forces "structural adjustment" on people who already have next to nothing, privatizing, into the hands of global capital, the few remaining public services to which the poor have access. It is not only the doctrine of third-world debt that forces billions of dollars in debt on ordinary citizens of third-world countries who never borrowed the money in the first place. It is also these five global monopolies, described by Amin, in which control of the fate of our planet and its resources has passed into fewer and fewer hands in the twentieth and twenty-first centuries.

No capitalist enterprise believes in "free trade." All capitalist enterprises attempt to grow faster than the competition in order to (a) put the competition out of business and so enjoy monopoly over the market or (b) absorb and appropriate the competition through buy-outs or mergers so as to enjoy monopoly over the market. Inherent in the very logic of production for private profit is the drive to eliminate free competition as quickly as possible and dominate the wealth-producing process for the benefit of the ownership class. The same is true of the system of nation-states, structured, as we saw, into a world of autonomous territories competing with one another for ascendency and wealth.

In his books *Economic Democracy: The Political Struggle of the Twenty-first Century* (2003a) and *Why? The Deeper History Behind the September 11, 2001 Terrorist Attack on America* (2002), economist J. W. Smith describes the centuries long historical interface between capitalism and the nation-state system. Adam Smith "free trade" has always been a mere ideological ploy, Smith shows, to cover up the reality that every nation has always acted to protect its own markets from competition. Nations get rich through "plunder by trade," through creating systematic advantages for their own capitalist enterprises to the detriment of other nations, never through free and equal competition with capital from other nations (2002b, pp. 22-27). Nation-states strive to control and manipulate markets for their own advantage. They strive to create monopoly conditions for their own capitalist enterprises.

Smith details the history of the "Adam Smith free trade" ideology as a cover for the true maneuvering of nations for advantage and ascendency. The advanced capitalism that today dominates the world (in league with the United States as the dominant imperial nation) operates its system of plunder by trade through four "subtle-monopolies" while simultaneously promoting the ideology of global free trade to the rest of the world. These are the subtle-monopolization of land (2003a, ch. 24), the subtle-monopolization of technology (ch. 25), the subtle-monopolization of money (ch. 26), and the subtle-monopolization of information (ch. 27). These are all "subtle" because their monopoly character is obscured by the "free-trade" rhetoric of their propaganda. These forms of economic domination allowing systematic "plunder by trade" of the world's wealth-creation process suck the natural resources and productive wealth from those who produce (in the poorer regions of the world) into the coffers of those who control these monopolies.

The four monopolies identified by J. W. Smith match the first four monopolies of advanced capitalism identified by Amin. First, for Smith, through unrestricted land titles and the power to appropriate vast tracts of public land (with the aid of government) for private purposes, big capital owns and exploits vast areas of the world that properly belong to the peoples and nations of the world. Amin calls this monopolistic control of the world's "natural resources."

Second, Smith examines the use of the global system of patents (intellectual property rights) to retain monopoly control over technologies that give superior efficiency and power to capital and simultaneously prevent development of poor nations to the point where they might be able to compete with corporations located in the developed world. Amin calls this monopolistic control of technology and links this with his fifth form of monopoly: weapons of mass destruction. Control of technology also means a monopoly on military power and weapons of mass destruction. Smith details the history of military repression in the service of protecting these monopolies of domination and exploitation (2003b, ch. 8).

Third, Smith and Amin agree that a key component in this system of exploitation is control of money. First-world financial institutions perpetuate the myth that only those with prior accumulations of wealth can loan money to those without capital. They perpetuate the myth that only the wealthy governments can create money for use in world trade and markets. If state banks in poor countries create their own money, first-world financial institutions will devalue that currency, making it more and more worthless in relation to the dominant, convertible world currencies (Smith 2003a, ch. 26). The poor must go further and further into unsustainable debt to the rich in a cycle that creates more and more wealth for the rich and greater and greater dependency in the poor. The monopoly on money is a key to global economic domination and exploitation.

Finally, Smith and Amin agree concerning a global media more and more controlled by fewer and fewer hands, concentrated in the developed world. This control of information is absolutely essential for perpetuating the mythologies and lies on which the global system of capitalism is based. The network of lies is interconnected and forms a matrix of interlocking ideas: the lie that Adam Smith free trade is essential to development, the lie that the developed nations believe in democracy, human rights, or economic justice for the world, the lie that only those who are already wealthy can create and control money, the lie that the only workable system of property rights is the absolute private property rights today enjoyed by the rich, the lie that the system of intellectual property rights is an expression of a free marketplace, the lie that military might is exercised out of the need for "self-defense," and, finally, the crucial lie that the mass media believes in free expression in a marketplace of ideas. The result is that every area of human life and every corner of the planet is under the monopoly domination of this system.

Planetary thinker Anthony Mansueto, Jr., describes the consequences of this nexus of monopolies of global capital:

> The penetration of market relations into every sphere of life, in every corner of the planet, is rapidly destroying the ecosystem and the social fabric on which human development and social progress depend, and undermining efforts to centralize the surplus necessary for technological, economic, political, social, and cultural progress. The result is an unprecedented social crisis, in which the vast majority of humanity is rapidly losing hope in its future, and even broader sectors of the population are resorting to random violence or self-destruction. (1995, p. 453)

The monopoly character itself of the global capitalist system must be emphasized, for the solution cannot be reform-directed toward curbing "random violence" or toward creating a better "social safety net." The solution can only be a new order founded on life rather than death. Theologian and philosopher Jürgen Moltmann presents a picture capturing this sense of the totality of a system organized against life that must be transformed as a whole. He quotes from a 1990 document expressing "third-world theology":

"Like a huge idol, like the Beast in the Apocalypse (Rev. 13), the present economic system covers the Earth with its open sewer of unemployment and homelessness, hunger and nakedness, despair and death. It destroys different ways of living and working, which are in antithesis to its own. In its hostility to the environment, it sullies nature. It enforces an alien culture on the peoples which it has conquered. In its insatiable greed for prosperity, it offers people themselves as a sacrifice in a bloody holocaust, pre-eminently in the Third-world but increasingly in the First-world too. The Beast has become a ravening monster, armed to the teeth with tanks and guns, atomic bombs, warships with computer-guided missiles, radar systems and satellites, and it is bringing humanity to the verge of total and sudden annihilation. But in the world-wide struggles of the poor and oppressed against all forms of dehumanization, there is a sign of life and of victory." (1996, p. 216)

This global crisis has not been brought about by an "advanced" capitalism without a history. This monopoly of a system of death over human life must be viewed in terms of its development as an integral part of the modern world of the past five centuries.

2. Historical Evolution of the Capitalist System

Advanced capitalism is an heir of its earlier forms that have evolved through several relatively distinct stages. The first stage involved the conquest and rape of non-European lands and peoples by European conquistadors beginning in the fifteenth century. In the lust for gold and conquest, and to enrich their royal sponsors in the courts of European nation-states, the conquistadors began a genocide of indigenous peoples that continued unabated as the nascent stage of capitalist "primitive accumulation" evolved into the "legal" rule of the conquering powers (Churchill, 1998). The second stage involved the institutionalization of slavery and colonialism by the dominating powers, who imposed exploitative laws on conquered lands (colonies) throughout the world for the next several centuries. These laws forced alien systems on indigenous peoples, systems designed to foster the accumulation process enriching the nation-states and wealthy "investors" in the colonial "ventures."

The third stage in the evolution of capitalism included the industrial revolution, the heyday of individual robber baron capitalists. In the industrial centers vast workers's proletariats lived in unspeakable poverty and misery with a life-expectancy into their 30s. Like the indigenous peoples in conquered lands, their lives were sacrificed to the private accumulation of wealth for the few, and the beginnings of a truly global market system. The workers often organized and fought back against this system of dehumanization and degradation, but as with the first two stages in the evolution of capitalism, the powers of their nation-states defended the ruling elite against the struggles of working people, preserving with their military and police powers the system of private accumulation by the few at the expense of the many.

The fourth stage in this evolution is characterized by the "advanced" capitalism that emerged in the twentieth and twenty-first centuries. Under this global economic system, a core of nation-states representing about ten percent of the world's population use their control of international trade regulations, international financial markets, international debt, and worldwide military supremacy to impose a global system of exploitation on the other ninety percent of the world. The countries representing the majority of the world's population are forced to sell their natural resources and labor of their starving millions cheaply to multinational corporations based in the first-world countries, who hold them hostage under this global arrangement. If people in poor countries do revolt against this system, first-world military or economic power is used to defeat popular movements, overthrow democracies attempting to regain control over their own economies, or destroy guerilla movements through "counter insurgency warfare" (see Dussel, 1990, pp. 9-15).

This is not the only narrative by which this history could be described, nor does this chronology insist that these are distinct "stages" that do not overlap and intertwine with one another. But the central point remains that the wealth sucked from the ravaged civilizations of these conquered peoples immediately entered a system of "law" within the conquering nations. This law, an elaborate system of interconnected principles as is any system of law, grounded itself in the principle that private accumulations of property may legally be used to increase themselves through exploitation of nature and other persons. The wealth stolen from the conquered peoples was inserted into the system of private property and, under this legal system, became itself private property.

The already powerful class structure of the European countries, in which their own poor were dominated and exploited at the whim of those who "owned" land, titles, or positions of power in government or religious hierarchy, was swollen by the pillaged wealth that flowed into the system from the ravaged peoples of the conquests. The character of this class system had evolved from a feudal one into one dominated by capitalists without so much as a break in the historical series of systems of domination and exploitation of the poor by the rich and powerful. And the conquered lands themselves were not ravaged and then left behind merely bleeding and pillaged, instead the system of law from the conquering nations was imposed upon the conquered. Huge estates were formed from the stolen lands of the conquered and became, under the imposed system of foreign

law, the "private property" of the conquerors (Galeano, 1973).
Jürgen Moltmann writes:

> In America and Europe, slave-trading companies were formed. In the Caribbean and in Central and South America the subsistence economy was destroyed and the colonial economy build up, with monocultures for the export of cotton, sugar-cane, rice and tobacco. Africa was "de-developed" economically and politically through the slave trade. "It lasted the better part of four centuries, during which it had involved, by a conservative estimate, the forced migration of fifteen million Negroes, besides causing the death of perhaps thirty or forty million others.... What it had produced in Africa was nothing but misery, stagnation, and social chaos. In England and France - also at a considerable cost of lives – it had created greater accumulations of wealth than had been known in previous centuries, and thus it had played its part in the Industrial Revolution...." According to Galeano, the silver brought to Spain between 1503 and 1660 was more than three times all European reserves. Gold and silver from America generated an accumulation of capital in Europe which was used for investment in industrialization. (1996, pp. 212 & 214)

Today's multi-dimensional monopoly of the global capitalist system is a consequence of five centuries of rape and destruction of nature and human beings worldwide. The conquistadors, the system of slavery, colonial exploitation, and the robber baron super-exploitation of the poor in the mills of France, England, the United States and elsewhere are primary sources of the vast accumulations of wealth that today globally suck the life from the poor and the precious ecological resources from our planet.

The process of vast accumulations of wealth over these centuries intensified the domination of the poor by the rich, but not particularly in the tremendous cruelty and inhumanity of specific acts of domination. During Roman times or the Christian middle ages in Europe, specific acts of domination could take forms of nearly unimaginable cruelty. Instead, with the swelling of the means of domination into vast accumulations of private wealth through the pillage and destruction of foreign peoples, the extent, institutional solidity, and scope of the power of the dominating classes increased immensely.

The system of slavery and colonization was a key transitional period leading to today's "advanced" capitalism. Through the imposition of European law on conquered nations, the legal system of private wealth had become international. Laws were made, in the Americas, India, Indonesia, French Indochina, and so on, that (1) promoted a class system favoring the "white" citizens of the colonial power over the native populations, a wealthy ruling elite unconcerned with the culture or welfare of the people in the conquered countries, and (2) promoted a system of trade favorable to the dominating country through which wealth produced in the colonial country flowed into the hands of the colonial class and back into the hands of "investors" in the dominating country. While the ideology of colonialism was the "white man's burden," the purpose of colonialism was to extract the wealth and resources of conquered peoples for the enrichment of the dominator. The process of accumulation of massive concentrations of wealth continued and built upon the already massive concentrations that had resulted from the rape and pillage of the conquered nations by the conquistadors.

The developing modern industrial system was a key focus for the investment of these accumulations of wealth. Under the system of private property steadily being elaborated since the sixteenth century, accumulations of gold or other forms of private wealth were stagnant or in danger of shrinking unless they were invested. The banking and finance industries arose in which experts in investment could make enough profit to pay interest in deposited accumulations of private wealth. This institutionalized a system in which capital formations and accumulations of private wealth circulate and re-circulate in the form of investment and in which the accumulated private wealth continued to grow into greater accumulations of private wealth. Modern law is based on this system, as is the so-called "science" of economics in which this system of capital formation and exchange with a view to accumulation, along with the "laws" of supply and demand, are formulated in mathematical and statistical terms.

The rape and pillage of foreign lands, roughly of the sixteenth and seventeenth centuries, and the colonization and exploitation of foreign peoples, roughly through the eighteenth and nineteenth centuries, and the evolution of the modern system of production, banking, and finance of the nineteenth and twentieth centuries, have globalized economics to the point where nearly all corners of the world are under direct control of this system or under ever mounting pressures tending to capitulation to this system. By the twentieth century the accumulations resulting from this process had reached astronomical proportions, giving the dominating class and first-world countries a systemic power over the entire globe unheard of in previous centuries. Each stage in the evolution of the system saw ever greater concentrations of private wealth, not only in the form of astronomically wealthy individuals, but in the form of institutions (corporations) possessing even more astronomical concentrations of private wealth and incredible power to the nation-states who fostered and defended this system.

Although some individuals may have dropped along the way from the class having immense economic and political power, and other individuals may have prospered through a combination of hard work, cleverness, ruthlessness and luck to the point where they effectively moved from the laboring classes into the dominating classes, by and large the phenomenon of the corporation or private company, together with the laws of inheritance of private wealth, served to insure the perpetuation and growth of capital formations and a relatively stable capitalist ruling class over these centuries.

Those corporations and individuals who possess vast concentrations of wealth today are the legal and institutional heirs of those who raped and pillaged entire civilizations in the sixteenth and seventeenth centuries, and of those in the eighteenth and nineteenth centuries who worked boys and girls as young as six and seven and men and women in their "satanic mills" literally to death. Marx documents this process in great detail throughout his writings, including *Capital*, which are available to anyone who cares to investigate the background of today's capitalism. The corporations and individuals who today dominate the Earth and its inhabitants may operate differently in method, but their system is no different in principle.

Vast concentrations of private wealth give immense political and economic power. Under the hegemony (or under the direct ownership) of these vast capital formations are the mass media of the world, the transportation systems of the world, the communication systems of the world, and the political governments of the world. Huge concentrations of wealth, today institutionalized and legalized in a global economic system (hence, protected and promoted by the police and militaries of the dominant countries of the world – the wealthy "first-world" industrialized nations) do not always need oppressive or totalitarian political forms to ensure their control and exploitation of their populations for the goal of further corporate profit.

To characterize this system as "a system of death" does not require the assumption that all valorization takes place through Marx's famous labor theory of value, although a large portion of the private accumulation of profit does accrue through exploitation of the labor power of human beings. Enrique Dussel, in *Ethics and Community* (1988), and Franz Hinkelammert in *The Ideological Weapons of Death* (1986), make this assumption and defend it eloquently. But "system of death" can have a larger and simpler meaning than capital sucking dry the life energies of countless generations of workers who are forced to sell their living labor to those who extract their surplus life energy from them in the form of profit. The ugly phenomenon of conquest has itself been integral to the capitalist system, using governments and military as the agents of private concentrations of wealth in their lust for the resources, lands, and labor of other peoples.

Exploitation of labor, military or cultural conquest and exploitation, or the rape of the Earth's resources in the service of the private accumulation of wealth all contribute to "profit" and the increase of private capital. Private capital cannot be accumulated except through some form of exploitation or theft. Private property or capital (as opposed to "personal" property that is entirely legitimate within limits) is theft, as Pierre Joseph Proudhon remarked. And theft is directly linked to the death of millions, for its basic premises are a system built upon death rather than life. In religious language, this "system of death" is identical with a "system of sin," as Liberation Theologians have pointed out repeatedly.

In this connection, Moltmann calls the global capitalist system "structural sin" and describes it as institutionalized violence:

> There are political and economic structures which are unjust because they are used to enforce the domination of human beings over human beings, the exploitation of human beings by human beings, and the alienation of human beings from one another. Within these structures, violence is practiced, not directly and personally, but indirectly, by way of laws and prices. Through structures of this kind, violence is legitimated. Through them, violent death is spread. Today impoverishment, debt and exploitation spread misery, disease and epidemics, an hence premature death, among the weakest of the weak in the Third-world. The mass death of children in Africa is just the beginning. There, the number of people dying a violent death through structural violence is greater than the number of soldiers killed by military violence in the great world wars. (1996, p. 95)

3. Democracy, Development, or Repression?

In the first-world, the hegemony of the capitalist class is so complete today that it can allow the so-called political freedoms of speech, press, assembly, due process of law, etc. Such freedoms are today used to promote the agenda of capital accumulation, for people need to be conditioned to become passive (use and discard) consumers of the goods and services spewed forth from corporate service, fast food, and industrial enterprises. The best way to make avid consumers out of the population is to condition them to desire ever more consumption, status, pleasure, and "fun" in a compulsive quest for happiness or acceptance.

They must think they are free. People cannot be forced to be compulsive consumers by totalitarian methods. They must have what they perceive to be political freedom even though the ruling classes understand that such freedom makes no effective difference. The hegemony over media, goods and services, law and government is so great that these "framing conditions" of the society are never even raised as a question (see Edwards, 1996, Chs. 1-2). These limitations on thought are out of the realm of discourse in the mass media and out of the realm of consciousness of most people in these societies.

In the third-world the situation is quite different. The people whose ancestors were raped and pillaged, and whose grandparents were enslaved and colonized in the service of the private accumulation of wealth are today left in economically devastated lands, in massive poverty, without health-care or education, on the edge of sickness, starvation, and death. They are often ruled by a tiny elite of landowners, thugs, local capitalists, and military officers whose ancestors were installed by their colonial masters.

These people often have little to lose and nothing to gain from allowing themselves to be the passive victims of the process of corporate indoctrination. To put this another way, the process or corporate indoctrination is making every effort – through advertising, television, radio, and print media – to indoctrinate them into the mindless pursuit of consumerism, and into the ideology of capitalism mouthing words like "freedom," "democracy," and "prosperity," but their starting condition is so wretched that the illusion does not embed itself so easily.

They watch their children die, and their lives slip by in sickness and misery, while being bombarded with the doctrinal myth that hard work and enterprise can make you too like the trivial shells of human beings, mindlessly comic and idiotically happy, that appear in the soaps, quiz shows, commercials, mass magazines and movies. Quite often these people do not buy the myth as naively. They are not so willingly enslaved as the passive and thoughtless citizens of the wealthy countries who have handed over their freedom and integrity to the corporate domination of their lives. That is why military domination of their countries is a necessary complement of economic domination.

Under third-world conditions, "democracy" as found in the affluent first-world will not work. Manipulation of information and ideological slant by the mass media is so complete in the first-world that people can be left entirely "free" to vote or speak, since there is little danger that they will even be aware that there may be alternatives to the system as they know it. But in the third-world, if people are actually free to vote, they may not vote for the tiny elites currently ruling their countries, remnants of the old colonial elite, who control all their country's wealth while millions die of sickness and starvation.

They may vote for people who promise a society based on human dignity, justice, and rights to housing, health care, education, even food. The material conditions of people in most third-world societies militate against their accepting the corporate hegemony over their minds and lives that exists in the first-world. The contradictions are too great. The promise of "prosperity" though "free enterprise" too easily exposed as a gigantic lie designed to foster the continued accumulation of wealth for the ruling classes at the expense of whoever and whatever gets in the way of this process.

A careful watch is kept by the United States on elections in the third-world. Money is poured into those candidates and parties believed necessary to continuing the system. CIA agents manipulate elections and candidates. The military of these countries, often trained in the United States, keeps careful watch. If the wrong candidate is nevertheless elected, a *coup* or assassination may well follow (see Blum, 2000).

Therefore, first-world "democracy" will not do under third-world conditions. The third-world needs rapacious dictatorships, installed or maintained in power by military and other forms of "aid" to their countries, who ensure a stable "investment climate" for the corporations whose transnational enterprises require the cheap labor, the cheap natural resources, and the cheaply grown food for export to the consumers of the first-world. Even better, from the point of view of the ideological smokescreen pretending that first-world countries believe in human rights, are "civilian" governments, or political systems sometimes referred to as "fledgling democracies," in which civilian leaders take their orders from the rich and the military.

In recent decades such governments have developed as a new political form that the North American Congress on Latin America (NACLA) (1998) calls "militarized democracies." In these countries, the military has a permanent role in every sector of life that endures regardless of the election processes that may change the trappings of the "civilian" government. The corporations, unlike their conquistador, mercantilist, or colonial forerunners, do not need to torture, exterminate, disappear, or bomb those who resist their rapacity in the third-world. Their power and the influence of their money is so immense that they can afford secondary agents (often military or paramilitary death squads) to perform these tasks for them.

To be sure, their goal is not to destroy people, or the environment, directly. Their goal is profit. The torture and extermination of dissidents is only an unfortunate consequence of the need to ensure a stable "investment climate" in the massively poor countries. See, for example, the description under the title "Indonesia: Mass Extermination, Investor's Paradise" researched and written by Noam Chomsky and Edward S. Herman (1979, pp. 205-217).

First-world governments serve as agents of this process. Under the leadership of the United States, they have formulated the doctrine of "internal security." The real enemy is not likely to be invasion from without (although this may be still possible and requires massive armaments sales to third-world nations to the enrichment of first-world corporations). The real enemy is within. The real enemy is "subversives," "traitors," "communists," or "terrorists," who want to destroy civilized stability and human decency as these are expressed in any "stable investment climate." How does one identify these heinous traitors to civilization? Military personnel are indoctrinated to believe that these internal enemies are everywhere. They are in the schools as concerned teachers, in factories as union organizers, in human rights offices, among laborers on the farms, and among the peasants who organize community projects in the countryside.

They can be identified because they are the ones organizing unions, or undertaking health-care improvement projects, or promoting education for all, or working to provide small plots of land or small irrigation projects for starving peasants. All people who promote the welfare of the poor are considered "communistic" or have "suspected links to terrorism." They are resisted, intimidated, and often brutally repressed (Blum, 1995). The corporations, along with their agents, the military and first-world governments, only want to help the poor and starving, as they profess. As U.S. Secretary of State Henry Kissinger said when the United States was arranging in 1973 to destroy the democratically elected socialist government of Chile and replace it with a brutal military dictatorship: "Why should we let Chile go communist just because the Chileans don't know any better" (Brown, 1986, p. 42).

The official propaganda doctrine is that the only possible way to end poverty and misery is by development through "free enterprise" (and this doctrine is militarily and politically enforced as an unwritten international law). People who have absolutely nothing are to compete in the free market with multinational corporations possessing billions in assets. Under the rules of such free competition only the wealthy will win, but the poor must believe that this is their only hope or face repression and extermination from a first-world backed military designed to enforce this system as their only hope. Under this new world system the corporations can easily evade responsibility for the murderous practices of the repressive regimes that protect a "favorable investment climate."

In a world system totally dominated by vast capital accumulations resulting from centuries of exploitation, the power of the dominating system is so great that responsibility is quite difficult to determine. Many of the sadistic El Salvadoran military personnel brutalizing their fellow citizens during the 1980s and early 90s were trained in the United States School of the Americas in Fort Benning, Georgia, just as the brutal and repressive military of Columbia is trained there today. It is quite difficult to know what goes on inside this top secret school, but spokespersons for the military say that the doctrine of "internal security" is taught concomitantly with respect for human rights. The School of the Americas is in turn part of the highly secret Pentagon system intimately connected with mega-corporations in which executives of the weapons-producing industries are often retired Pentagon personnel, industries that have numerous lobbyists and liaisons with the Pentagon and the government, and that make large routine campaign contributions to elected officials.

These huge corporations, in turn, are secret entities (because they are "private" concentrations of wealth) in which the planning and strategy of their controlling bodies is hidden from the public. Villagers are massacred in Guatemala by the Guatemalan military (whose planning operates in secret), but who are accused of being advised by the CIA (which operates in secret), that is directed by the Pentagon system (a secret system), who are intimately related to the governing boards of transnational corporations (who operate in secret). How then are we to assess the situation when someone claims the domination of global capital is ultimately responsible for the massacre of those peasants in Guatemala? Democracy, by any stretch of the imagination, is a sham under this system. And the system itself breeds corruption. For a more detailed description of this corruption, see Greg Palast, *The Best Democracy Money Can Buy: The Truth About Corporate Cons, Globalization and High-Finance Fraudsters* (2003).

When Columbus began the genocidal massacre of the Arawak Indians it was possible for an individual like Bartolome de Las Casas to witness this. Columbus, the direct agent of Ferdinand and Isabella on a mission to amass gold for the Spanish Crown, could be understood to be a brutal torturer in the service of the accumulation of wealth (see Gutierrez, 1993). Under today's system, which is in many ways a perfection and refinement of the same system of rape and pillage in the service of the accumulation of wealth, how is responsibility to be assessed? The boards of directors of corporations in the first-world wear expensive suits, drive luxury cars, and live in sumptuous homes with beautiful children, gentle refined manners, and sophisticated, cultured friends and relatives. They may have never even seen a torture chamber or a death squad. Like the U.S. government that serves them, their entire existence is built around "plausible deniability."

Their influence is not usually a product of conspiracies on their part, but instead the inevitable workings of the system of private accumulation in which they are dominant. Hence, they may plausibly deny responsibility for torture and repression in the countries where their investments are located, which over the past several decades includes Argentina, Bolivia, Brazil,

Chile, Columbia, Dominican Republic, East Pakistan, East Timor, Greece, Guatemala, Haiti, Indonesia, Iran, Mexico, Paraguay, Peru, Philippines, Saudi Arabia, South Korea, South Vietnam, Thailand, Tunesia, Turkey, Uruguay, Venezuela, and others. *The Washington Connection and Third-world Fascism* by Chomsky and Herman (1979) provides details about the political use of torture in the service of global capital within each of these countries.

When there are massacres in El Salvador, these are a consequence of mechanisms institutionalized over the centuries. Cuba and Vietnam are blockaded and strangled for decades by the United States to ensure that they do not thrive. There must be no good examples of societies that have found alternative means to the health and well-being of their citizens (see Chomsky, 1996, pp. 22-24). The global economy must be entirely dominated by big capital with the help of first-world governments and military power. Even one example of a truly alternative society would serve as an inspiration to the wretched masses of the Earth. But as long as the system remains truly global, then poor peoples (or any peoples) have no choice but to try to survive and thrive within the system geared toward ever greater capital accumulation.

The clean, gentle, educated elites who dominate this system, do not need to conspire to massacre the people of El Salvador or starve the people of Cuba who simply want a system in which they can survive. The global system is automatic. The United States government serves to protect its "strategic interests" (corporate interests) within other nations, and serves to protect a "secure investment climate" for the transnationals worldwide. Therefore, this system will automatically try to destroy any people who struggle for a system that works to their benefit instead of to the benefit of the foreign investors.

The clean, beautiful, wealthy people who dominate the corporations, often know little or nothing of the massacres in El Salvador, Guatemala, or Indonesia. They are "apolitical." Even the people of the U.S. know little or nothing of these massacres since the media automatically ignore atrocities in the countries of our "official friends" and focus only on the atrocities of countries of our "official enemies" (e.g., Cuba, Iraq, Libya, Sudan, Vietnam, Yugoslavia, etc.) The system of rape and pillage has been brought to perfection, at least from the point of view of the dominating class whose hands and minds are seemingly innocent of the human nightmare fostered by their system.

4. Immorality and Instrumental Irrationality

In a system of private accumulation of wealth, neither the common good of people, nor the welfare of future generations, nor the integrity of the environment has economic value in itself. A system of supply and demand addressed through private business activity is not concerned with any of these values. Therefore, what is ultimately valuable is of *no concern* to the system. The only planning that occurs is planning for the maximization of private profit in the relatively short term. There is no ethical consideration of what is intrinsically valuable, since all intrinsic value (for example, human dignity) is of null value to a system of private profit.

There is an observable responsiveness between demand and supply in the capitalist system that is the foundation within the amoral and immoral workings of this system. Only sheer ideology is capable of manufacturing the fantasy that this system fosters the common good. The ideology states that the law of supply and demand will automatically, as a mechanistic side effect of production for private profit, create the famous "invisible hand" of Adam Smith, a "hand" that works for maximization of the common good, or, in the utilitarian formulation, for "the greatest happiness of the greatest number of people."

Yet even supposing a "free market" where large corporations do not use their hegemonic powers to regulate supply and demand in their favor, the law of supply and demand is observably a very poor tool for achieving anything remotely approaching the common good. If there is a demand for slaves to work the plantations of South Carolina, then someone will find a way to supply that demand, despite the human cost, and such "entrepreneurs" will develop an ideology to justify what they do to supply that demand. If there is a demand for inexpensive clothing among the poorer sectors of the first-world nations, corporations will turn to semi-slave labor in the sweatshops of third-world nations to fill that demand. If there is a demand for luxury automobiles among the wealthy, corporations will build them, even when the cost of one automobile could provide life for thousands of starving children in the poorer nations. If there is a demand for air-conditioning and refrigeration using chemicals that destroy the ozone layer, air conditioning will be supplied, even if it means ultimate destruction of the viability of the planet itself.

The proponents of "free market environmentalism" who argue that the recognition of the danger to the ozone layer will bring about new developments in these products that do not seem harmful to the planetary environment have missed the point. Market mechanisms may or may not address the danger and develop new forms of air conditioning and refrigeration. The decisive factor is not rational planning for the future or human concern for the good of the planet or human welfare but greed for profit. If there is no profit to be made from developing new forms, then it will not happen. Neither reason (other than a narrow technical reason in the service of greed) nor moral values are decisive operating forces in the "free market."

For many years, it has been widely known that solar, wind, and water energy are the only possible routes to the ending of global warming and the preservation of thermal balance for the planetary environment, but this rational demand has had little or no effect. By far the greatest profit is still to be made from oil, and oil corporations produce immense quantities of environmentally destructive plastics as well as unimaginable quantities of gasoline and fuel oil with the corresponding advertising pressure to use these environmentally destructive commodities. Consumers still demand gasoline powered automobiles, governments still build mainly roads and refuse to invest in alternative forms of transportation. Big corporations still promote that sale of automobiles, gas, and oil worldwide in the face of the widespread knowledge that if the entire world depended on gas and oil the way the first-world does there would be no environment left to protect.

In the face of the destruction of the planetary environment these commodities are creating, the market demand for these things is blatantly irrational, ultimately deleterious to the common good. But roads, automobiles, gas, oil, and plastics will be supplied even if it means planetary self-destruction. The market is not driven by rational planning or moral considerations, but by greed and institutionalized mechanisms of private profit. The allusion to "freedom" in the slogans "free market" or "free enterprise" is wrongly used.

There is no freedom in what ignores rational planning for the future (as Plato pointed out in the *Republic*) and there is no freedom in what indulges inclinations, greed, and desires at the expense of moral reasoning (as Kant pointed out in his ethical writings). Because it is immoral and irrational as a system, capitalism is also ultimately self-destructive. It has nothing to do with authentic freedom, but everything to do with human beings refusing to take responsibility for their freedom through designing rational and moral economic institutions.

By contrast, under ethical-based socialism human individuals as ends-in-themselves and the environment as intrinsically valuable will be the goals of economic, social, political, and cultural life. We have seen Marx contrast the "blind supply and demand laws" with the principle of "socialist foresight," rational planning directed toward a society based on the value of individual human beings and their planetary home. Reason is not only to be directed toward realizing human freedom, but rational planning is itself a primary mode of human freedom within history.

We can use our scientific understanding of nature and ourselves to promote truly human ends and attain ever greater freedom within the context of nature, or we can be the victims of blind seemingly mechanical economic "laws." When people contract tuberculosis, they can be the victims of the blind workings of the disease, or they can use their knowledge to treat the disease and hence exercise freedom in relation to these otherwise blind workings. They may also use their knowledge to eliminate the disease altogether and attain a still higher level of freedom. The fact that the globalized system of "free trade" has not eliminated preventable diseases like typhoid, cholera, tuberculosis, and polio that still ravage the majority of the world's population is living proof that there is nothing "free" about this system.

This "still higher level of freedom" will be realized only with authentic socialism, for under capitalism the major determinants of people's lives remain blind market forces, so-called laws of supply and demand, of recessions and booms, of scarcity in the midst of plenty, and of massive worldwide joblessness in the midst of monumental tasks to be accomplished. Capitalism is instrumentally and substantially irrational and therefore unfree (see Wolff, 1989, pp. 126-137). As "instrumentally irrational," it appears a poor instrument for achieving economic goals.

As "substantially irrational," by its very nature capitalism reflects, as Marx saw, irrational and humanly destructive premises. To be irrational in these ways means capitalism is not and cannot be based on human freedom. Mere self-indulgence, doing whatever one feels like, is not freedom. Authentic freedom, as we saw in earlier chapters, requires intelligence, planning, and foresight in conformity with practical moral reasoning.

In an early essay of 1842, Marx writes the following: "Liberty is so much the essence of humans that even its enemies realize it when they attack its existence. They wish to expropriate as a precious jewel for themselves what they reject as an adornment of human nature...." Marx chose to have this essay republished in 1851, as he was entering his mature period (Miranda, 1986, p. 58). It reflects his consistent affirmation of human freedom throughout his life, not only as one human attribute, but as our human essence comparable to the most "precious jewel." Those philosophical "materialists" or "determinists" who attack freedom must exercise that very freedom to attack it, showing the absurdity of their position. In the first volume of *Capital,* regarding Malthus' law of geometric growth in human population, Marx writes, "An abstract law of population exists for plants and animals only, and only in so far as man has not interfered with them" (Miranda, 1986, p. 55; Foster, 1998, pp. 1-18).

Human beings are liberated from the necessary operation of abstract laws insofar as they comprehend and "interfere" with these laws. Even today the world remains faced with an exploding population and still has not moved to a rational system in which the blind laws of population growth are replaced by rational, free incentives for people to limit the number of children born in their families. Rational understanding of natural laws and the possibility of human freedom go hand in hand for Marx.

The population explosion today remains primarily in the third-world where the crushing poverty produced by five centuries of systematic exploitation under the cover of "blind market forces" has created an economic necessity for producing large families in each new generation. Capitalism is the refusal to use human intelligence and foresight to create a truly human world of freedom. It is "instrumentally" and "substantially" irrational. Let us look in more detail at these aspects of irrationality that define the capitalist system. Let me begin with instrumental irrationality.

First, the "market" is a poor instrument for distributing goods and services (food, clothing, shelter, health care, etc.) to society. Wages are necessarily kept low enough for capitalists to make a profit, yet these very wages are necessary for people to buy the goods and services essential to life. And masses of people are without jobs and therefore without a source of livable income, since under capitalism jobs are only created in response to a "demand" that allows owners to make a profit in some sector of social existence. If there is no profit to be made, the starvation of masses of people is not their concern. As we saw in Chapter Three, "scarcity" under capitalism is not a so-called natural scarcity, like famine, or a shortage of resources. Instead, scarcity is artificial. It is necessary to allow the few to continue to exploit the many.

Second, just as market forces are forces of scarcity, so scarcity may increase or decrease depending on these same blind, irrational forces. Competition leads to cycles of overproduction, then to layoffs and recessions (or depressions). This is the most famous aspect of the instrumental irrationality of capitalism and needs the least discussion. Even with twentieth century government intervention in these cycles, the system remains unstable, as the near worldwide collapse of the economic system in 1998 and 1999 made clear. Distribution of the basic needs of life is left to depend on the fluctuations of "the market." The goal of the system is profit for investors and owners, not rational concern with human need or fulfillment.

Third, capitalism is also a poor economic instrument because it requires massive duplication of production efforts, distribution systems, and advertising. It involves a massive waste of time, effort, and resources in the face of a world of crying misery and scarcity. As Miranda writes:

And in fact how can we talk about overproduction when millions of human beings lack the most basic necessities? Doesn't such talk prove that there is a complete inversion of ends and means in capitalist production? How can humanity continue to put up with a system that channels all the resources of the world (including humanity itself) into obtaining a profit rather than into satisfying the needs of human beings? (1986, p. 127)

Production according to market forces dictates that billions of dollars are spent each year in research and development, for example, by auto makers in their attempt to get the market edge on other automakers. This does not necessarily make better automobiles since the number of lemons and failures is notorious. Nor does it make reliable autos since companies would go out of business if they built a car to last more than a few years. Yet we know well that a comfortable, reliable, inexpensive automobile could be developed that would be fuel efficient (perhaps using solar energy), strong, safe, and run for 300,000 or more miles. But such development would require production for human need, not for profit within a competitive market.

The same principle holds throughout the system. If everyone needs a refrigerator, then rational planning would build a basic set of refrigerator models, designed to last for decades, and distribute them through a carefully designed system of accountability to everyone who needs one. Could this be done using some market mechanisms? Certainly. But the premises of the system would have to be different. The premises of both the economic and political systems must be human beings as ends-in-themselves.

Instead, billions of dollars in time and resources go down the drain of competition (and then results in a system of scarcity where only the well-off can afford the products developed) rather than into developing and producing what everyone needs anyway. We do not need a choice between ten brands of refrigerators all offering the same set of models, each with its own private set of research and development facilities duplicating the others. We need a choice between different models of refrigerators designed to last, designed to protect the environment, and designed to serve human welfare. Nor do we need monopoly conditions where one company extorts from us prices way beyond the cost of production in order to further enrich its wealthy investors.

This is true not only in research and development, but in distribution systems and advertising. Private distribution systems duplicate trucking systems, rail systems, bureaucracies, and communication systems, wasting billions more in the pursuit of private profit for the wealthy owners of these systems. In *Capital*, Volume One, Marx writes: "The capitalist mode of production, while it enforces economy in each individual business, also begets, by its anarchic system of competition, the most outrageous squandering of labour-power and of the social means of production, not to mention the creation of a vast number of functions at present indispensable, but in themselves superfluous" (1990, p. 667). For a contemporary analysis of this phenomenon, see *The World's Wasted Wealth 2* by economist J. W. Smith (1994).

5. Ideological Control and Substantial Irrationality

Advertising alone spends billions in developing moronic and hypnotic messages to steer and manipulate consumers toward one kind of automobile or hair conditioner or high fat, low nourishment beef burger instead of another. The precious resources of the planet are squandered in a glut of imbecilic messages that pollute the minds of their recipients and interfere with the development of true human intelligence or spirituality. Yet advertising has become inseparable from corporate propaganda that, since the First-world War, has spent billions of dollars for the explicit purpose of manipulating the minds of United States citizens and people worldwide in the interests of the corporate system. Let us examine briefly the development of this system of corporate propaganda in the United States.

Noam Chomsky (1989) and others have given detailed accounts of this process. One excellent summary is found in Chapter Eight of Helen Caldicott's book *If You Love This Planet* (1992). In this chapter, called "The Manufacture of Consent," she tells the story of a congressional committee being established to investigate the activities of the National Association of Manufacturers (NAM) that had been formed just prior to the First-world War. With the vote in the United States being extended from about fifteen percent to fifty percent of the adult population during the period between 1880 and 1920, the power of the rich was threatened by the possibility that people would vote "for laws that supported their own health, education, and welfare. For the first time, their tax dollars would be used to support the majority of the population and not just the rich" (1992, pp. 150-51).

But propaganda techniques had been developed by the United States government during the first-world war to convert the reluctant U.S. population into war hysteria for joining that carnage. These techniques were so successful that big business was quite interested. Scholars supporting the corporate system at the time wrote: "Popular election may work fairly well as long as those questions are not raised which cause the holders of wealth and power to make full use of their resources. If they do so, there is much skill to be bought, and the art of using skill for the production of emotion and opinion has so advanced, that the whole condition of political contests would be changed for the future" (1992, p. 151).

NAM and other corporate organizations, such as the Committee on Public Information created gigantic media campaigns to convince the people of the United States to hate and fear communism or socialism and to accept the rule of big business (1992, p. 151-2). In order to counteract the effect of Franklin Delano Roosevelt's New Deal, which to many corporations indicated a tendency toward socialism, and to convince the public to support the corporate framework for life in the U.S., in 1935:

> The renowned National Association of Manufacturers (NAM) organized another massive propaganda campaign. The president of the NAM told business leaders in 1935, "This is not a hit or miss program. [It is] skillfully integrated...to...blanket every media.... It pounds the message home." In 1939, the La Follette committee of the U.S. Senate reported that the NAM had blanketed the country with propaganda that relied on secrecy and deception. The NAM employed radio speeches, news cartoons, editorials, advertising, motion pictures, and many other propaganda techniques that did not disclose its sponsorship. One business-sponsored agency distributed a steady supply of canned, ready-to-print editorials to twelve thousand local newspapers, and some 2.5 million column inches of this material were published. (1992, p.155)

While today hundreds of thousands of people go homeless in the streets, while forty percent of U.S. citizens are without adequate health-care insurance, while millions are unemployed or marginally employed, corporations spend billions of dollars in precious resources for propaganda purposes designed to keep the population compliant to their system of private profit and greed. Caldicott's chapter traces this process right though the Reagan and Bush eras, and shows the same techniques used by the U.S. government to engineer consent to the Gulf War of 1991. Caldicott's story of the engineering of war and the "war on terrorism" is continued to the present by Gore Vidal in *Perpetual War for Perpetual Peace: How We Got To Be So Hated* (2002).

Corporations have gained great influence over educational institutions to promote an agenda which includes massive arms sales worldwide and "perpetual war" so they can supply the Pentagon with lucrative weapons contracts (Vidal, 2002). They have funded the creation of "think tanks" staffed by highly educated pundits who write news reports, editorials, and even legislation for the U.S. congress. They have created a special kind of propaganda called "tree tops propaganda" directed toward members of Congress and other leaders of U.S. society (Caldicott, pp. 163-178).

By 1978, Caldicott writes, "according to a congressional inquiry, U.S. business was spending one billion a year of tax deductible money for "education," to convince people that big government was bad for them. "The truth is," she writes, "that government regulation is bad for corporations. It is amazing how corporate advertising can turn truth on its head" (1992, p.163). Hence, the great suck-up of wealth from the poor to the rich continued throughout the Reagan years, and down to the present. Congressional Budget Office figures say the poorest ten percent of U.S. citizens earned nine percent less income in 1990 than in 1980, while their tax rate increased by twenty-eight percent. By contrast the richest five percent of all citizens saw their tax rate decrease by ten percent while they received forty-five percent more income before taxes in 1990 than they did in 1980 (1992, p.171).

Under the conditions of advanced capitalism, such squandering of the precious resources of the Earth is inevitable. It cannot be stopped, for in a system of merely "political democracy" corporations will insist on their right of "freedom of speech." With billions of dollars to squander on their "free speech," and with corporate ownership of the mass media, and massive influence over educational and political institutions, the rational discussion of political and economic options, essential to real democracy, becomes impossible. Rational discourse is inundated by corporate propaganda.

Capitalism is not only a very inefficient instrument for providing the necessities of life to people, as we have seen, it remains utterly incompatible with democracy. It cannot promote the free rational discourse essential to democracy, for tremendous resources are necessarily directed toward propagandizing the population in the interests of the system. As Caldicott concludes: "It is interesting that since 1918 the Soviet government brainwashed its people by consistently lying to them, but its techniques were so clumsy that the people knew they were being brainwashed. By contrast, in the United States, corporations became expert manipulators, so most people have swallowed the corporate doctrine whole" (1992, p.161).

Yet poor as capitalism is as an instrument, as we have seen outlined above, utilitarian considerations are not the most decisive. More fundamental is the "substantial" irrationality of capitalism. Capitalism in this regard is a complete inversion of ends and means. Instead of a system in which the end of economics and politics is human well-being (humans as uniquely valuable in themselves), capitalism is a system in which human beings are sacrificed to the profit-oriented ends of production.

Even the rich are dehumanized in this respect and made the slaves of the system of profit and accumulation. Under the iron laws of capitalism, they must compete for profit and ever more profit. If they do not, they go under, bankrupt. This is the basis of the famous fourfold alienation described by Marx: capitalism alienates human beings from their own products, from their productive lives, from their own "species nature" or human nature, and from their fellow humans. Even those who have more wealth than they can use in a lifetime must continue to exploit their fellow human beings. They have had their human nature corrupted to the extent that they lack both compassion and wisdom. Their humanity is deadened by an inhuman system.

First, the above example of the way capitalism destroys democracy is an example of this "substantial irrationality." The founding principles of democracy are precisely the value of human beings in themselves. The U.S. *Declaration of Independence* reads, "We hold these truths to be self-evident, that all men are created equal, and endowed by their creator with certain inalienable rights." Democracy is a social philosophy based on *moral* principles (whether these are articulated in Lockean, Kantian-Rousseauean, or other terms). To found a society on equality and inalienable rights is to found a society on the moral value of human beings as ends-in-themselves. Democratic theory often elaborates these assumptions. It may spell out the notion of "equality," for example, as equality before the law or equality of opportunity, but its founding assumption usually remains the prior moral equality of all persons.

It may spell out the notion of freedom in terms of the relation between "truth" as the result of free inquiry and discussion and the possibility of justice for all within society. It may spell out the role of government as not only protecting the rights of all (minorities included) but as being an agent of the common good independently of special interests within society. Yet in none of these ways can capitalism exist within a viable democracy. "Equality" before the law becomes a simple myth when a segment of society possess such vast wealth and power. "Freedom" as a framework of free inquiry and rational discussion becomes an outright lie when corporations spend billions of dollars per year to control and manipulate the public mind. And the notion of government acting for the "common good" is a complete impossibility when government, as is the case today, is the servant, protector, and promoter of the interests of the ruling class.

Second, human labor occupies the heart of a productive life. Yet under capitalism most labor is not only not meaningful or rewarding, but positively exhausting or deadening, as human beings become appendages to a machine or a computer and conform their productive lives to its inhuman demands. The product a person creates in this laboring process, whether an intellectual product on a computer or a physical product, is then owned by someone else, and is appropriated by the corporation for use in generating ever greater accumulated capital.

In this situation a person is forced into competition with other persons, nearly any other person could replace one at one's job and the source of support for one's self and family would be lost. We are always in competition with the others, and we fear the others who can replace us at a moment's notice. We are forced into a life and death struggle with our fellows, whether we are rich or poor, all of us slaves to the imperatives of capital.

Third, capitalism is inherently anti-ecological. It depends on the perpetual and unlimited economic and industrial "growth" (an ever increasing "gross national product," and so on). Yet the science of ecology tells us that all life systems must be in balance with their environment, that the health and survival of species are inseparable from the health and viability of the ecosystems that support them. It tells us also that resources, like ecosystems, are finite and limited, and that the planet itself is a delicate balance of systems that are inevitably destroyed by unlimited growth and "development." As Tom Athanasiou, author of *Divided Planet*, puts it:

> Another reason capitalism isn't sustainable is that, at least so far, it must grow or die. Like a cancer.... It might be theoretically possible on some other planet to have a form of capitalism deeply and soundly committed to green technology.... The truth is that it doesn't matter, because none of us are living theoretically. We live historically. Global warming and the biodiversity crash aren't theoretical. The children worldwide who die every minute from starvation or easily preventable diseases aren't theoretical. None of this is necessary, which only makes it worse. It doesn't have to be that way. (1996, p. 48)

A more technical formulation of the anti-ecological character of capitalism is given by philosopher James O'Connor under the heading of "the second contradiction of capitalism." The first contradiction of capitalism, which is integral to the crises-ridden character of this system, involves the struggle between productive forces and production relations in which vast socially organized systems of production are in private hands and used to extract surplus value from laborers who do not own private property (1996, p. 200). The second contradiction involves the fact that capitalism destroys the natural and social conditions that make production possible, instead of reproducing and protecting these conditions of production as would be the case under a genuine socialism.

As examples of the destruction of natural conditions for production, O'Connor cites global warming, destruction of species, acid rain destroying forests, lakes, and buildings, destruction of water tables, massive soil erosion, and toxic wastes. All of these destroy profitability as well as the ability to sustain production in the long term. The destruction of the social environment of production includes decaying infrastructures, the "urban renewal treadmill," "which impairs its own conditions and therefore profits, for example through congestion costs and high rents." It includes "the welfare treadmill," "the health-care treadmill," and so on, which are connected with "capital's destruction of traditionalist family life." It includes "the introduction of work relations that impair coping skills, and the presently toxic social environment generally" (1996, p.207).

In the light of our discussion of the variety of instrumental and substantial ways in which capitalism is irrational, unstable, and destructive, it should appear quite unlikely that there would be even a "theoretical possibility" of a green capitalism. Just as capitalism involves a destructive contradiction between the forces of production and the relations of production, it also involves a destructive contradiction with the conditions of production, with the social and natural environments that make its production for profit possible. Unless the ruling principle of a social order is the value of human beings themselves, in harmony with the precious planetary system that supports them and the ecosystems within which they are embedded, there can be no end to the self-destructive growth of capitalism other than planetary suicide. Only a socialism based on human beings as ends-in-themselves and nature as valuable in itself can realize democracy and ecological sustainability.

6. The Mature Dream of Socialism

The early Marx speaks of alienation from our "species-being." The latter Marx writes of alienation from our "human end-in-itself to an entirely external end" (Bologh, 1979, p. 123). The "domination and exploitation of the producers," Marx writes in *Capital,* "distort the worker into the fragment of a man, they degrade him to the level of an appendage of a machine" and "alienate him from the intellectual potentialities of the labor process" (1990, p. 799). The former concept of alienation is more abstract and seemingly more metaphysical than the latter, but the dynamics are the same. Capitalism alienates human beings from their moral status as ends-in-themselves and from our potential for a community in which all are recognized as ends-in-themselves. Capitalism has developed technology, machines, and the forces of production in general but, as Brenkert and others have pointed out, it actively hinders individual and human self-realization and therefore human freedom:

> What, then, is it to be free in Marx's sense? Stated most concisely, it is for one to live such that one essentially determines, within communal rela-tions to other people, the concrete totality of desires, capacities, and tal-ents, which constitute one's self-objectification.... There are three different, though interrelated, aspects of Marx's view of freedom: (a) self-determi-nation requires self-objectification through one's desires, capacities, and talents; (b) one's self-objectification must be a concrete self-objectification with regard to other people and nature; and (c) self-determination is only possible within harmonious, communal relations to others.... Marx insists that man's essence has to be captured by an account of his relations. Fur-

ther, if what is uniquely human about a person is captured in his relations to others, then only if those relations are positive and co-operative, i.e., communal, will people be free.... Thus Marx comments that "as long as a cleavage exists between the particular and the common interests, as long, therefore, as activity is not voluntary, but naturally, divided, man's own deed becomes an alien power opposed to him, which enslaves him instead of being controlled by him." (1983, pp. 88-89 & 128)

Human fulfillment is inseparable from the nexus of relationships within which we live. No person is an island, and all must work to produce the necessities of life. This work can be fulfilling, creative, and voluntary or it can be a form of slavery, brutalizing us and preventing the realization of our human potential. Marx does not give extended accounts of the fulfilled relationships very often, although they are implicit in all that he wrote. But we saw in Chapter Seven one such account in his Comments on James Mill's *Elemens D'Economie Politique* (Hewitt, 1995, p. 52) . Marx links our "human dignity" with one's ability to "affirm" one's self and the other person in mutual production for the common good. Our true human dignity (as moral "ends-in-ourselves") shows when the expression of my creative life supports and makes possible the expression of your creative life, a relationship that he characterizes as mutual "love" that is simultaneously the fulfillment of our human nature.

We see in Marx's thought the dual aspects of freedom that Brenkert pointed out above. Individual voluntary creative self-fulfillment is inseparable from fulfillment of our social nature through communal cooperation and interdependence. What appears a violation of human dignity, Marx says, is in reality the fulfillment of that dignity, to "carry out production as human beings" instead of as commodities who dehumanize one another through exploiting another's labor for the private accumulation of wealth or competing with one another for scarce jobs or resources.

This "production as human beings" can even be called "love," for our social nature of mutual cooperation and affirmation becomes inseparable from "the individual expression of my life" or "your life." This passage is from the early Marx of 1843-44 but the fundamental assumptions concerning the four-fold alienation (from our true individual and social selves) produced by capitalism remained unchanged in the later Marx. In *Capital*, the mature Marx writes:

The worker always leaves the process in the same state as he entered it – a personal source of wealth, but deprived of any means of making that wealth a reality for himself. Since, before he enters the process, his own labour has already been alienated [*entfremdet*] from him, appropriated by the capitalist, and incorporated with capital, it now, in the course of the process, constantly objectifies itself so that it becomes a product alien to him [*fremder Produkt*]. Since the process of production is also the process of consumption of labour-power by the capitalist, the worker's product is not only constantly converted into commodities, but also into capital, i.e. into value that sucks up the worker's value-creating power, means of subsistence that actually purchase human beings, and the means of production that employ people who are doing the producing. Therefore the worker himself constantly produces objective wealth, in the form of capital, an alien power that dominates and exploits him; and the capitalist just as constantly produces labour-power, in the form of a subjective source of wealth which is abstract, exists merely in the physical body of the worker, and is separated from its own means of objectification and realization; in short, the capitalist produces the worker as wage-labourer. This incessant reproduction, this perpetuation of the worker, is the absolutely necessary condition for capitalist production. (1990, p. 716)

The worker is "a personal source of wealth" for others but is "deprived of any real means of making wealth a reality for himself." Just as the worker's production of surplus value for the profit of the capitalist is the essence of capitalism, for capitalism could not exist without such workers, so this relationship is reciprocal. The worker reproduces the capitalist and the capitalist reproduces the worker. This is why there can be no reform of capitalism in the direction of even bourgeois standards of justice.

Even if the worker receives better wages and working conditions, the essential relationship, as Marx points out, is "a hierarchically organized system of exploitation and oppression" (1990, p. 695). Institutional transformation is the only option, the founding of human life on entirely different principles free of class exploitation and dehumanization, principles in which creative and fulfilling labor produces value that is appropriated by the cooperative producers for the individual and common good, or, put in ethical terms, the founding of society on the equality, dignity, freedom, and self-realization of human beings. This passage from *Capital* expresses at least three of the four-fold aspects of alienation discussed by the early Marx: alienation from a person's life activity (one's own labor), since that is purchased by the capitalist, alienation from the product of a person's labor, since that is appropriated by the capitalist, and alienation from our social being or most essential human possibilities, since these are destroyed by the reciprocal relation itself.

Therefore, capitalism is ultimately destructive of civilized human relationships. As Anthony E. Mansueto, Jr. puts this, "the market system is so destructive of social organization precisely because it treats human beings as individual atoms related to each other in a purely external fashion, and therefore undermines the mutual determining relations by which social systems sustain and develop their complexity and that of their constitutive elements" (1995, p. 51). The ideological system attributes racism, fear, greed, terrorism, war, social chaos, violence, drug use, and crime to a mythical "human nature." But a close examination of economic institutions clarifies the real sources of these terrible social ills.

We often hear that socialism has never worked. When pressed on this, people refer to the Soviet model or the East German model or the Chinese model. But none of these could possibly have been the dream of socialism as it was envisioned by the great utopian socialists, and none of these was even close to the dream of socialism envisioned by the scientific socialists, Marx and Engels. One fundamental reason for this is that a fully-articulated socialist alternative cannot possibly exist in a world dominated by capitalism. A socialist country or block of countries in a world dominated by the market and capitalism is a contradiction in terms.

Economic arrangements were already global in scale in Marx's day. He called for the worldwide solidarity of the exploited class in the transformation of capitalism. Socialist countries within the context of global capitalism will be isolated, defensive military and political fortresses struggling for their very survival within a capitalist world bent on their destruction. Naturally such conditions distort government and the human beings within these countries struggling for a decent social-economic-political system.

In the twenty-first century, economy is global in every way, and there can be no more a fulfilled socialism within countries than there can be a fulfilled and happy human being within the context of the greedy, deceitful, and alienated human beings that today dominate and destroy the planet. Those who care about their brothers and sisters around the world will suffer intensely from this system fostered by the ruling class and ruling nations of the world and the immoral systems of greed that they perpetuate. Human freedom and fulfillment can come to humanity as a whole or it cannot come at all. We are one at the deepest level, and as long as this oneness goes unrealized in social-economic-political forms, then the values of freedom, community, human dignity, true diversity, and justice cannot be realized on Earth.

How foolish for people to fear this movement to oneness that is the ascent to our true destiny as mature human beings, one species and one community to whom the Earth and its precious resources and delicate future are entrusted. People claim they fear a world totalitarian society, and any move we make toward world unity or world government may lead to this eventuality. But there exists no decent, effectively working world system now. Nor has one ever existed. The world reflects a chaos of greed, destruction, weapons proliferation, ethnic, racial, national, and economic conflicts. It is a nightmare of human rights abuses. And it represents a total economic failure where one fifth of the human population, more than a billion people, face starvation and death because they have not been and cannot be incorporated into a global economic system devoted to private accumulation of wealth.

The twenty percent of the human population who are doing well and who say they fear a planetary society under the rule of law seem to have little or no human compassion for the other eighty percent. Let them rot, die, starve, endure torture, murder, disappearances, bombings, genocidal economic sanctions, and other forms of a living hell on Earth (much of this misery promoted by the so called "free" societies that our citizens are so fearful might become unfree if a world system were realized). Let them eat their cake of living hell, the small portion of humanity who are privileged and well fed seem to say, we will resist with all our effort giving up our power and privilege to a world system that might not give us as much "freedom" (undemocratic power and privilege) as we now have. The moral cynicism and self-serving nature of this argument is there to see for anyone who cares about truth.

The attainment of unity for the human species on our planet will not come about without action on the part of human beings to take this crucial historical step toward planetary maturity. We will only realize a common human consciousness, or species-being, when steps are taken that make this possible. The human project and the precious natural environment on Earth are facing imminent destruction through a global system carrying forward the momentum of five centuries of greed, death, and destruction. But great hope arises through the realization of our unity as a species in intimate balance with our global planetary environment. The imperative to create a practical social utopia worldwide, predicated on the value and dignity of persons as persons (democratic socialism) coincides with the imperative to an ecologically sustainable economy worldwide.

Jürgen Moltmann expresses the imperative for social and environmental transformation of the world system in the following way:

> If the political form of liberty is democracy, the economic form of equality is socialism or communitarianism. If all human beings are created free *and* equal, then the task of modern societies is to harmonize between the right to individual freedom and the right to social equality. Without equal conditions and equal opportunities for living no democracy can function. Without the development of individual freedom no system of social justice can function. The universalism of these declarations can be put into practice only in a world-wide community of states which make these human rights the fundamental rights of their citizens. Of course this was, and is, largely a utopia but it will increasingly become a historical necessity if humanity is to survive. What began as a utopia of messianic humanism is becoming an ecological necessity: the unity of the human race is inexorably required by

the unity of the Earth as organism. (1996, pp. 190-191)

If the possibility of this transformation appears utterly "utopian" in the negative sense to many well-meaning people, it may be because they have not yet become open to the "eschatological," future-oriented energy urging history toward its true fulfillment in a free, socialist world community. In the first epigram at the head of this chapter, Carl Jung insists that our most fundamental problems are not solved but *out-grown*. We must make conscious efforts to grow toward planetary maturity. The time is more than ripe, and we are ready for this transition in which the seemingly "insoluble" problems of the past will "lose their urgency" and future generations will wonder what all the fuss was about.

In the second epigram, Dominique Barbé speaks of "the utopian function in every human being" as essential to politics, economics, and morality. The possibility of growing up through a transformation of human consciousness open to the eschatological and utopian demands at the heart of our human situation is quite real. And this eschatological energy moving history forward is easily accessible by any person willing to open their heart and mind in this direction. Marx's critique of capitalism, outlined above, is not the only force moving us toward the practical utopia of authentic socialism. Marx also recognized the eschatological energy urging us as individuals, and history as our collective reality on this planet, toward genuine fulfillment, or in religious language, toward a practical anticipation of the kingdom of God on Earth.

7. Eschatology and the Dream of Socialism

The notion of "eschatology" here means the possibility of a real transformation and fulfillment within human history. It means an end to history as we know it and the realization of our human potential for peace, freedom, and joy in living. In this respect, my use of the word "eschatology" does not necessarily mean that such fulfillment is our ultimate "metaphysical" destiny, beyond history. The subject of this book is our historical destiny, the end and goal of human life within history, within emergent evolution, and within the scope of a fully-realized human freedom and our concrete potentialities as human beings. Within history, practical utopia is fully realizable, but only if we combine transformatory critical theory with an openness to the deepest sources of compassion that flow from the depths of the universe.

The same is true, according to José Miranda, of the teaching of Jesus Christ and the comparable teaching of Karl Marx:

But there is another teaching of Jesus Christ that is even more central and equally pervasive in its revolutionary impact on everything. It is his proclamation of the final end and outcome of history. The Greek term for it is *eschaton;* the Latin term is *ultimum.* Now it is true that one branch of later theology gave an ultraworldly cast to eschatology. It is also true that those around today who thrive on the opiate of the people understand the term in that unEarthly sense. Yet the fact remains that in the Bible this end of history is viewed as something within history itself, something occurring not in another world but in this very world where the historical process has unfolded.

Some individuals – the postponers – interpret this statement to mean that the *eschaton* is approaching, that it is not as far away as it was yesterday. But that is hardly news. Such escapist interpretations would turn Jesus into a common fool who puts enormous enthusiasm and passion into announcing a trite commonplace as big news.

Many Christians as well as official Christian churches have refused to accept this message, and continue to do so today, even though the term "Messiah" can have no specific meaning without it. We find, all the same, that the most striking feature of Marx's thought is its full eschatological awareness. What is more, no one who lacks this awareness can be a revolutionary. (1986, pp. 265-266)

The awareness of the concrete demand in the here and now for human beings to transform their lives and their social relationships is the eschatological awareness, and persons who have this awareness can be called "eschatological persons." This awareness arises from a direct and immediate openness to the flow of compassion from the depths of existence and the sources of the ethical imperative confronting every normal human being. Jesus Christ expressed it in his every breath, and that is why the people around him recognized him as the Messiah, as the incarnate God.

This awareness may be called awareness of the voice of God in us, or it may be expressed, as in Marx, as awareness of the non-commodifiable dignity of every human being and the demand that we create social and economic relationships predicated on that dignity. This awareness, lacking even in critical thinkers like Jürgen Habermas, is what differentiates mere liberalism or evolutionary socialism from authentic transformative socialism. Revolutionaries manifest the eschatological awareness that the demand for transformation is, like the categorical imperative of Immanuel Kant, an absolute demand in the here and now, not an inevitably postponed "ideal" projected into some vague and never-quite-realized future.

Much of the bourgeois philosophical thinking of the twentieth century, mired as in a false notion of rationality tied to immediate empirical phenomena, restricts itself to abstracting from the data of experience as the basis for its generalizations. To remain with the "evidence" in this sense is to be unable to generate any vision of human fulfillment. Insofar as philosophers abstract from the data of history and experience, the result is often profound pessimism about the future of humanity. Many, without the courage to face and transcend this pessimism, turn away from the human situation in crisis by burying their thought in narrow esoteric specialties, unwilling and unable to speak concerning our present situation of being at the crossroads of history.

One of the great exceptions to this trend toward philosophical shallowness is Nicholas Berdyaev, who characterizes our situation in the following words:

> Historical pessimism is justified to a remarkable degree, and there are no empirical grounds for historical optimism. But the ultimate truth lies beyond pessimism and optimism. It all goes back to the mystery of the relation between time and eternity. There are such things as moments of communion with eternity. These moments pass, and again I lapse into time. Yet it is not that moment which passes, but I in my fallen temporality: the moment indeed remains in eternity. (1952, pp. 209-210)

Here we find an intimation of the roots of the dream of that socialism that is the political form of love. This eschatological dream arises from an awakening into the mysterious depths of existence that confront us on every side and that are repeatedly encountered in "moments of communion with eternity." With the realization that time is penetrated by eternity, by a mystery not "in time" at all, thought is freed from the limitations of natural necessity and from dependence on a lost and despondent human freedom such as that posited by the early Jean-Paul Sartre. Human freedom exists, to be sure, and Marx took his stand on this freedom and on the need to increase our self-conscious understanding of the mythologies and fetishes, products of the human mind, to which we bow as if they were forms of natural necessity or eternal laws of "economic reality."

For Marx, the more we realize the extent of human freedom, and the more we understand the mechanisms of nature and the fetishes that we project upon nature, the more we will be liberated from slavery, injustice, and stupidities like capitalism. But this is not optimism, which often involves a shallow assessment of the human situation. Marx's vision was eschatological. There is no way to read ordinary hope from the facts of our situation. The eschatological enters human life through a different dimension to which optimism and pessimism are inapplicable.

Pessimism, and the tragic sense of history that may inform it, is a deeper assessment of the human situation than optimism. But pessimism may also be permeated with a sense of the miraculous, the unspeakable mysteries that give rise to miraculous hope, eschatological hope. Berdyaev writes that "what is revolutionary in a really profound sense, is not optimism, which in the last resort is conservative, but rather the pessimism that cannot come to terms with the world. But this pessimism is not absolute, it is relative, and the messianic hope remains in it" (1952, p. 249).

Berdyaev is a great visionary philosopher of freedom, eschatology, personality, and mysticism within the twentieth century. He deeply understands, through his own set of categories, the depths of our situation that illuminate the eschatological meaning of history. Yet despite being one of the great philosophers of freedom, Berdyaev does not remain faithful enough to the Earth, to the blessed and sacred character of creation. His vision of eschatology ultimately leaves time behind in an anticipated transformation of the world in which personality and spirit are lifted up to eternity.

Eschatology need not envision an end to time, however, but can mean the potentiality for genuine fulfillment for nature and humanity within our sacred terrestrial home, and within human history. But this "within history" must include access to the depths of the present moment that are always beyond history, for these depths show that transformation is available to us any time and any place and is not limited to the causal conditions that we inherit from the past. And openness to these depths makes possible ecstatic living that makes faithfulness to the Earth and the body an integral part of our eschatological insight. As we saw in the epigraph to Chapter Five, D.H. Lawrence understood this ecstasy: "What man most passionately wants is his living wholeness and his living unison, not his own isolate salvation of his 'soul.' Man wants his physical fulfillment first and foremost, since now, once and once only, he is in the flesh and potent" (1976, pp. 125-126).

However, in history, freedom alone would be relatively helpless to realize an authentic practical utopia unless human freedom recognizes and opens itself to the flow of compassion from the depths of existence into the human heart. This flow is not limited to "moments of communion with eternity," although these are often crucial. The more open we become, the more the flow becomes incessant and the more we understand the miraculous possibilities of transformation that lie at the heart of the human situation.

Freedom may progressively or dialectically liberate human beings ever more fully from slavery to natural necessity and make possible the elimination of capitalism and the advent of socialism. For in our day, capitalism (in league with the sovereign nation-state) is the most fundamental force inhibiting the progress of human freedom, pretending, as it does, that economics means conformity to natural "economic laws" instead of intelligent planning to meet human needs. But freedom is only fulfilled and transformed when compassion flows out of the eternity from the depths of the present moment and into the human heart. Berdyaev gives the metaphysical designation "spirit" to this flow from the depths into human awareness: "And in so breaking in, spirit seeks to order society after a different pattern, to introduce freedom, the dignity and value of personality, compassion and the brotherhood of men" (1952, p. 220).

Marx understood that alienated human beings under capitalism are shut up in the self-enclosed egos, encouraged by the system itself to commodify one another and to see themselves and others only in terms of isolated divisive relationships, fracturing society and human potential in a nightmare of predatory and self-encapsulated encounters. Compassion opens us up to a deeper human reality where my suffering is your suffering and my joy is your joy. Compassion is systematically blocked within capitalism. But it can inform a human life, as it did Marx's life and that of his wife, Jenny, both of whom voluntarily renounced self-interest, living in squalor out of their compassion for suffering humanity.

When this occurs, the reality of our common life becomes more fully apparent, making simultaneously clear the false and twisted character of the petty self-interested ego. In calling this common life our "species-being," Marx was not making a claim about some preexisting "essential" human nature. Instead, our "species-being" may connote the eschatological potential we hold within us to be open to others and to the depths of existence. The sense of deep community, deep mutual oneness, flows into our lives with this realization. Berdyaev gives the name "God" to the transforming compassion that flows into an open and deeply attentive human life:

> The problem of the shared life, of overcoming the state of being shut up in oneself, and living in isolation is a fundamental problem of human life. Solitude is a late product of advanced culture. Primitive man knew no solitude, he lived too much within his social group for that. Collectivism is earlier than individualism. The experience of solitude raises the question of the shared life in a new way. And for man of the present day, who has fallen away from his organic life, there is no more painful problem. Man lives in a disintegrated world and the final truth is in the fact that the true sharing of life, a true sense of community is a possibility only through God: it comes from above not from below. (1952, p. 215)

This eschatologically realized shared life of the human community is very much the antithesis of the collectivized life found within totalitarian societies, and worlds apart from the mechanized and fragmented life found within the bourgeois democracies today. We must distinguish true personality and true individuality from the adolescent, compulsive self-image or divisive ego that assumes the role of a false individuality under capitalism.

The self-encapsulated ego is to a significant extent a product of the commodification and objectification of human beings. Marx often refers to human beings as "subjects," as free subjectivities. This free subjectivity, which Søren Kierkegaard and Ludwig Wittgenstein understood as prior to language, as the unsayable uniqueness of our human reality, constitutes the ground of the human personality. This principle within us grows toward ever deeper awareness of the miraculous depths of existence and becomes the source of the deepest springs of authentic action. True human community involves the mutual realization of oneness and uniqueness. But this is only possible when compassion flows into our lives from the unspeakable mystery in which we are immersed.

When this openness to the depths of the present moment begins to happen in the human heart, a person realizes that the nexus of causal factors inherited from the past and seemingly determining the present is not the end of the matter. Reason begins to understand that the depths of the universe transcend a merely temporal continuum and that we can be open to a transformative energy that unifies us as one compassionate human reality and lifts us toward our true destiny, which is to live in peace and harmony with one another and with nature on our planetary home. Reason can more clearly and honestly admit that the modern world system of death is at the end of the line if it can also see some alternative, an avenue of hope beyond imminent destruction of humanity and nature.

Eschatological awareness illuminates the possibilities for total transformation that confront us in every present moment. This is the "principle of hope" itself, as Ernst Bloch (1986) realized. The idea of "practical utopia" loses its negative connotations and is understood as integral to our human destiny. Mere reformism and evolution toward a better world are neither possibilities nor viable options in the face of cataclysms faced by humanity today.

Mahatma Gandhi understood this imperative to live in terms of our eschatological possibilities:

> The world of tomorrow will be, must be, a society based on non-violence. That is the first law; out of it all other blessings will flow. It may seem a distant goal, an impractical Utopia. But it is not in the least unobtainable, since it can be worked for here and now. An individual can adopt the way of life of the future – the non-violent way – without having to wait for others to do so. And if an individual can do it, cannot whole groups of individuals? Whole nations? Men often hesitate to make a beginning because they feel that the objective cannot be achieved in its entirety. This attitude of mind is precisely the greatest obstacle to progress – an obstacle that each man, if he only wills it, can clear away.
>
> Equal distribution – the second great law of tomorrow's world as I see it – grows out of non-violence.... I see no poverty in the world of tomorrow,

no wars, no revolutions, no bloodshed. (1987, pp. 458-460).

When accused of being "utopian," Gandhi answered that each of us should live our utopias at all times (Jesudasan, 1984, p. 32), for these constitute our highest, God-realizing, moral nature. Socialism or "equal distribution" is a necessary aspect of any nonviolent society with "no poverty, no wars, no revolutions, no bloodshed." It is primarily a matter of realizing who we actually are, of awakening from our current nightmarish sleep.

Through every historical age and within nearly every culture, people have attested to this sense of a flow into their lives from out of the depths of existence, as Chapters Four, Five, and Six discussed at length. It has been given many different names, and sometimes it has been allowed to remain unnamed. It is the source of our sense of morality, of our sense of mystical oneness, and of our sense of the eschatological meaning of human history.

For the person who has experienced "moments of communion with eternity" the realization begins to dawn that every moment of our lives bear within them the possibility of this same communion. And out of this realization eschatological hope arises. For the depths of existence, which permeate our everyday lives, portend a total transformation, the transformative possibility of a new heaven and a new Earth.

Berdyaev makes this point clear: "Here the human tongue keeps silence. The eschatological outlook is not limited to the prospect of an indefinable end of the world, it embraces in its view every moment of life. At each moment of one's living, what is needed is to put an end to the old world and to begin the new" (1952, p. 254). The transformative possibility portended by a deep awareness of the here and now of our lives is the possibility of true community, of relations of love, compassion, without greed, violence, or hatred.

We intimate our extraordinary potential for a planetary community characterized by the joy and deep fulfillment of living fully and simply on the Earth. The depths and concrete possibilities of our present awareness portend a compassionate, democratic socialism as the political and economic form of love, as planetary maturity and the eschatological fulfillment of our human project.

PART FOUR

Practical Utopia and Democratic World Government

Chapter Ten

The Principle of Unity-in-Diversity and
Three Sources of a Revolutionary Spirituality

Disillusionment with the world knows nothing of the sacrament of coexistence. It can find no place for the sacramental act. It can conjure out of itself no philosophy of action, for its ultimate implication is inaction. If we fail to find finality in the world we will ultimately fail to find it necessary to do anything; and all that we have done will come to seem senseless. But if we can act on faith that is an appreciation of the finality of things, we may come to understand that neither ourselves nor any finite being should be counted at naught. We all stand only together, not only all men, but all things. To abandon things, and to abandon each other, is to be lost....

But as we learn to take things in their darkness, their utter density and darkness, as we can acknowledge them in the intimation of their finality, then we stand upon the threshold of receiving the ultimate gift of things, and obscurity within us gives way to utter light.

Henry G. Bugbee

The mystery of the future and the mystery of the past are united in the mystery of the present. Our time, the time we have, is the time in which we have "presence." But how can we have "presence"? Is not the present moment gone when we think of it? Is not the present the ever-moving boundary line between past and future? But a moving boundary is not a place to stand upon. If nothing were given to us except the "no more" of the past and the "not yet" of the future, we would not have anything....

The mystery is that we have a present; and even more that our future also because we anticipate it in the present; and that we have our past also, because we remember it in the present.... The riddle of the present is the deepest of all riddles of time.... We live in it and it is renewed for us in every new "present." This is possible because every moment of time reaches into the eternal. It is the eternal that stops the flux of time for us. It is the eternal "now" which provides for us a temporal "now".... Not everybody, and nobody all the time, is aware of this "eternal now" in the temporal "now." But sometimes it breaks powerfully into our consciousness and gives us certainty of the eternal, of a dimension of time which cuts into time and gives us our time.

Paul Tillich

Journal entry, 10 January 2000. *It is a vertical axis on which all human value lies. On the horizontal axis lies science, fact, utility, and so on, but running through each human being, wherever they are, is a vertical axis that is the axis of value. Our age is focused on the horizontal. And insofar as it thinks about value, it tries to ground value in the facts, in utility, pleasure, personal satisfactions, social conventions, and the like. This grounding is absolutely impossible and its attempt leads to the immense confusions that characterize our age. Value is encountered only when one faces the vertical axis of our being. This facing has been put in different ways by different thinkers.*

Socrates referred to it as "waking up." Plato called it a "conversion of the soul," a turning round and looking in an entirely different direction. Eric Gutkind in Choose Life called it "standing upright." It has been spoken of by St. Augustine, Meister Eckhart, Kant, Thoreau, Kierkegaard, Wittgenstein, Levinas, Tillich and others. The essential feature of it is a willingness to look "above ourselves," so to speak, or "below ourselves" into the depths, to open ourselves up to where there is only a courageous looking and a certain vertigo, for there is no grounding for the vertical axis. We must have the courage to stand upright and realize that in standing upright we transcend the world of facts, evidence, and grounds.

These are by no means irrelevant. But within the immense complexity of the facts, we can only see our way clear to action if we are "standing upright." Ethics and spirituality flow through us along the vertical axis. To stand upright is accept the mysterious fullness of our human destiny, which is to harmonize and integrate the horizontal and the vertical.

Glen T. Martin

A coherent public policy directed toward world peace for the global civilization confronting us at the dawn of the twenty-first century cannot come out of the institutions presently dominating our planet that are premised on outdated Cartesian and Newtonian conceptions of the individual and society. We must draw instead on the great paradigm-shifts that have characterized the most advanced thinking of the twentieth century but as yet do not inform our institutions, paradigm-shifts summarized here under the heading of "unity-in-diversity." The paradigm-shift required is not simply a shift from one way of seeing the world to another. It is a fundamental transformation from our present stage of human adolescence to planetary maturity. Within the present oppressive world-order, human maturity is profoundly revolutionary.

Deep existential recognition of unity-in-diversity as foundational for human existence involves drawing in one way or another on the three sources of revolutionary spirituality discussed in this volume: the ethical sense of human dignity, the mystical sense of wholeness, and the utopic-eschatological sense demanding fulfillment for our personal lives and for human history. "Revolutionary and compassionate spirituality" is a way of identifying the realization of religious and spiritual maturity in human beings as they become more fully aware of these sources of awakening, whereas "unity-in-diversity" is a principle deriving from the process of spiritual awakening that can be rationally applied as a criterion for global government. In subsequent chapters of Part IV, I will apply this principle concretely to our present world-order. First, it is important to examine the conceptual and spiritual foundations for a revolutionary praxis.

1. Unity-in-Diversity as a Basis for Public Policy

The principle of "unity-in-diversity" operates on many levels, as we have seen. It can be understood as a social, ethical, and cosmological principle recognized by a compassionate spirituality. In Chapter Two, we explored the twentieth-century paradigm-shifts in science (involving relativity theory, quantum mechanics, ecology, and social theory) that have led many to see this century as the "age of unification," of synergism and the integration of whole and part. Individuals do not appear to be independent of the "field" or environment within which whole and part arise together. In the social theories of Karl Marx, George Herbert Mead, and Jürgen Habermas, for example, individuals are understood as profoundly social, what we call "the self" being inseparable from the social matrix that forms and sustains it. Scientifically, philosophically, and socially we are moving toward unity. As Raimon Panikkar puts it, "this thirst for unity is not only ontological and epistemological (unity of being, unity of intellection), it is also sociological and political (unity of humankind, unity of civilizations)" (1993, p. 7).

Yet care must be taken if we are to formulate a viable public policy on this principle. False unities and irresponsible reductionisms are not impossible, as postmodern skeptics and pluralists are quick to point out. We do not wish to move from an ideologically motivated nominalism and Cartesian individualism into the hands of an equally ideological universalism. We require what Raimundo Panikkar calls an "open horizon" in the face of our planetary need for a unified "vision of reality," an horizon that does not close off the vision with some form of reductionism or dogmatism. What is required, he argues, is a philosophical synthesis showing the inseparability of whole and part, and not emphasizing either one at the expense of the other (1993, pp. 5-7).

As Wittgenstein would remind us, the notions of whole and part might be expressed in several ways on a number of different levels. These would necessarily overlap and interconnect as part of the family resemblances of various language games involving these concepts. For philosophical purposes we will distinguish five ways these concepts can be expressed. First, whole and part could be considered ethically, for example, in Kantian terms. What is the relation of the individual, with specific needs and inclinations, to the universality of moral laws? We have seen Kant argue that every individual ethical decision necessarily places the individual under universal ethical laws applicable to all persons. Habermas extends the Kantian ethical theme with the question of the relation of moral laws to society: can we formulate a "discursive" version of universal moral law that involves the whole of society, as well as the individual, in its legislation?

Second, we might speak of whole and part on a human or planetary level, as Marx does, for example. What is the relation of the unique individual to our species-being or our social and human nature, the principle that makes us all human, a principle larger than cultural, racial, or individual commonalities? Erich Fromm expresses this idea as follows: "One individual represents the human race. He is one specific example of the human species. He is 'he' and he is 'all'; he is an individual with his peculiarities and in this sense unique, and at the same time he is representative of all characteristics of the human race" (1947, p. 47).

Third, whole and part are often today discussed "organically." Human beings can be understood in relation to the ecosystems of our planet, the whole being larger than human nature and involving what some have called "Gaia," the planetary system itself. Human beings are an inseparable part of the ecological web of life on this planet. Fourth, "synergistic" accounts of whole and part often extend this interconnectedness to the universe itself, understanding the individual, the human species, and the Earth in relation to the cosmos, wholes and parts existing in mutual interrelations on various levels within the whole of the cosmos (see Mansueto, 1995).

Finally, there is what might be called the expression of whole and part found in many accounts of mystical experience. On these accounts, there is often the conviction that the whole and part mutually interpenetrate in a simultaneity of unity and difference, or oneness and manyness, in ways utterly inexpressible and beyond conceptual language (in an experience of what is often called "God," "Brahman," "Allah," or "Dharmakaya"). There is an unspeakable depth of existence, pointed to by mystics, which should not be forgotten in discussing the relations of whole and part of any of these other levels. For practical purposes in this chapter, my argument will draw primarily upon the first, or ethical, and the last, or mystical, understandings of whole and part.

However, given this complexity of overlapping possibilities in reflecting on the relations of whole and part, and the contemporary concern to express the new paradigm emerging from the sciences, we must take care to observe Panikkar's warning to preserve the inseparability and interdependency of unity and diversity. In this task we also need formulations that preserve what he calls an intellectual "open horizon," free of dogmatism. Finally, with Panikkar, we need to take seriously the experiences of the mystics who point to the depths of the interpenetration of whole and part, beyond language, knowledge, and being.

We not only wish to preserve the sense of open horizon, but also to communicate the inadequacy of all formulations in the face of the absolute mystery of existence and point to these depths, beyond knowledge, in which all things participate. We need to avoid *systems* that see the relation of the whole and part as solely a matter of knowledge, and *closed* systems that deny the infinite depths of the world. With respect to this project of attending to the dangers inherent in considering the relations of whole and part, we should at this point consider the thought of Emmanuel Levinas who expresses significant philosophical criticisms of the ontological-totalizing tendencies of many nineteenth and twentieth-century formulations of this issue.

2. The Thought of Levinas in Relation to Unity-in-Diversity

Levinas' critique of idealism might appear as an objection to any principle linking whole and part in a social system, such as democratic world government discussed below. This objection is sometimes also voiced by anarchists who posit local cooperative communities over and against what they fear as the threat of an authoritarian "totality" (see Chomsky, 1994). Levinas says that "the idealist intelligible constitutes a system of coherent ideal relations whose presentation before the subject is equivalent to the entry of the subject into this order and its absorption into those ideal relations" (1969, p. 216). He fears the implications of this totalization that may lead to the notion of "the universal State in which multiplicity is reabsorbed and discourse comes to an end, for lack of interlocutors" (1969, p. 217).

Any conception of the primacy of the whole over the parts (or of the parts derived from a knowledge of being, which he calls "ontology"), as was the case, for example, in the Soviet Union, can serve as a foundation for tyranny. "Ontology as first philosophy," he writes, "is a philosophy of power....which appears in the tyranny of the State. Truth, which should reconcile persons, here exists anonymously. Universality presents itself as impersonal; and this is another inhumanity" (1969, p. 46). This is a danger to be given careful consideration. For Levinas, only if the uniqueness and particularity of persons is prior to the system of universal relations, or reason, can we avoid such absorption and implicitly totalitarian results. The ethical dimension, he asserts, is also the absolute obligation encountered in the infinity reflected in "the human face."

The freedom of persons confronts us as infinitely transcending what might be contained in any ontological, factual, or rational description of them as persons. It exists prior to any political dimension, and is the primary relationship among persons, preserving their uniqueness in contradistinction to any rationalist or idealist system. Panikkar stresses a related idea:

> Nothing which stifles human freedom can endure or be called truly human. Humanness demands the free fulfillment of Man. There is no justice if

liberty is not respected. But there is no freedom where justice is violated. No monistic system or uniform worldview will ever satisfy the inexhaustible versatility of Man, whose greatest dignity is inseparable from his or her freedom and personal uniqueness. (1993, p. 8)

The warnings of Levinas and Panikkar are well-taken. Yet there is no *a priori* reason why world government, or any government, cannot be founded on precisely this understanding of the absolute uniqueness of persons. We have seen Levinas point to the "infinity" of persons that places them beyond all knowledge and beyond any system attempting to derive understanding of persons causally or analytically from a conception of the totality. Similarly, he says God is "infinite" in the sense of a mystery, akin to persons, beyond knowledge and beyond any conception of totality (1969, pp. 292-294).

Yet "wholeness," as attested to by many who have experienced the mystical identity of whole and part, is a living experience of oneness beyond all knowledge and conceptual totalities. It is not identical with any conceptual totalities, as we have seen twentieth century mystic Jiddu Krishnamurti point out (for example, 1978). Levinas' own thinking moves beyond being, understood as the conceptual totality, to the unknowable "infinite." There is no *a priori* reason why "wholeness" cannot point beyond human knowledge and conceptual totalities in the same way the uniqueness of persons does. Spiritual masters within every world religious tradition have testified to this idea, among them Rumi, Plotinus, Śankara, Lao Tzu, Buddha, and Meister Eckhart.

Krishnamurti recognizes this wholeness beyond all conceptual totalities that arises directly from the fullness of human awareness. "The particular by itself," he says, "has very little meaning, but when you see the total, then that particular has a relationship to the whole.... So the real question is: does one see the total process of life or is one concentrated on the particular, thus missing the whole field of life?" (1977, p. 44). And in spite of his tremendous compassion and attention to individual detail with respect to nature and people, Krishnamurti is led to associate human ethical corruption with precisely our lack of wholeness: "So what is one to do," he asks, "in this disintegrating, corrupt, immoral world, as a human being – not an individual, because there is no such thing as the individual – we are human beings, we are collective, not individual" (1978, p. 55).

This living, compassionate wholeness, for Krishnamurti, is not a merely conceptual totality and cannot serve as a ground for the intellectual derivation of the individual from such a totality. Part and whole arise together, for him, beyond language and all conceptual totalities, as they do for most whose lives participate in the processes of mystical awakening.

Access to this fundamental awareness is the heritage of every person born on this planet and constitutes our fundamental possibility as human beings. In mystical awareness the depths within each absolutely unique person are inseparably linked to the depths of our oneness. If God is beyond knowledge, for Levinas, like the human individual made in the image of God, then this applies just as much to that dimension of God traditionally called "immanent." Levinas does not explicitly recognize the sense in which what were traditionally called the "immanence" and "transcendence" of God were beyond knowledge for those who experienced these mysteries directly. He does not recognize that the traditional sense of the "immanence" of God always involved the realization that the one and the many arise together in some fundamental way that can only be "experienced" and never conceptualized. According to Panikkar,

> Every being has an abyssal dimension, both transcendent and immanent. Every being transcends everything – including and perhaps most pointedly "itself," which in truth has no limits. It is, further, infinitely immanent, i.e., inexhaustible and unfathomable. And this is so not because the limited powers of our intellect cannot pierce deeper, but because this depth belongs to every being as such. (1993, p. 61)

Compare the way Teilhard de Chardin expresses this principle using the concept of "Omega" to represent the completed wholeness and endpoint of emergent evolution. In the whole, we find:

> Each particular consciousness remaining conscious of itself..., and (this must be absolutely understood) each particular consciousness becoming still more itself and more distinct from others the closer it gets to them in Omega....In every organized whole, the parts perfect themselves and fulfill themselves..., the grains of consciousness do not tend to lose their outline and blend, but, on the contrary, to accentuate the depth and incommunicability of their Egos. (Happold, 1970, pp. 400-401)

Oneness and individuality can be seen to arise together in mutual fulfillment prior to all knowledge, totalities, and systems. Human awareness can be said to "shade off" from a practical and ethical insight into the inseparability of the one and the many as expressed by thinkers like Kant, Marx, and Habermas to an awareness beyond knowledge of the depths of this inseparability as expressed, for example, by Krishnamurti, Panikkar, and Teilhard.

In his essay "The Ultimate State of Consciousness," scholar of mysticism Ken Wilber writes:

> As Seng-t'san points out, "Not two" does not mean just One. For pure Oneness is most dualistic, excluding as it does its opposite of Manyness.

The single One opposes the plural Many, while the Nondual embraces them both. "One without a second" means "One without an opposite," not One opposed to Many. Thus, as we have already hinted, we mustn't picture the Absolute as excluding diversity, as being an undifferentiated monistic mush, for Brahman embraces both unity and multiplicity with equanimity. (1995, pp. 199-200)

Levinas' fears of a totality that eliminates diversity or the infinite mystery of the individual human being are unfounded. Unity and diversity are not only compatible, they are inseparable on the deepest level of existence. The unity of existence is a "non-dual" unity. It is not opposed in any way to diversity but is the ground and source of the very possibility of diversity. I agree with Wilber that this was also fundamental to Wittgenstein's thought.

According to Benedictine theologian and Zen Master Willigis Jäger, "the whole universe is none other than the correspondence between the two poles of individuality and totality.... Here mysticism," he says, "has to avoid two extremes above all: an excessive stress on the individual and a dissolution into the One and Only. As human beings we are quite individual structures of the primal principle, irreplaceable and unique" (1994, p. 53). The ethical principle of the relationship between whole and part elaborated by Kant, Marx, and Habermas is understood at the profoundest level beyond ego-consciousness and beyond knowledge to be constitutive of the depths of existence itself. Levinas' critique misses the crucial insight that genuine wholeness, like genuine individuality, is beyond knowledge, beyond ontology, and beyond all potentially totalitarian conceptual systems.

3. Reason in Relation to Knowledge and Being

As Enrique Dussel points out, human beings are near the end with their long obsession with knowledge and being (1985, chs. 1 and 5). This obsession was a crucial part of our growth from the pre-maturity period that ranged from several centuries before the common era to the twentieth century. It raised us out of mythology into the era of reason and objectivity, gave us natural law theory, the notion of universal equality, human rights, and universal justice.

But the deepest truth of the human situation, the intersection of ethical awareness, compassion, and eschatological hope, is beyond knowledge and being. For these dimensions of our situation come to us "as if from God," as Plato expressed it in the sixth book of the *Republic*, for the good, he understood, is "beyond being" (*hyperousía*). These ever-present dimensions of our existence ("the good" understood as ethical, mystical, and eschatological) confront us at every moment, but, entangled, as we are, all unknowing in the net of language, we do not often recognize them as such.

When we do on occasion experience, for example, the total responsibility for the other through our response to the face of the other, or experience the unsayable immediacy of the spring flower, we mistake these for mere subjective experiences. We are lost in the untenable ideological disjunction between "objective reality" that is the object of knowledge and the sciences and "mere subjectivity," which includes everything else. The aesthetic, ethical, religious, mystical, and compassionate dimensions of our lives are all reduced to "mere subjectivity."

One fundamental theme of the Bible is the demand of God that we "stand upright," becoming vertical creatures, inheriting our destiny as creatures made in the image of God. This idea is found, for example, at Nehemiah 9:5, Isaiah 51:17, Ezekiel 2:1, Daniel 11:4, Luke 6:8, Acts 14:10, and so on. Yet we cling to what we perceive as solid, secure, and safe, looking beneath us into the "horizontal" dimension of existence. We cling to a blind, ritual performance of "the law" if we are Jews of Biblical times, or to a "literal interpretation of the Bible" if we are their modern heirs. Or, if the progress of knowledge has led us to overthrow what we take to be Biblical superstition, we cling to knowledge, science, facts, and become lost in the modern totalitarian nightmare of valuelessness, relativism, and one-dimensional consumer existence. And we cling, all of us, to money and economic security in a world where our security is always someone else's misery, where first-world retirement investments exploit the poverty and misery of third-world citizens while simultaneously promoting the ecological destruction of the planet.

The maturity of human beings will involve creating systems (economic, social, and cultural systems) that put human beings first. It will involve creating systems that are founded on the dignity and value of each human being. The concern and fulfillment of each mature person on the planet will be with the others, will consist in seeing that all the others are treated with dignity and respect, having food, housing, medical care, education, personal security, the right to personal property, the right to family and participation in the community, and so on. But this maturity is not possible for people unwilling to "stand upright" and open themselves to the vertical dimension of existence.

The "facts," knowledge and being, are themselves no grounding for the recognition of infinite value in other persons and the need to preserve our planetary environment. Fact and value are in some respects separate dimensions, metaphorically speaking, one horizontal, the other vertical.

Yet our human destiny is to harmonize and integrate these dimensions through transforming our political, social, and economic worlds. Here is a fundamental role for reason recognized neither by positivists nor by critical theorists in the Marxist tradition. Here lie the foundations of revolutionary theory.

There are those who worry that moving beyond knowledge will mean that reason will also be transcended and all manner of evils will be justified by the appeal to passion or unreason. How do we distinguish Hitler's nightmarish appeal to blood and soil from the Buddhist appeal to the unsayable unity-in-diversity of things? How do we distinguish the sham preacher who enriches himself by preying on people through a claim to inspired experiences of God's will from the inspired speech of a Martin Luther King, Jr., who has a "dream" of a world of equality, dignity, and freedom?

The answer was given by Jesus and many other great spiritual teachers: by their fruits you shall know them. The fundamental truth of the dignity, freedom, and worth of each individual person cannot be abridged by any claim to the rights of a collective over and against individuals. And this untenable domination of the collective is asserted not only in societies lacking political freedoms, but when individuals claim the special privileges of accumulated private property (beyond their immediate personal property) or power or status when there are others who are denied even the basic necessities required for personal dignity and freedom.

The rights of each individual over the collective consist in the claim that the collective must create economic, social, and cultural institutions that provide dignity and freedom for every citizen on the planet. Once everyone has clean water, decent food, housing, and the rest, within a sustainable world economic order, then we can discuss variations of cultural or economic privilege beyond that point. The present capitalist world-order is so utterly corrupt (in the institutional sense based on exploitation of people and the planet for private profit rather than on human dignity), so utterly unsustainable, and so utterly incapable of providing basic necessities to all citizens of the Earth that it cannot be reformed but must be abolished through social revolution.

These are the fruits of a true wisdom and insight. By these fruits we can distinguish true compassion and wisdom beyond language from false irrational claims. Any ideology that benefits only one group, nation, race, sex, religious sect, or class is a false ideology, whether or not it claims to be beyond knowledge. Ultimately, a world society based on human dignity and freedom will not be beyond reason, even though it will include an awareness beyond knowledge. Critical and communicative forms of reasoning are necessary for creating a just and peaceful world-order. Scientific and dialectical reasoning (so eloquently discussed , for example, in the works of Errol E. Harris) are absolutely necessary. But they are not sufficient. They must be complemented by a breakthrough beyond knowledge and being to the ethical, mystical, and eschatological.

Our notion of reason must be enlarged and extended yet further. Reason recognizes universals, sees patterns, draws conclusions, assesses equality and difference of cases, synthesizes into wholes, functions dialectically, and so on. But reason is unable to ground human life and it is asking too much of it to do so. People will always use reasoning in their daily lives, and ultimately reason exerts a "normative pull," as Habermas argues, toward ever greater degrees of communicative rationality and ever greater limitations on strategic and instrumental forms of rationality. But our current notion of rationality is much too narrow. If "rationality" is supposed to be embodied in our current professors of philosophy in universities, or in their faculty in general, or in people with Ph.Ds, then the world is in even deeper trouble than we are supposing.

Most contemporary professors of philosophy, as well as other university faculty, are utterly complicit in the vicious system of worldwide exploitation. They seem to be quite devoid of wisdom, complacent ideological clones, using "reason" to justify their privileged and corrupt lives lived at the expense of the exploited masses in their own countries and the third-world. Practical reason does not reside with such people but with ordinary people, as Kant pointed out, who often have more wisdom, insight, and practical rationality than the professors who scorn their ignorance. Communicative rationality, as Habermas asserts, arises within the lifeworld.

But even the communicative rationality of Habermas cannot be grounded in any "being" beyond language and cannot justify our sense of the absolute dignity of each human person and the absolute responsibility that we experience for one another. Communicative rationality cannot produce an ethical imperative or command that we do what is right regardless of social pressures, personal advantage, or the systems of privilege to which we belong. This is why neither critical nor communicative rationality can articulate a revolutionary imperative, an absolute duty to subordinate egoistic self-interest to action for a transformed world for all citizens of the planet and for future generations.

One meets many academic Marxists who lead lives of personal self-indulgence rather than lives of revolutionary action. Rationality must one day work in harmony with the ethical, mystical, and eschatological that comprise the deep truth of our situation. From these sources, absolute responsibility and non-self-indulgent action, connected with a deep experience of unity-in-diversity, flows into human life.

Here the role of rationality is enlarged. Beyond its obvious uses in science and technology, reason, we have seen, can expose the ideological self-justifications of exploitative institutions. It can also understand the limits of language and its own sphere of operation, as it does for example in the thought of Wittgenstein, thereby making possible awareness of what is beyond language. Yet, finally, reason can understand the processes of human growth and maturity (which are linked to the processes of cosmogenesis and the evolution of human consciousness on Earth). In doing so it can work to cooperate with the cosmic process and seek to harmonize all aspects of our being into wholeness as we continue to evolve.

The "integral philosophy" of Sri Aurobindo (1872-1950) emphasizes this role for human reason, harmonizing and promoting the ever greater realization of unity-in-diversity that is our cosmic destiny and vocation. Scholar of Indian thought J. N. Mohanty describes this process:

> It is Sri Aurobindo's singular vision that this mode of self-awareness is beyond the separative mental consciousness and nearer that divine self-consciousness – towards which man is growing – for which unity and plurality do not jar.... It is possible now, and indeed it is his spiritual responsibility, that man should consciously co-operate with the cosmic process. The *urge* is towards a higher (in the sense of being more integrated, harmonious, all-comprehensive and based not on separation but identity) mode of consciousness. The *task* is to prepare the ground for the emergence of such a mode of consciousness, morality, individual and social, religion, personal and institutional, art and literature, science and technology, education and social ordering – all these activities of man may be understood and evaluated in the light of this most fundamental responsibility that is placed on man by virtue of his unique position in the evolutionary process. (1960, pp. 162-163)

Reason cannot ground human existence or human knowledge in any absolute certainties beyond language, whether these be called the "facts" or the "ontological structures of being." However, this very insight can lead reason to its proper role as facilitator of the processes of human-divine-cosmic evolutionary maturity.

4. The Mystical Source of a Revolutionary Spirituality

The ethical-mystical implications of Buddhist compassion (*karunā*) or Christian love (*agapē*) make capitalism an impossibility. The selfishness and greed at the heart of a system designed around the private accumulation of wealth is in direct contradiction to the deep meaning of the human situation that is compassionate oneness with all sentient creatures, and most fundamentally with human beings. The mystic directly experiences this unity-in-diversity with the result that he or she also experiences the grace of *karunā* or *agapē*, genuine compassionate oneness, or genuine unselfish, other directed love. In Sermon 6, Meister Eckhart asserts:

> There is something in the soul which is only God and the masters say it is nameless, having no proper name of its own.... For herein the soul takes its whole life and being and from this source it draws its life and being, for this is totally in God.... So you might say that all things and God too are yours. That is to say – empty yourself of your ego and of all things and of all that you are in yourself and consider yourself as what you are in God.... For your human nature and that of the divine Word are no different – it's one and the same. (1980, pp. 103-104)

And in Sermon 31 he adds that "The highest work of God is compassion and this means that God sets the soul in the highest and purest place which it can occupy.... Reason can never comprehend him in the ocean of his unfathomableness. I say that beyond these two, beyond knowledge and love, there is compassion. In the highest and purest acts that God works, God works compassion" (1980, pp. 441-442).

Wealth, in Buddhism or Christianity, should always be other-directed, just as my ethical obligation for Kant and Levinas is directed to the other. Just as the Bodhisattva does not seek a private *nirvāna* but vows never to enter final *nirvāna* until all sentient beings are liberated, so the Christian fathers affirm the other-directed nature of compassion. As St John Chrysostom (c. 349-407) wrote, "The rich are in possession of the goods of the poor, even if they have acquired them honestly or inherited them legally" (Cort, 1988, p. 45). Or as St. Thomas Aquinas wrote, "Do not say, 'I am using what belongs to me.' You are using what belongs to others. All the wealth of the world belongs to you and to the others in common, as the sun, air, Earth, and all the rest" (Cort, 1988, p. 45). For a morally healthy human being, other persons claim priority over my self-interest.

This means that most wealth must be social wealth, generated and distributed by the community to its members, and ultimately, the community includes the sentient creatures inhabiting the entire planet. Each creature manifests an absolute uniqueness beyond knowledge, just as each creature in its uniqueness is inseparable from the whole, from its Buddha or Christ nature. Only democratic socialism combines these features that are realized within awakened minds: the democratic valuing of each individual (who has infinite value because he or she is a human being), and socialistic valuing of the whole of humanity within which our individuality emerges and from which it is ultimately inseparable.

Wholeness means the following: as long as any human being is deprived of her humanity through poverty, exploitation, privation of educational opportunity or health care, no person has the moral right (no matter how lost she may be in the ignorance of private egoism) to accumulate unearned capital. Nor is there any moral right to generate "advertisements" that attempt to manipulate people into consuming at the expense of others. Our genuine human fulfillment as well as our personal integrity lies in the opposite direction.

The welfare of others is the source of my moral integrity (Kant and Levinas), and my fulfillment consists in realizing the unspeakable fulness-emptiness of existence in which the others, like all things, are experienced as holy and fulfilling of my spirit. The community is prior to the individual, in one sense, but this must not be understood as the sacrifice of individuality but as its fulfillment, since as the fulfillment of each consists in the welfare of others, my welfare is assured. It is utterly dependent on their good will, just as their welfare is utterly dependent on my good will. Unity-in-diversity is the very structure of existence, as Meister Eckhart understood, although language tends to ontologize what must be directly realized beyond knowledge.

5. The Ethical Source of a Revolutionary Spirituality

Despite the fact that Wittgenstein effected his famous turnabout from the picture theory of language of his early *Tractatus Logico-Philosophicus* (1921) to the philosophy of ordinary language in the later *Philosophical Investigations* (1953), the spirit and framework of his life-work was all of a piece, reflecting the great intensity and seriousness of his mind and the often unspoken religious and ethical insights behind his reflections concerning language. "I am not a religious man," he wrote, "but I cannot help looking at every problem from a religious point of view" (Rhees, 1981, p. 94).

Wittgenstein expressed much of the spirit of his life's work when he wrote: "Those who have found after a long period of doubt that the sense of life became clear to them have been unable to say what constituted that sense" (1961, p. 73). The reason that the sense of life cannot be expressed is because the good can only be apprehended through direct apprehension outside of language. The depths of existence are not within the grasp of everyday meaning and sense, nor of science. This is also true of the ethical dimension for Wittgenstein. "You cannot lead people to what is good;" he wrote, "you can only lead them to some place or other. The good is outside the space of facts" (1980, p.3e)

Wittgenstein could never have written an entire book on "ethics," as his friend G.E. Moore, for example, had done. He could only delineate what can be said, the dimension of ordinary meaning and sense, and gesture to something that must be seen or encountered, prior to knowledge, with respect to the good. Yet Wittgenstein's "Lecture on Ethics" (1930) stresses the absolute importance of this enquiry, for it is "the enquiry into the meaning of life, or into what makes life worth living, or into the right way of living" (1965, p. 5).

With respect to statements about the good, he distinguishes the "trivial or relative sense" of expressions from the "ethical or absolute sense" and concludes that we cannot express the latter in language, that "nothing we could ever think or say would be *the* thing" (1965, p.7). Ethics, he says, "is supernatural and our words will only express facts" (p.7). No book on ethics can be written. If a person could "write a book on Ethics which really was a book on Ethics, this book would, with an explosion, destroy all the other books in the world" (p. 7).

Such statements by one of the greatest thinkers of the twentieth century give us pause. It would seem that positivism, science, and technology have all omitted what is most fundamental about human life and that what is most fundamental must be encountered directly in an immediacy prior to language and thought. It is not impulse, or emotion, or "irrational." Nor for Wittgenstein is this "far away" in some mystical other world. "God grant the philosopher," he writes, "insight into what lies in front of everyone's eyes" (1980, p.63e).

His "Lecture on Ethics" attempts to point to what he means by "absolute value" with three examples. The first, which he calls "my experience *par excellence,*" is the experience of "wonder at the existence of the world." When he has this experience, Wittgenstein says, he is inclined to use phrases like "how extraordinary that anything should exist" (1965, p.8). His second absolute experience he calls "the experience of feeling *absolutely safe,*" and the third experience he mentions is that of "feeling guilty."

One significant feature of Wittgenstein's "Lecture on Ethics" is that these "absolute experiences" that gesture toward the ethical dimension in which "the sense of life" has become clear to him do not themselves discuss the social relation between persons. Yet his lecture includes this social relation within what he means by "absolute value." In distinguishing between the "trivial" and the "ethical or absolute" sense of certain phrases, Wittgenstein makes a distinction similar to Kant's distinction between hypothetical and categorical imperatives, the former being non-moral and the latter absolute or ethical imperatives.

Wittgenstein distinguishes senses of "good" that are "trivial," such as "a good pianist," the "right road," "playing tennis badly," from ethical senses, such as "telling a lie" in which case the proper response is "you ought to want to behave better" (1965, p. 5). But if a person does not see this "ought," no reiteration of the facts will make a difference. In the sense of absolute value, or the special case of the ethical imperative in relation to other persons, we are confronted with something that cannot be encompassed within the conceptual world of knowledge or science. Yet for Wittgenstein this is the dimension of "absolute value" (1965, p. 7). It is "what makes life worth living" (p. 5).

Wittgenstein died in 1951. In our day, the work of such thinkers as Levinas and Enrique Dussel has carried forward this recognition of the ethical in an "infinity" or unsayable dimension beyond knowledge, beyond even phenomenological description. Genuine value, whether the absolute value of persons or that expressed in the astonishment that anything at all exists, is apparent to us in an immediacy prior to conceptualization or language. But it hears the cry of the poor, "I am hungry; give me something to eat." As Wittgenstein put it in his notebooks of 1929: "What is good is also divine. Queer as it sounds, that sums up my ethics. Only something supernatural can express the Supernatural" (1980, p.3e).

The absolute imperative to treat other persons as ends-in-themselves, experienced as divine, Wittgenstein suggests (precisely because it is absolute) is equivalent to acting out of *agapē* or compassion. In Kantian language, compassion is not an "inclination" that may or may not be there, depending on how we happen to feel at the moment. Instead, compassion, like the "absolute good" of ethics, is non-attached. It is not a mere feeling. This is the reason Jesus can command *agapē* (Matthew 22:39), whereas a subjective feeling cannot be commanded. For Wittgenstein, this imperative that confronts human beings with an immediacy prior to language can only be called "supernatural."

6. The Eschatological Source of a Revolutionary Spirituality

Eschatology is present in Marx. He sees a break between the history of causality and determination within class societies toward the full realization of human potential (which is also the potential at the heart of history) in the classless society. In the case of Marx this is due to his insight into the hidden depths and possibilities of humanity, evinced in many passages cited, for example, in George Brenkert's book *Marx's Ethics of Freedom* (1983). Marx has a social understanding, similar to Freud's understanding in the psychological realm, that our life in society is governed by blind laws that destroy human dignity, freedom, and potential for the fulness of life precisely because we are not conscious of these blind forces.

For Marx, the eschatological fulfillment of history and of human potential comes about through an increase of human self-consciousness of historical-social-economic processes as well as through recognition of the dignity and value of other persons. Self-awareness frees us from the blind forces, for example, of capitalism, where people are trapped within a network of "market forces," laws of supply and demand, destructive competition, inflation, and commodification, unaware that these blind forces to which we feel we must submit as if they were laws of nature are in reality created by us and can be transformed by us.

Self-consciousness breaks the power of these laws over us and frees us for an entirely transformed world based on human dignity, freedom, and the development of human potentialities for the fulness of life. Self-conscious freedom and dignity themselves, if actualized in society, carry within them the eschatological potential for a transformed world, an end to history as it has always been, the beginning of true human fulfillment and fulfillment of the hidden potential within history (see Martin, 1998).

Similarly, there is an eschatological dimension within the thought of Levinas. As with Marx, a break with all previous history is possible. But Levinas in *Totality and Infinity* is even more explicit: this break is made possible by something within our human situation that is not more of "the same," more of the causality, determinism, and domination of the sameness of "being" over the entire process. The entire Preface and Chapter One of this book involves an extended discussion of eschatology. Levinas argues that if "history itself [is] an identification of the same" (1961, p. 40), and like all knowledge, presupposes a totalization in which self and other are encompassed by a being that is sameness, then eschatology cannot be understood in terms of history.

"The absolutely other," he writes, "whose alterity is overcome in the philosophy of immanence on the allegedly common plane of history, maintains his transcendence in the midst of history" (1961, p. 40). There may be some ambiguity in what Levinas means by "the philosophy of immanence." But if this phrase carries connotations of the traditional Western notion that God is being and that God as being is immanent and transcendent, then the "philosophy of immanence" is poorly understood if it assumes that immanence within the totality compromises the otherness of God or of humans made in God's image.

Although much traditional Western thought is limited by its articulation under the thought of "being" and through expression in terms of "being," as we have seen, the experience of immanence was quite often simultaneously that of a transcendence unassimilable to the categories of knowledge, as, for example, in the writings of Meister Eckhart. The other person confronts us within an immanence (an immediacy or closeness) that is simultaneously transcendent. The "proximity" of Enrique Dussel (1990) is simultaneously the unsayable transcendent mystery.

The transcendent (beyond the world) and immanent (within the world) dimensions of God are beyond language and beyond totalization and sameness. But this does not obviate the possibility that the immanence of God or other persons as infinite is at the heart of history. By contrast, Levinas reserves the notion of "transcendence" for this feature of our human situation: "Transcendence designates a relation with a reality infinitely distant from my own reality, yet without this distance destroying this relation and without this relation destroying this distance, as would happen with relations within the same" (1961, p. 41).

Similarly, for Levinas, eschatology can be understood as otherness entering time without losing its otherness. It is the hope of incarnation, the kingdom of God on Earth, a hope precisely not comprehensible within the limits of cause and effect, historical forces, or a *telos* determining the direction of history. Rather it is a hope involving the non-concept of "grace," the transcendent infusing the world without losing its character as transcendent:

> Eschatology institutes a relation with being *beyond the totality* or beyond history, and not with being beyond the past and the present.... It is a relation-ship with *a surplus always exterior to the totality*, as though the objective totality did not fill the true measure of being, as though another concept, the concept of *infinity*, were needed to express this transcendence with regard to totality, non encompassable within a totality and as primordial as total-ity.... The eschatological, as the "beyond" of history, draws beings out of the jurisdiction of history and the future; it arouses them in and calls them forth to their full responsibility. Submitting history as a whole to judgment, exterior to the very wars that mark its end, it restores to each instant its full signification in that very instant. (1961, pp. 22-23)

Here Levinas points to the mysterious depths of the absolute present moment that contain, in his words, "a surplus always exterior to the totality" that reason attempts to comprehend under the category of "the same." This surplus submits "history as a whole to judgment" and indicates the possibility of a genuine "peace" beyond the "wars" that have characterized the oppressive "sameness" of all of history.

In this book I have pointed to the "depths" that fall away from us on every side: in the human Other, in the immediacy of concrete things, in the mystery of creation, the experience of beauty, in temporality and futurity, and in human experiences of breakthrough to oneness. These depths undermine the totalistic character of the deterministic and causally conditioned view of the future. Transformations and breakthroughs are possible at any time. Eschatological hope intuits this uncanny nature of existence: the unimagined and transfigurative possibilities of existence that can never be encompassed within the sameness of the past.

Since it is impossible to give an account of what precisely goes beyond all accounting and all language, different understandings of the grounds of these possibilities are common. Ultimately only phenomenological description (or what Levinas calls "meta-phenomenological description) would seem possible, but here, description itself can lend to differing accounts. At some point, interpretation must enter and the same descriptions of mystical experiences can be used in a Freudian reductionistic account (regression to infantilism) or in a religious account (union with God). What is not an "interpretation," because it is beyond language and the perspectival ego, is the direct experience of the depths of the absolute present.

No ultimately decisive decision procedure is possible with respect to these differing accounts. That is why the description must be used in conjunction with a philosophy of the limits to language (such as that provided by Wittgenstein) in order to illuminate the unsayable character of these depths (see Martin, 1989, Chs 5-9). Therefore, the need to stop! Therefore, the need for silence! To stop talk and interpretation and bring persons up against the unsayable. Then, and then only, can we begin to talk once again, this time with a stammering, tentative attempt to assess our human situation in the light of not only knowledge but knowledge always in confrontation with the unsayable depths that encompass our situation. These depths include the eschatological, the sense of "a surplus always exterior to the totality," which indicates the possibility of a genuine transfiguration of our human situation from the history of the same (war) to genuine newness (peace).

It is fascinating to reflect, in this regard, on the controversial final thoughts of Jean-Paul Sartre published as *Hope Now* (1996). Sartre was one of the brilliant minds of our time. He dedicated himself since the 1940s to the praxis of revolution and authored the *Critique of Dialectical Reason* that attempted to do for the Marxist tradition what Kant's *Critique of Pure Reason* did for early modern epistemology. In the Introduction to *Hope Now,* Ronald Aronson calls him "one of the geniuses of Western Marxism" (p.24). Yet in these interviews, Sartre says he is embarking on a project "with the idea of rediscovering a guiding principle for the left as it exists today" (p. 60), a left for whom original Marxist categories are no longer sufficient:

A left that has given up on everything, that currently is crushed, that allows a wretched right wing to triumph....When I use the term "right wing," for me it means dirty bastards. Either this left is going to die, in which case man dies at the same moment, or new principles must be discovered for it. I would like our discussion here both to sketch out an ethics and to find a true guiding principle for the left. (p. 61)

New principles are needed for the left, Sartre says, because what unites people in the struggle for equality, fraternity, and justice is something deeper than "the bonds of production...the fact of being producers;" what unites people "is that they are human beings." "Society as being the result of a bond among people," he says, "that's more basic than politics" (p. 86). He calls this bond "fraternity" and its basis is "ethics."

After a lifelong intellectual adventure, Sartre has gone beyond his early notion that the most basic human modality is our egoistic desire to be God, to be solely concerned with ourselves even at the expense of the other, a theme prominent in *Being and Nothingness* (1956; see 1996, p. 59). He now sees that we also have a modality of concern for the other that can be called "ethics." "By 'ethics,'" he says, "I mean that every consciousness, no matter whose, has a dimension that I didn't study in my philosophical works and that few people have studied, for that matter: the dimension of obligation....By obligation I mean that at every moment that I am conscious of anything or do anything, there exists a kind of requisition that goes beyond the real and results in the fact that the action I want to perform includes a kind of inner constraint, which is a dimension of my consciousness" (pp. 69-70).

Unlike his earliest works where there was no genuine "other," Sartre now says that "each consciousness seems to me now simultaneously to constitute itself as a consciousness and, at the same time, as the consciousness of the other and for the other. It is this reality – the self considering itself as self for the other, having a relationship with the other – that I call ethical conscience" (p. 71).

The "other" ultimately means all others, and the goal implicit in this ethical awareness is a universal "humanity" or "fraternity" in which "you need to extend the idea of fraternity until it becomes the manifest, unique relationship among all human beings" (p. 93). This, he says, is "the goal that all men have within them" (p. 90). The revolutionary struggle against the current world system of material scarcity is precisely also an ethical struggle and an eschatological struggle. Revolution, Sartre says, means "doing away with the present society and replacing it by a juster society in which human beings can have good relations with each other" (p. 107). This struggle, the struggle for the "ethical end" that is "the beginning of the existence of men who live for each other" (p. 106), is the effort to engender what he calls "Humanity." This is the goal, he says, that all people have within them "which is to say, what I have is yours, what you have is mine; if I am in need, you give to me, and if you are in need I give to you – that is the future of ethics" (pp. 90-91).

Sartre says in these interviews, shortly before his death, that his final project will be the working out of these ideas to establish a new grounding for the revolutionary left in this ethical relationship with the other. It may be that in these interviews Sartre has not done adequate justice to Marx, whom we have seen assumes this ethical dimension in all of his works and whose repeatedly expressed moral outrage at the exploitation and dehumanization of capitalism is based on the understanding that all persons are ends-in-themselves. Ethics, the dimension of value and obligation, is a fundamental aspect of the spiritual foundations of revolutionary theory, for Marx, as well as for the late Sartre.

What needs to be stressed, however, is the radically nonconceptual character of the ethical dimension and its eschatological implications. Marx, like Sartre in the *Critique of Dialectical Reason*, can go a long way toward grounding socialism in history, science, and human knowledge, making it a "scientific socialism." But the ethical dimension itself, the living sense of value, relationship, and obligation, cannot be made an object of knowledge, as we have seen. For this insight, we need to turn to the great philosophers of the limits of human language and knowledge, Kant, Wittgenstein, and Levinas. In his final reflections, Sartre intuits a "hope now," eschatological in character, linked to the Jewish messianic tradition in which he had then become interested. "It's through a kind of messianism," he says, "that one can conceive of this ethics as the ultimate goal of revolution" (p. 107).

In the same interview, he comments further on his messianic hope: "We must try to explain why the world of today, which is horrible, is only one moment in a long historical development, that hope has always been one of the dominant forces of revolutions and insurrections, and how I still feel that hope is my conception of the future" (p. 110). Sartre concluded his life by opening his awareness to a dimension beyond language from which an insurmountable eschatological hope is derived, intuiting the possibility of a truly transformed world and an absolute ethical obligation to move beyond egoistic self-interest and "engender Humanity," which he calls "unification" – "the unity of the human enterprise is still to be created" (96).

The mystical experience of the absolute oneness of all things and the ethical sense of absolute value and dignity, beyond language, must be complemented by the eschatological sense of the mystery of the simultaneity of present and future in that aspect of the present moment that is outside of time and language. Time, as St. Augustine affirmed, confronts us as an absolute mystery that cannot be comprehended. The penetration beyond linguistic forms into the absolute present prior to language is simultaneously an experience of the eschatological fulfillment that impels us to speak in terms of a practical utopia, anticipation on Earth of the kingdom of God.

This fulfillment is not only possible but immanent within history and implicit in our divine-human potential for planetary maturity. Practical utopia is a transformed world beyond oppression and exploitation, or, in the words of Levinas, an era of peace as opposed to the history of war. Seeing clearly the limits of language, as Wittgenstein urged, allows us to encounter the absolute mystery at the heart of the universe and to intuit the possibilities of revolutionary fulfillment implicit in that dimension.

We do not have to engage in Eastern forms of meditation to gain an insight into the eschatological dimension that confronts us at every turn of our lives. Enrique Dussel has identified many of the concrete events of life that can open us up to the eschatological dimension implicit in our human situation (1988 and 1990). In life, we are often confronted with the possibility of a radical "proximity," a timeless immediacy, a nearness without distance in which we encounter the "eschatologically utopian" as our basic human reality.

Such events are "metaphysical experiences," in his language, that may break open our closed world of everydayness (as well as our closed "ontological" world-views). They allow us to encounter "the other," true exteriority, as an epiphany, the beginnings of a realization that our world is shot through with absolute mysteries from which we can intimate the possibilities of a totally transformed planet lifted to its true destiny, not by the blind causal forces of nature but through incarnations (descents) into nature of the ultimate meaning and possibilities of existence.

As with Levinas, "metaphysics," for Dussel, indicates an infinite surplus beyond our closed ontologies of sameness, causality, and determinism of the future by the past. Dussel speaks of "the timeless joy of being together in proximity" (1990, p. 19), of the awakening experience to one's own freedom (pp. 41-44), of the mystery of true compassion (pp. 64-65), of coitus as one of the "privileged metaphysical experiences of a human being" (p. 81), of the metaphysical moment revealed in the birth of a child (p. 89) of the experience of the cosmos as suspended from a creative freedom that places it at the disposition of the liberator and the oppressed (p. 101), and of the poor as the "epiphany of the revelation of the Absolute" (p. 102). In these experiences of proximity we understand the immense hidden possibilities within existence and we yearn for the realization of these possibilities in a new "order of proximity": "Archeologically timeless and eschatologically utopian," he writes, "proximity is the most essential reality of a person, the beginning of the philosophical discourse of liberation, and metaphysics in its strict sense" (p. 21).

In the epigraph to this chapter, I wrote that all genuine value comes into human life from the "vertical axis." Yet in our investigation of the mystical, ethical and utopic-eschatological sources of revolutionary imperative, we have seen that the mystery of temporality – the mystery of origins, of the astonishing present moment, and of the call of the future – all issue, in one way or another, in "absolute responsibilities." The vertical axis is not some dimension of "spirit" in dualistic opposition to the "horizontal axis" of matter. Such language functions as a metaphorical pointing to certain aspects of our human situation. The emergent powers of our universe, come to consciousness in human life, arise out of a unity-in-diversity that ultimately cannot be expressed in dualistic ontologies.

We are not bound into a causal development determined by the past. We are not trapped into a one dimensional "now" sliding helplessly toward a meaningless death. Instead, we are confronted with demands, with "absolute commands," on every side that portend the dignity and meaning of our emerging divine-human project. As Paul Tillich expresses this, we are under a command to create "something unconditionally new." This new creation is the fulfillment and meaning of our human project on planet Earth:

> The demand calls for something that does not yet exist but should exist, should come to fulfillment. A being that experiences a demand is no longer simply bound to the origin. Human life involves more than a mere development of what already is. Through the demand, humanity is directed to what ought to be. And what ought to be does not emerge with the unfolding of what is; if it did, it would be something that is, rather than something that ought to be. This means, however, that the demand that confronts humanity is an unconditional demand. The question "Whither?" is not contained with the limits of the question "Whence?" It is something unconditionally new that transcends what is new and what is old within the sphere of mere development. Through human beings, something unconditionally new is to be realized; this is the meaning of the demand that they experience, and which they are able to experience because in them being is twofold. For the human person is not only an individual, a self, but also has knowledge about himself or herself, and thereby the possibility of transcending what is found within the self and around the self. This is human freedom, not that one has a so-called free will, but that as a human being one is not bound to what one finds in existence, that one is subject to a demand that something unconditionally new should be realized through oneself. (1987, p. 143)

In the epigraph to this chapter, Tillich correctly affirms that we have a place "to stand upon" within the flux of time and motion. We are situated, as Bugbee says, within "the finality of things." Yet for Tillich and Bugbee, our place is ultimately intelligible only as a mystery of infinite depth. We cannot secure the world for ourselves through our grasping, greedy fearful egos. We cannot "master" our situation through weapons, insurance policies, accumulated possessions, or domination of people and things.

Our situation calls instead for response. It calls for living with a certain perpetual "vertigo" that is neither madness nor irresponsibility but a mature responding to the call resounding from the depths. It requires of us a "standing upright" within which we encounter the call of the mystical, the ethical and the utopic-eschatological and wherein we experience the unconditional promise and demand for a transformed world of peace, justice, and fulfillment. This is not a "regulative ideal" guiding our evolution into a better future. This is an "unconditional demand" in the now for revolutionary transformation.

Any thinker who recognizes this ever-present possibility of breakthrough or transformation is an eschatological thinker. Sri Aurobindo writes:

> Man in himself is little more than an ambitious nothing. He is a littleness that reaches to a wideness and a grandeur that are beyond him, a dwarf enamoured of the heights. His mind is a dark ray in the splendours of the universal Mind. His life is a striving, exulting, suffering, an eager passion-tossed and sorrow-stricken or a blindly and dumbly longing petty moment of the universal Life.... This cannot be the end of the mysterious upward surge of nature....But this greater spirit is obstructed from descent by the hard lid of his constructed personality; and that inner luminous soul is wrapped, stifled, oppressed in dense outer coatings. In all but a few the soul is seldom active, in most hardly perceptible.... If earth calls and the Supreme answers, the hour can be even now for that immense and glorious transformation. (1974, pp. 56-57)

The permanent "expectation of the dawn," the perpetual hope that "the hour can be even now for that immense and glorious transformation" is the eschatological hope. Similarly, Mahatma Gandhi lived as an eschatological person in the public world of political and revolutionary action. Wherever he went, he expected the apparently impossible (*ahimsā* and transformation), and he forever expected the ordinary *satyagrahi* to do the apparently impossible. In his *Autobiography* Gandhi wrote:

> What I want to achieve – what I have been striving and pining to achieve these thirty years – is self-realization, to see God face to face, to attain *Moksha*. I live and move and have my being in pursuit of this goal.... But as I have all along believed that what is possible for one is possible for all, my experiments have not been conducted in the closet, but in the open.... The further conviction has been growing upon me that whatever is

possible for me is possible even for a child, and I have sound reasons for saying so. The instruments for the quest of truth are as simple as they are difficult. (1927, pp. x-xi)

For the awakened person all the fundamental experiences of life are shot through with eschatological potential, with the possibility of a totally transformed world realized in time through our openness to dimensions of our experience beyond time and language. For "the instruments for the quest for truth are as simple as they are difficult." Here lies the continuous possibility of revolutionary transformation at the heart of our human situation.

The principle of unity-in-diversity arises here, as well, in the realization that the absolute multiplicity and diversity embedded within the temporal flow is unified and made whole by the unity of the non-discriminative infinite that may break into our awareness through all the primal experiences of our lives. Like the ethical and the mystical, radical, utopian futurity is a fundamental form of human spirituality and another source of the principle of unity-in-diversity.

The "grace" of the eschatological promise is like a benediction on our compassion for the suffering of others. Compassion is not without the promise of genuine fulfillment. The ethical, the mystical, and the eschatological interpenetrate in direct awareness. The great compassion of the Bodhisattva in Mahāyāna Buddhism is simultaneously an ethical imperative to realize the oneness of humanity and the eschatological vow to renounce final salvation until all sentient beings have found liberation. Here are the foundations of the revolutionary imperative. The unity-in-diversity of the absolute present is simultaneously a "grace" or "surplus" capable of transfiguring human beings and their history.

7. Integration of the Three Sources of Revolutionary Spirituality

The three sources of revolutionary spirituality infuse the background experience of every normal human being. They are normally ignored by the majority of people who never realize the stage-six or seven-maturities discussed in Chapter Seven. The fractured human ego filters out as irrelevant all aspects of awareness not related to its violence, anxiety, and self-promotion.

Historically, there have always been a few attaining to ethical, mystical, or eschatological maturity. Once awareness opens to any of these dimensions, persons experience a powerful awakening. The power of the insight or awakening reflected in any of these aspects of our existence led many to advocate or elucidate one or the other of these dimensions at the expense of the others. Kant, for example, elucidates the absolute imperative of the ethical at the expense of the eschatological and the mystical. Levinas powerfully elucidates the ethical and the eschatological, but at the expense of the mystical.

Thinkers experiencing mystical awakening may also explain the mystical at the expense of the ethical and the eschatological. For example, in *What is Enlightenment?* Ken Wilber provides a description of the "ultimate state of consciousness" that has been repeated at least 2600 years since the *Upanisads*:

> And so proceeds meditation, which is simply higher development, which is simply higher evolution – a transformation from unity to unity until there is simply Unity, whereupon Brahman, in an unnoticed shock of recognition and final remembrance, grins silently to itself, closes its eyes, breathes deeply, and throws itself outward for the millionth time, losing itself in its manifestation for the sport and play of it all. (White, 1995, p. 208)

In this rendering of the insight of "enlightenment" presented in the language the Hindu tradition, there is a hint at the possibility of an "evolutionary" movement that relates the emergent levels of diversity in the universe in some small way to the matrix and ground of absolute unity. But this connection is withdrawn in the use of the traditional Hindu metaphors of "sport" and "play."

The tremendous ethical and existential seriousness of a Wittgenstein or a Kierkegaard is undercut in such classical renderings of awakening through seeing the diversity of the world as *māyā*, illusion, or *līlā*, play. The unspeakable suffering of the world's oppressed appears to lose its claim upon us, for the only thing "real" and worthy of awareness is the "One without a second," Brahman, who "dreams" the vast multiplicity of the world for the millionth time. We regress to the traditional Hindu acceptance of the horrors of "untouchability" or similar social and economic institutions that engender immense suffering century after century when metaphors for spiritual awakening characterize the world in these ways. The eschatological promise of a fulfillment through deep transformation is also lost. The great hope of humankind on this planet as announced, for example, by Jesus and some of the Hebrew prophets is abandoned through such metaphors. We watch "the passing show" with detachment and equanimity.

Such metaphors for the unsayable dimension focus on the mystical aspect of our awareness at the expense of the ethical and eschatological. They lead to a deeply conservative and even immoral attitude toward the diversity of the world and the struggle of the exploited and dehumanized toward a decent existence. It does not redress this problem to assert, "if everyone were enlightened, there would not be any exploitation or degradation." For the mystic thereby justifies his or her lack of ethical action to change oppressive institutions or create an institutionally and spiritually decent world-order.

We saw the ethical demand in human life as an absolute command that we somehow live our lives differently, that we realize the mysterious purpose of existence on this planet in ways that we are now avoiding. This demand is a real feature of our human situation available to any and all who attend carefully to their awareness. We also saw the eschatological dimension as present in the ever-present background of awareness, joining with the ethical demand in the insight that fundamental transformation is available in every moment of our lives. Non-attachment no longer need vitiate our ability for effective ethical and eschatological action through misleading metaphors. Our lives arise from groundless depths beyond determinism, causality, and conditioned existence.

Nicholas Berdyaev is excellent on this aspect of experience, as are Sri Aurobindo, Ernst Bloch, Enrique Dussel, James Fowler, Eric Gutkind, Emmanuel Levinas, Jürgen Moltmann, and others. A consciousness evolving toward planetary maturity is a revolutionary consciousness in so far as it integrates all three dimensions of our deep background awareness. As we saw José Miranda assert of Marx, a person cannot be a true revolutionary without awareness of this eschatological dimension of our existence. Marx's eschatology may have been occasionally articulated in misleading idioms such as "immutable dialectical laws of history." Nevertheless, his ethical outrage at commodification and dehumanization of people and his sense of the possibility of genuine transformation of human existence were right on target.

Neither can a person be revolutionary without experiencing the "absolute command" to change the structure of human existence to make possible human fulfillment on this planet. Without experience of this moral imperative, we lapse into a Habermasian or liberal "evolution" toward a better world in the vaguely distant future. The Kantian sense of an imperative to create a "kingdom of ends" on planet Earth is at bottom a revolutionary command, a demand for the here and now.

Finally, the revolutionary consciousness cannot be fully activated as long as we have not transcended the anxiety-ridden, fearful, violent ego through mystical identification with the other and the realization of genuine compassion. The experience of "the One without a second" must result in the vow of the Bodhisattva not to leave the endless round of existence until all sentient beings have been saved from suffering. To see the suffering of others as "not fully real," as the play or sport of Brahman, is to make of God a moral monster and ourselves complicit in the immense institutionalized suffering wracking our planet.

The universe only makes sense, in terms of our intuitions of its unsayable depths and in terms of rational reflection, if its primal origin is intrinsically related to its evolutionary upsurge. We saw the strictly rational arguments of philosopher Errol E. Harris draw this conclusion. We also saw in Chapter Five that "integrative mysticism" draws this connection while "primal mysticism" often treats the precious diversity of the world and the uniqueness of persons as *māyā*, illusion.

We must attend to the deepest aspects of our existence, the ethical, the eschatological, and the mystical so that we may intuit the kind of lives we should be living and transform our fragmented selves in the direction of ecstatic and revolutionary fulfillment. Models and teachers, from Jesus Christ and Lord Buddha to Mahatma Gandhi, are not lacking. The primal matrix of the world, what Whitehead would call its "antecedent nature," is intrinsically related to its evolutionary and transformative direction (its "consequent nature").

Only through attending to all three aspects of what Aurobindo terms "integral awareness" do we intuit the meaning and purpose of human life on Earth. Our "faith" becomes more than faith. It becomes a living wisdom and compassion. Our religion becomes more than dogma and doctrine. It becomes a living spirituality. We realize a perpetually "open horizon" as we journey into a forever transformed future without fear. We become non-attached in the sense that we no longer base our lives on the "ordinary hope" of predictions based on past perceptions of causality and probabilities. The principle of unity-in-diversity, arising from integral awareness as a criterion for mature economic, political, and social life, becomes the self-evident basis for action.

In the integration of the three sources of a revolutionary spirituality, we find the revolutionary upsurge of the depths of existence for a transformed world. Practical planning for rational and free institutions within a revolutionary society will not succeed without many inspired citizens who have realized this integration and deep revolutionary awareness within their lives. Transforming the systems that now constrict the possibilities for revolutionary awareness in citizens (trapping even adults in adolescent modes of being) will liberate human awareness for a perpetual journeying into ever freer existence. At the same time, individually liberating ourselves within the present systems of domination and death will foster a revolutionary transformation of these systems.

Our great, ecstatic hope is "eschatological hope." It does not arise from the fragmented ego with its projections designed to ensure personal security and safety. Eschatological hope arises from the foundations of existence. Fully compatible with non-attachment, it is the promise and certainty of God manifested in a living spirituality. In integral awareness, the three sources of revolutionary spirituality are one. For the universe itself has exploded in a multidimensional fusion of unity-in-diversity.

Chapter Eleven

The Principle of Unity-in-Diversity
and Democratic World Government

There was, perhaps, a time before our own when individuals could still try to better themselves and fulfil themselves, each on his own, in isolation. That time has gone for ever. We now have to make up our minds to recognize that at no moment of history has man been so completely involved (both actively and passively), through the very foundations of his being, in the value and betterment of all those around him, as he is today. And all the evidence indicates that this regime of interdependence can only become more pronounced in the course of the coming centuries.

Pierre Teilhard de Chardin

Contemporary science has announced that its own operation is accessory to the existence of the physical universe, and today the technology that it has empowered threatens to destroy the biosphere and to eliminate all scientific activity. In a world politically organized so as to be perpetually threatened by war, science and technology have put into the hands of men weapons of total destruction – nuclear weapons, the uncontrolled use of which could fatally and finally disrupt the ecology of the planet....

Those who recognize the threat to human existence and the consequent necessity for the conservation of the environment, as well as the policies they advocate, are becoming "green." Could mankind succeed in this endeavour, the course of history would reinforce the Anthropic Principle, and the fulfillment of the cosmic principle would cease to be endangered. But this seems possible only on one condition: namely, that national sovereignties can be superseded and a world authority established which could act globally with legal right and efficiency....

The organizing principle unifying the cosmic whole issues, in the process of its self-enfolding, as the course of human history. The contemporary political structures which that has developed have now precipitated a crisis which can be relieved only by the unification of the human race under a global world constitution.

Errol E. Harris

T he wholeness of the universe unfolds through time in a dialectical process of concurrent complexification and unification (Teilhard de Chardin, 1970, pp. 167-168). The anthropic principle in its broadest form states that human life, an advanced manifestation of the concurrent process of complexification and unification, has been implicit in the cosmic process from the beginning (Harris, 1991). Unity and diversity are not only fundamental to the dynamics of human life and civilization. They are fundamental principles of the cosmogonic process itself.

Philosophically, human beings have been reflecting on the issue of the one and the many since the very beginnings of philosophic thought. The principle of unity-in-diversity that we will see expressed in the *Constitution for the Federation of Earth* has its roots in the earliest sources of philosophical history in the West. It has come to self-conscious realization only in the most advanced thinking of the twentieth century.

1. The Principles of Unity-in-Diversity, Whole and Part

The problem of the one and the many goes back to the so-called "axis period in human history" (circa 800-200 BCE) in which humankind began to emerge from mythic consciousness into what might be termed the "linear" consciousness of analysis and abstract thought. In the west, the Presocratic philosophers first struggled with the problem. For the Ionian cosmologists, Thales, Anaximander, and Anaximenes, this took the form of looking for the primal substance or origin from which the diversity of secondary substances that we find in everyday experience might be traced. Heraclitus took his stand on the reality of the process itself, a world-process throwing up ever new forms, in eternal tension with itself, swallowing the particulars back into itself in a never-ending cycle of birth and death, harmony within conflict and tension.

Parmenides found the One in the opposite conception of reality, in eternal, immutable being, without parts, without before and after, without beginning or end. For Plato, the one and the many took the direction of the radical distinction between forms (universals) and particulars (multiple individuals constituting a class or category identified by its separately existing, eternal form). Aristotle worked to overcome the radical duality of Plato's model and to embed the forms within the material world that provided the principle of individuation for the forms. Beyond this level of unification of the many, Plato and Aristotle reflected on a One beyond the forms, a unifying principle toward which all motion and all activity gravitated.

Yet Aristotle's "Unmoved Mover" lacked the depth of Plato's "Idea of the Good," for Plato's Good was "beyond being" (*hyperousía*) and became a fundamental source for the idea of the unknowability of God in later centuries. This sense of the unknowability or ineffability of the ultimate oneness of the universe continued through Plotinus' "One," to the "Divine Darkness" of Pseudo-Dionysus, to Eriugena's "that which neither creates nor is created," to Aquinas' idea that the "Being" of God is "being" in a sense only analogous to that of the world, to the "Godhead" of Meister

Eckhart, to Nicholas of Cusa's idea of the incommensurability between infinity and finitude.

Plato's unknowable Good beyond being became a source not only for the apophatic (negative) theology asserting the unknowability of God but also for the transforming and redeeming positivity of the mystical union with God, so clearly expressed, for example, in Plotinus, Pseudo-Dionysus, and Eckhart. The "problem" of the ultimate whole in relation to the parts was resolved in these thinkers, not in a newly-formulated metaphysical doctrine, but in an encounter with the ineffability and unsayability of the One beyond being. Whether or not they ontologized the intelligible structures apparent in the cosmic order, they placed the ultimate Source "beyond being," as the unifying and integrating principle of the whole.

Yet an opposing movement ultimately dominated in the medieval West that slowly developed into the doctrines of nominalism and conceptualism, culminating in a powerful articulation within the context of a new psychologism by William of Occam in the 14th century. Only individuals are real. Classes, categories, or universals are only names in language (nominalism) or concepts in the human mind (Occam's conceptualism and psychologism). This movement obviated not only the intelligible forms, but obliterated any possible awareness of a Source beyond being.

The doctrine of nominalism, however untenable in the face of an emerging science appearing to articulate the universal structural features of the natural world, caught on in the West in part because it lent itself ideologically to the emerging predatory capitalism of the next three centuries that *wanted* human life to be the predatory struggle of isolated, atomistic individuals with one another. This ideology of nominalism was forcefully articulated in the seventeenth century by Thomas Hobbes, resulting in a conception of the natural state of human beings as a "war of all against all." The doctrine was soon expressed in a more refined but equally damaging way by John Locke with each individual having the inalienable "right" to accumulate property over and against all others. The dogma was soon to be synthesized with evolutionary doctrine in the brutal nineteenth-century philosophy of social Darwinism.

This doctrine that "only individuals exist" denied not only the Platonic and Aristotelian belief that unifying form and structure permeated the world, integrating all individuals into more and more comprehensive realities, and linking unity and diversity within a complex hierarchy of intelligible wholes. It also tended to deny the unifying mystery of the One beyond being that can embrace and make gentle even the violent atomism of isolated individuality. After several centuries in which violent atomism has dominated, spawning such destructive corollary doctrines as positivism, analytic one-dimensionalism, naïve materialism, and empiricism, the twentieth century saw the problem of the one and the many re-emerge in surprising new forms. The integrative intuition of Plato and Aristotle has been recovered in entirely new ways, and atomism discredited, as the philosophical works of Anthony E. Mansueto, Jr., (1995), Errol E. Harris, and others have revealed. This was not done through the assertion of metaphysical hierarchies of forms embracing particulars, but through an even deeper realization of the bonds between wholes and individual parts. We have seen that twentieth-century paradigm shifts in science involving relativity theory, quantum theory, ecology, and social theory have led many to see this century as the "age of unification," of synergism and the integration of the whole and part.

And we have recognized that we do not wish to embrace a vision of the whole to the exclusion of diversity or diversity unredeemed by an encompassing wholeness. We require what Raimundo Panikkar calls an "open horizon" in the face of our planetary need for a unified "vision of reality," an horizon that does not close off the vision with some form of reductionism or dogmatism:

> The greeks formulated it as the One and the Many: *hen kai polla*. The problem lies not in unity or plurality, but in that *kai* (and) which joins them, in their synthesis. Is there any link between an ultimately rigid and deadly monism on the one hand, and an ultimately anarchic and equally fatal plurality on the other? At our present juncture in consciousness we cannot irresponsibly accept either of these two human experiences as a solution. We have lived through the consequences of both options long enough and intensively enough to put us on our guard lest we make the same mistakes. (1993, pp. 5-7)

Neither whole nor part may be separated from one another if we are to understand the world aright and act to realize the eschatological possibilities of our existence within a transformed world order.

Mansueto points out that the contemporary movement to articulate a new global paradigm is based on the relational, evolutionary universe derived from contemporary science, in such fields as "unified field theories, complex systems theory, post-Darwinian evolutionary biology, and anthropic cosmology" (1995, p. 13). All these fields show us a universe deeply interrelated in which whole and part are inseparable. We have seen Emmanuel Levinas' philosophy resist the tendency to reduce human life to an expression of the whole, and phenomenologically attempt to show the fallacy of such reductionism.

Levinas is steeped in the Jewish tradition with its foundational separation of the three domains of God, world, and human beings made in God's image. None of these is reducible to the others, and, most emphatically, in this tradition, humans are not derivable from the world. Even Jewish mysticism rarely went as far as the mystical traditions of the other great religions in meditatively promoting the direct experience of God in which only unity and the three principles of God, world, and human beings are experienced in some fundamental way as one (Stace, 1960b, pp. 221-224).

Yet it should now be clear that the new global paradigm of a relational universe in which whole and part are inseparable is not in conflict with the thought of Levinas to the extent its proponents make clear that the experience of cosmic consciousness or oneness goes beyond all knowledge and beyond any possibility of rationally or scientifically deriving the part from the whole. Metaphysics often speculates about ultimate matters beyond human knowledge, and to indulge such language can be useful if we understand this. Metaphysical language can be used as a pointer to the depths of things beyond our closed systems of thought. Let us use metaphysical language for the moment to suggest that God, world, and human beings are irreducibly separate at one level and yet simultaneously one at another level, just as God has traditionally been said to be transcendent and immanent at once. Yet God simultaneously remains only one, and at both levels ultimately transcendent to human knowledge.

In *Towards Synergism - The Cosmic Significance of the Human Civilizational Project* (1995), Mansueto appears to come close to the ontological totalizing of human knowledge feared by Levinas. Although this book represents a fine expression of the new global paradigm expressing the interdependence of whole and part, it does not fully recognize the unknowable infinite at the heart of humans and God. Mansueto writes "for the fist time in its history, humanity is in a position to grasp being as relationship, structure, and organization, to comprehend the cosmos as an organized totality developing toward higher and higher levels of complexity and integration – and thus to recognize human civilization as an active participant in the cosmohistorical evolutionary process" (1995, p. 1).

On the basis of this understanding, Mansueto articulates the meaning and purpose of human life, society, and the cosmos. On this understanding, he says, "we need to reestablish the logical-ontological, cosmological and axiological foundations of the human civilizational project. Only on such a foundation can we attempt to chart a course for the future of humanity" (1995, p. 6). To comprehend and participate in the cosmos as an organized totality is what Mansueto calls "spirituality": "This active participation in the self-organization activity of the cosmos, become conscious of itself as participation, is spirituality" (p. 83). "Spirit," he says, "is nothing other than the realized potential for organization" (p. 442).

Lacking in this expression of the new paradigm is the deep, experiential realization of God (or the "void" of Buddhism) as the infinite, unsayable depth at the heart of whole and part. Mansueto calls the "complex, synergistic unity" of the universe "God," but if the universe can be understood as a process of emergent evolutionary totalization, this is not identical with what has been called "God" by awakened people of the world's great spiritual traditions. Nor is this equivalent to "spirituality" as understood by these traditions.

We saw Jiddu Krishnamurti maintain that spiritual awareness cannot be expressed, but only experienced as emptiness, as silence. Similarly, in *Encountering God*, Diana Eck says, "whatever we may think of God, the referent of that word, that symbol, is a mystery. God is finally beyond our grasp. God is not ours – even with the grace of God's revealing" (1993, p. 46). In *The Contemplative Life,* Joel Goldsmith writes, "there is nothing you can know about God that is God. There is no idea of God that you can entertain that is God. There is no possible thought that you can have about God that is God. It makes no difference what your idea may be or what your concept may be, it remains an idea or a concept, and an idea or a concept is not God" (1990, p. 22).

This sounds very much like Krishnamurti's distinction between the radical unsayability of the meditative state and anything expressible in language. Donald Evans, in *Spirituality and Human Nature,* suggests why this is so:

> The mystical God cannot be experienced, for an experience is always an experience of some content, whereas God is not a content, however sublime. God is the creative pure consciousness, the pregnant void, out of which all particular existents continually arise. God as such is known only in a state of pure consciousness, devoid of all particular contents. (1993, p. 176)

The world may well be the "body of God" as Eric Gutkind expresses it, but in this case Mansueto is confusing the body of God with God (1969, pp. 77-86). God (or the absolute mystery at the core of existence) is beyond all discursive, demonstrable, or empirical knowledge (at least in God's aspect as Godhead, *Eyn Sof, Nirguna Brahman,* or *Dharmakāya*), and the interpenetration of the whole and part in all spheres of existence participates in this infinity. Levinas' objections, and his suspicions of all mysticism that speaks of "union with the One," are ultimately unfounded. By contrast, Levinas takes his stand on the uniqueness of Jewish mysticism that avoids the notion of "union with God." (see 1994, pp. 6-11). Even a strictly scientific account of the relation of whole and part will do well to recognize the "depth" beyond knowledge only experienced in "cosmic religious feeling."

Let us recall that in their book *The Conscious Universe – Part and Whole in Modern Physical Theory* Menas Kafatos and Robert Nadeau affirm precisely this:

> If theoretical reason in modern physics does eventually refashion the terms of constructing our symbolic universe to the extent that it impacts practical reason, then conceiving of a human being, as Einstein puts it, as "part of the whole" is the leap of faith that would prove most critical...[for widening] "our circle of compassion...." Yet one cannot, of course, merely reason or argue oneself into an acceptance of this proposition. One must also have the capacity, in our view, for what Einstein termed "cosmic religious feeling." (1990, p. 182)

Here the depth beyond knowledge experienced in "cosmic religious feeling" is linked with the capacity for an all-embracing "circle of compassion." Mansueto does not speak of compassion very often, and the reason is clear. His identification of whole and part is primarily conceptual and does not seem to recognize the possibility of an experiential identity with the other beyond the individual ego (with the knowledge and "intuition" of its participation in totality), an identity going to the unsayable depths of existence.

Neither does Levinas speak of compassion very often, but, instead, of "absolute ethical demands" communicated in the face of the other. But this is for a different reason. A sense of my deep identity with the other is required for compassion, yet Levinas will not allow this. And only the fact that the other and myself are identical in the unsayable oneness of things beyond knowledge makes possible the experiential reality of compassion, whether we are fully realized mystics or not. Such identity with the other in no way obviates the infinite unknowability of the other, the other as utterly unique, which Levinas wishes to preserve.

Again Levinas may well have a legitimate concern that no group should come to power assuming it has knowledge of the cosmohistorical process (the ontological totality) and the relation of individual human beings to that process. And, appropriately, the *Constitution for the Federation of Earth* makes no such assumptions. The *Constitution* is *compatible* with the cosmogonic process of the universe as expressed by thinkers like Pierre Teilhard de Chardin and Errol E. Harris, but is not premised on assumptions about this or any other metaphysical process.

2. Unity-in-Diversity as a Founding Principle in the *Constitution for the Federation of Earth*

The *Constitution for the Federation of Earth* was developed over a period of thirty-three years through four constitutional conventions and the participation of numerous world citizens. In 1958, Professor Philip

Isely and three others began circulating a petition worldwide requesting national governments and citizens of each country to send delegates to a World Constitutional Convention. By 1961 this petition was adopted with the signature of thousands of world citizens and five national governments. The first World Constitutional Convention took place in 1968 in Interlaken, Switzerland, with two hundred people's delegates from twenty-seven countries, although no governments participated.

The result of this convention was a committee to draft a constitution for the Earth. By 1974, the first draft was ready and circulated worldwide for comment, together with the call for the second session of the convention, now called the "World Constituent Assembly." In 1976 a second draft was circulated worldwide in the light of comments received. The second session of the World Constituent Assembly met in Innsbruck, Austria, in 1977 and debated the proposed *Constitution* paragraph by paragraph. The *Constitution* was amended through this debate and signed by one hundred thirty-eight world citizens from twenty-five countries.

It was then circulated to the United Nations and all the national governments of the world. A third session of the World Constituent Assembly was held in Colombo, Sri Lanka, in 1979 where a rationale was adopted for the right of the people of Earth to develop this *Constitution* in the light of the failure of the national governments to bring the world closer to environmental sustainability, peace, democracy, respect for human rights, or justice. Under rights granted by the *Constitution* (Article XIX), the people of the world began holding sessions of the Provisional World Parliament to work on world legislation and move forward the process of ratification for the *Constitution*.

Eight sessions of the Parliament have been held to date: in Brighton, England, (1982), New Delhi, India, (1985), Miami Beach, Florida, (1987), Barcelona, Spain, (1996), Malta (2000), Bangkok, Thailand (March, 2003), Chennai, India (December 2003), and Lucknow, India (August 2004). Some final amendments were made to the *Constitution* at the Fourth World Constituent Assembly that was held in Troia, Portugal, in 1991. Today, the *Constitution* has been translated into twenty-two languages and a network of organizations and individuals in many countries has developed to support democratic world government under this *Constitution* and to work for its ratification.

This *Constitution* provides a *framework* for the democratic enfranchisement of all Earth's citizens and the preservation of the planetary ecosystem. Its principle of unity-in-diversity, its understanding of the necessary interdependence of whole and part, says nothing about the direction or purpose of either the cosmos, or human social activity.

Nor does it suggest that the whole/part distinction be understood in ontological, metaphysical, or mystical terms. No constitution should do this. Nevertheless, on a legal and social level, it does reflect the paradigm shift that has characterized the twentieth-century scientific revolutions in microphysics, astrophysics, ecology, and the social sciences. For it explicitly affirms the principle of unity-in-diversity.

The *World Constitution* provides a viable *legal* framework for the growth of human beings toward planetary maturity. Its universality remains at the ethical level that rationally requires inclusion of *all* human beings as ends-in-themselves or as citizens with universal human rights. It carefully preserves freedom of thought, religion, and expression as essential to a unified humanity in which justice is a primary concern. My own earlier descriptions concerning the cosmogonic *telos* of the universe and of the eschatological direction of the human project are nowhere found in the *Constitution*. The evolution of human beings toward planetary maturity cannot be mandated by any legal framework.

But a truly democratic and dialogical legal framework can *make possible* the rapid growth and transformation of human beings toward compassion, critical social awareness, and recognition of the principle of unity-in-diversity. *The World Constitution makes possible, within a context of democratic freedom, first, planetary ecological survival, second, planetary elimination of poverty and control of the population explosion, third, global disarmament and world peace and, finally, a genuine movement toward spiritual simplicity and practical utopia.* The last of these cannot be dictated by any constitution, but can be made possible. Without this framework, none of these today appears even remotely within the realm of possibility.

The *Constitution for the Federation of Earth* (promoted by the World Constitution and Parliament Association, the Institute on World Problems, and other organizations working toward the emerging Earth Federation) stresses the principle of unity-in-diversity in an open way that can be understood on differing levels. The *Constitution* offers a concrete and practical solution to our apparently insoluble global problems while at the same time envisioning the possibility of a transition to a totally transformed world. The Preamble to the *Constitution* reads in part:

> Aware of the interdependence of people, nations and all life... Conscious that Humanity is One despite the existence of diverse nations, races, creeds, ideologies and cultures and that the principle of unity-in-diversity is the basis for a new age when war shall be outlawed and peace prevail; when the earth's total resources shall be equitably used for human welfare; and when basic human rights and responsibilities shall be shared by all without

discrimination.... We citizens of the world, hereby resolve to establish a world federation to be governed in accordance with this constitution for the Federation of Earth. (Harris, 1993, p. 122)

The ethical awareness of unity-in-diversity embodied in this proclamation should be apparent. The unity-in-diversity affirmed in this *Earth Constitution* provides the first viable premise for a human freedom and a world peace that makes possible the further development of the human project. Its unity is the sovereignty of the people of Earth, its diversity is the sanctity of the individual and the multiplicity of differences protected and made possible by the practical unity of humankind under the sovereignty of all. As such, its affirmation of unity-in-diversity can serve as the principal foundation for public policy and good government, since the ethical basis of good government must include the Kantian principle of respect for each individual as an end-in-his-or-her-self within the framework of a universal morally legitimate legislation.

On the ethical level, we have seen the unity-in-diversity implicit in Kant's categorical imperative that commands us to "treat all persons as ends-in-themselves." "All persons" here recalls the demand for universalization expressed in the first formula of the categorical imperative expressed as "judge your every action as if it were to become a universal law, applicable to all." A universal law is a law of the whole, of "all persons." Similarly "ends-in-themselves" here refers to unique individuals, with immeasurable dignity beyond all price. The part cannot have this immeasurable dignity without the whole, without the free legislation of universal law to which it itself is subject. The whole could not be a whole without the autonomy and dignity of the parts.

To emphasize the parts alone (political liberalism) is to effectively deny the possibility of justice. To emphasize the whole alone (through either socialist totalitarianism or state-capitalist fascism) is to deny freedom. Only the two inseparably together, part and whole, can give us justice as well as freedom and fulfill the ethical and spiritual requirements of human life. For Kant, through moral experience, rather than through knowledge, human life comes in direct contact with the "noumenal" ultimate reality. In the realm of knowledge, direct, experiential contact with the whole is not possible. Nevertheless, the idea of the whole serves as a "regulative ideal of reason," constructed through the forms and categories of the knowing intellect and necessary to all progress in science (1965, pp. 402-409).

Ethically, whole and individual require one another as a foundation for a sound global public policy directed toward overcoming the rule of power and violence and establishing peace. In today's world, the individual cannot be protected, since there exists no legitimate corresponding whole.

This holds true whether the individual is a small nation confronted by the might of a powerful nation, or an ethnic, tribal, or religious minority confronted by a more powerful grouping, or individual persons, whose rights are violated with impunity by oppressive governments or giant profit-seeking corporations.

Only the organized lawful will of the sovereign people of Earth, with a moral force comparable to Jean-Jacques Rousseau's "general will," can protect and justify the parts and individuals of this planet. For the first time in history, human beings have the opportunity to establish government premised on the inseparability (as well as the non-identity) of whole and part, and by this means to free themselves from chaos and tyranny. This principle is the foundation of freedom. As Indian philosopher Sri Aurobindo expresses this, "a FREE world-union must in its very nature be a complex unity based on a diversity and that diversity must be based on free self-determination" (1997, p. 517).

And it should be stressed that the *Constitution* rests on this principle *as a framework only* for the human project, maintaining that intellectual "open horizon" affirmed by Panikkar. It provides *a framework*, not a system, a framework of unity-in-diversity that alone can actualize a deeper human freedom than that which has hitherto existed. The fragmented forces of pseudo-wholeness that now dominate the Earth: economic class, culture, race, nation-state, gender, or religion can never give rise to authentic political or dialogical peace and freedom. These provide no true unity under which respect for these parts of our human reality can flourish, but only divisions and power blocks resulting in a disfigured peace and freedom for some at the expense of domination and dehumanization for others.

The *Constitution's* principle of unity and diversity as a framework providing an open horizon for human thought does not therefore mandate a further direction for the human project. It solely provides the peace and freedom, the presuppositions, through which a direction for the human project might be dialogically worked out. Levinas' fears of a totalitarian system cannot be addressed by blocking all unity in the name of an anarchic individuality, for unity is the condition of any genuine peace and freedom not premised on the domination or exclusion of some by others.

Instead, these fears should be addressed by affirming the freedom of dialogue in which the open horizon of the human project, beyond closed and totalitarian systemizations, can be properly discussed and articulated. Unity-in-diversity as affirmed in the Preamble and elsewhere in the *Constitution for the Federation of Earth* need not be understood on mystical or eschatological levels. Its affirmation of this principle can remain on the concrete practical level of the ethical demand to create a decent world-order for all inhabitants of Earth and the clear understanding that the present world order cannot possibly achieve this.

Yet the ringing affirmation of unity-in-diversity includes the eschatological intuition that a new world is imminently possible in the here and now if human beings were willing to recognize it. For with the simple ratification of this constitution by the people of Earth, with the recognition of the sovereignty (wholeness) of humanity, the *Constitution* would provide the basis for a truly "new age when war shall be outlawed and peace prevail." The eschatological intuition recognizes that such a practical utopia is easily within our present possibilities, should we choose to allow it to happen.

3. Freedom and the Danger of Totalitarian Totalization

Reflection on the concept of unity-in-diversity reveals that we cannot protect and maintain true diversity until we have reached a certain level of genuine unity, which also involves a certain level of universality. For example, "all persons are ends-in-themselves," or "every person is a citizen of the Federation of Earth." If my unity is Christianity, defined in any of the traditional exclusivistic senses, then this necessarily excludes all that is non-Christian. If my unity is being British, then this excludes everything not British. If my unity is my race, then this excludes the diversity and individuality of what is not of my race. Only an all-inclusive unity with respect to human beings (and ultimately beyond human beings to other sentient beings and our planetary ecosystem) can fully affirm the variations and diversity of all the members, precisely because we are all one at the deepest level.

We have little to fear and everything to gain from the idea of the "totality" or "unity" of human beings as long as this is understood, within an "open horizon," in its mutual relationship with authentic individuality. No legitimate, free government can function if it does not affirm the oneness and sameness of humanity with respect to equality, dignity, freedom, and principles of justice as well as the absolute value and uniqueness of each person, beyond knowledge and beyond all systems. Philosophers and governments must deal with the concrete dilemmas posed by this duality in everyday practice. Government must foster the universal equality of all and the universal applicability of the law to all persons (no one is above the law), yet it must also treat people as concrete individuals formed through specific cultural, religious, and historical circumstances and not as mere faceless ciphers subjected indiscriminately to universal laws (see Habermas, 1994).

But what ordinary people as well as philosophers like Levinas seem to fear most is that democratic world government may become totalitarian.

This fear is not well-founded. Levinas does not deny equality, although he founds equality on the ethical relation of responsibility in the claim of others upon us, prior to any sameness deriving from a totalizing system. But he fears the loss of individual uniqueness implicit in, for example, the Hegelian model of the state where the individual is derived from and subordinate to the ontologically conceived totality. But good government can recognize all this and be designed to provide and protect a framework for authentic freedom and discourse among unique individuals. As Habermas insists, democratic theory at its best promotes just this (1979, pp. 186-187; see 1994).

Government must be institutionalized to avoid all forms of tyranny: the tyranny of the majority or popular opinion, the tyranny of the state, tyrannies of anarchic individuality, the tyranny of religion or dogma, the tyrannies of fear, hatred, or prejudice, the tyrannies of capital and wealth, or the tyrannies of power politics among nation-states. Correspondingly it must also be institutionalized to promote universal peace, freedom, and justice. It can only do these things by affirming the principle of unity-in-diversity that science has shown to be the organizational matrix of our world at every level.

We cannot allow the horrible possibilities apparent within our current nightmarish human condition to paralyze us. Fear that this constitution would lead to tyranny is most basically a first-world assertion of our hidden desire to maintain our privilege at the expense of the rest of humanity. We privileged few exhibit a maturity fear, in which we are unwilling to grow toward mature ethical-spiritual awareness, unwilling to recognize the principle of unity-in-diversity as the basis of authentic human relationships.

Yet Levinas has a legitimate concern that no group should come to power that assumes it has knowledge of the cosmohistorical process (the ontological totality) and the relation of individual human beings to that process. But how are we to prevent this from happening except through democratic discussion and dialogue? Using any other means would sink to the same violence that we were hoping to prevent. In our present world of mass suffering, exploitation, and oppression, it makes little sense to block efforts to achieve wholeness out of a speculative fear that wholeness will deny individuality.

The dogma of the U.N. and the so-called "world order" of the late twentieth and early twenty-first centuries has been the clear contradiction that peace is to be kept through the means of war, through "peacekeeping" forces of the Security Council, the self-appointed violence of NATO, or the unilateral arrogance of the United States. The *World Constitution* abolishes all weapons of war, since these are not the way to peace, and legislates a rule of law in which *individuals* are apprehended for violations of the law. The insane idea that wars, bombings, invasions, or economic blockades must be used against whole peoples to stop the criminal activity of a single group or leader within these societies is abolished for the travesty of "peacekeeping" that it is.

Yet the *World Constitution* goes beyond the legal abolition of war, that barbaric phenomenon so rightly abhorred by Levinas and all decent human beings. It also makes possible the exposure of totalitarian ideologies through the process of discussion and dialogue by enfranchising all of Earth's citizens. It provides a viable *legal* framework for that "open horizon" advocated by Panikkar or the corresponding "authentic dialogue" promoted by Habermas. World peace is not possible without an enforceable *framework* creating enfranchisement and dignity for every citizen on Earth. For the alternatives to dialogue are the opposites of authentic peace: manipulation, deception, exploitation, propaganda, stereotyping, coercion, bigotry, emotionalism, and violence.

Even philosophical dialogue in the ivy tower of today's universities is distorted and inundated by a world writhing in manipulation, deception, exploitation, coercion, and violence. By creating a legal framework of the equality and sovereignty of all persons, the *World Constitution* creates for the first time the priority of communicative discourse over instrumental and strategic forms of discourse. For the *World Constitution* provides precisely that "open horizon" in which human beings can work out their destiny and future within a framework of peace, equality, and dialogue. It does not even mandate democratic socialism, although to the present writer the framework of peace, equality, and dialogue would inevitably lead in that direction.

The present writer very much agrees with Harry Van Der Linden (1988) that Kant's notion of a possible "kingdom of ends," implicit in the categorical imperative binding on all persons, implies the longer range goal of global democratic socialism. Ethically speaking, political, social, and economic life is under the imperative to socialize, to become whole through overcoming the lack of universality that characterizes the political and economic power blocks dominating our current world system. Although the proposed *Constitution for the Federation of Earth* does not mandate any specific economic system, leaving nations free to organize their own systems within the framework of peace, freedom, and universal human rights, it does provide for the first time the freedom for genuine dialogue concerning the implications of ethics for the human project, a freedom that is radically curtailed within the current world-system (see Chomsky and Herman, 1988).

At the dawn of the twenty-first century, such freedom of dialogue requires as a first step non-military, democratic world government. This principle in the *World Constitution* supplies the *necessary* conditions for freedom and peace that makes possible genuine dialogue about the meaning and future of the human civilizational project. Making these conditions *sufficient* must be left to the people of Earth, once the necessary conditions are created. The question of the meaning and direction of the human project must be worked out through free dialogue possible only when unity-in-diversity is the framework for planetary government. Here is where the danger of totalization is properly addressed, not by blocking planetary attempts to create democratic world legal unity, but by creating a framework where planetary dialogue is actually possible for the first time.

On a less abstract level than that offered by Levinas, one often hears from even educated people challenges like the following. "If any world government, adequately empowered, were established, would not this create the potential for appalling abuses of power and disenfranchisement?" The import of this question shows tremendous naivete about this issue. Yet such naivete is promoted and encouraged by the dominant ideological system that does everything possible to denigrate the idea of democratic world government in the minds of citizens worldwide.

First, we must recognize that "disenfranchisement" is now the condition of the majority of people in the world, most of whom, whether under "formal democracies" or totalitarian governments, do not enjoy even the most minimal "enfranchisement." Democratic world government is precisely the beginning of meaningful enfranchisement for the majority of the world's population. These kind of worries only occur in the minds of people who have not seen for themselves the appalling misery and disenfranchisement experienced by most persons on Earth. In this regard, for the majority of persons on Earth, there is nothing to lose by democratic world government and everything to gain.

Second, even those who believe themselves presently "enfranchised" are deluded in this respect. Only limited forms of democracy are possible under the system of class domination, as we have seen. In addition, in a world where global economic, environmental, population, and military forces are operative, and where there are 190 other territorial entities vying for ascendency or survival, "enfranchisement" within any of these territories means very little. Citizens have no political power over the issues that affect their lives since these issues are rarely exclusively internal to territories but are global in nature. "Enfranchisement" is meaningless if it does not give citizens some means of political participation into the real issues that affect their lives.

Third, "appalling abuse of power" is a potential inherent in any and all government. As long as there exists a mechanism for enforcing the law that has real power to enforce the law (or abuse the law), then any government has this potential. In today's world, even tiny governments have terrorized their populations. Most people are prisoners in their countries of birth. Only a few privileged first-world people can travel or get visas. No escape exists from the terror of even tiny governments. The problem has nothing to do with "world government."

In reality, many first-world people fear equality with non-white people, with the vast majority of humans who are so many more than them, with cultures and ways of life that are so different from their own, and with religions that seem alien. These are the real motives behind our fears about a possible totalitarianism. In reality we are already in a totalitarian relationship with the rest of the world – as dominators. What we really fear is giving up our position of privilege and exploitation that we erroneously call our "freedom."

The real issue is how we can build into government (any government) protections, limits, checks on the abuse of power, accountability, lack of secrecy, and democratic control and oversight by the population. Under the nation-state system, none of these can be built into government because governments claim they live in a dangerous world requiring state secrecy, secret national security arrangements, secret military arrangements, and so on. Therefore, the potential for abuse of government is greater in a world of nation-states requiring military arrangements, secret preparations against "terrorists," and other corresponding secrets.

Under the *Earth Constitution*, public accountability is possible for the first time – since there are no enemy governments and all nations are now federated (like states within the U.S.). Under the *Earth Constitution*, the main causes of terrorism will also be eliminated. These causes are apparent to all thoughtful persons: (1) imperial domination of some nations over others, (2) imperial domination of some religious groupings ("Christian" nations) over others ("Moslem" nations), (3) centuries of economic exploitation by certain world groups over the majority of the world population, backed up by vicious military repression whenever these dominated peoples make a break for freedom, and (4) immense global poverty and misery for the majority in the face of unjustifiable wealth, luxury, and privilege for the few.

Under the global system of capitalism and nation-states, none of these root causes of terrorism can even begin to be addressed. We saw that they are built into the global system from the beginning. Under the *Earth Constitution*, they are all addressed, since all persons, cultures, nations, and religions are for the first time in human history respected and given equal rights within the framework of the *Constitution*. The *Earth Constitution* is predicated on creating global economic, social, and personal justice for the entire planet, not through forcibly redistributing wealth, but through transforming the undemocratic mechanisms by which the present system is perpetuated into the future (see Chapter Thirteen below). Only when this is achieved will the root causes of terrorism be eliminated.

If some terrorism remains, it will be relatively impotent to operate, since it will not be able to hide within supposedly "sovereign" nations or through any network with access to weapons of war, since these will be illegal. Nor will fighting terrorism require the repressive and massive military measures that now give sovereign nations the excuse to violate human rights, due process of law, and the integrity of persons "suspected" to be terrorists. There will be no need for "total information awareness" systems spying on the population, since only unjust authorities and concentrations of power need fear their own citizens as possible enemies.

Governments become totalitarian and abuse power because they find some excuse, some "enemy" that must be eliminated or exterminated, whether "Jews," "Moslem extremists," "rogue states," "armed revolutionaries," "enemy combatants," or "Communist subversives." Once the lie of some "axis of evil" entirely different from ourselves is overcome through an enforceable constitution embracing the unity-in-diversity of all people, the potential for governmental abuse of power through the ruse of "national security" is significantly diminished. The real potential for "abuse of power and disenfranchisement" does not lie with world government. It lies with the current world-system of territorial nation-states and global monopoly capitalism.

In his 1946 book, *The Anatomy of Peace*, Emery Reeves summed up our world situation in the following way:

> It is a strange paradox that at any suggestion of a world-wide legal order which could guarantee mankind freedom from war for many generations to come, and consequently individual liberty, all the worshipers of the present nation-states snipe: "Superstate!" The reality is that the present nation-state has become a super-state. It is this nation-state which today is making serfs of its citizens. It is this state which, to protect its particular vested interests, takes away the earnings of the people and wastes them on munitions in the constant fear of being attacked and destroyed by some other nation-state. It is this state which, by forcing passports and visas upon us, does not allow us to move freely.... And we shall become more and more subject to this all-powerful super-state if our supreme goal is to maintain the nation-state structure of the world....
>
> At the present state of industrial development, there can be no freedom under the system of sovereign nation-states. This system is in conflict with the fundamental democratic principles and jeopardizes all our

cherished individual freedoms. (1946, pp. 160-163)

The last half of the twentieth century and first events of the twenty-first century have amply confirmed Emery Reves' insight into the false principle of sovereign territorial nation-states. These are the real breeding ground of totalitarianism, not democratic world government.

4. World peace and the Possibility of Human Fulfillment

The *Constitution* states that "the World Government shall be non-military and shall be democratic in its own structure, with ultimate sovereignty residing in all the people who live on Earth" (Article II, 2). Only this principle of non-military, universal sovereignty can effectively legislate world law. This principle directly opposes the current global system in which the agreements of "sovereign nations" are in reality only treaties to be broken at will by the powerful nations and their corporations while being obeyed only by the weaker nations and other victims of this system.

And it is only on the corresponding affirmation of diversity that individuals, peoples, or small nations can be respected and protected, as the *Constitution* explicitly states. For without the sovereign moral authority of the whole of the citizens of the Earth, the weak are always going to be victims in the chaos of power struggles that comprise our current world. A viable global public policy directed toward peace must be premised on these principles.

The *World Constitution* provides this legal-philosophical context for the whole of humanity, which includes the guarantee of political rights and free expression for all citizens of the Earth and of those economic and social rights that promote the equality necessary for peace and justice. No closed "totalities" are dictated by the *World Constitution*, but instead open discussion is made possible precisely by the principle of unity-in-diversity. Without this framework for a global public policy, we are left with our current systems of power and domination that tend to impose either an arbitrary totality or the chaos of aggressive individualism on their victims. Within either of these alternatives neither genuine openness and dialogue, nor genuine peace, lies within the realm of possibility.

The *Constitution* makes possible for the first time in history the authentic free dialogue inclusive of all human beings that is the presupposition for debate about the future and meaning of the human civilizational project. "In every organized whole," Teilhard de Chardin writes, "the parts perfect themselves and fulfill themselves." No fulfillment is possible under the distorted and closed horizon implicit in the present system of fragmentation and domination. Ideologues of the system of domination assert that we are at the "end of history," for all alternatives to the present system have been exhausted. See, for example, Francis Fukuyama's book *The End of History and the Last Man* (1989). At the same time over one billion of Earth's citizens live in the nightmare condition of semi-starvation that the U.N. calls "absolute poverty."

Human beings are not isolated units whose fulfillment can be unrelated to the dehumanization and misery of others. And we have seen spiritual teachers such as Panikkar, Krishnamurti, and Jäger testify that there is no individual fulfillment without a corresponding wholeness. Without the "open horizon" of political unity-in-diversity, there can be no movement toward this deeper fulfillment for humankind. The "end of history" in the sense of the realization of a practical utopia on Earth is certainly possible, but not within the present set of institutions that actively prevent the actualization of these possibilities.

This *World Constitution* provides for a public policy that carefully preserves freedom of thought, religion, and expression as essential to a unified humanity in which peace and justice are primary concerns. For as Habermas points out, genuine dialogue, like the authentic quest for justice, is only possible within a context of the mutual equality and individual respect for all participants, within a context of unity-in-diversity (see 1994, pp. 107-148). Human individual fulfillment can come about through no source other than sufficient recognition of our oneness to the point where we can freely discuss with one another the meaning of that fulfillment.

As long as my neighbor in Afghanistan, East Timor, Columbia, or Iraq is being tortured and oppressed, I may enjoy a truncated freedom and quest for fulfillment, but one which ultimately leaves me disfigured and dehumanized. Global public policy under the *Constitution for the Federation of Earth* would supply, for the first time in history, that wholeness in which individual human beings have the opportunity to "perfect and fulfill themselves." The deepest meaning of world peace lies in this possibility alone.

The step to world government, like the step to democratic socialism, can be taken on the structural-practical level or on the spiritual-transformative level. If on the structural-practical level only, the step will be a very important one, but it will not actualize practical utopia until human beings have also transformed themselves spiritually. For the *Constitution of the Federation of Earth* to say that "Humanity is One despite the existence of diverse nations, races, creeds, ideologies and cultures and that the principle of unity-in-diversity is the basis for a new age when war shall be outlawed and peace prevail" is one thing. For this unity-in-diversity to be realized in genuine world peace is quite another. It provides the necessary, not the sufficient condition, of world peace.

Yet I have tried to show that we are not locked into the "horizontal" dimension only. At every moment we are confronted with a depth dimension to which human beings can be more or less open. This is the dimension of love and compassion, the *agapē* of Jesus or *karunā* of Buddha. This vertical dimension would be necessary and sufficient for revolutionary transformation of our human condition to a free, loving socialist society *if* the majority of humans were to experience this dimension more or less spontaneously. But today this is not likely to happen (despite the ever present *possibility* of eschatological breakthrough) because the current structural conditions of the world create and perpetuate a false consciousness of nationalism, egoism, greed, competition, self-indulgence, and emotional violence.

In his *First Address of the General Council on the Franco-Prussian War,* Marx describes the basic principles of the First International that he helped to found: "We defined the foreign policy aimed at by the International in these words: 'Vindicate the simple laws of morals and justice, which ought to govern the relations of private individuals, as the laws paramount of the intercourse of nations'" (Miranda, 1986, p. 160). Similarly, the mass media rarely question the barbaric system of sovereign nation-states all competing with one another for wealth, power, and position. They inculcate a fragmented and distorted world-view into each subsequent generation, preventing "the simple laws of morality and justice" from entering into human life.

That is why, given our present situation, critical theory and revolutionary social action are necessary (although not sufficient) for human liberation. We must radically transform the structures that perpetuate our false, distorted awareness and create new structures based on the oneness of all human beings under non-military democratic world government and under the idea that the free development of each is the condition of the free development of all. Human consciousness is not automatically transformed by the transformation of social institutions as some Marxists have claimed. But nonviolent social revolution is a necessary precondition for the transformation of human consciousness for most of the human population.

Such a transformed society would then allow people much more access to the vertical (depth) dimension and make possible the realization of the mystical experience of the identity of whole and part, the ethical experience of absolute responsibility for the Other, and the eschatological awareness that intuits the possibility of a genuine fulfillment for the human project. Simple adoption of the *Constitution for the Federation of Earth* by the nations and peoples of Earth would go a long way toward effecting that structural transformation *necessary* if human beings are to take the next step in the process of becoming spiritually mature. This *Constitution* can supply the framework, the basis, not the final result. It can then truly be the "basis for a new age when war shall be outlawed and peace prevail."

5. Bourgeois Idealism, Human Survival, and Practical Utopia

Only a well-formulated and constitutionally binding principle of unity and diversity, therefore, focusing on the need for institutionalized equality and the rule of good law, on the one hand, and the need for respect of individual freedom and difference, on the other, can give us a world of justice instead of the anarchy of individualism or the totalitarianism of some system of domination. And this could only be realized on a planetary scale, for the alternative is precisely our present world that is an unstable mixture of anarchy and totalitarianism and within which authentic democracy nowhere exists. The goal of praxis must be a balanced, dynamic, and open interrelationship of unity and diversity.

In *The Ideal of Human Unity,* Aurobindo expresses this idea as follows:

> While diversity is essential for power and fruitfulness of life, unity is necessary for its order, arrangement and stability. Unity we must create, but not necessarily uniformity. If man....could realize a secure, clear, firmly-held unity in the principle, a rich, even an unlimited diversity in its application might be possible without any fear of disorder, confusion or strife. (1997, p. 401)

Yet the concrete transition to the practical utopia inherent in the human situation must be premised on the fact that most people have not yet reached cosmic consciousness and are not yet capable of the life of simplicity, gentleness, compassion, and contentment that arise from that awakening. Secondly, the concrete transition to practical utopia must also take into account that global measures must be taken immediately if the current destruction of the global environment is to be brought to a halt and reversed before the collapse of the entire global ecosystem occurs. Thirdly, the transition must take into account the immense global poverty to be dealt with economically and institutionally before the planet can even begin to think in terms of a practical utopia consisting of widespread simplicity, contentment, and peace (see also Maheshvaranda, 2003).

There must be transitional stages and they must be democratic, never putting power into unaccountable hands in an over-hasty rush to address the crushing global problems faced by the citizens of the Earth. Praxis cannot skip lightly over the concrete transitional stages on the way to practical utopia. Yet we must never forget that genuine liberation is both possible and imminent within our situation, and our transitional stages must never abandon the practical conditions that make this possible. As Jesuit liberation theologian Sabastian Kappen points out, liberation movements today spring from the utopian impulse that does not buy the lies of the powerful who claim that all utopias have been disproven by history and banished from the Earth.

Where humanizing action exists – creative, subversive, or celebrative – there is the utopian at work, not as a blueprint for action or as a state of affairs to be realized once and for all but as an encompassing horizon of hope and promise. As the adverse effects of middle-class capitulation to corporate, neo-colonial fascism begin to be felt by the marginalized majorities of Asia and Africa, there will definitely emerge a second wave of national liberation movements, Kappen claims. This time, he says, these movements will aim at recovering "cultural identity and national sovereignty."

With these movements, the utopian impulse of the less industrialized people will redefine itself as a new world-order in which there will no longer be the dualism of center and periphery. The ideological lie of "developed and developing" will be exposed. A new world will emerge, he claims, in which there will be as many centers as there are peoples and nations, each pursuing its own model of growth and refusing to measure themselves by borrowed or imposed standards of development (Jäger, 1994, pp. 32-33).

Practical utopia is implicit in the human longing for liberation. Present struggle is a practical step toward the perhaps ever-receding horizon of peace, justice, and community. Yet Kappen, too, appears to skip lightly over the tremendous difficulties blocking the realization of "the dormant utopia" of the less industrialized people of Earth. How, we wonder, could these marginalized majorities recapture their cultural identity and national sovereignty in a world where global capitalism is beyond the control of any nation?

How could they regain control of their destinies in a world where their nations are held hostage to international debt or economic leverage from the first-world nations? When those who control the finance of the world force them to open their countries to "the market," or to blackmail techniques practiced by the World Bank and IMF forcing them to expose their people to the predations of multinational corporations while cutting services to the poor? How can they take an independent course when the mass media of the imperialist first-world stand ready to demonize attempts to break for freedom? When the armies of the first-world stand ready to bomb or invade any small nation that attempts to take an independent course?

How could marginalized peoples develop "cultural identity" if their only source of income in an irrevocably global economy is to sell their cheap labor and resources to the rich in the first-world? The rich relentlessly use their military, economic, and political power to maintain their unsustainable, consumer-oriented standard of living that *necessarily* requires exploitation of third-world poor and their resources. The economy of the industrialized peoples of the world is inseparably linked to the poverty of the less industrialized. How can they regain "national sovereignty" when this very principle opens up weak countries to the domination of powerful countries?

The people of East Timor, for example, whose simple sustainable village life existed entirely outside the predations of the global economy, were genocidally murdered by the Indonesians for two and a half decades since Indonesia's 1975 invasion with the complicity and cooperation of the big governments and many big corporations of the world. Utopian dreams of breaking out of the "iron cage" of this system remain idle fantasies without the authority of the sovereignty of the people of the Earth. Democratic world government is the only hope of marginalized peoples for abolishing the dualism of center and periphery and recovering their cultural identities and national integrity. They must give up false pretensions to territorial "national sovereignty" for a federal system capable of protecting cultural identity and national integrity precisely because their independence and individuality have the authority of the whole behind them.

Otherwise the poor majorities of Asia, Africa, and Latin America are helpless in a world where the only real law is the power of the big fish to eat the little fish. The utopic impulse for liberation does not have a chance without the protection of a constitution that recognizes the right of peoples to self-determination and cultural and economic liberation. The whole and the part are mutually interdependent and ultimately inseparable. Such visionary eloquence as that of Kappen is not very useful without a corresponding practical vision about how practical utopia might be realized. Yet our so-called "visionary" thinkers have been astonishingly naive as they call for a global change of heart that appears at present far from likely, since they have little to suggest in practical structural terms that might make possible such a change of heart.

Peter Russell, in *The Global Brain Awakens*, tells us that what is required is a realization of the basic wisdom (of non-attachment to our egoistic needs) already existing in the spiritual traditions of the world, and his suggestions under such headings as "A Spiritual Renaissance" and "The Dawning of a New Era" amount to nothing more than the challenge, "can we live it, instead of just talking about it? Can it permeate our minds and hearts, enabling us to put this wisdom into practice? This is the real challenge facing us as we move into the next millennium" (1995, p. 25).

In the face of his account of the cataclysms facing the Earth if we do not change soon, he gives not a hint that simple structural changes might make possible just those momentous spiritual changes that he advocates. Russell quotes with approval Vaclav Havel's address before the U.S. Senate and Congress in which Havel reinforced those legislators' capitalist complacency in the face of their self-created nightmare of global destruction with the usual idealist rhetoric claiming that "consciousness precedes being, and not the other way around, as the Marxists claim. For this reason the salvation of this human world lies nowhere else than in the human heart, in the human power to reflect, in human meekness, and in human responsibility" (1995, p. 22). Without concrete structural changes to make possible this "change of consciousness," this doctrine serves as reactionary propaganda.

Such "visionaries," who fail to complement their idealism with proposals for concrete structural changes, only distract us from the task at hand. Like the Buddhist tale of the man hit by a poisoned arrow who reflects philosophically on the kind of arrow, who may have shot it, for what reason, and so on, while he is suffering and dying, visionaries like Russell urge upon us a pious ideal world of spiritual transformation but lack the courage to express the immediate structural need for removal of the poisoned arrow if there is ever going to be spiritual transformation at all. Similarly, Barbara Ward and Rene Dubos in *Only One Earth – The Care and Maintenance of a Small Planet* trace the impending global disaster and, like Russell, present us with another bourgeois idealism, which they call "the vision of unity" as the only solution:

> If this vision of unity – which is not a vision only but a hard and inescapable scientific fact – can become part of the common insight of all the inhabitants of planet Earth, then we may find that, beyond all our inevitable pluralisms, we can achieve just enough unity of purpose to build a human world.... Today, in human society, we can perhaps hope to survive in all our prized diversity provided we can achieve an ultimate loyalty to our single, beautiful, and vulnerable planet Earth. (1972, pp. 219-220)

Such ineffectual idealism, which fails to call into question the structural violence of the capitalist system and carefully avoids revealing those structural features of the dominant world system principally responsible for the present global crisis (global capitalism and sovereign territorial nation-states) might be excusable for a 1972 book, but much less so in Havel's 1990 speech or Russell's 1993 book. This same complicity in the present structural world hegemony responsible for the crisis makes these "visionaries" silent about the common sense and relatively simple solution of democratic world government.

Yet the relatively simple structural change to a democratic federal world government would go a long way toward inspiring the "vision of unity" among the peoples of Earth advocated by Dubos and Ward. A concrete constitution that gave legal expression to the principle of unity-in-diversity would be likely to be studied by millions of school children the world over, just as they now study their national constitutions. Under the *Earth Constitution*, children the world over might well also study the implications of the new paradigm of interdependency fostered by field theory, ecology, systems theory, and so on. The required "change of heart" would very possibly rapidly occur.

The same complicity in the dominant system of exploitation of human beings and the environment is found in the 1995 "Report of The Commission on Global Governance" entitled *Our Global Neighborhood.* Like the others cited here, this book documents the global environmental and human crises in detail. It states plainly that "the new generation knows how close they stand to cataclysms unless they respect the limits of the natural order and care for the Earth by sustaining its life-giving qualities." It calls for new leadership and new vision to emerge before it is too late, for "the alternative is too frightening to contemplate" (1995, pp. 357 and 356), and recognizes that "the world over, people are caught in vicious circles of disrespect for the life and integrity of others" (p. 17).

Yet in the face of this awareness of the present global crisis, the document pusillanimously calls for gradual modifications in the structure of the U.N. (which we have seen is totally helpless to deal with the crisis) and a new commitment by citizens, non-governmental organizations, nations, and multinational corporations to the global "neighborhood values" of "respect for life, liberty, justice and equality, mutual respect, caring, and integrity" (pp. 48-54). These fairly meaningless platitudes are all this commission of renowned planetary citizens can manage, for they do not dare raise any substantial criticisms of the ruling world powers of multinational corporations and sovereign territorial nation-states.

After detailing the crisis situation of the world, they assert that "global governance does not imply world government or world federalism. Effective global governance calls for a new vision, challenging people as well as governments to realize that no alternative exists to working together to create the kind of world they want for themselves and their children" (p. 336). Like lemmings rushing headlong toward destruction, these "visionaries," living in their first-world societies of affluence and luxury, deftly draw the ideological veil over the obvious simple structural changes necessary for survival on this planet. Democratic federal world government is the only concrete hope for survival precisely because it represents a simple but basic structural change in the current anarchy of "global governance" and not merely a visionary exhortation for people globally to activate within themselves a miraculous change of heart.

My argument has been that the democratic, non-military federal world government offered by the *Constitution for the Federation of Earth* not only provides the best concrete means for dealing with the immediate global problems of survival, but that it also provides the necessary framework, if we can preserve the global eco-structure reasonably in tact, for then moving in the direction of a practical utopia. It provides a framework, not a blueprint, for the further evolution and transformation of human life.

We have seen the *Constitution* state that "The World Government shall be non-military and shall be democratic in its own structure, with ultimate sovereignty residing in all the people who live on Earth" (Article II, 2). Only on this principle of universal sovereignty can effective world law be legislated. And only on the corresponding affirmation of diversity can individuals, peoples, or small nations be respected and protected.

Finally, only on these principles can the world begin to move in the direction of a humane and decent democratic socialism as we will see in the next chapter. The *Constitution* does not mandate socialism or any other economic order. It provides a framework predicated sufficiently on universal political and social equality, justice, and human rights, that makes possible the transition to a truly mature and human economic order. This is precisely what the present world system makes impossible. The *Constitution* makes possible transition toward fulfillment and planetary maturity – toward that world of justice, peace, freedom, and diversity that many have understood as the ultimate hope for our common human project.

Chapter Twelve

Practical and Revolutionary Implications
of the *Constitution for the Federation of Earth*

*It took hundreds of centuries for man simply to people the earth and cover it with a first network: and further thousands of years to build up, as chance circumstances allowed, solid nuclei of civilizations within this fluctuating envelope. Today, these elements have multiplied and grown; they have packed themselves closer together and forced themselves against one another – to the point where an over-all unity, **of no matter what nature,** has become economically and psychologically inevitable. Mankind, in coming of age, has begun to be subject to the necessity and to feel the urgency of forming one single body coextensive with itself....*

Either a single nation will succeed in destroying and absorbing all the others: or all nations will come together in one common soul, that they may be more human.

Pierre Teilhard de Chardin

The development of technology and of the implements of war has brought about something akin to the shrinking of our planet. Economic interlinking has made the destinies of nations interdependent to a degree far greater than in previous years. The available weapons of destruction are of a kind such that no place on earth is safeguarded against sudden total destruction. The only hope for protection lies in the securing of peace in a supranational way. World government must be created which is able to solve conflicts between nations by judicial decision. This government must be based on a clear-cut constitution which is approved by the governments and the nations.

Albert Einstein

"Either a single nation will succeed in destroying and absorbing all the others: or all nations will come together in one common soul, that they may be more human." These prophetic words today ring of literal truth as one nation works to militarize space in order to control the entire world from what it terms "the ultimate high ground." Advocates of world government have understood the profound thought of Einstein, Teilhard de Chardin, and others as far back as World War One when it became clear that humans had immense potential to create weapons of mass destruction and stockpile them for use in every one of their "wars to end all wars."

A number of groups and movements developed that worked toward democratic world government through much of the twentieth century. But as we saw in Chapter Nine, they were working to spread clarity of thought and action around the world in the face of an immense propaganda system dedicated to preserving the unquestioned assumptions of the nation-state system and monopoly capitalism. The world had to wait for the militarization of space, endless proliferation of weapons of mass destruction, uncontrollable global warming, environmental collapse, massive species extinction, food supply collapse, and accelerating global poverty and misery before the need to unite behind the principle of unity-in-diversity became absolutely clear. At the dawn of the twenty-first century more and more people are recognizing that "a clear cut constitution" is our only option.

1. The Struggle for Democratic World Government

In general, all of the movements for world government understand that the system of sovereign territorial nation-states is not natural, rational, or moral. However, among the several organizations working for world government, there are vast differences in orientation, strategy, and world-view. The World Federalist Movement (WFM), for example, has done much good work for the past five decades in promoting the idea of global citizenship and educating humanity about the urgent need for viable federal world government, which is in all likelihood the only route to ending the scourge of war forever (see Harris, 1999, pp. 183-196). The limitations of this association (and the several other associations working toward world government), I believe, center around the twin poles of naivete and timidity.

It naively assumes the world will eventually listen to reason (and the reasons for democratic world government are compelling, urgent, and decisive) and eventually call a constitutional convention or reform the U.N. in the direction of democratic world government. However, in the light of our discussions in this book, it should be clear that the unimaginable power of the dominant global institutions will forever subvert these possibilities in spite of the compelling reasons given. What we need is revolutionary, transformative action directed toward a new world. Rational arguments given to members of Congress or some parliament, themselves up to their eyeballs in this twisted social and economic system, amount to little but timidity compounded by naivete.

Second, many world federalists lack a critical perspective into the institutional structures of monopoly capitalism and therefore are sanguine as to the power of reason to effect change in people's attitudes, while they do not see the need for basic changes in the global economic system. Similarly, world federalists often do not see the ways in which the system of sovereign nations is manipulated by global capitalism in its own interests and are naive about the ability of nations (or their representatives to the U.N.) to listen to reason. The world cannot be made to evolve toward a more rational system because, we have seen, the very foundation of the institutions now controlling the world is irrational power and greed.

The only option is revolutionary change in existing institutions arising from the impoverished masses of the world and those who stand in solidarity with them. But this revolutionary change need not be limited to a country by country socialist revolution, a scenario consciously defeated and prepared for by the imperialist nations and their corporate allies. It can, however, be effected though a global mass movement for a non-military, democratic constitution for the Earth, an excellent example of which already exists and is promoted by the World Constitution and Parliament Association (WCPA) and its sister organizations, the Global Ratification and Elections Network (GREN), the Graduate School of World Problems (GSWP), and the Institute On World Problems (IOWP).

This combined effort is also known as the Earth Federation Movement (EFM). A new beginning can and must be made through the simple, basic structural change of adopting the *Constitution for the Federation of Earth* that limits the control of irrational power and greed and places democratic authority in all the citizens of the Earth, the only place where this authority is legitimate and rational.

The constitutions of many nations today claim that sovereignty resides with their people. They claim that people have universal human rights that are expressed in these constitutions. But the truth is that all nations are territory-based, not people-based. This notion of sovereignty residing in the people has a long history in Western thought, going all the way back to Greek and Roman times, which finally found preliminary concrete embodiment in the democratic revolutions of the eighteenth century (Hinsley, 1986). However, the ideal of the genuine sovereignty of people has never yet been fully realized, for it cannot be realized apart from the sovereignty of all the citizens of Earth.

Emery Reeves understood this principle as early as 1946. In the *Anatomy of Peace* he writes:

> We cannot have democracy in a world of interdependent, sovereign nation-states, because democracy means the sovereignty of the people. The nation-state structure strangulates and exterminates the sovereignty of the people, that sovereignty which, instead of being vested in institutions of the community is vested in [approximately 190] separate sets of sovereign nation-state institutions. (1946, p. 162)

The great proclamations of universal human sovereignty and human rights from the eighteenth century to the present affirm a universal ideal but tacitly assume sovereignty is limited and territorial, not people-based. Countries worldwide are concerned to defend their "sovereign territory," not the primacy of human beings and their rights. And territory-based assumptions ignore the reality of imperialism, as well as veil the active complicity between global capital and the dominant world powers who use the territorial system for their advantage.

Citizens within various "sovereign" territories may be powerless to act on their duty to ensure that their respective governments protect their human rights, since their rights are ultimately being violated by foreign sovereign territories or multinational corporations over which they have little or no control. And if citizens's rights are generally respected within a world imperialist center, as in the United States before the Patriot Act of 2001, what is the obligation of its citizens with respect to their country's violation of other peoples' rights? I have cited the facts of these violations several places in this book. As long as nations are territories that operate as sovereign, this system itself tends to deny the equality, rights, and sovereignty of all those outside their territorial boundaries.

The only viable hope for humanity is social and spiritual revolution involving the de-legitimizing of these institutions and the establishment of new institutions premised on the sovereignty of the people of the Earth, and the dignity, rights, and responsibilities of every person who lives on the Earth. We have seen in this volume that the present institutions cannot be reformed and extended since their very nature denies these principles. Most world federalists fail to grasp this insight despite their well-intentioned and energetic efforts to create a decent world within which future generations can live. The United Nations cannot even begin to deal with either of these problems, first, because it does not have the power of making law, second, because it is not democratic, and third, because it is premised on the very principle (of territorial sovereignty) that is at the core of the most fundamental global problems.

At present no such thing as genuine "international law" exists, if one means by "law" the legitimate, enforceable legislation of principles of conduct to which citizens, groups, and nations must conform. The U.N. is premised in its Charter on the sovereign rights of territorially independent nation-states that, by definition in its charter, cannot be regulated under any superior law (see Harris, 1993, Ch. 5). All agreements by member states of the U.N. have only the status of "treaties" voluntarily followed and from which nation-states may withdraw at any time.

The International Court of Justice or "World Court" in the Hague does not have mandatory jurisdiction over alleged violations of international law or other disputes between nations. It can only decide cases if all parties to the dispute agree ahead of time to submit to the court's jurisdiction, and even then the parties might refuse to abide if they do not like the outcome, as happened when the U.S. refused to pay the several billion dollars in damages assessed by the court in 1986 for its aggression against Nicaragua during the early 1980s. Further, it deals with disputes between nations only, while the real issue involves creating a court system to try individuals. Nations do not break laws, individuals do. We need a fully developed system of courts for the world if we are ever to have the rule of law on Earth.

The newly created International Criminal Court by the Assembly of States Parties (strongly opposed by the United States) represents a positive step toward the development of world law. Yet the Rome Statute of this Criminal Court is hamstrung by the system of sovereign nations. It does not have the authority (of a real court) to order arrests, to subpoena witnesses, demand information, or force individuals to stand trial for their crimes. It can only "request" these things from sovereign nations within which suspected criminals are living.

The General Assembly of the U.N., with one representative from every nation, big or small, is in no way representative of the peoples of the Earth. Not only are vast numbers of people grossly under-represented (for example, China or India with their huge populations), but the ambassadors represent only nation-states, not people, and many of the nation-states in the U.N. are undemocratic in the extreme, oppressors, not representatives of their people. In addition, the existence of the Security Council defeats even the slightest pretense to a democratic U.N. in that no resolutions, agreements, or treaties can be passed by the U.N., no matter how universally they are assented to by nearly all the nations of the world, if these are vetoed by any of the five permanent members of the Security Council.

This situation has happened repeatedly in the history of the U.N., where a large majority of the world's nations have passed a resolution only to have it vetoed by the United States or one of the other permanent members of the Security Council. The General Assembly, for example, has repeatedly passed near-unanimous resolutions calling for an end to the U.S. economic blockade of Cuba, only to have the U.S. veto the resolutions in the Security Council. Finally, the budget of the U.N. is woefully inadequate to the global crises we face. Payment of dues is voluntary and dependent on the good will of participating nations. Payment can be withdrawn (as in the case of the U.S.) if sovereign territorial nations do not perceive the U.N. as acting sufficiently in their self-interest.

As we saw in Chapter Eleven, in the 1950s, a group of world

citizens realized time was running out for the planet in the facing of the ever increasing severity of the global problems of population explosion, increasing poverty and misery, environmental degradation threatening the very ecostructure of the planet, rampant militarism, and the threat of nuclear annihilation. These visionaries and pioneers, under the leadership of Philip and Margaret Isely, Dr. Terence Amerasinghe, Dr. Reinhart Ruge, Ms. Eugenia Almand, Mr. Sarwar Alam, and others, may or may not have had the critical insight into the intractability of the present global institutions. However, they had a crucial insight into the naivete of waiting for a global constitutional convention or the futility of trying to reform the U.N. that is predicated squarely on the principles of sovereign national territories and the power of the dominant world nations to control everything done by the U.N. through their veto on the Security Council.

This group of global citizens, working with many others, collectively created the *Constitution for the Federation of Earth* over a period of several decades and formed the above named organizations to promote the ratification and adoption of this constitution as the basis for non-military, democratic federal world government. This constitution is a brilliant document with deep insight into the nature of democracy, the principle of the sovereignty of people, not territories, and the rights of all people to a real and visible measure of equality, freedom, dignity, and justice. This movement signals that we have "come of age," as Teilhard de Chardin asserts in the quote at the head of this chapter. Peoples all over the Earth are beginning to face the "necessity and to feel the urgency of forming one single body," one united Earth, "that they may be more human."

2. The *Constitution for the Federation of Earth*

The *Constitution for the Federation of Earth* is not socialist in the sense of government ownership of the means of production, nor does it specifically envision the practical utopia required for a fulfilled human community. In our present historical situation, however, this *Earth Constitution* provides the only immediately viable framework that can make a fulfilled human community even possible for future generations. It abolishes the spurious notion of territorial sovereignty and establishes the sovereignty of the people of the Earth. All actions taken by the world government are responsible to the people of the Earth. This fundamental and guiding principle effectively ends the anti-democratic notion that territorial nations can be responsible to a portion of the people of the Earth while denying or ignoring the rights and dignity of those outside their territories.

Second, it establishes the sovereignty of the people of the Earth, through their representatives in the world parliament, over the central resources of the Earth necessary to providing a decent life to all citizens of the planet and to preserving the global environment for future generations. A market economic system is accepted by the *Constitution* (as are some socialist principles) as part of the right of individual nations within the federation to determine their social and economic arrangements within the limits of protection for human rights and the environment.

However, the power of global monopoly capitalism to hide behind the system of sovereign territorial nations and to use its massive accumulations of private wealth and power for private gain regardless of consequences to the environment or peoples' lives is broken by this principle of the sovereignty of all the Earth's people. The universal human rights defined by this constitution, the power of eminent domain over key resources, ecosystems, and the oceans by the people of the Earth, and the mandatory demilitarization of all aspects of the world system, effectively break the power of sovereign nations and global corporations to destroy the Earth as they are now doing.

This process of a revolutionary change in the world-order from the limited and antiquated territorial nation-state system to global democracy itself can and must be done democratically, through popular participation, although it requires on the part of citizens a massive campaign to de-legitimize the current oppressive territorial system. The *Constitution for the Federation of Earth*, like all constitutions that establish a new system, has a set of clauses that are to be used only once, the clauses that provide a mechanism for democratic ratification and legitimation of the constitution. The *Constitution* will have three stages of implementation and ratification, granting increasing authority and democratic powers at each stage.

Each stage provides some options in the ratification process depending on whether nation-states themselves, or the independently acting citizens of the Earth, or a combination of both, satisfy the specified criteria for ratification. At present, several related organizations are working to coordinate and promote this process as we have seen. The transition to non-military democratic world government can be accomplished with a minimum of disorder. The present world condition of disorder could hardly get worse, since the current anarchic system maximizes disorder in the form of human and animal suffering and global destruction of the environment.

The first step is clearly to de-legitimize the sovereign nation-state system, transferring sovereignty to the people of the Earth where it belongs, and to retain the nation-states as political units within the democratic world government. Within this role they can protect the cultural diversity and identities of their respective peoples, promote local self-determination for their citizens, and perhaps begin to play a positive and constructive role within the world system. Once this step is accomplished, and it must be accomplished soon if the planetary ecosystem and its ability to support higher forms of life is to be salvaged, then people would be free to work toward realization of the second step: the building of institutions that make possible a free process of growth toward human ethical-spiritual maturity and the realization of a fulfilled community.

Step two would involve efforts to de-legitimize exploitative human relationships, especially those institutionalized within the capitalist system. But this step in the revolution toward a truly human world-order can be done with even less disorder than the first step of ending the rule of the parts and initiating the rule of the whole (the sovereignty of the people of Earth). For within the framework of a constitution that asserts the rights of every citizen of Earth to a life of dignity and to economic-social-political conditions that make possible a life of education, creativity, and free self-fulfillment, the stage is set for creating economic institutions that actually allow the emergence of a fulfilled human community.

While our very survival depends on the first step, the possibility of a fully human world-order depends on the second. The democratic world government promoted by the World Constitution and Parliament Association under the *Constitution for the Federation of Earth* is something that should be advocated and actively supported by democratic socialists as well as by all people of compassion and good will. It is essential to viable revolutionary praxis in our historical moment at the dawn of the twenty-first century, and is essential to the very survival of the planetary ecostructure and its ability to sustain higher forms of life. There are many good reasons to support such a democratic world government, some of them independent of socialist values.

These reasons for supporting democratic world government can be divided into four broad categories. First, the multifaceted global crisis we are facing in the early twenty-first century is utterly beyond the capability of any individual nation, socialist or not, to handle. Such vast problems such as destruction of the oceans and fisheries, ozone depletion, global warming, world deforestation, widespread destruction of agricultural lands, diminishing fresh water supplies, rapidly growing desertification, population explosion, world militarism, world repression of freedom and human rights, lack of clean water and sanitation for the majority, and world-wide poverty and starvation can only be dealt with on a global level with democratic planetary forms of enforceable legislation.

Second, the notions of the sovereignty and human rights at the heart of democratic theory (whether bourgeois or socialist) point, as we have seen, beyond the idea of limited national sovereignties to the sovereignty of the people of the Earth and universal principles applicable to all. Third, I am arguing that the proposed democratic constitution would promote a transition to world democratic socialism (the only option for a truly just and compassionate world) far more effectively than revolutionary changes within individual nation-states could do. Finally, only democratic world government can make possible the ascent to planetary maturity.

The words of the greatest scientific genius of the twentieth century apply directly to our situation at the dawn of the twenty-first century and to the *Earth Constitution*. In Chapter Two we saw Einstein expressing the cosmic consciousness of planetary maturity. No other option exists today. The so-called "political right wing" offers us no option beyond more of the same nightmare. The so-called "political left" offers no clear vision of the future, only endless resistance to everything the right stands for. In the epigram at the head of this chapter, Einstein writes, "world government must be created which is able to solve conflicts between nations by judicial decision. This government must be based on a clear-cut constitution which is approved by the governments and the nations." We know the solution (the rule of law and judicial decision) and we have this clear cut constitution. It is time for all those who embody some degree of compassion, critical theory, or nonviolence to act for a decent world order.

3. Socialist Values and the *Earth Constitution*

Socialists within most sovereign nation-states today, especially those of the first world, most often find themselves working not for a revolutionary transformation of the economic-social-political system (since this is not even remotely a viable immediate option) but for organizing, educating, and implementing progressive resistance in defense of the oppressed, whether this be human beings or the environment. They work for labor rights, progressive taxation, defense of civil liberties, war resistance, campaign reform, universal health care rights, environmental legislation, defense of the poor and homeless, prison reform, abolition of nuclear weapons, and so on.

The battle is Quixotic because such legislation, reform, or protest will in no way endanger the global system that produces these very injustices and oppressions. Socialists struggle defensively within the framework of unjust class society without much immediate hope of creating a class-free society. The more success progressives have in reforming this system to protect labor, the poor, or the environment, the more the system is legitimized in the eyes of the population as being "not so bad." We have a catch-twenty-two situation. The capitalist system has overwhelming power in its hands, including the power of the state that it largely controls. As Jürgen Habermas points out, entitlement legislation, such as welfare for the poor, social services, or environmental legislation, serves the greatest need of the system at this juncture in history, which is "legitimation" in the eyes of the population (Habermas, 1975, Ch. 6).

In the face of this apparently hopeless situation, it can only be of benefit to socialists to examine the possibility of an alternative route to labor rights, protection of liberty, the ending of war, universal health care, protection of the environment, and the ending of poverty. A much more viable option for creating a class-free society would be to first legitimate a federal world government that is constitutionally mandated not only to protect labor rights, liberty, and the environment but to create universal health care, education, and social security.

From this set of constitutional mandates, socialists could for the first time begin to effectively work for genuine worldwide democratic socialism. If their progressive energy were transferred at least in part from defensive local struggles, which are not likely in the long run to overturn the system itself, to the creation of a progressive democratic world government, they might well enlist as their allies the disenfranchised peoples of the world who are tangential to the capitalist system and facing starvation and/or oppression in their local situations.

With the collapse of so-called "actually existing socialism" as a real alternative to the nightmare of monopoly capitalism, the left has floundered without a vision and without being able to articulate a genuine alternative. They have ignored the one real option available to the world that is more easily created than endless "resistance" that in the end changes little as it is repressed, disappeared, bombed, or jailed by the ever-expanding world "security" apparatus. Nearly all the values the left claims to cherish are embodied in the *Earth Constitution*. Without challenging fundamental assumptions, resistance within the Neanderthal framework of the present world-order of monopoly capitalism and territorial nation-states is utterly self-defeating. The institutions themselves prevent progressive change, no matter how many noble minded individuals die in Colombian torture chambers or languish in United States federal prisons or perish in the Pentagon's Iraqi concentration camps.

The overwhelming majority of human beings, the disenfranchised of the world, have nothing to lose and everything to gain from democratic world government where their rights are constitutionally recognized. Such a constitutional federal system would level the playing field tremendously and provide them with constitutional grounds to pursue their rights to a life of dignity, freedom, and opportunity. A federal world government under the *World Constitution* would not provide a panacea or magical solution to the problem of exploitative institutional relationships, but it would make success possible (whereas success in the present situation hardly appears possible) through the ability to use the World Courts, the World Ombudsmus, the World Parliament, the World Executive branch, and the World District Attorneys in the struggle for the protection and progressive implementation of a just, socialist world order.

Article I of the *Constitution for the Federation of Earth* lists the six most basic primary functions of the Federation. Let us examine them in turn. (1) "To prevent war, secure disarmament, and resolve territorial and other disputes which endanger peace and human rights." No longer could the "cycle of violence" exist where rebellions because of the structural violence of extreme poverty meet with repression from third-world governments financed and supported by first-world governments or with "interventions" by first world military to prevent progressive social change from occurring. Nation-states, like the federal government, would be disarmed by law, and the process of changing the structural violence of poverty would be open to non-violent methods of conflict resolution such as the courts, demonstrations, social organizing, creative economic policies, and so on.

(2) The second primary function of the federation will be "To protect universal human rights, including life, liberty, security, democracy, and equal opportunities in life." Again, the very foundations of the world federal government would allow the progressive transformation of institutionalized violence and exploitation, protecting the "security" of those who militate for change, and allowing them to legally base their claim for just economic and social institutions on the right to "equal opportunities in life" (an idea that is a bold-faced lie under the capitalist system).

(3) "To obtain for all people on Earth the conditions required for equitable economic and social development and for diminishing social differences." The constitution specifies its affirmation of cultural diversity and local autonomy in other places (for example, Article XIII-16), but here we see concern to diminish the "social differences" of the present system of wealth and power versus the poor and exploited. The mandate of the world government, stated repeatedly in the *Constitution*, is "equal opportunity for useful employment for everyone, with wages or remuneration sufficient to assure human dignity" (Article XIII-1), in other words, to end the extremes of poverty and wealth worldwide as we know them.

The remaining three "broad functions" of the Federation would again work in favor of the socialist struggle for a fully realized human community: (4) "To regulate world trade," (5) "To protect the environment and the ecological fabric of life from all damage," (6) "To devise and implement solutions to all problems which are beyond the capability of national governments, or which are now or may become of global or international concern or consequence." World trade would no longer easily interfere with the rights of every person to a life of dignity with a home, security, health care, and opportunity (Article XIII, numbers 4-7 and 11-13). The exploitation of the poor by multinational corporations would be brought to a rapid end with the regulation of world trade, and the destruction of the global environment though multinational exploitation of resources would be quickly ended (and can only be quickly ended) through the power of the Earth Federation.

For the first time, a consistent set of worldwide laws regarding the environment, enforced by the world police armed only with weapons sufficient to apprehend individuals, could be enacted.= ("World Police shall be armed only with weapons appropriate for the apprehension of individuals responsible for the violation of world law" (Article 10-C-5).) No longer would the poor nations have to sacrifice their environmental standards to attract rapacious corporations to their resources. International debt will be assumed by the Federation and rapidly paid off (see Chapter Thirteen), and a government concerned with global prosperity within the framework of environmental sustainability would be initiated for the first time in history.

These articles also give the world government the means to raise capital to be used for the global common good through taxes, fees, and other ways of generating federal income. The present system of capitalism unregulated by enforceable world laws cannot create investment capital capable of promoting the common good, whether within nations or globally, with any effectiveness. For competition (which is directed to private advantage) will always force private investment capital in the direction of a high enough rate of return to (1) stay in business and (2) make a profit for the private benefit of the wealthy investors. The pressure of the market also mandates (3) continual growth, for as technology and competitors evolve and the rate of return drops, without a continual eye to growth businesses will tend to fail.

Sustainable development is not likely under this system, for the incentive is to neglect, for example, the impact of production on the environment or communities in order to maximize growth and protect the rate of profit (Daly, 1996). World government, on the other hand, will be free of this irrational and destructive pressure now compromising corporations and territorial nation-states. It will be able to invest directly in the common good (the good that makes possible the survival and flourishing of all the parts of the whole) (Martin, 2003).

On the planetary level, the "common good" has taken on a deeper meaning than within nation-states where it rarely has the seriousness of survival itself. Many global problems, including global wealth and poverty, global militarism and lawlessness, and global environmental preservation, are "beyond the capacity of national governments" to address. The *World Constitution* provides the only viable hope for humanity to move in the direction of non-military democratic world of justice and peace.

Study of the *Constitution for the Federation of Earth* shows the proposed democratic world government would specifically possess or actively work for many features we associate with socialism (or with any decent, equitable society). Article IV, number 12, and article XIII, numbers 4, 5, 6, and 11, give it the goal and authority to provide free and adequate education, health care, housing, food, water, and social security to everyone on the planet. Individual nations, no matter what their economic system, would be required to tax the rich and/or legally appropriate enough of their resources to provide, probably with the help of the global federal government, adequate education, health care, housing, food, water, and social security to all their citizens. Profits will no longer be funneled to off-shore bank accounts to avoid the taxes that contribute to the common good.

By law, no longer could nations exist (as in most of today's world) where five or ten percent of the population controls ninety percent of the land, wealth, and power. In all likelihood, the educational systems of most nations would encourage study of the *World Constitution* and the assimilation of its values of universal equality and dignity. People would study the supreme law of the world as they now study the constitutions of their respective territorial nation-states, and this could in turn contribute to the successful implementation of a more just and equitable world order, one more and more beginning to take on democratic socialist features.

Article IV, number 14, of the *Constitution* gives the world federal government the power to regulate all transnational corporations, finances, and industry. Just as territorial nation-states now have the legal power to regulate corporations, finances, and industry, so would the world government. But currently transnational corporations hold their governments hostage with the threat to move their resources and productive facilities to other nations if they are not given favorable tax breaks or environmental liberties. In addition, given the inadequate forms of democracy in territorial nations, large corporations at present buy, control, and manipulate politicians and other people with the authority to regulate them.

Under democratic world government, their ability to use these tactics would be seriously limited. The *Earth Constitution* is designed with multifaceted checks, balances, and institutional mechanisms to deter the corruption of those in power and ensure the realization of the common good. Even private corporations, finance, and industry would be required to be more responsible to the public domain and less secret and totalitarian in their operations and methods. Individuals would regain their right to privacy (today destroyed in the so-called war on terrorism). Corporations would have to assume public accountability.

Article IV, numbers 23, 27, 28, and 30, effectively mundialize the Earth's oceans and sea beds, all transnational power systems, all essential natural resources, and all fossil fuel production in the world. These actions are necessary if the constitutional goal of a decent life for all planetary citizens is ever to be realized, along with the constitutional goal of preserving the planetary environment. The ecological and human harm done by the big oil corporations during the twentieth century defies imagination, including the extensive destruction of rain forests, ecosystems, and the lives of people living in these regions, including substantial complicity with murderers and torturers in places such as Brazil, Indonesia, or Nigeria.

In addition, the burning of fossil fuel promoted by these corporations has been a major cause of global warming and the on-going collapse of the planetary ecosystem. It is absolutely essential to take these domains out of secretive private hands and place them in hands democratically responsible for the people of the Earth and future generations. These measures are therefore significant and necessary features of democracy and good world government. But they also point in the direction of socialism insofar as this is understood as a system in which essential resources and production are placed under democratic control for the common good.

4. Bureaucracy and the Common Good

Would these functions of world government require the development of a large federal bureaucracy that would entangle petitioners in an interminable bureaucratic labyrinth? Bureaucracy, yes, interminable labyrinth, not likely. Go to the web site of any state government within the United States and examine the number of agencies necessary to the functioning of complex society even at this level. In this regard the proposed constitution deserves careful study, for it outlines in detail much of the structure of the world federal bureaucracy.

The bureaucracy is not hinted at or covered up, but is there for us to see. There would necessarily be a federal bureaucracy. The world is a large and very complex place. However, there would be significant differences from, for example, the U.S. federal bureaucracy that has proved to be a nightmare for the poor and powerless (while the rich negotiate it fairly easily through their corporate lawyers and other connections). When government actually represents the people, bureaucracy will function to their benefit.

First, if there are going to be fair global elections using fair campaign practices and proportionate representation, there must be a federal system to allow democracy to function at the global level. Second, no doubt exists any longer that our world is one ecosystem and its maintenance necessarily requires many qualified people in an executive branch who can monitor atmosphere, oceans, fisheries, forests, rain cycles, natural resources, arable land, erosion patterns, pollution trends, quality of water, air, sanitation, spread of disease, population trends, transportation, trade, human rights protection, and so on. For our planet must be coordinated to maintain sustainability, ecological balance, and social justice.

If the population of the Earth returns to three or four billion, the limit currently sustainable, this number of people necessarily has a tremendous impact on the environment beyond what can be monitored and assessed locally (Cohen, 1996). And if there is to be international trade, more equitable distribution of key world resources, sufficient non-destructive power systems of sun, wind, water, and magnetic fields, or the monitoring of Earth's population with well-constructed incentives for its control, an executive bureaucracy will be necessary. There is no reason why it cannot be efficient and economical.

Third, there will continue to be disputes between cultures, individuals, groups, or corporations at the international level. Human beings are far from perfect and will have many conflicts among themselves. A federal judiciary and their support persons will be necessary. The *Constitution* mandates eight benches of the Supreme Court for human rights, criminal cases, civil cases, constitutional cases, international conflicts, and so on. Fourth, if there are going to be violations of world human rights, environmental or other world laws, there will need to be world attorneys general, police, and their support persons.

Finally, if there is going to be careful monitoring of human rights implementation and protection worldwide, including remedies addressing any violations by the police or federal bureaucracy itself, there will have to be a world ombudsmus and staff of qualified support persons. I have just described the four independent branches of the federal government provided by the *Constitution* plus the mechanism necessary for the World Parliament to function. The Earth has become a tiny place, a planetary spaceship, and no matter how insulated a culture may wish to be, there is no more any possibility of independence from the whole.

Yet the principles behind this federal bureaucracy would be different. First, the *Constitution* makes ample provision for removing corrupt or incompetent people from office, while protecting their rights. Second, the premise of the bureaucracy would be the authority delegated by the Parliament (representatives of the peoples and nations of the Earth), and the mandate would be to serve the people faithfully through the spirit and letter of the *World Constitution*. Unlike national bureaucracies (which are controlled by wealth and power and to which the poor or middle classes are often helpless petitioners who are often insulted and degraded by the red tape and attitude of the bureaucrats) the federal world government would be instituted on entirely different premises. Third, the executive branch of world government (like the other independent branches) would be directly responsible to Parliament and would not have nearly the power (and corresponding arrogance) that, for example, the executive branch of the United States government has presently.

Finally, one independent branch of world government would be the "World Ombudsmus," functioning as a watchdog and advocate for the peoples of the Earth with respect to the protection or neglect of human rights and to "promote the welfare" of all peoples "by seeking to assure conditions of social justice and of minimizing disparities are achieved in the implementation and administration of world legislation and world law" (Article XI-4). This organization would have the power to initiate legal action in defense of individuals or groups and is mandated "to protect the People of Earth and all individuals against violations of this *World Constitution* by any official or agency of the World Government, including elected and appointed officials or public employees regardless of origin, department, office, agency, or rank" (XI-2). Of the eleven separate powers and functions listed for the World Ombudsmus, one is directly concerned with bureaucracy: "To ascertain that the administration of otherwise proper laws, ordinances and procedures of the World Government do not result in unforeseen injustices or inequities, or become stultified in bureaucracy or details of administration" (XI-6).

Bureaucracy is necessary at this stage of history since the planet is too small, too fragile, and too complex not to require a single legal system and a system of careful monitoring of environmental and social factors, as well as trained professionals in the various agencies of government whose specializations include concern for the good of the whole. The *World Constitution* does everything possible to see that this works to peoples' benefit and does not become a hindrance to the freedom, peace, and justice that are among its fundamental principles.

None of these features of the world bureaucracy need become entangled in prolonged paper trails or endless levels of rote approval-seeking, or hopeless confusion concerning information and details. The information technology revolution of the last several decades has given human beings the tools to eliminate all these features of former bureaucracies, whether on the model of the oppressive U.S. welfare system or bureaucratic decision-making in the former Soviet Union.

Supercomputers that can process a trillion or more bits of information per second can be interfaced with PCs and other computers at every level of the world government and of society itself, making a truly democratic and responsive government (as well as effective socialist economic management) possible for the first time in history (see Pollack, 1997). An effective federal bureaucracy using the immense information processing capabilities of today's computers (currently used by the rich to become more rich and by governments to create military machines to destroy yet more people) will be able to monitor very complex environmental and social factors, be responsive to human and environmental needs worldwide, and create effective, fair, and speedy electoral procedures for the global population.

The *Constitution for the Federation of Earth* institutionalizes neither capitalism nor socialism, although we saw that its protection for basic human economic rights requires it to go a long way in the direction of socialism. Article XIV, number 2, gives each nation the right to determine its own internal economic and social system consistent with human rights and dignity. The federal world government could not interfere with nations wishing to go even farther in the direction of socialism in their internal affairs. Here is the place for the internal struggle within nations for true democratic socialism: under conditions of democratic dialogue and debate, with guaranteed rights of assembly, protest, and petition, not in the guerilla battlefield or in a war of propaganda slogans.

Some nations could be shining examples to the others in the extent to which they had realized a truly compassionate and fulfilled human community. Once the principles of democratic participation, freedom, and human rights have been established through the *World Constitution*, it would remain for revolutionaries to demonstrate socialism as inseparable from true democracy. For these reasons, adoption of the *Constitution for the Federation of Earth* is as practical as it is revolutionary.

Habermas, like Marx, argues that the universal cannot be separated from the particular in terms of metaphysical theory or social-political application. Concrete persons, for Habermas, whose identities have been formed through specific cultural traditions and communities, have the moral right to demand an equality not negating those very traditions and differences that have participated in the formation of their identities. Equality must be equality of particular persons whose individuality is nurtured through specific influences and who engage in discourse in the political arena precisely from the perspective of this situatedness. As Habermas puts it, "we ascribe to the bearers of individual rights an identity that is conceived intersubjectively.... A correctly understood theory of rights requires a politics of recognition that protects the integrity of the individual in the life contexts in which his or her identity is formed" (1994, p. 113).

Habermas suggests true legitimacy in any social order can only rest on authentic democracy, on the autonomy of its citizens who feel the legislation enacted in their name is self-generated legislation (see also Coicaud, 2002). I have shown that under the present system of sovereign nations such democratic autonomy is impossible in at least two fundamental ways. First, the separation of the political sphere of citizenship from the civil sphere of accumulated private property and other massive social and political forces necessarily makes much legislation result from the influence of these non-democratic forces and not the enactment of a discursively formed collective will among equal citizen participants. As Antonio Gramsci pointed out, the cultural hegemony of the capitalist class generates a self-legitimating ideology ensuring that legislation will protect the interests of this class (Forgacs, 2000).

Second, the fact of other nation-states in a so-called "world order" existing outside of all democratic and procedural frameworks for the possibility of democratic decision making confronts citizens within each nation with pressing factors beyond any possible democratic control: international economic rivalry, massive poverty and injustice, military threats and arms-trading, the global destruction of the environment, the need for a national security state independent of citizen scrutiny, economic exploitation of the poorest nations by the rich, and so on. In neither case within the present world order can the democratic-socialist value of the fullness of life of a person within a community be realized. On both these grounds, the current system of sovereign nation-states is illegitimate.

The federal bureaucracy outlined by the *Constitution for the Federation of Earth* is designed to implement the equality, freedom, and prosperity for the entire planet and to end the present system of exploitation and domination of nation by nation and class by class. It is designed for accountability on the part of government officials and with carefully thought-out checks and balances among government agencies. Without such a bureaucracy the domination of larger nation-states and/or the domination of the rich cannot be prevented. Insofar as the *Constitution* has socialist features, it is designed to protect equality, freedom, and the common good. Without a carefully designed federal bureaucracy, such a goal would be unrealizable.

4. Sovereignty of the People of Earth

One might almost say that the most fundamental issue is not that of capitalism versus socialism but the question as to who is to be sovereign. Are we to have democracy that treats every person as an end-in-herself within community, or are we to have some form of illegitimate power determination for our lives, the empty form of democracy without authentic content? The government of Cuba, despite its democratic socialist ideals, attributes its restrictions on freedom of speech to self-defense against the imperialist designs of the United States. Above we saw Emery Reeves underline this dilemma. One cannot create democracy and liberty premised on the sovereignty of the people at the same time that sovereignty is based on a multiplicity of territorial nation-states.

Only the true sovereignty of the whole can affirm the particularity of each one of us instead of leaving us prey to a chaos of forces that dehumanize, manipulate, and devalue our humanity. And no territorial nation-state can truly represent the whole and take its constitutional stand on the right to live and flourish for every human being. The only legitimate sovereignty is that of the whole of humankind, and only such an affirmation of wholeness can fully affirm the freedom and individuality within community of each person. For this reason, the affirmation of wholeness in the *World Constitution* is the crucial factor in the transition to a world-order where the capitalist division between private self-interest and our common humanity is overcome.

The affirmation of the *human community* as sovereign makes possible creating a world in which every individual on the planet has sufficiency of goods, dignity, security, health-care, and education. This represents a key paradigm-shift, the internal logic of which will lead to a future worldwide democratic socialism in which the community affirms the individual and the individual, in turn, enriches and supports the community. The principle of unity-in-diversity affirms the sovereign community (the whole of humankind) and the dignity and freedom of every individual. In Chapter Seven, I quoted Mortimer Adler's crucial insight: "'All' – when what is meant is *all without exception* – is the most radical and, perhaps, also the most revolutionary term in the lexicon of political thought" (1991, p. 90). For the first time in human history, the *Earth Constitution* applies the values of democracy, human rights, and freedom to *all*.

The fact that the proposed *World Constitution* explicitly affirms the principle of unity-in-diversity in relation to the sovereignty of humanity shows, I believe, that it was written with an awareness of the principles I have attempted to articulate in this chapter. It mandates "the Earth's total resources shall be used equitably for human welfare," thereby institutionalizing a goal for world government that must inevitably lead to a transformed world-order. "Unity-in-diversity" implies nothing less. Contemporary Japanese philosopher Masao Abe affirms similar principles with his call to recognize the sovereignty of humankind. He writes, "a human community which has overcome...the existence of the nation-state... serves mankind by transcending distinctions between races and between people" (1985, p. 256).

Yet by the very token of overcoming these distinctions among people in the awareness of the unity of humankind, Abe is able to continue with the assertion that "sovereignty which is established therein, takes self-negation as a basic principle and encompasses all races and all peoples in their respective particularity." Sameness and difference, wholeness and particularity, coextensively arise as the roots of authentic sovereignty. The Preamble to the *Constitution for the Federation of Earth*, quoted above, specifies "the principle of unity-in-diversity is the basis for a new age," and so on. In the light of this chapter, we see this "new age" is not merely a pious ideal, but a genuine possibility embodied in this *Constitution*. This genuine possibility is premised on a clear seeing of the human situation.

PART FIVE

Practical Utopia and
Transformative Praxis

Chapter Thirteen

A Paradigm Shift

to Universal Peace, Freedom, and Prosperity

*Saint Paul spoke of "madness" (1 Cor. 1:18-2:16): that which is absurd for the prevailing morality. For the dominant, present rationality, which dictates the true and the false (as does Karl Popper in the **Open Society and Its Enemies**), the construction of the new Jerusalem is the absolute **evil** (because it calls in question the current system in its totality).... The poor set out on their journey. They pass **beyond** Egypt's frontier, they transcend the horizon of the system, they cross the barrier of death. Now there is nothing to follow, no one to heed, but the Lord. They have now embarked on the **nothing**-of-the-system, the non-being of the prevailing morality. They are on the road to the "wilderness"....*

*Praxis, as an action and a relationship of the members of the community, of a people that has transcended the morality of sin (as Nicaragua, after its 1979 revolution, became a "new land" – an earthly one, it is true, but nevertheless a historical "new land"), is utopian, meaningless, absurd, mad, subversive, destructive, **dangerous**, for the system left behind, left in the past: "But they cried out the more: Crucify him!" (Matt. 27:23).... The practices of the liberators, those complying with ethical **demands, have no meaning** for the system.... The Israelites, however, who have moved out into the wilderness, know that God is **with them.***

Enrique Dussel

The vision of "what should be" – independent though it may sometimes appear of personal will – is yet inseparable from a critical and fundamental relationship to the existing condition of humanity. All suffering under a social order prepares the soul for vision and what the soul receives in this vision strengthens and deepens its insight into the perversity of what is perverted.

Martin Buber

I have been presenting a holistic philosophy of human liberation, apprehending our human situation in the light of our highest possibilities. In doing this, I have integrated several themes illuminating the possibility of revolutionary transformation toward planetary maturity and a new world-order of universal peace, justice, and prosperity. Three themes in particular need to be emphasized at this juncture. All three point in different ways to the same conclusion. The world and human life are part of an integrated whole that science as well as religion have revealed as deriving from utterly simple, fundamental principles. If we want to survive on this planet, we must reach the point of self-conscious maturity very rapidly. We can no longer afford to evolve slowly into the future, limping along with botched and broken institutions inherited from a compulsive and adolescent past. We must establish a planetary society upon principles that allow our highest human possibilities to rapidly unfold.

1. Praxis – from Fragmentation to Integration

The first theme articulates the eschatological or transformative potential inherent in the structure of the human experience of time and its intersection with a dimension transcending time. As the great religions have always understood, we are capable of being "reborn" at any time. We are capable of breakthrough to a new level of being and a new way of being in the world. Each of us experiences this possibility daily in moments of awakening and annually in spurts of growth toward holistic awareness and stage-seven maturity. Human history shows similar leaps forward and breakthroughs at particular junctures. Witness the astonishingly rapid and progressive transformations of the golden age of fifth-century BCE Greece, the high middle ages of thirteenth-century Europe, fifteenth-century Renaissance Italy, the eighteenth-century Enlightenment, and the twentieth-century global peace and justice movements.

In the above quote, Enrique Dussel describes the liberating exit from complicity with the systems of perverted, false morality that have hitherto dominated in history. To encounter the "wilderness" beyond positivism, relativism, fundamentalism, capitalism, nationalism, and thoughtless conformity is to enter upon a process of perpetual realization of our highest human possibilities. It is to be labeled "subversive" by the imperial morality, for our true possibilities come from God, not from the "realism" of the dominant classes. Practical utopia is now very near realization.

We need but drop our egoistic illusions and allow the "grace" inherent in the structure of existence to inform our lives. Our eschatological destiny on Earth can be understood in the humanistic terms of an Eric Fromm as becoming "fully human" (1962, pp. 156-158). Or it can be understood in the religious idiom of Dussel and others. Christianity speaks of allowing the kingdom of God to descend upon Earth. Islam speaks of the realization of the true *sharia*. Judaism awaits the coming messianic age. Hinduism looks forward to restoration of the golden age. Buddhism focuses on the promises of the Bodhisattva for universal enlightenment.

The breakthrough in every case moves from fragmentation to wholeness. Our world today carries forward the outdated modern paradigm assuming a plurality of fragmented egos emphasizing their differences from other egos. It assumes an inevitable economic competition based on self-interest at the expense of others. And it assumes a world divided into collective cultural, racial, religious, ethnic, and nationalistic egos. This structure of fragmentation remains institutionalized in global capitalism and the nation-state system, institutions, we have seen, currently carrying our planet toward ecological and militaristic destruction. We examined the revelations of twentieth-century science revealing a paradigm shift from an atomistic and materialistic universe to one informed by unity-in-diversity at every level, from the microscopic to the biological to the cosmic.

"Praxis" means action inseparable from, and integrated with "theory," that is, from the vision of a community. "Theory" means here a coherent account of the most fundamental principles by which we organize our experience. Our consciousness (theory) and our action dialectically influence one another and move us into a future at least partly self-created (and partly the result of a new openness to the "grace" of existence). "Transformative praxis" means self-conscious action and theory directed toward liberation. Eschatologically, we can cultivate and facilitate the emergence of a transformed world of peace, freedom, and prosperity for our planet.

The second theme I have emphasized is the concept of emergent evolution. In Chapter One, I outlined the successive transformations of human consciousness we have undergone in our two- million-year history on this planet. I suggested (following such thinkers as Samuel Alexander, Nicholas Berdyaev, Errol E. Harris, Dada Maheshvaranda, Pierre Teilhard de Chardin, and Alfred North Whitehead) that this emergent evolution of our consciousness is but a continuation of the process of emergence within the universe itself. The universe is fostering within itself an ever-increasing complexity, unification, and levels of awareness, exhibiting emergent properties not reducible to previous levels of existence.

This process has led from the level of the atom through the level of the molecule to the one-celled organisms to higher forms of life. It has led through the development of sentient awareness in complex organisms and beyond to the emergent levels of reason and value. It points forward to cosmic consciousness and planetary maturity. Our ascent beyond the isolated ego of domination and separation now informing our consciousness can liberate us to wholeness and integration. Universal peace and prosperity is not an empty ideal violating the known structures of "reality."

Peace and prosperity are implied in the realization of the real potential within us. The awareness of unity-in-diversity now emerging on a planetary scale within culture, poetry, literature, non-governmental organizations, and personal attitudes is the foundation of a new realism within which there will be universal peace and prosperity on the Earth.

Transformative praxis means we can make our lives a dynamic force facilitating the emergence of this new level of human consciousness. Mahatma Gandhi said we must be the change we want to see in the world. Transformative praxis means the simultaneous transformation of ourselves and our institutions.

The third theme we examined involves the concept of paradigm shift. Human beings have cognized their world through a series of paradigms. A paradigm is a set of fundamental presuppositions through which we organize and understand our world (Harris, 2000b, ch 1). Chapter One described the fundamental assumptions of the mythological age of human consciousness, approximately 10,000 to 500 BCE, as being quite distinct from the new consciousness emerging during the "Axis Period" between 600 and 200 BCE. The Greek thinkers of the Axis Period developed a set of presuppositions for understanding the world and human existence significantly different from the mythological outlook, establishing what can be termed the "Ancient" Western paradigm. After the collapse of the Ancient World, the emerging Medieval World integrated the Ancient paradigm with Christianity in the West and Middle East and with Islam in other parts of the Middle East extending to north India and North Africa.

The Ancient and Medieval paradigms were superseded by the development of the mechanistic and atomistic (Modern) paradigm from Nicolas Copernicus through Galileo Galilei to Sir Isaac Newton. This paradigm included a set of presuppositions about the universe, nature, and human beings now superseded by a holistic paradigm arising from all aspects of twentieth-century science. For a detailed account of this process, see *Apocalypse and Paradigm* by Harris (2000b). For a briefer account, see my article "A Planetary Paradigm for Global Government" (1999b). All paradigm shifts historically have been relatively slow to occur. Yet historical change has been accelerating rapidly to the point where the present transformation may take decades rather than centuries. In Chapter Fourteen, I will explore several ways that aware and committed people can contribute to the speed and integrity of this transformation.

Chapter Two discussed the paradigm shift our generation must accomplish. We must rapidly move from the fragmented and atomistic Newtonian set of assumptions to the holistic and integrated assumptions behind the scientific breakthroughs of the twentieth century. Chapter Four demonstrated the need for a similar paradigm shift with regard to our understanding of religion and spirituality. The scholarship and universal theologies developed by twentieth-century thinkers have created a "Copernican Revolution" in our understanding of religion, liberating us to a new level of existence. In every case, the presuppositions under which we currently understand human life and the world are outmoded and obsolete. The current militarized chaos in the political world and the on-going ecological destruction of the biological world make the failure of our current paradigm obvious.

The transition to the new paradigm of unity-in-diversity will not require further chaos or violence. Instead, it will rapidly eliminate the chaos and violence resulting from our current inadequate paradigm. The madness of the world's currently dominant institutions for "security" will only create further violence and insecurity. Our present world's most basic assumptions comprise the root causes of these evils. The institutionalization of our assumptions in monopoly capitalism and the nation-state system constitutes the primary source of violence, destruction of nature, and most terrorism on Earth.

As Martin Buber affirms in the quote at the head of this chapter, "all suffering under a social order prepares the soul for vision and what the soul receives in this vision strengthens and deepens its insight into the perversity of what is perverted." In Chapter Seven, we saw Jiddu Krishnamurti affirm with Buber that the seeing clearly of what is perverted leads to spontaneous transformation beyond fragmentation to wholeness. Insight into the perversity of what is perverted leads to changing our assumptions. Transformative praxis means adopting institutions based on holistic assumptions. It means liberation for human beings and nature.

Part Three of this book clarified in what ways the premises behind democratic socialism embody the paradigm shift to economic unity-in-diversity. Part Four examined how the paradigm shift to political unity-in-diversity is embodied in the *Constitution for the Federation of Earth*. These institutionalized embodiments of unity-in-diversity require one another. Human beings will not be able to realize universal prosperity under democratic socialism without the authority of federal world government. Economic regulations cannot legitimately be decided in secret by elite groups behind closed World Trade Organization doors. And they cannot be legitimately decided by nearly two hundred differing "sovereign" territorial entities. They must be legislated democratically by the representatives of all the Earth's citizens.

There is no liberation unless both forms of institutionalized fragmentation are replaced with institutions premised on integration and wholeness: non-military democratic world government and democratic socialism. We have examined above in what ways the *Constitution for the Federation of Earth* embodies both. The powers now dominating the world are not going to suddenly transform their economic practices to benefit the majority of the Earth's population. Advocating a more just and democratic economics for the Earth (as, for example, do Herman Daly, David Korten, and Vandana Siva) amounts to pie-in-the-sky idealism without a World Parliament to legislate and enforce these changes.

The required paradigm shift can also be understood in terms of a shift from the empty forms of democracy to authentic democracy. Under class society and the nation-state system, governments do not and cannot fully serve the needs of the people. Nor can they maximize the effective participation of people in the process of governing. Class domination in and between nations and imperialism between nations (which includes inevitable militarism within nations) make peaceful, prosperous, democratic living impossible. Transformative praxis means radical action for authentic democracy from the local to the global level.

For more then two hundred years, the people of Earth have been in the midst of a paradigm shift emerging from Enlightenment thought. Chapters Seven and Eight emphasized eighteenth-century Enlightenment thought (refined and deepened by nineteenth-century critical social theory) formulating the standard for legitimate government as liberty, equality, and community for all citizens. The affirmation in the United States *Declaration of Independence* that "all men are created equal, and endowed by their creator with certain inalienable rights" is a proclamation of a new paradigm for morally legitimate, democratic government. Government exists to protect these rights and maximize the good of citizens. The subsequent lines from this *Declaration* asserting that "whenever any government is in violation of these rights it is the right of the people to alter or abolish it" make clear the criterion of legitimate government as the ability to assure the "life, liberty, and pursuit of happiness" for all citizens within a framework of equality and justice.

For more than two centuries, this new paradigm struggled to be born in the face of class-dominated society and the militarized nation-state system. The paradigm affirms these rights for all, *all human beings*. Yet under class society and nation-states, the world faces ever greater global crises, intractable in terms of our present institutions. Global militarism, imperialism, human rights abuses, environmental destruction, poverty, and population explosion destroy the quality of life and the capability of all individual nation-states to provide anything resembling authentic democracy for their citizens. The paradigm shift to authentic democracy has yet to be realized and cannot be realized under the present world system. As Harris expresses this:

> National sovereign independence therefore has proved fatally inimical to
> the solution of world problems. Yet it is on the resolution of these global
> difficulties that the welfare of peoples and the very survival of humankind

depends. The national sovereign state can no longer effectively protect its citizens from devastation in war, nor can it protect their living standards and maintain the amenities of life in the face of environmental deterioration.... In short, the national state now lacks the one and only justification for the exercise of sovereign power, the fostering of national prosperity and security. Its ethical character has been undermined, and its title to be juristically supreme is no longer valid. (2002b, pp. 70-71)

The paradigm shift we must effect we are to survive on this planet much longer is the shift to authentic democracy under the concept of the universal right of all to peace, freedom, and prosperity. At this point in history, the only political sovereignty capable of realizing this goal is the sovereignty of the people of Earth expressed in non-military, democratic federal world government. Legitimate government requires democratized economic and political institutions. Praxis here means a multiplicity of actions struggling to create, for the first time in history, planetary self-understanding based on the principle of unity-in-diversity as the foundation for global democracy. The paradigm shift envisioned by the Enlightenment thinkers finds its realization under the *Constitution for the Federation of Earth.*

All three themes of eschatology, emergent evolution, and paradigm shift point to the possibility and necessity of concrete institutions such as those proposed by the *Earth Constitution* and outline appropriate praxis for the dawn of the twenty-first century. Undoubtedly, under the *Earth Constitution* human beings will continue to mature toward ethical existence and planetary maturity once these emergent qualities are no longer blocked by monopoly capitalism and the nation-state system. The adoption of planetary institutions premised on unity-in-diversity will *make possible* further transformation of human life in the direction of practical utopia. In the twenty-first century, it will be necessary to self-consciously *found* planetary institutions on the practical and ethical principles that are at the heart of the democratic ideal.

2. A Planetary Society Founded on Principle

Whatever "spiritual" transformations people undergo, a liberated society will still require, at this stage of history, a well-written democratic constitution for the entire planet specifying limitations on powers, balance of powers, due process, and other institutionalized features designed to prevent totalitarianism. But such a constitution must also embody the ends or the goals of government and economics (since the latter ultimately cannot operate independently of careful, democratically organized planning and oversight). Such a constitution is our only practical hope. As Jawaharlal Nehru, India's Prime Minister, expressed this: "I have no doubt in my mind that World Government must and will come, for there is no other remedy for the world's sickness" (Habicht, p. 22).

If the goals written into this constitution are economics and politics in the service of preserving and enhancing human liberation, if society is directed toward the satisfaction of everyone's individual basic human needs and the development of their potentialities as human beings, then the *Constitution* itself can be used to ensure that the mechanisms of government and economics remain devoted to this end. It can be used to see that these goals do not become sidetracked into serving the interests of the few at the expense of the many. Such a society would be a *founded* society, not one that has evolved. It would be a conscious reorganization of society according to liberating principles.

In his *Grundrisse*, as in the *Communist Manifesto*, Marx distinguishes his thought from those forms of socialism believing a gradual transition to socialism is possible through progressive reforms within the capitalist system. For Marx, the alternative was not necessarily violent overthrow of existing societies, since democratic means of change might suffice. In either case, Marx advocated the *founding* of a new social and economic order in which private ownership of the means of production was replaced by socially constituted relations of production

A founded society, based on self-conscious principles, is necessary for human liberation. A "founded" society is one established according to principles embodied in a founding document. It is entirely different from an "evolved" society in which slow changes blend new principles with older ones with the resulting lack of self-understanding, lack of self-consciousness, and lack of a clear moral foundation for society. "Respectable" thought, in today's world, insists on just this sort of slow, counter-productive evolution of global society. As Dussel asserts in the epigraph at the head of this chapter, awakened thought, premised of the founding of real justice in human affairs, is considered "subversive" by the dominant, imperial powers and their "respectable" thinkers.

The world situation has changed in many ways since Marx wrote, and we have seen some difficulties in his notion of the historical agent of the transition to socialism, the proletariat (see Gottlieb, 1987). On the global scale of capitalist domination today, along with automation and downsizing of work-forces, along with contracting work out to other countries, with the conditioning and cooptation of the industrial work force in the first-world nations, and so on, there remains little hope for an industrial proletariat leading a transition to socialism through political revolution or other means. I have argued that solidarity and a liberated consciousness are not dependent on the industrial proletariat alone.

The agents of revolution must be the people of the world in their vast multiplicity, working through their local groups with the dual and interconnected purposes of resisting the oppression of their group and of liberating the planet from all forms of domination and exploitation. The industrial proletariat remains crucial in this struggle, but the struggle must involve all oppressed peoples and groups, including the disenfranchised *Lumpenproletariat* of those unemployed and in absolute poverty, on the one hand, and the middle and upper classes, on the other hand, who have awakened to the terrible spiritual and moral price they must pay to maintain their lives of comfort and privilege.

The praxis of this multiplicity of agents of liberation must continually work to delegitimize the capitalism system (interconnected with all systems of domination) as well as the nation-state system. Political revolutions within specific countries are not likely to change the framework of global capitalism, now operating autonomously, independently of any particular nation-states, yet simultaneously protected and promoted by the imperial, first-world nation-states. The so-called "Domino Theory" of one nation after another becoming socialist until there is a united world is pure mythology. Socialism alone within a system of sovereign nation-states will not create a world of peace, freedom, and justice. History has repeatedly seen the power of nationalism distort and overcome the universal ideals of socialism centered on persons as ends-in-themselves.

The revolution must be worldwide to truly establish a just and free order for individual groups, for no group today escapes the global domination of capital and the tyranny of the nation-state system. The disastrous effects of the present global system must be repeatedly pointed out, and it must be made clear that the system itself is the source of these effects. There can be no gradual reform as long as the principle of production for corporate private profit is maintained and the principle of governance is the nation-state. The transition to socialism and democracy can only occur through a global "revolution," yet this revolution must go deeper than the ordinary political revolution (as we have seen), and it should *not* be a violent, armed revolution. It must, as Marx puts it, be "a conscious reorganization of society." Of capitalism, he writes:

> It squanders human being, living labour, more readily than does any other mode of production, squandering not only flesh and blood, but nerves and brain as well. In fact it is only through the most tremendous waste of individual development that the development of humanity in general is secured and pursued, in that epoch of history that directly precedes the conscious reconstruction of society. (1991, p. 182)

Human history has moved to ever greater self-awareness. Peoples are now in a position to create a founded world-society. This is a crucial point. Instead of living in societies that are the product of a kind of blind social evolution from one social form through another, often retaining vestiges of earlier forms of domination (for example, titles of royalty, exclusivistic private property rights, class privilege), human beings have become capable of founding societies based on principles: ethical, legal, political, and economic.

A founded society is one in which the founders have moved to the level of a conscious determination of the nature of the social world in which they are to live. We no longer accept the lie asserting "natural laws of economics and society." We now self-consciously realize that human beings choose their economic and social relations. This moves human life, in Kantian language, from the level of social life based on inclinations, to the level of social life based on the free decision to live by principles. Our level of self-awareness has increased since the 18th century, in part through the work of great thinkers like Kant, Marx, Nietzsche, Wittgenstein, and Habermas as well as the many others examined in this book.

At the dawn of the twenty-first century, we are, for the first time, in a position to self-consciously *found* a just, democratic, peaceful, and enduring planetary society. As we saw Roslyn Wallach Bologh express this: "Marx formulates history from within a form of life characterized by the possibility of self-conscious community.... He reads history in terms of repressed community (capitalism) versus natural community (pre-capitalism) and self-conscious community (post-capitalism)" (1979, p. 237). Today, enough persons manifest planetary consciousness to a sufficient degree to understand the need to begin a global, founded society. Only a self-conscious society can be free, just, and peaceful. Promoters of the system of domination, from universities to mass media, sense this. That is why representatives of the "repressed community" (educational institutions, businesses, and governments) work so hard to keep the population in a condition of childlike lack of self-awareness.

The *United States Constitution* is one example of a founded society. The document spells out not only the balance of powers and the framework for the laws of the founded society, but also the rights and freedoms and privileges (as well as duties) of the citizens of that society. With this eighteenth-century development of a founded society, human beings had discovered some elements in the equation of human liberation, for example, checks and balances, guarantee of political rights and liberties, and so on. For its time, this founded society was a great step forward. Today, it serves as a reactionary fetter on the next great step.

We now understand the society that they founded excluded some essential aspects of human liberation such as an economic system predicated on the common good. This is where the *United States Constitution* fails. It was founded on the principles of formal, political democracy and did not alter the exploitative framework of the economic system of its day. Nor did it challenge the fragmented and unworkable system of sovereign nation-states.

The intention was never to create a full democracy enfranchising those referred to by some founding fathers as "the rabble." And the intention was never to transcend the nation-state system but to create a "great nation." A system was created in which the domination of government (by royalty or monarch) was replaced with domination by the rich, a system existing to this day, and continuing to spread its domination across the globe.

Noam Chomsky appeals in this regard to Bertrand Russell and John Dewey, "who disagreed on many things but shared a vision" of what a truly human, decent, self-conscious society would be like. For Dewey, Chomsky writes,

> The "ultimate aim" of production is not production of goods, but "of free human beings associated with one another in terms of equality." The goal of education, as Russell put it, is "to give a sense of the value of things other than domination," to help create "wise citizens in a free community" in which both liberty and "individual creativeness" will flourish, and working people will be masters of their fate, not tools of production. Illegitimate structures of coercion must be unraveled. (1996b, pp. 75-76)

A founded society is predicated on ethical goals such as these and understands that institutions infected with "illegitimate structures of coercion" must be abolished. At the dawn of the twenty-first century, we have developed a degree of self-awareness allowing us to see the illegitimacy of monopoly capitalism and the system of nation-states. Both are based on "structures of coercion." Both are illegitimate. Our praxis at this point in history must be advocacy of the founded society under the *Constitution for the Federation of Earth* and the praxis of delegitimation of the current world order.

Loyalty to the old illegitimate system dehumanizes and demeans us. As Philip Allott expresses this, *"A legal system which does its best to make sense of murder, theft, exploitation, oppression, abuse of power, and injustice, perpetrated by public authorities in the public interest, is a perversion of a legal system"* (1990, p. xvii, italics added). The legal systems of nation-states claiming sovereignty are illegitimate. People must see that we are all "pilgrim citizens" of the new order. Our human integrity and dignity is related to our commitment to live under a free, just, and peaceful world-order.

This does not entail giving up multi-cultural group identifications or the diversity of voices across the planet. It means giving up the notion that partial groupings can be sovereign, along with the notion that my identification with this group must entail the objectification and dehumanization of other peoples. Revolutionary transition to a liberated society will require the massive delegitimation of the system as it now exists, leading toward the "conscious reorganization of society."

For Marx, internal contradictions within the capitalist system portended its eventual demise. Like Hegel before him, and like the pragmatists, the process philosophers, and other critical thinkers who followed him, Marx attempted to understand the social-economic-political world as a process, a dynamic movement whose confluences of identity and difference followed certain patterns of development and dissolution, a totality in the process of perpetual transformation. That is why socialism cannot be entirely defined before-hand. The world is a process and cannot be defined in terms of fixed essences. For Marx, however, the capitalist system was rife with internal contradictions that repressed and destroyed our eschatological potential for planetary maturity (Miranda, 1986).

The praxis required at the dawn of the twenty-first century relies on a quantum leap in the creativity and self-aware input of human beings into their destiny (for the sake of our survival as well). Instead of relying on the working out of contradictions in the dialectical processes of economic and social transformations (another mythology), humans must act self-consciously on behalf of themselves and future generations. From the works of the great thinkers, and through our own understanding of the global nightmare to which corporate capitalism and the system of autonomous nation-states has brought the world, we are now able to extrapolate the basic parameters of a non-exploitative, truly human, global society.

These parameters are no mystery. (1) Establish authentic democracy, not the massive manipulation of public opinion by the mass media and the rich. (2) Create the other aspects of authentic democracy such as separation of powers and built-in protection against tyranny or governmental abuses. (3) Assure political rights: assembly, speech, press, privacy from government surveillance, due process of law, *habeas corpus*, and so on. The system must provide these rights for all equally, not only for those who can afford outrageously expensive lawyers. It must actively promote freedom of the press (not only for those who can afford to own one). (4) Guarantee a demilitarized world free of the horror of wars of all kinds. Peace is very much a human right as the International Philosophers for Peace *Document on World Peace* (2001) affirms. (5) Guarantee economic rights: every one having a right to health care, a job, social security, a family, security and safety, adequate housing, and educational opportunities.

(6) Protect diversity: cultural, individual, racial, ethnic, and religious diversity. (7) Protect the planetary environment so no business, nation, or group can legally destroy our planet that sustains the fragile life upon it or compromise the precious heritage of future generations. (8) Guarantee freedom of religion and spirituality (or to assert no religion or spirituality), and establish a cultural, political, and economic environment that enhances (rather than, as now, destroys) the possibility of spiritual exploration and mediation. Freedom of religion is practically meaningless in the present environment that systematically destroys most authentic spirituality and in which human spiritual needs must attempt to satisfy themselves within a system promoting the very opposite in the form of greed, selfishness, egoism, hatred of others, fear, and hopelessness.

(9) Provide a preamble, or statement of the most general principles, which founds the planetary society on the protection, enrichment, fulfillment, and dignity of all human life (and planetary life that we understand today is inseparably connected with human dignity). (10) Design an economic system that produces prosperity and sustainable efficiency without destroying any of the above principles. None of these principles are far fetched or out of easy reach if we wish to self-consciously found a planetary society based upon them (see Marchand, 1979, pp. 10-12).

What must be founded here is something without precedent in history, although it appears in limited, distorted forms in documents like the French *Declaration of the Rights of Man*, the *United States Constitution* and *Declaration of Independence*, the United Nations *Universal Declaration of Human Rights*, and the *Cuban Constitution* of 1976. All of these documents speak of something "universal" to all human beings. Yet they make these universalist claims from within fragmented systems destroying their own possibility of realization. With advanced computers, communications, transportation, and global society, we are now in a position to abolish the fragmentation and realize these universal principles in an effective manner.

For the first time in human history a non-exploitative, non-destructive society can be founded, precisely because we are more fully aware of our historical situation, and aware of our impending doom if we do not transform our ways. The founded society must include the social, economic, and political dimensions of human existence. Human freedom must be assured, and this must include the minimum requirements for being free in terms of food, housing, and social opportunities. An environment allowing development of spirituality must be created so human greed, hatred, and delusion can be overcome and people's lives can turn to simplicity, contentment, and creative fulfillment. The unity-in-diversity of humankind will seem simple and self-evident to future generations, who will revere us as the founding fathers and mothers of a decent world-order.

Historical "socialist" contradictions between economic equality and totalitarian political systems must be abolished, just as much as capitalist contradictions between political equality and economic domination. In a society self-consciously founded to eliminate such contradictions, a new era and human history will have truly begun. The immense distortions and problems of the older historical societies, whether "capitalist" or "socialist" will no longer be seen as inevitable facets of "reality" or "human nature." The distortions of "reality" or "human nature" now appearing all around as if they were inevitable features of life will be minimized in a society founded consciously on the welfare of human life and on our interdependence with all other creatures on this planet.

No society in history has ever been founded squarely on these principles. No society could have been, since these principles can only be implemented at the planetary scale. Our praxis must revolve around a multiplicity of activities making possible the move from here to there, including delegitimation of the present system in every way possible. Sri Aurobindo writes: "The Nation in modern times is practically indestructible – unless it dies from within" (Basu, p. 109).

This is why the concept of "sovereign nations" must be delegitimized. Nation-states must federate under genuine federal world government, and we *pilgrim citizens* must be loyal to our planetary citizenship (Falk, 1992). We are pilgrims precisely because, as Guy Marchand writes, "the world laws that the world citizen has the duty to respect have not yet been enacted" (1979, p. 13). We need a founding ratification convention for the *Constitution for the Federation of Earth.*

3. Immediate Economic Prosperity under the *Earth Constitution*

The *Constitution,* as a framework predicated on the common good, making possible the growth of human beings toward planetary maturity, must provide for a *transitional economics* directed toward universal peace and prosperity. The central principle of the transitional economics will be to begin the process of restoring and protecting the global commons in land, technology, money creation, and information (Smith, 2003a). The economics of absolute property rights that now dominates the world through monopolies on land, technology, money creation, and information will be transformed over time to *an economics of conditional property rights* (derived, among others, from the principles of American economist

Henry George (1946)) in which the common good and prosperity of the diverse peoples of the Earth will be ensured. The first steps in this process (the initial economics of the Earth Federation) will involve only a few, simple, common-sense changes in current economic practices.

At the founding ratification convention, it will be necessary for perhaps twenty-five nations to *simultaneously* ratify the *Constitution* and initiate federal world government immediately among themselves. For under the current global system of domination, any individual nation making a break for freedom by ratifying the *Constitution* would almost certainly be economically punished by the powers now managing the system (see Isely, 2000). One or two nations attempting to begin the Earth Federation would experience the devaluation of their currencies, withdrawal of investments, foreclosure of loans, economic sanctions, or blockades. As with Cuba, which attempted to make a break for freedom in 1959, economic penalties would be implemented ensuring the enterprise was largely unsuccessful.

However, twenty-five nations ratifying the *Constitution* together at a founding ratification convention will have among themselves sufficient resources, capacity for trade among themselves, productive strength, collective prestige, and capability to publicize the significance of their actions to the world at large to make them together fairly independent of the current world system of control and domination. Almost certainly they will achieve an immediate economic prosperity unimagined by the majority of the world's poor nations. They will have the poor nations of the world knocking at the door to join the Federation. Naturally, the Earth Federation is for all nations and none willing to ratify and submit to the *Constitution of the Federation of Earth* would be excluded. Poor nations under the current world order have nothing to lose and everything to gain by joining the Earth Federation.

The first twenty-five or so nations who join together to simultaneously ratify the *Earth Constitution* will immediately achieve prosperity and an economic well-being undreamed of under the nation-state-monopoly-capitalist systems of the past five centuries. Achieving prosperity is not the difficult part, as we will see in this section. The difficult part is overcoming the economic myths and lies ingrained in the minds of the world's citizens for centuries. These myths and lies are the core of the propaganda spewed forth by the dominant super-wealthy class controlling the world-order: from the World Bank, IMF, and WTO, the multinational corporations, the corporate owned mass media, the first-world imperialist governments, the CIA, and other national propaganda machines (see Smith, 2003b, ch. 3).

The new federated world government created at a founding ratification convention by an initial twenty-five or so nations will immediately act to make these nations economically autonomous from the present global system of domination and exploitation. Among themselves they will possess the technology, the resources, and the labor power to create healthy local and regional markets very rapidly through the assistance and guidance of the federal government. (Cuba's wonderful progress toward food independence and food security over the past few years should be carefully studied in this regard (Koont, 2004).) Multinational corporations operating within the new federation can cooperate in the drive toward universal prosperity or they can risk being mundialized by the Federation or nationalized by the nations within the federation.

The federal government will immediately supply substantial lines of credit to all peaceful enterprises and all governments within the Federation to activate the available technology, resources, and labor power. Through the inflow of substantial credit, the economic multiplier factor at the heart of every healthy economy will rapidly create a substantial prosperity impossible under the development model now controlled by the world's wealthy classes through the World Bank, the IMF, and other institutions. From the wealth created by activation of regional and local economies, the principal borrowed through these lines of credit will be repaid along with only a small administrative fee. Exploitative interest on loans leading to massive international debt will be immediately abolished (Isely, 2000).

One role the federal government must assume in this process of rapid economic development is to ensure the process does not further destroy the local and global environments. The government must facilitate the progress of rapid economic development while carefully monitoring and regulating the process to ensure the costs of production are not externalized into hidden social costs for the environment, society, and future generations (Daly and Cobb, 1994). The *Constitution for the Federation of Earth* is carefully designed to play both roles. It is the vehicle for a truly transformative praxis with regard to development and sustainability.

The Earth Federation will assume the former international debt of its member nations and begin payment on this debt at reasonable rates of return. Seeing the rapidly-developing prosperity of the new Earth Federation, other nations (of the world's poor majority) will rapidly join until the Federation comprises the overwhelming majority of nations and people. People within the former imperialist nations will soon recognize the liberated nature of the federated nations. The propaganda machine owned by the wealthy in the imperialist nations will not be able to hide the healthy, non-militarized enterprises, protection for universal human rights, and new spirit of global peace and community within the

Federation. Citizens of these nations will also soon clamor to become part of the Federation. Lastly, the governments of these first-world nations, which represent the tiny minority of human beings who profit from global exploitation, will be forced to take their place within the democratic Federation of Earth.

Neither corporations nor individuals will lose their accumulated private wealth. The economics of the initial Earth Federation is not about mandating equality of wealth, but about creating prosperity for all. The rich will retain their personal wealth (which may suffice them and their children for generations to come). The rich will lose only the means of continuing their exploitation into the future. The system of exploitation itself will be rapidly transformed to the point where the power of those who own but do not work to exploit those who work but do not own will be brought to an end.

The World Parliament of the Earth Federation will take a few practical steps to foster global liberty, equality, and fraternity in the economic sphere. In doing this, as discussed in Chapter Seven, it will be making possible not only universal human prosperity but also the emergence of greater human maturity. These practical steps do not change the present economic system in any radical way. (Eventually, an emergent human maturity may almost certainly evolve substantially new economic forms.) These steps use the authority of government to universalize the opportunities for development and to break what economist J.W. Smith calls the "subtle-monopolies" of domination masquerading under the ideology of "global free trade" (2003a). In taking these steps, however, the Earth Parliament will be using self-conscious social foresight. It will be taking the first steps away from the repressed self-consciousness of monopoly capitalism.

There are at least six simple economic principles that must be adopted by the Federation to rapidly create universal prosperity. As we will see, these six principles oppose six mythologies (sets of lies) perpetuated by the wealthy nations and financial institutions in today's world. I will list these principles here, then discuss each of them below. (1) Create vast lines of credit available for development on the basis of people's ability to work and produce goods and services. (2) Eliminate the bizarre legal fiction of corporations having the rights of persons, and restore to democratic government the power to regulate them for the common good. (3) Eliminate the absolute right of corporations over so-called "intellectual property," so technology and productive techniques can spread rapidly throughout the world.

(4) Eliminate the corporate monopoly on media (radio, television, news publications, and so on), thereby effectively ending the propaganda

system controlled by the wealthy. This will make many of the airwaves available for public health and development education. This will also activate real democratic dialogue and debate within the Earth Federation. (5) Write into law the principle of equal pay for equally productive work for all people. This will immediately end much of corporate domination over governments and regions while providing workers with the cash to buy goods and services. (6) Break the present global monopoly over land and resources through restoring a multiplicity of local land-owners and converting land ownership rights to conditional rather than absolute rights. All of these steps together will activate the "multiplier factor" at the heart of any prosperous economy.

The orgy of greed and destruction convulsing the world since the last half of the twentieth century can only come to an end through the advent of a democratic world government acting on these or similar principles. Under the nation-state system, we saw, the tiny elites controlling wealth and finance through their agents in the World Bank and elsewhere act to enrich themselves and the already wealthy elites in the countries whose resources and export economic potential is targeted. Catherine Caufield, in *Masters of Illusion: The World Bank and the Poverty of Nations,* describes the result of this system:

> The past half-century of development has not profited the poorest people, nor the poorest countries. Rather, they have paid dearly – and their descendants will continue to pay dearly – for the disproportionately small benefits they have received.... Fifty years of development have left the rich countries – and especially their richest citizens – richer than before. (1996, p. 338)

Only federal world government, representing, for the first time in history, all the world's citizens, could possibly have the authority to end this system now controlling individual governments, the mass media, and the world's gigantic financial institutions. Bruce Rich, in *Mortgaging the Earth. The World Bank, Environmental Impoverishment, and the Crisis of Development,* describes the environmental consequences of the global system of greed and exploitation centered on "development" as engineered by the World Bank and the IMF:

> Massive internationally financed development schemes were unleashing ecological destruction and social upheaval in areas larger than many American states or European countries. Huge forests had been destroyed, gigantic river basins filled with dams, and vast agricultural expanses consolidated into larger holdings for export production at tremendous ecological cost. What was occurring was not a reasonable, measured process to increase economic welfare, but the destruction of natural and social systems whose

endurance are the prerequisite, and the goal, of any sane project for longer term human development. (1994, p. 25)

A world of unmitigated and unregulated diversity without any true political, social, or economic unity is a world in the process of self-destruction. Only the power of federal government under a quality document empowering the Earth's people (such as the *Constitution for the Federation of Earth*) can turn around the disastrous course the wealthy and powerful have chosen for our planet. The Provisional World Parliament and other organizations working on behalf of the *Constitution for the Federation of Earth* have worked out a clear, common sense economics based on human realities instead of lies designed to accumulate further wealth for the already powerful. The principles of this economics are described below. The first of these global economic myths that must be overcome is underlined by Michel Chossudovsky in *The Globalization of Poverty: Impacts of IMF and World Bank Reforms*:

> The question remains whether this global economic system based on the relentless accumulation of private wealth can be subjected to a process of meaningful reform.... Meaningful reforms are not likely to be implemented without an enduring social struggle. What is at stake is the massive concentration of financial wealth and the command over real resources by a social minority. The latter also controls the "creation of money" within the international banking system (1998, p. 27)

The central myth is the grand lie of money and loan-creation. On this lie the entire system of global economic domination and exploitation is predicated. This lie is exposed in *Immediate Economic Benefits of World Government* (2000) by Philip Isely and in *Economic Democracy: The Political Struggle of the Twenty-first Century* (2003a) by J. W. Smith. The lie states that only governments or banks with wealth can create or print money, and only financial institutions with wealth can lend money. The lie asserts that accumulated capital is necessary for creating or lending money.

Under this system, when poor governments try to print money to activate their economies, their money is devalued by world financial institutions until practically worthless. In Ghana, in the summer of 2002, my colleagues and I had to fill plastic shopping bags with bundles of paper money at the bank to pay our modest hotel bill because the national money of that country was so worthless. Simultaneously, these poor governments are offered loans in convertible first-world currencies from already wealthy financial institutions with interest rates making a profit on the loan for the wealthy lenders. Those who have stolen the world's wealth for five centuries, now use the wealth they stole from the world's poor to increase their own wealth by offering to lend what they have stolen back to their third world victims.

All genuine wealth is created through a productive combination of capital, labor, and natural resources (Smith, 2003a). Wealth is created from resources through human productivity. A government does not need preexisting funds to create money or lines of credit. It can create these (for loans as capital investment) on the basis of the ability of people to use this credit, along with labor and natural resources, to produce goods and services. These loans can be repaid to the government from the wealth produced at a nominal additional cost for the administration of the loan. The Earth Federation does not have to bow to the Lords of the Earth to achieve rapid prosperity. All that is required is the political will of the initial group of ratifying nations.

The world federal government will also necessarily be a major employer itself as it activates agencies for fundamental economic conversion to sustainable energy uses, for reforestation of our denuded planet, reclamation of degraded agricultural land, restoration of fisheries, development of sustainable technologies, development of energy sources, transportation systems, and for the systematic demilitarization of the nations within the Federation. There is no danger of loss of employment for the many now engaged in military-related production and deployment.

The number of jobs required to restore our planet to ecological, social, productive, and cultural health will be immense. Large numbers of scientists (now engaged in the horrific work of designing ever more effective machines of death and destruction) will be required for developing sustainable engineering designs for housing, industry, transportation, sustainable sources of energy, and the restoration of integrity to our planetary environment. *The "brain drain" will be reversed, as scientists from non-federation countries flee their nightmarish war-related jobs for employment within the Earth Federation using their skills for peaceful and productive purposes.* People will work with energy and a sense of fulfillment, since they will be engaged in the project of saving the Earth and creating democracy for our planet for the first time in history.

When twenty-five or so nations simultaneously ratify the *Constitution for the Federation of Earth*, they will create a common currency (call it "Earth Currency") and will immediately be able to receive ample lines of credit for rapid development based on their productive capability, resources, and labor supply. Twenty-five or so nations combined together as the initial Earth Federation will have plenty of all three and will be able to eliminate money scarcity and devalued currency immediately. Their economies will be regional, emphasizing local, autonomous development and activating the economic multiplier factor that is the key to every healthy economy. And their economy within the Earth Federation as a whole will be large enough to function independently of the financial centers of control of the present world-system.

The economic multiplier factor means that goods produced make a profit for the local producers that is reinvested in the local economy. It requires good pay for workers who can then afford the products they produced and circulate their money through consumption of more goods and services. When this happens, all local consumers and services prosper because the money is spread widely among the population and re-circulated throughout the regional economy. There is a "take off" in which capital, labor, and resources, activated locally and regionally into production, enrich the region and reinvest the wealth produced back into the same region. Millions of new jobs are created in the private sector and in the governmental sector responsible for converting the emerging productive capacity to ever more sustainable forms.

This is exactly what is prevented by the globalized so-called "free trade" economy. In this economy, the already poor are in debt to the already rich and are forced to sell off their natural resources and cheap labor to wealthy foreign corporations (through structural adjustment programs) who then drain the profits (and resources) from the poor regions into the coffers of the already wealthy. Barriers are maintained between nations and regions protecting accumulated wealth in certain nations and regions who do business in the exploited nations. There is no one to tax or regulate the process of exploitation. The nation-state system makes a decent economic world-order impossible.

In this process, the poor of the world are in competition with one another for the business of the rich and must continually lower labor wages and the price of natural resources to try to attract business and stay afloat in their international indebtedness. There is a race to the bottom in which the multiplier factor can never operate since wages are never enough to allow the population to consume the goods they produce and since the wealth is siphoned into the coffers of first-world multinational corporations. If wages in Indonesia are lower than those in Central America, corporations will demand lowering wages in Central America or they will follow the "free market" and switch production to Indonesia.

Resources are sold off ever more cheaply as poor nations compete with one another to earn convertible currencies to pay off their international debt to stay afloat. Resources and services are privatized and purchased by the rich for a fraction of their value. The poor are paid starvation and dehumanizing wages. The IMF and World Bank, backed by massive first-world military capability, ensure the maintenance and continuity of this nightmarish system. Environmental destruction and militarism continue unabated.

We saw that it is imperative that the initial Earth Federation assume the international debt of all joining nations immediately, to be paid off at a reasonable rate of interest by the Federation. The Federation will be careful not to throw the non-ratifying nations into economic turmoil, only to show them by example how much they would benefit from joining the Federation. The principle behind the *Earth Constitution* is the good of all humanity, not the initiation of a new competition between the Federation and non-Federation nations in the early stages of world government.

Simultaneously with the assumption of the international debt of member nations, the Federation will issue ample lines of credit to activate the economies of its members. Trade outside the Federation would have to be done in Earth Currency, the value of which would not be regulated by present global financial institutions. Trade outside the Federation would not depend on offering concessions to exploitative corporations, since the Federation would be self-sufficient and economically independent. Investment within the Federation from outside would have to be done in Earth Currency and follow Federation laws. The global system of exploitation would immediately be transformed. Other poor nations would begin joining the Federation in great numbers upon seeing the freedom and prosperity activated by the Federation.

Is this "socialism"? Or is it "cooperative capitalism," so-called by J. W. Smith (2003b)? Or should we term it the initial stages of "economic democracy"? We have seen that "socialism" most basically means institutions predicated on human beings as ends-in-themselves, not the exploitation of human beings by others. Why quibble over words or slogans when what we all want is peace, freedom, prosperity, education, health care, and social security for human beings everywhere on the planet? This can be done easily through democratizing the global economy and empowering regions to activate local economies to produce and exchange services, whenever possible, at the local level.

As J. W. Smith points out, a mere forty billion dollars a year "would provide clean water and sanitation, care for women's reproductive health, basic health and nutrition, and basic education for all the world's citizens," while the world now spends an astonishing $800 billion a year on militarism (2002, p. 2). Activating local and regional economies can easily produce the equivalent of forty billion per year to provide these necessities to all persons, especially since all nations within the Federation will no longer be spending money on militarism. Global trade can be reserved for those commodities and resources not available within the industrially developed, healthy, local and regional economies. The Earth Federation will have no trouble fulfilling these guaranteed economic and social rights (Article XIII), since it will activate a prosperous economy while eliminating all costs formerly dedicated to war and militarism. Under the present system of domination (nation-state-monopoly-capitalism), there is no intention of creating a prosperous world economy. Trade, like militarism and everything else, is directed toward preserving the system (see Chomsky, 1996a, pp. 7-28). Twenty percent of the world population benefit while the other eighty percent remain in perpetual poverty as the exploited source of wealth for the few.

Under the Earth Federation, personal private property is protected by law, and, within limits imposed by preserving the environment and the good of all, the quest for private accumulation within reasonable bounds is retained. The government does not own all business and industry, nor are decisions made in a "command economy" fashion. The goal of government is to activate regional and local economies and coordinate use of resources and development so no nation or group benefits at the expense of others. Only a planetary government can achieve this, since individual nations under the present system are subject to economic forces over which their governments have little or no control. And under the present system, nation-states promote their own economic interests at the expense of all others.

The transition toward economic democracy, therefore, will not mean transition to government ownership but to economic systems where the least labor and least waste is expended so all may live reasonably well (sustainably) and get on with valuable and meaningful living. Economist J. W. Smith predicts that once prosperity is rapidly achieved, efficient economic production with prosperity for everyone will result in a work week of two or three days for most people on Earth (2003a). Our planet is extremely rich in resources (even after half a century of diminishing resources under monopoly capitalism). And the technology for conversion to renewable or alternative resources already exists (Daly, 1996, chs. 5-9; Brown 2001). We can create reasonable prosperity for everyone if we begin to democratically and self-consciously organize the economy under a democratic world government mandated for this goal.

The transformation of the Earth's globalized economy will not mean massive economic dislocation such as we have witnessed from the "structural adjustment" programs of the World Bank and IMF that have taken the land from millions of poor people in order to convert it to gigantic export crop operations or in order to create massive dam and irrigation

projects (see Caufield, 1996). The changes needed are as simple as they
are fundamental. Former World Bank economist David C. Korten, in *The
Post-Corporate World: Life After Capitalism*, presents a list of some of
needed changes closely related to the ones proposed here:

> Curing the capitalist cancer to restore democracy, the market, and our
> human rights and freedoms will require virtually eliminating the institution
> of the limited-liability for-profit public corporation as we know it to create
> a post-corporate world through actions such as the following:
> 1. End the legal fiction that corporations are entitled to the rights of
> persons and exclude corporations from political participation;
> 2. Implement serious political campaign reform to reduce the influence
> of money on politics;
> 3. Eliminate corporate welfare by eliminating direct subsidies and
> recovering other externalized costs through fees and taxes;
> 4. Implement mechanisms to regulate international corporations and
> finance; and
> 5. Use fiscal and regulatory policy to make financial speculation
> unprofitable and to give an economic advantage to human-scale, stakeholder-
> owned enterprises. (1999, p. 15)

The Earth Federation, predicated for the first time in history on
the welfare of all rather than the benefit of particular nations or classes,
will also found its economic and political system free of the other lies or
mythologies now serving global domination. The list offered by Korten
expresses the same insight as the list I offered above. The global economy
must be democratized. The power of exploitation and domination must
be taken from the transnational corporations and imperialist governments
protecting them. There is no force in the world capable of this other than
the legitimate sovereignty of the people of Earth expressed in federal
world government.

These practical steps are nearly impossible to implement under the
current world-order. No amount of "world social forums," international
people's movements, or guerrilla insurgencies can overcome the power of
those who now control the world-order. On the other hand, these common
sense changes would be easy for the Earth Federation to implement and
enforce. Under the Earth Federation, people would no longer be trapped
within a global economy beyond the power of individual governments. The
corporations could no longer prevent government from enacting simple
laws to democratize economics and ensure sustainability. For the first time
in history, the Earth would have a federal government representing all
people, directed toward creating universal prosperity as well as ensuring
the sustainability of the Earth for future generations.

As soon as corporations are stripped of the fiction of being legal persons with all the rights of legal persons, they can be regulated by government in a sensible fashion, as Korten recommends. The question of the "absolute right of private property" for corporations can then be debated and modified as necessary by the World Parliament. But in a federated world, corporations will no longer be able to blackmail nations by threatening to move elsewhere if environmental laws and labor laws are not weakened to their satisfaction.

For the first time in history, businesses would assume their rightful place as contributors to the common good of society through the production of needed goods and services. There is nothing wrong with corporations or businesses in themselves. The world needs intelligent, inventive, and creative business persons. What is wrong is the current system that forces our business persons to sacrifice the common good in order to survive and flourish. What is wrong is the current system that encourages profit achieved through externalizing and transferring the true costs of production to society, the environment, and future generations. Sustainable production is sensible and possible (see Brown 2001).

In addition to the lie of money-creation and the lie of corporations having legal human rights, there is a third lie now promoted by the wealthy of the world. *The lie of "intellectual property rights" is directly connected to their claim that corporations are legal persons.* This mythology asserts their absolute right to control patents and their "intellectual property" as if they were human persons like authors, inventors, or artists. It asserts their right to use technology and ideas for corporate gain at the expense of the common good. Rapid development cannot take place for the poor of the world until this falsehood is fundamentally changed.

A slight change in the present patent laws, now favoring the rich and powerful at the expense of the poor, will end the monopoly on technology now enforced through the World Trade Organization by its system of global patents (intellectual property rights). As Vandana Siva (1997; 2000), David Korten (2001), Michel Chossudovsky (1999), and others have shown, the global patent system prevents technology from disseminating, prevents poor countries from developing, and serves a system of domination creating starvation and misery for millions. Under the Earth Federation, a simple system of allowing any patented ideas to be used by any enterprise for a reasonable royalty fee would give everyone access to needed technological innovations.

The fourth myth, the lie of a "free press" through the corporate mass media, could easily be overcome under the Earth Federation by encouraging a multiplicity of media voices and not allowing media monopolies to be concentrated in the hands of the rich as they are today (McChesney, 1997;

Edwards, 1996; Chomsky, 1994). Breaking the monopoly on information held by the dominant nations and classes is essential for activating genuine democratic dialogue and debate within the Earth Federation. Korten's related point above is fundamental to activating real democracy within the Earth Federation. The Federation must "implement serious political campaign reform to reduce the influence of money on politics." The *Constitution* is already written to significantly reduce this danger.

The Earth Federation provides the same campaign possibilities for all candidates for office. Privately funded public relations campaigns now masquerading as a "political process" are eliminated. However, the initial World Parliament must take the further step of ending the corporate monopoly on information, and other forms of corporate influence on politicians. If the information monopoly can manipulate public opinion as it easily does today, then eliminating private campaign funding is not sufficient. Honest, decent journalism must be promoted. The election of representatives to the House of Nations, the House of Counselors, and the House of Peoples cannot be democratic as long as such media monopolies exist.

If the airwaves are repossessed by the people instead of given away to the corporate monopolies, the immense potential of radio and television for public education, heath education, economic development, and free expression of ideas is activated. The corporate propaganda hold over the public mind will be broken. The common good of all (as ends-in-themselves) becomes the criterion for leasing the airwaves to a multiplicity of individuals and organizations. Education and skills for a prosperous economy are free to all and widely disseminated. Education is no longer the private privilege of the rich who can afford to pay tuition, room, and board at some university. It is available to all the world's citizens for free over numerous public radio, television, and computer systems provided to enrich life and foster sustainable development.

The fifth myth now promulgated by the Lords of the Earth, that wages must be determined by the "free market" just as the price of ham hocks and pork bellies are so determined, can easily be eradicated by the Earth Federation on the simple, common sense principle of "equal pay for equally productive work." On this principle, and with a Federation government concerned to maximize the economic multiplier factor through good wages allowing money to circulate freely through the economy, the exploitation of poor countries by wealthier countries comes to an end. In *Economic Democracy,* economist Smith describes the effect of today's wage differentials between nations:

> The equally-productive worker in the poorly-paid Third World produces a unique widget, is paid $1 an hour, and is producing one widget per hour.

The equally-productive worker in the developed world produces another unique widget, is paid $10 an hour, and produces one widget per hour. Each equally-productive worker likes, and purchases the other's widgets.... The $1 an hour worker must work 10 hours to buy one of the widgets of the $10 an hour worker, but, with the money earned in the same 10 hours, the $10 an hour worker can buy 100 of the widgets of the $1 an hour worker.... *At this ten times wage differential, in direct trades between each other – or between countries – there is an exponential 100 times differential in retained wealth.* (2003a, p. 15)

The Earth Federation's first goal is to create a global economy promoting prosperity for all. Under the lie of "free market" determined wage levels, exponential rates of exploitation are maintained and the economic multiplier factor is circumvented in poor countries. How to create economic prosperity through the multiplier effect is well known. All that is required is an Earth Federation dedicated to this principle and premised on the welfare of all. Equal pay for equally productive work is the fifth key to the initial transformation of the economic world order. Within the Earth Federation, the ability of businesses to move to poorer regions to exploit cheaper labor would be eliminated. Their ability to funnel their funds to off-shore tax-free accounts would be eliminated. Their ability to blackmail governments would be eliminated. The exponential rate of exploitation described by Smith would be eliminated.

Sixth, the mythology of the absolute "natural right to private property" is promoted world-wide through the media monopolies owned by the global corporations in cooperation with imperial nation-states. This is pure seventeenth-century and eighteenth century mythology taken from the social contract theory of John Locke and others who wrote to justify the legitimacy of the rising bourgeois class of property owners against the king and the declining aristocratic class. The World Parliament will enact carefully crafted laws to promote world-wide land reform so that the land and its wealth can be returned to the people of Earth. Under the present system of global absolute property rights, corporations can own huge tracts of land everywhere on the planet that are effectively out of the control of national and local governments (since property rights are considered absolute). Governments attempting land reform are overthrown or economically punished by the military might of the imperial governments in order to protect this system of absolute property rights.

Everywhere, the dominators have demonized attempts at land reform in the service of the common good as "communism" and have bombed, overthrown, or economically blockaded all attempts at breaking the concept of absolute property rights. This suppression of the move to conditional property rights was a key factor in dozens of imperial interventions and wars. Among these are the overthrow of democracy in Iran in 1953, in Guatemala in 1954, and the economic punishment of Cuba, North Korea, and Libya for many years. This brutal history includes the destruction of Vietnam, Cambodia, and Laos in the 1960s and 1970s, the overthrow of Sukarno in Indonesia in 1965, in the destruction of democracy in Chile in 1973, the wars against Nicaragua, El Salvador, and Guatemala in the 1980s, the bombing destruction of Iraq in 1991, the wars against the people of Columbia since the 1980s, the military attack on Yugoslavia in 1998, the recent invasions of Iraq and Afghanistan, and the sabotage and destruction of the economies of the Soviet Union and Eastern Europe during this entire period.

Under the system of nation-states, genuine land-reform is impossible not only because of imperial military domination of the world in the service of private monopoly wealth but because no nation attempting an alternative economics could succeed within an economic world-order predicated on absolute property rights and monopoly capital principles. The only force capable of creating an economics of sustainability and universal prosperity is federal world government. As we have seen, the initial economics of the Earth Federation is not "communism" but a mixed economics predicated on unity (recognition of the common good and the vital need for a sustainable future) and diversity (recognition of self-interest, rewarding individual initiative, and a multiplicity of forms of ownership).

The first step the Earth Federation must take will be to purchase (or appropriate from uncooperative corporations) unused land or large concentrations of land at its tax value. Corporate and other forms of land monopolies can be broken up by law, with due compensation to the owners. Much of this land will be transferred to the poor using lines of credit charging only an accounting fee. In some cases, huge private plantations with workers living in poverty upon them must be converted in stages to cooperatives, the workers becoming co-owners who share in the profits produced from their labor. Eventually today's system of monopolistic private ownership to the exclusion of the well-being of others will disappear. Society will collect the land-rent from all people, as Economist Henry George suggested (1935). Land and resource ownership will be converted to conditional ownership, for the most fundamental imperative of the Federation will be the common good of the Earth, all its citizens, and the welfare of future generations.

Programs will be initiated for the hundreds of millions of Earth's citizens now unemployed or underemployed to integrate them into their newly activated local and regional economies. The Earth Federation itself would employ millions of the currently unemployed in replanting the forests of the Earth and the hundreds of other environmental tasks necessary to restore the integrity of our planetary ecosystem. George understood that *conditional property rights* (rather than absolute property rights) would place the good of the planet and society at the heart of property law. Laws would be enacted (along with massive education) protecting *sustainable* development and prohibiting business, industry, and farming from externalizing costs to society, nature, or future generations.

On these six principles alone, the twenty-five or so nations in the initial Earth Federation will be liberated to rapidly create universal prosperity and democracy for themselves. Money-creation can and must be premised on the wealth that ample lines of credit for peaceful productive purposes can bring to the entire Federation. Eliminating military spending will provide an immediate influx of funds within the initial Federation. Private property, including intellectual property, would be a limited right of persons, and it would be carefully regulated for the common good, as in any truly democratic society.

There must be sharing of developmental technology and knowledge through a rational system of intellectual property rights predicated on the good of all, not the monopoly of the multinational corporations. There must be true freedom of information and dialogue through a media system not in the hands of media monopolies. There must be equal pay for equally productive work world-wide. And there must be meaningful land reform under a new, socially responsible, conception of property. On the basis of these six, simple principles, the economic multiplier effect will produce rapid development and virtually universal prosperity. The Earth Federation must encourage this process, monitor it for equatability and sustainability, and employ millions of citizens in the task of reversing the environmental destruction proceeding everywhere on Earth.

A truly efficient planetary system of production could provide enough for all (food, clothing, housing, education, health care, social security) within a sustainable system of production with a work week of two or three days distributed equitably among the Earth's adult working population (Smith, 2003a). There is no mystery about this. "Human nature" does not have to be drastically changed. It is only necessary to found planetary institutions under the Earth Federation premised on this goal. None of these simple changes can be implemented on a planetary scale without the authority of democratic world government. None could be implemented among the initial twenty-five or so nations unless they federated under the *Earth Constitution*. This simple paradigm shift results in practical action for a new world order.

4. The Transition to Planetary Maturity

As I stressed throughout this Part Four, the *Constitution for the Federation of Earth* supplies the framework making possible the practical utopia of planetary maturity through moving toward a new level of human existence. It cannot do this until the global system benefiting the few has been eliminated and genuine prosperity for all has been achieved. As a framework, the *Constitution* is absolutely essential to activate a process of rapid sustainable, development. The basic needs of all must be met before we can begin to talk seriously about a more mature consciousness for the majority. The *Constitution* does not enforce any vision of "utopia" on the citizens of Earth. It provides a framework through which basic needs can be met and the free quest for planetary maturity can be activated.

The economic principles outlined in the previous section are derived from the work of Michael Chossudovsky, Herman Daly, Henry George, Michael Hudson, Philip Isely, David Korten, Dada Maheshvaranda, Vandana Siva, J.W. Smith, and others. All these thinkers agree that global poverty can only be eliminated though democratizing the world's economic operating principles. None of these thinkers assume that a fundamental change in human consciousness or so-called "human nature" is necessary. The "immediate economic benefits of world government" (Isely) require only the formation of the Earth Federation and initiation of freedom for sustainable development through eliminating the present global monopolies on money creation, corporate "human" rights, information dissemination, technology, wage levels, and land. This is as it should be, since the Earth Federation will make possible further transformation of consciousness. It does not require transformation in any substantial way prior to ratification and initiation of a fundamentally democratic political and economic order.

At the moment our goal must be the immediate elimination of poverty, militarism, imperialism, environmental destruction, human rights abuses, and control of population growth. Transformation to practical utopia will likely come speedily once we have dealt with our planetary crises. Errol E. Harris confirms our most immediate need:

> At the present time, because the customary way of thinking is molded by the Newtonian paradigm, few people give serious consideration to the establishment of world federation; but if, in accordance with the new scientific holism, global thinking were to prevail, that would be our immediate political goal; for it is the only condition under which global measures could be

enacted to cope with the global problems which face humanity and threaten the survival of the species. Clearly, such all-embracing actions cannot be accomplished by the individual efforts of private persons and organizations. They must be universally enforced, and that requires global legislation and the global maintenance of a rule of law, which is possible only under a world government. (2002b, p. 109)

The creation of world government under the *Constitution's* guiding principle of unity-in-diversity will soon lead to a different conception of economics. The principles of Chossudovsky, Daly, George, Hudson, Isely, Korten, Maheshvaranda, Siva, and Smith will be further "socialized" so worker participation in productive decision making will increase and the concept of production itself will increasingly focus on what is needed and how to contribute to the common good instead of private accumulation of wealth regardless of what is needed for the common good. Harris describes this development in the following way:

The economic health and success of every country is dependent on that of all others, so the world economy has to be seen as a single system and must be treated as a whole. Further, the conception of profit must be transformed: It must be socialized rather than individualized. Production and supply have to be viewed as a cooperative enterprise rendering service to the community, rather than a venture undertaken for personal gain. Likewise labor is not to be exploited to ensure profits, but has to be employed in partnership with capital for a common good. (2002b, p. 107)

The conception of profit will quite likely be further "socialized" as human consciousness adopts ever more fully the principle of unity-in-diversity. Once universal prosperity and efficient sustainability are achieved, and under the Earth Federation this would not take many decades, people will likely begin to lose interest in spending their lives grubbing for money. Mature people will want to spend their time with other, more serious, and important pursuits. Eventually, practical utopia will emerge on planet Earth. Once the *Constitution for the Federation of Earth* is ratified and the Earth Federation has brought our planetary crises under control, transformative praxis will act to bring about planetary maturity.

The obsession with material wealth and domination will probably disappear from our planet. The nihilism now dominating intellectual life will disappear with a new sense of fulfillment and joy in living. In previous chapters, we examined the intellectual and spiritual poverty of positivism, post-modern relativism, scientism, and fundamentalism. All of these ignore or distort the paradigm shift at the heart of twentieth-century science, theology, and philosophy. The fulness of life will soon come flooding back into existence soon after we have founded the Earth Federation and overcome the global crises threatening our existence on Earth.

In *Fashionable Nihilism – A Critique of Analytic Philosophy*, Bruce Wilshire frames this issue in terms of our present intellectual nihilism and the alternative of a fulfilled and meaningful existence as mature human beings:

> Nihilism means: to mangle the roots of our thinking-feeling-evaluating selves, to lose the full potential of our immediate ecstatic involvement in the world around us. It means to lose full contact with our willing-feeling-valu-ing life-projects: to have a shallow sense of what is valuable in human life. It means to be arch, smug, dried out – to be a talking head among other such heads. Speak and reason as we will, we are no longer moved in our depths...
>
> What passes as education is not the *educing (educare)* of our needs, yearnings, questionings as beings who must develop our-selves or rot in boredom.... But it is rather *instruction* in data and methods for amassing more of it: *instruere*, structuring into....
>
> For William James....all meaning and truth are a species of goodness, and this is the fruitful building out of the past into the present and future. Meaning-making and truth are essential features of being vitally alive and centered, of fully being, and philosophy is meant to nurture and feed us – we who are ecstatic body-minds. (2002, pp. 6 and 35)

Philosophers such as John Dewey, Errol Harris, William James, Alfred North Whitehead, and Bruce Wilshire understand the need for a fundamental paradigm shift beyond fragmentation to an integrated fullness of "our thinking-feeling-evaluating selves." This change will be made possible by the simple mechanism of ratifying the *Earth Constitution* and institutionalizing the principle of unity-in-diversity politically and economically for our planet.

In Chapter Five, we saw Henry David Thoreau express this principle of planetary maturity:

> Those things which now most engage the attention of men, as politics and the daily routine, are, it is true, vital functions of human society, but should be unconsciously performed, like the corresponding functions of the physi-cal body. They are *infra*-human, a kind of vegetation.... Thus our life is not altogether a forgetting, but also, alas! to a great extent, a remembering, of that which we should never have been conscious of, certainly not in our waking hours. (1967, pp. 372-73)

The evolution of the economic system under the *Constitution for the Federation of Earth* may take on entirely unexpected forms once global and equitable prosperity has been achieved. We cannot predict, but can surely imagine, a beautiful system such as was envisioned by Karl Marx. We can imagine a transformation of our entire experience of life attendant upon an equitable and planetary economy based on human dignity and sustainable efficiency. Marx writes:

The transcendence of private property is therefore the complete *emancipation* of all the human senses and attributes, but it is this emancipation precisely because these senses and attributes have become subjectively and objectively, *human*.... Only through the objectively unfolded richness of man's essential being is the richness of subjective *human* sensibility...either cultivated or brought into being. For not only the five senses but also the so-called mental senses – the practical senses (love, will, etc.) – in a word, *human* sense – the humanness of the senses – comes to be.... (1978, pp. 87-89)

The possibilities for humanization of our being, for transformation of our being toward planetary maturity are immense. For Marx, they included a liberation of the senses to the point where the meaning and richness of existence flows into human lives through an awakened and living sensitivity to the inexhaustible depth and beauty of our precious Earth.

Marx writes of the liberation of our senses. He intuits their constricted nature under capitalism. Similarly, in *The Listening Self: Personal Growth, Social Change, and the Closure of Metaphysics* (1989), David Michael Levin finds that the modern "hegemony of vision" constricts and delimits our deep possibilities for listening and attunement with being. In Chapter Three, we saw Jean-Paul Sartre describe our world system as an institutionalized "structure of scarcity." Once the Earth Federation has eliminated the "structure of scarcity" dominating our thinking-feeling-willing selves, the possibilities for a transformed mode of being in the world are immense.

These possibilities cannot be realized under the present world-order of nation-state-monopoly-capitalism. For the perpetuation of exploitation and domination require that people be kept in a state of childish adolescence. These possibilities can only be realized within true economic democracy for our entire planet. Transformative praxis acts to make this happen. We need a planetary framework premised on the political and economic unity-in-diversity of all people, nations, and cultures.

We need practical, simple steps like those outlined here to create economic prosperity for all the world's citizens. Peace, freedom, and prosperity are relatively easy to create once the institutions preventing their emergence have been transformed. The ratification of the *Earth Constitution*, plus these simple, common sense, economic steps implicit in the *Constitution*, is all that is required to make possible the realization of our higher divine-human destiny on this planet.

Chapter Fourteen: Conclusion

Barcelona Reflections

on Revolutionary Praxis

for the Twenty-first Century

Modern history and the development which is taking place within it constitute an enormous wealth of new experience for mankind. The human soul has become more complex and at the same time more fully developed. The harshness and cruelty of earlier periods have been diminished and there is much greater humanity; there is a new compassion abroad in the world not only towards men but even towards animals. There is more refinement and sensitiveness of conscience in the world, a greater opposition to cruelty, falsehood, and violence, and more demand for love and liberty.... No power on earth can stop evolution with all the contradictions which it brings in its train. God himself wills it, and desires the realization of every sort of possibility; He wills that human freedom should be put to the test and that experience should be deepened and widened.

Nicholas Berdyaev

In the blind-alley we find subjective man. He is shut up within himself; autistic, inwardly broken, though outwardly secure – the burgher. Nothing is alive in his world. Everything is closed, everything dead.... No – we must venture again and again upon that highest union, that source of all other unions, that meeting of God, man, and world.... And he is best fitted to speak with God who knows how to speak with man and who can proclaim the fullness of the glory of the world. The absolute unity of all beings which is reached in the gathering together of men who have become completed in their humanity, free from fear, nature and ideology.... The present is free both from the passage of time and from the "world beyond." The world is there. Man is raised up.

Eric Gutkind

From Parc Guell on one of the hillsides overlooking Barcelona, the city and Mediterranean lie open below. From here (in the warm September sun) I can see the castle on Montjuic rising on another hill on the right, and behind to the East in the higher hills surrounding the city rise the spires of the Basilica of Tibidado. "Tibidabo" is Latin for "Unto you I will give...," recalling the temptation of Christ in Matthew's Gospel in which Satan brings him to the top of a mountain overlooking the kingdoms of the world (Matt. 4: 8-10).

Looking east to the Basilica, with a tram car carrying tourists up to it and the nearby amusement park for children, it becomes clear that they have built this basilica on the mountain in praise of Satan, for they have accepted all he offered. The wealthy and beautiful city of Barcelona is spread out in the valley below, within which the struggle for ownership of the wealth and power of the world flourishes as big corporations inundate the people with their propaganda, under the reassuring presence of the Basilica of Tibidabo. "All this I will give to you."

1. A Tour of Barcelona

The sights of Barcelona are tributes to this struggle. Parc Guell was built by the architect Antoni Gaudi (1852-1926), whose monumental works dot the city where he lived. Much of this work could not have been done but for Gaudi's patron Count Eusebi Guell, after whom the park is named and whose wealth served well the slogan "All this will I give to you...." The park includes distinctive, monumental walls of unusual shapes and dimensions and is an attraction for thousands of tourists each year. Where did the fortune of Eusebi Guell that built this park come from?

Where do all concentrations of wealth come from? Thousands come each year, and no one asks these questions. Satan has offered to some (through the temptations of Christ) great concentrations of wealth and power. "All this will I give to you...." At what price? What did we give back in return? What are the people of Barcelona giving today? In what ways are we at the dawn of the twenty-first century selling our souls, as Thoreau put it, for a mess of pottage? All this is given to those few today who are the "owners" and to the untold millions of "tourists" worldwide who are their followers and passive supporters. Yet all will be taken from us tomorrow as the ecology of the Earth collapses and the environment loses its ability to support our unsustainable civilization.

The difficulty is to stay focused on what is most simple and most basic and not be distracted by the many "tourist" distractions of Barcelona and the global commercial world Barcelona represents. Barcelona has visitors from all over the first world, speaking a variety of languages. They are titillated by its sights, sounds, and wonders – those unique features of the world that attract them as tourists. There would be nothing particularly invidious in this if it were not for the half of the people of the world who cannot be tourists, who literally cannot afford even to leave the town where they are born because they do not have a peso or rupee for the local bus or even adequate food for themselves or their children.

Within this political and economic situation, tourism functions as a distraction from the real. As with professional sports as a spectacle and the "entertainment" industry, tourism has a very important political function.

It keeps people focused on what is secondary, trivial, and insubstantial, so they live out their lives without ever encountering the "real." An encounter with the real is inherently revolutionary. The ruling classes of the world, the business classes, have a vested interest in people encountering only the ideological appearances of things, never penetrating to the real. They have a vested interest in creating beautiful, attractive cities like Barcelona.

What, then, is the "real"? The real is certainly revealed in the cry of the poor, "I am hungry; I have no food; my children are starving." But to really hear this cry requires an awakening consciousness. The "real" is revealed to the awakening consciousness beyond the limits of language and cognitive rationality (although not beyond deep intelligence). The real includes the ethical dimension of human life realized through encountering the other as other, as a person like myself but inherently unique and valuable in his or her own right as other. This recognition of the other as a personal awareness reflective of a deeper infinity, as a bottomless inwardness like myself, identical with myself as person, yet utterly unique and deserving of autonomy as other, constitutes the ethical dimension and the encounter with the real.

The cry of the poor is then understood to be the "real." When we hear this cry, we are no longer tourists, indulging our superficial curiosity at the wonders of the world, travelers outside of life, gawking at its spectacles. The awakening consciousness encounters ever more fully the inseparability of the ethical, the mystical, and the eschatological, three aspects of the absolute present moment ever-present to our lives, sources of the overwhelming fullness of life. To hear the cry of the poor is to become real ourselves. All of life becomes this ecstatic, astonishing process of transformation, a perpetual journeying and ever fuller encounter with the real.

In Barcelona, I now stand in the park confronting of the magnificent edifice of *Sagrada Familia,* begun by Gaudi in 1883 and worked on by him until his accidental death in 1926. This monumental project is still under construction. With the great religious edifices of the church, two hundred years is nothing. Yet we are in the twenty-first century, when time is looked at quite differently than it was in the twelfth century. What is the impulse today behind this awe-inspiring project? In the religious statuary, the icons, the *bas reliefs*, the columns, and the intricate designs on surfaces, every detail appears lovingly worked out, much of it made in Gaudi's own workshop on the premises, all preserved and open to the public.

Gaudi himself was a devout Catholic, a lover of religious music and a devoted servant of Christ. Yet the time, energy, and immense wealth invested in this project reflects the symbolic consciousness of an other-worldliness that devotes its energy to projects of symbolic value and fails to call into question the economic and social structures of power and wealth that characterize the world as we know it. "All this I will give to you" stands above the city as a reminder that the Church has given away this world in favor of a symbolism leaving the rule of Mammon and imperial power firmly in control.

This symbolic consciousness does not engage the concrete suffering of real human persons in this world, but romanticizes the religious feeling for Christ in a non-threatening, symbolic form. So non-threatening is this stance that when you buy an admission ticket at the gate to walk through the unfinished cathedral, the ticket is stamped with the logos of two multinational fast-food corporations. Apparently there is no contradiction in the mind of those who control *Sagrada Familia*. Religion here holds no threat for those destroying the Earth through the massive production of beef in the service of private profit. The immense energy and wealth invested in *Sagrada Familia* could have been used for revolutionary purposes (which are not those of a charity perpetuating the system of domination) to change the world in the direction of the kingdom of God.

Changes in the direction of the kingdom of God focus on the real sufferings of human beings, which are the focus of ethical solidarity and all authentic ethical action. Work for realization of the kingdom of God on Earth challenges all structures of domination and dehumanization. It acts from an ethical and eschatological, not a symbolic consciousness. Unlike the bourgeois reformist impulse that feels the need for justice and ethical solidarity in a merely tangential way, the eschatological consciousness realizes the transformative possibilities in the present as a source of its revolutionary action. Instead of the symbolical consciousness, which projects a kingdom of ethical solidarity into another dimension ("heaven"), or the reformist consciousness projecting ethical solidarity into a distant evolutionary future, eschatological consciousness understands the ethical unity-in-diversity of all persons as the "real," the starting point of the human-divine-cosmic situation, not as an "ideal" to be perhaps realized one day.

2. Postmodern Relativism

On a level similar to the tourists who flock to the city of Barcelona are many of today's philosophers and intellectuals. Trapped within language and lacking a direct, unmediated awareness of the "real," they travel the cognitive world titillated by its sights and wonders in a life of bourgeois self-indulgence. This helps explain the limitations and successes of postmodernists and pragmatists like Richard Rorty as well as of positivists and many versions of analytic philosophy discussed in previous chapters. They rightly see the groundlessness of the human situation and the failure of correspondence versions of truth throughout history.

However, they retain Cartesian subjectivity in its untranscended form. They are not free of a bourgeois subjectivism that sees all truth relative to points of view, the vast morass of skepticism and relativism that refuses to listen to the silence at the heart of our groundlessness. Postmodernist relativists and pragmatists often critique the idea of a grounded rationality and argue that reasoning is groundless and will tolerate, as they put it, no "grand narratives." Yet in their one-dimensional intellectualism, they miss the groundless depth beyond cognitive reason in the dimension of ethical solidarity that, once realized, is encountered as real in a way not reducible to conceptualized theories of truth, be they correspondence, coherence, or pragmatic. They miss the "fullness of the glory of the world."

Postmodern subjectivism is lost in the maze of conflicting narratives, in language, and never frees itself from language to encounter real suffering in the life of the other. Positivists cling blindly to the "facts" and find all value, all compassionate encounter with the life of others, "merely subjective." It is true, as Enrique Dussel (1990) insists, that one must hear the cry of the other and must be able to respond to "I am hungry, give me something to eat."

Subjectivism of all forms, whether Cartesian or postmodern, does not truly hear the cry of the other or feel her pain and therefore does not ever fully respond to her cry. To truly respond would be a revolutionary act, because only revolution can transform the system (and the bourgeois consciousness the system cultivates) that has caused her hunger in the first place. Class society, and a world where class society is defended by the might of the imperialist first world-nations, is society where the precious resources of the Earth are appropriated as the "private property" of the few. This is the fundamental cause of hunger. There is no other fundamental cause, since even famine would be easily overcome in a world directed to the satisfaction of basic human needs on the premise that all human beings are valuable in themselves.

To hear the cry of the other in a deep way requires beginning to live life from the real dimension of human solidarity. Individualized bourgeois consciousness knows nothing of this living oneness, which involves living from a unity-in-diversity prior to language or conceptual thought. Socialist materialism, on the other hand, often attempts to establish oneness on the basis of a false metaphysics as well as a *de facto* denial of diversity. But authentic oneness is not monism, nor is it "totality" in Levinas' sense, and it is never mere collectivity. Oneness is always inseparable from diversity. Errol E. Harris (1991; 1992; 2000a; 2000b) has demonstrated this at great length as the ultimate implication of twentieth-century science.

Universality and diversity arise together in phenomenal existence. But this is also true on the groundless-ground of the unsayable oneness-in-multiplicity that becomes overwhelmingly present in direct awareness. The two dimensions, unity and diversity, arise simultaneously and are inseparable. This is why for centuries the Buddhists have spoken of the simultaneous "fullness-emptiness" (*śūnyatā*) of all existence.

To breakthrough to the living awareness of human solidarity is simultaneously to gain a critical perspective toward one's own subjectivity. One's subjective life is now seen as an ephemeral "noise" on the surface of the ethical dimension, an epiphenomenon, like the squeaking of the wheel of awareness, which may eventually become silent, smoothly working, and ever more fully aware. The fuller the awareness, the quieter the wheel of consciousness. The "I" orientation begins to loosen its compulsive grip.

The "I" is no longer seen as "my reality" but becomes a mere utility, something useful when needed in everyday functioning, like a hammer or a pair of shoes. The free-arising of solidarity, the unity-in-diversity of all persons (and in another sense) of all creatures, and finally of all things, begins to permeate consciousness, transforming the "I"-fixation through an ever-deeper non-cognitive understanding. This is the source of transformative praxis. Here one can proclaim the fullness of the glory of the world.

Postmodern subjectivism, lost in the chatter of language and the subjective perspectivism of individual narratives, is a consciousness liberated from the logocentric narratives historically used to ground oppression, exploitation, and domination (as Michel Foucault and others have made clear). But its retained subjectivism and its concomitant relativism keeps the postmodern and the positivist locked into the patterns of oppression. The postmodern relativist or positivist, despite his or her rhetoric of small acts of "resistance" to the system, finds no standpoint from which to critique the *institutions* of exploitation and domination. In rejecting "grand narratives," he or she rejects anything that might authentically be said in response to the cry of the suffering person, to the voices crying "We are hungry, we do not have food."

Our knowledge and understanding must be *lived* knowledge and understanding, based on our willing-feeling-valuing selves that take real action within the concrete world in which we find ourselves. How can we recognize the system of death for what it is, or feel the interconnectedness of the real, pulsing life about us, as Ralph Waldo Emerson so eloquently insisted, if we have always remained cloistered within our intellectual suburbs?

Action is with the scholar subordinate, but it is essential. Without it, he is not yet man. Without it, thought can never ripen into truth. Whilst the world hangs before the eye as a cloud of beauty, we cannot even see its beauty. Inaction is cowardice, but there can be no scholar without the heroic mind. The preamble of thought, the transition through which it passes from the unconscious to the conscious, is action. Only so much do I know, as I have lived. Instantly we know whose words are loaded with life, and whose not. (1965, p. 230)

It is not difficult to travel to some of the many nightmare regions of our world and become involved directly with the agonizing lives of those condemned by accident of birth to live in these hell-holes. We are not as likely to find such lives in Barcelona or any of the many tourist centers of the bourgeois world. First-world hotels carefully screened from the nightmarish lives of the mass of humanity exist in every tourist center of the world. I have personally walked the slums from Managua in Central America and Mumbai in India to Dhaka in Bangladesh. We can travel to Mumbai, Dhaka, or Managua without ever seeing and feeling the immense suffering surrounding us. But it is not difficult to visit such places as a guest of the poor who open their arms with a generosity we cannot begin to imagine. Such action makes it possible for us to experience the "real," to experience the fullness of life, and to see in what ways we live within a system of death.

Postmodern subjectivity remains conformed to bourgeois individualism and self-indulgence. In the absence of anything real from which it can act, it lapses into personal indulgence, pleasure seeking, and a none-too-courageous intellectual adventurism. In doing so, it concedes to the system exactly what its laudable initial impulse had grappled with. It correctly points out that the logocentric narratives of the medieval church justified the exploitation and domination within the medieval system. However, it has overcome logocentric domination only to sink into relativist domination. It has no sense of the "real" on which to base a critique of the present system.

But it is precisely "cultural diversity" (without genuine solidarity), relativism, and skepticism that form the narratives of the transnational corporations sucking the life resources from our human brothers and sisters in the third world and channeling the profits drained from their dead or dying bodies into the coffers of first-world concentrations of wealth and power. Universities around the first world are promoting "internationalizing of the curriculum." For the future executives and managers of transnational capital graduated by these universities very much need to be "multicultural" and tolerant of diversity. Postmodern relativists have no resources to fight these insidious forces of economic and cultural domination and exploitation, for they share many of the same premises.

To reject all "grand narratives" means, for postmodernism and positivism, also to reject critical analyses of the vast institutions that exploit and dominate the world today. This to be tolerant of the ideological hegemony masking a system of dehumanization and death as the dominant institutions put private profit above human suffering while destroying the environment that future generations need to sustain them. Logocentric narratives are trapped within a form of language easily appropriated by systems of domination benefitting the few at the expense of the many. Postmodern critiques of logocentrism are well taken in this respect, but if the result is relativism, skepticism, or multiculturalism as the opposite extreme, then this form of language-use is also easily appropriated by systems of domination.

There is no power-structure more affirming of multiculturalism than McSuper Corporation, with its fast-food chain locations in practically every nation and culture on Earth. Yet this vast system, devoted to the private appropriation of wealth and to promoting the world-wide consumption of beef, is sacrificing the ability of future generations to survive on this planet. Diversity unredeemed though genuine unity is often a mere cover for imperialist assimilation of the other. Within the unredeemed clash of diversities, the stronger always predominates and assimilates the weaker.

All power systems ideologically justify their domination. Capitalism is especially flexible in that the extensive multi-billion-dollar propaganda networks of its immense concentrations of wealth will say whatever is necessary to sell its products and its ideological self-justifications to the public. All major corporations now have multi-million-dollar greenwashing departments. Corporate propaganda has made them not only into multiculturalists but also into environmentalists, while the Earth and its inhabitants are sacrificed to the pursuit of private profit.

Unlike medieval systems in Europe that were largely locked into religious language to mask domination, modern corporations will use religious language or not depending on the needs of profit. They use the language of environmentalism similarly, or the language of individualism, or of relativism – whatever works. In this system, truth in the moral sense has no place; there is only propaganda in the service of profit. Postmodern rebellion against logocentrism plays directly into the hands of these exploiters and indirectly into the death and misery of untold millions of the Earth's citizens.

Postmodern relativism and positivism are unable to develop any fundamental critique of capitalism or the nation-state system, just as they are unable to critique any system that operates insidiously, since both are based on individual diversity and subjectivist self-centeredness. Without the overcoming of subjectivism, the temptation to self-interest and greed is overwhelming. Subjectivism thrives in the absence of the claims to objectivist moral or social values once proffered by the great objectivist narratives. At the least, the institutionalization of these grand narratives had a restraining effect on the subjectivist dimension.

In the absence of institutionalized logocentric narratives, subjective personal preference, greed, and license find no clear restraints. The religious right and religious fundamentalism understand this, however limited their understanding in other respects. We must not react to relativism and subjectivism by sinking into any form of blind dogmatism or bigotry. We saw in previous chapters that the interconnections of all these movements represent perverted reactions to modernity. We must rise to a new level of existence.

3. Solidarity

The only possible restraint at this point in history would involve the discovery of human solidarity of the one and the many prior to subjectivity. Once the real dimensions of human solidarity appear, the subjective is under a perpetual critique that not only restrains its indulgences but progressively diminishes and ultimately abolishes the subjective to the level of the "squeaky wheel" of consciousness. Awareness remains, but now a silent awareness free of subjective noise and the illusion of the autonomous "I."

The "I" becomes a utility to be used, not a "reality" pretending to be the sole access to all other "reality." If there is a spiritual and historical dialectic, it moves from logocentrism, to postmodernist diversity of language-games, to silence. Neither a single narrative nor the plurality of narratives reveals the "real." Even the word "real," since it appears in language, can only serve as a pointer to the primordial silence beyond all language. For the distinction between the "real" and "unreal" is a linguistic distinction. Nevertheless, one can gesture toward the "real" prior to language in the transformative silence apprehending the mutual arising of the one and the many, the source of revolutionary solidarity with the poor and our suffering planet.

For this reason, what I am writing here is not meant to be another narrative, but a fumbling gesture at the fullness of life encompassing our willing-feeling-valuing selves beyond mere intellectual cognition. This use of language is one way of gesturing toward the transformative silence that is the "real" of the world and human awareness. The "real" is pure silence, and no language is involved. No narrative is involved but rather the spontaneous arising of the ecstatic immediacy prior to thought and language.

Here is the most basic source of human solidarity, and here is the source of a revolutionary critique of all systems of oppression. The unity-in-diversity revealed as the basic structure of the universe by twentieth-century science can point in the direction of solidarity. But by itself it cannot activate authentic love and compassion. True human freedom cannot arise without authentic solidarity opposing any and all oppression of persons by other persons. Human solidarity requires an analysis arising from the great thinkers of liberation, especially within the Marxist and liberation traditions. We not only identify with the suffering of others. We must analyze why they are suffering. Why is there poverty on this beautiful, wealthy, and bountiful planet?

It is not necessary to "buy into" any logocentric metaphysics that such an analysis might on one level imply, especially to dogmatic thinkers. If the analysis is revolutionary and promotes human solidarity, it is an important use of reason. As we saw in the work of Jürgen Habermas, language and communicative rationality play an absolutely vital role in the foundations of democracy and human liberation. And as we saw in the work of Errol E. Harris, the ultimate presuppositions of science reveal unity-in-diversity at the heart of the universe. Yet the ground of solidarity is not analysis or science alone, but the ethical realization in silence prior to any and all analyses. We are one with one another at a much deeper level than that to which intellect can penetrate. For the first time, one begins to really hear the cries of the hungry and the oppressed.

Here we come upon the authentic meaning of praxis, the inseparability of theory and practice. Theory does not and cannot give a final analysis of the hidden and overt relations of domination against which we struggle. What we say in terms of an abstract characterization of our situation will necessarily arise from our practical action as we move into an ever-new and ever-renewed future. What we say, theory, is never final. Process philosophy has understood some of this – the universe and human beings are in a process of emergence characterized by a genuine newness that cannot be captured in any final way by static metaphysical formulas.

Yet much of process philosophy remains mired in bourgeois subjectivity and appears incapable of moving to a revolutionary stance. In spite of this, the newness recognized in much process philosophy is the genuine newness of a universe that cannot be predicted, of a future that cannot be theoretically encompassed and formulated in any final way. This principle is true of all three sources of revolutionary praxis examined in Chapter Ten. Integral awareness, intuiting the ethical, mystical, and eschatological dimensions of existence, comprehends our highest human possibilities – possibilities arising not from any mutable "human nature" but from the deepest sources of existence itself.

This radical futurity, always emerging from the silent present prior to thought and language, makes our analyses and linguistic formulations dependent on the emergence of concrete relationships. Yet there is no *a priori* reason why "grand narratives" may not be used to illuminate hidden patterns of domination and exploitation. Nearly everything in traditional metaphysics provides insight and is worth studying today. But we study it not to find a final, timeless metaphysical truth but rather to educate ourselves on the interdependency of partial truths in the whole pattern of truth, so that we can better act out of human understanding in the present.

The coherence conception of truth associated with Marxism, critical theory, or much philosophy of liberation, can illuminate our situation and promote the critical consciousness necessary for revolutionary action. The coherence of truth can be clarified through communicative rationality to a certain extent, to be sure. But ultimately, our "truths" must be evaluated in the light of the utopian mandate at the heart of eschatological awareness. To what extent do they promote a world of justice, freedom, equality, dignity, and ecological harmony in which each and every person has sufficiency of food, clothing, shelter, education, health care, and the other minimum conditions for a decent, creative, and fulfilled human life?

The postmodern refusal to engage in "grand narratives" has, in its most authentic spokespersons, an authentic integrity based on truthfulness. Yet the impulse to liberation behind this truthfulness is compromised by the inability of postmodernism to discover a genuine source of human solidarity. (Traditional philosophy often included such indicators of solidarity in its grand narratives, for example, "human rights," "human dignity," "humans made in God's image," and so on.) To be free of big language is still to be trapped in little language. Solidarity arises from a groundless source prior to language and becomes an unspoken non-linguistic criterion for all language-games. To what extent does the language in question reveal domination and exploitation? To what extent does the language lead to action promoting a transformed world? How can we live authentic lives of transformative praxis?

This evening I have been sitting for a long while on the steps of the monument to Columbus that towers over Barcelona harbor, a harbor long since developed with fountains, boardwalks, shops, and boat rides for tourists. People speaking many languages have stopped to gaze at the elaborate sets of statues and relief figures that crowd the monument beneath the dominating figure of Columbus at the top with outstretched arm and finger, as if pointing to land or some new discovery of civilization. Bishops, royalty, and dignitaries from the life of Columbus mingle with romantic figures representing justice, civilization, progress, and virtue. It is a whitewash of a genocidal murderer and the greedy Spanish ruling class complicit in his crimes. All this is itself a language, a use of one of the endless perspectives possible in language to deceive and cover over the ethically reprehensible reality of the situations depicted. The *bas reliefs* show sequences of Columbus and his soldiers ushering their half-naked indigenous conquests into the presence of their royal patrons, on bended knee before the high priests of civilization and the representatives of the eternal Church. The beauty of the monument hides the hideousness of its lie. It dominates the harbor in Barcelona just as the Basilica of Tibidado dominates the city beyond.

The ideological mask of capitalism in league with the imperial ruling classes of nation-states uses every resource to divert us from solidarity with the oppressed and to seduce us into becoming tourists, mere *petits rentiers*, roaming the Earth in search of pleasure, titillation, and bourgeois self-indulgence. It seduces us into complicity with its murderous system of exploitation and the genocidal murderers who enforce its inhuman imperatives in Vietnam, Iraq, Indonesia, Columbia, El Salvador, Guatemala, Yugoslavia, Afghanistan, and elsewhere. For historically, through complicity with our class societies and imperial systems, we have accepted not only one but all three temptations offered by Satan to Christ. We have accepted worldly wealth, Mammon, as the deepest criterion of life. We have accepted imperial power as the "norm" on which human institutions are to be based, averting our eyes from the massive state terrorism and military repression practiced against others by our own societies.

And we have accepted a magical, symbolic mode of understanding the world, limiting "reality" to what we can imagine and encompass within our limited cognitive rationality and projecting our redeemed future into a merely symbolic dimension. Postmodern relativism, like its cousin traditional skepticism, has no resources that can bring us to a realization with the real fullness of life, to an encounter with the "real." And such relativism has no resources that can bring us into a revolutionary solidarity with the oppressed, for it is caught, in Wittgenstein's words, "all unknowing in the net of language."

4. Ten Aspects of Revolutionary Praxis for the Twenty-first Century

I have attempted to itemize here ten fundamental aspects of an integral revolutionary life. They are not given in order of importance but together form an integrated whole. Some persons may emphasize certain ones while other persons focus on others. Nor are they meant to be exhaustive. However, they do serve as a summary of much of the praxis articulated in previous chapters, since in one sense this entire book has been about praxis. "Praxis" means that theory and practice cannot be entirely disentangled, certainly not when we examine the direct, existential transformation of human consciousness involved in the process of awakening. As our discussion of mysticism has shown, for example, there is no way to "prove" many scholarly issues within mysticism through theory or additional scholarship.

The only option is the direct, existential realization that the mystics themselves practice. The same is true of revolutionary compassion. The motivation to take the side of the poor and the oppressed cannot be activated through any theoretical account of their exploitation. Many scholars read Marx's passionate accounts of the degradation of the poor and remain entirely unmoved. One must discover compassion in one's life, and then the motivation becomes self-evident. One realizes that to be a full human being involves such commitment. But one also needs a more complete philosophical account of what it means to be a full human being. The aspects of "praxis" articulated here presuppose many of the theoretical discussions in this book, and vice versa.

(1) Promote and develop truly critical thinking. Think and live as a revolutionary heir of the philosophers of human liberation. Expose the hidden premises of class society in every way possible and in every possible forum. Learn to read the mass media, the manifestations of culture, the symbols of the dominant system, and the pronouncements of government critically, with insight into their ideological cover-up of the system injustice and death from which they benefit. Use a "class analysis" and an analysis of the "territorial nation-state" to understand the workings of governments, corporations, the media, and the other dominant institutions of the world.

No thinking is truly critical without being revolutionary. The title "Critical Thinking" in most courses offered in universities today is deeply misleading. To be critical, thinking must be able to penetrate beneath the ideological veil of capitalism and the nation-state. And to be revolutionary, thinking must direct itself to a social reality in which human beings are first, in which dignity, security, freedom, and the satisfaction of basic human needs are the founding principles.

To be revolutionary means that praxis must direct itself toward creating global institutional embodiments of these values, toward making them the founding principles of a living institutional reality, and not merely holding them as "ideals" to be worked for in some distant future. Critical revolutionary thinking is not only democratic and socialist in orientation but is also necessarily global in scope, freeing humanity from monopoly capitalism and the territorial nation-state.

(2) Delegitimize the system of territorial nation-states and global capitalism in every way possible and on every occasion possible. Work to expose the illegitimacy of the institutions claiming to be the only legitimate ones in a world in which there exist no other alternatives. We must make clear everywhere the inadequacies and injustices of the system of nation-states and of the global capitalism with which it is intertwined. Show the interdependent complicities in this system of domination over education, communications media, culture, charity, business, the arts, and politics.

Expose the many absurdities of the system, while showing the many practical alternatives immediately available to any reasonably sane society (see Holland and Henriot, S.J., 1993). Make clear that the world has no future under the present system of ecological destruction and exploitation of the poor by the rich. Promote in every context the clear, universal principles of non-military democratic world government as expressed in the *Constitution for the Federation of Earth.*

(3) Commit to solidarity with the poor and the oppressed. Engage in organized struggle for liberation from all poverty and oppression. Commitment to the poor is not an external addition to the fullness of life. It is integral to a full and fulfilling way of existing, for unity-in-diversity with its concomitant awakening to the ethical dimension that recognizes persons as ends-in-themselves is at the heart of existence. Some people happen to have been born into these circumstances, with this hunger and malnutrition, with this lack of opportunity for education or health care. I could just as well have been born there and be experiencing these horrible sufferings and deprivations.

My struggle alongside the poor and oppressed and against the systems that oppress them is an essential part of my being human. It is inseparable from a life at the heart of the world where the struggle of human beings to emerge from their present state of barbarity. cannot be sundered from an authentic process of living. Always act in solidarity with others around the world who are struggling for a just and prosperous world-order. Actively promote the simple principles of a transformed economic order outlined in countless books and studies, some of which are listed in the Works Cited section below.

(4) Educate for human and planetary liberation. Everywhere and in every situation, strive to educate others, with sensitivity and thoughtfulness, about the possibilities and processes and necessity of human and planetary liberation. Show the interconnections between the political and the spiritual and between humanity and nature. Apply the process of education to yourself as well as to others, since education is truly a life-long process

and is never finished. Emphasize the inseparability of authentic education and truly critical thought. Think always in terms of the ways, the means, and the possibilities available for human liberation and the creation of a decent future for our children and the precious Earth on which we dwell.

(5) Become a planetary citizen: think both globally and locally, and act both globally and locally. Explore the connections; recognize that the only solution to many local problems will be planetary. Understand that it is not "globalization" in itself that provides an answer (since capitalism has been doing this for centuries) but rather a planetary solution based on a founded society, a global non-military democratic world government. Distinguish critically between the misleading ideology of "global governance" or "new world order" in which nothing substantial has changed and a founded, planetary society in which human liberation has been substantially institutionalized. Transfer your primary loyalty to the Earth and its inhabitants. Be a citizen of the Earth before all else, for only then can we become truly good citizens of the local communities of which we are a part.

(6) Organize and resist; organize for political and economic effectiveness, and resist through nonviolent direct action. Use the inseparability of critical theory, compassion, and active nonviolence as the basis for action as well as the theoretical framing of a new social order. Active nonviolence includes speaking out, editorial writing, voting, organizing, strikes, boycotts, protesting, street theater, revolutionary music, wall murals, disrupting the system, conferences, educating, teach-ins, and refusal to participate (for example, in paying war taxes, military registration, corporate military contracts, corporate exploitation of the third-world poor, and so on). It includes expressions and actions of solidarity with others in their revolutionary struggles, whether these be environmental defense actions, labor movements, or third-world struggles of liberation. Be very clear that none of the struggles by themselves can lead to a just world order without democratic world government.

(7) Practice meditation and mindfulness. Meditate: set time radically apart, free from all interruptions, to quiet the mind, and practice mindfulness in daily activities. The emergent evolutionary history of humanity is precisely the history of transformations of consciousness, often linked with the material conditions of existence. A person imbued with revolutionary ideology who is not self-aware and lacks sensitivity to others and to the fullness of the present moment is likely to be an incomplete revolutionary. The process of living itself is inseparable from a perpetual growth of awareness, a growth requiring effort, discipline, and conscious choice.

Meditate as often as possible without sacrificing the time of competing revolutionary activities. Continue the process of awareness cultivated in meditation into daily activities through mindfulness, the practice of self-awareness. Watching ones reactions, emotions, compulsions, and "inner chatter" without judging them is in itself liberating and helps make us free, rational, awake persons, no longer driven by hidden motivations or obsessions. Observe the many ways the dominant systems try to inhibit awareness and promote mindless, knee-jerk reactions in the population.

(8) *Cultivate compassionate solidarity; think and live compassionately.* The word "compassion" is used here as a symbol for a spiritual awakening to the inseparable unity-in-diversity of all things that is the source of our revolutionary solidarity with the poor and oppressed. As such, the realization of compassion is the inseparable compliment of social revolution and a fundamental dimension of revolutionary praxis. As the Fourteenth Dalai Lama, Tenzin Gyatso, insists in his writings, compassion does not need to come in a blinding light of something called "enlightenment" for those who follow the Buddhist path (see the Dalai Lama, 1995; 1994; 1985).

Instead, compassion, kindness, and love (three intertwined concepts) can be cultivated in daily actions, by attention to the way we treat others, though mindfulness of our own egoistic and selfish impulses, and through going out of our way to help, consider, and empathize with others. The realization of compassion is a process just as the other aspects of a revolutionary life are processes. This realization intertwines with our life-long education, meditation, and spiritual growth and becomes ever fuller, possibly in a series of breakthrough experiences. Ultimately, we must discover compassion that can identify with others we have never seen, simply because they are sensitive beings who are suffering. When this process begins to happen, we are beginning to discover true revolutionary solidarity and well as the fullness of our own humanity.

(9) *Think and live with an awareness of the silence encompassing our lives: be apart from all the world.* Such awareness is simultaneously to be at the heart of the world, living from the depths of silence in the fullness of the present moment. But it gives us the non-attachment, the objectivity, and the critical relationship to our own subjectivity that are essential requirements for effective revolutionary praxis. This awareness is also linked to other aspects of praxis: to the meditation, mindfulness, compassion, and ethical awareness discussed at many places in this book. But it must be emphasized in its own right, for ultimately the process of realizing this silence, available to us as the background to all our experiences, leads to the transcendence of the compulsive and

fractured ego so fundamental to capitalism and nationalism. The silence is transforming, so we become revolutionaries not only in our actions and commitments, but also through being transformed and awakened persons ourselves.

(10) *Think and live eschatologically, and cultivate the utopian imagination.* Celebrate daily the new time of human fulfillment being born in the present, or the realization of Buddha nature in all things, or the coming of the kingdom of God, or the coming and ever-present pleroma, or the realization of the messianic age, or the cosmogonic birth of the Omega Point, or the new era of peace and prosperity beginning in the here and now. The eschatological present-future informs the fullness of the absolute present and points to the wondrous, transformative depths at the heart of reality.

Available to us all as part of the depths of present existence, this awareness is a source of overwhelming joy and ecstasy in living. It is the bubbling up in us of the ultimate promise of the universe whose cosmic processes have led to the emergence of human beings over billions of years, not as the final goal but as the key to further realization of the divine-human project. It is the source of the authentic revolutionary imperative in us precisely because it sees the radical futurity of the absolute now and is no longer seduced into a perpetual postponement of a peaceful, just, and transformed world. Like the participants in the Jewish seder, we live as pilgrim citizens who celebrate daily our place in the liberated world to come.

While eschatological awareness involves the unsayable aspect of the fullness of the present, its partner, the utopian imagination, is free to use language, symbol, or story to express its vision. The utopian imagination can be freed from the ego and can articulate a future more "realistic" and intelligent than is possible for the egoistic imagination (see Moltmann, 1996; Fox, 1988). For we have seen that the utopian imagination is not the negative working of idle fantasies (as the forces of the present empire, which strives to freeze history and make itself eternal, would have it). The utopian imagination freed from the ego is one avenue of access to "reality." It can point to the possibilities implicit within the eschatological dimension of human existence. It can articulate the parameters of a practical utopia entirely available to human beings if we are willing to choose it.

These ten principles are, in brief form, the ten primary elements in a revolutionary praxis for the twenty-first century, transforming one's own life and the institutions of the world simultaneously: think critically, delegitimize the system, commit to the poor and oppressed, educate, adopt planetary citizenship, organize and resist, practice meditation and mindfulness, cultivate compassion, live from the silence of the absolute present, and live eschatologically. While one or more may predominate in daily life, I believe all of them are essential to the fullness of life and a truly revolutionary praxis. They are a result of a further development of revolutionary theory from the time of Marx as well as a fuller understanding of the notion of spirituality since the twentieth century. In this sense, they are uniquely the features of a twenty-first century revolutionary praxis.

5. Barcelona at the Crossroads of Human Existence

And all of these ten principles of a maturity oriented praxis are essential if we are to participate as vehicles of the divine-human-cosmic processes of emergent evolution taking place on planet Earth. The integral revolutionary awareness described in this book need not be fully present in our lives at every moment. We are always in the process of growing toward maturity, wisdom, and compassion. The central issue is our praxis, how we act, what we do to transform our broken and fragmented world-order and ourselves. The central issue does not require any claims to some "enlightened consciousness." People who care deeply about our planet, our children, and our world will be engaged, in one way or another, in all or most of these ten forms of praxis.

Yet none of them seem to be practiced by the tourists who pass me by as I sit beneath the monument to Columbus near the harbor in Barcelona. Barcelona is a wondrous city to visit. It is not far from the ancient monastery of Montsurat, carved from the side of the mountains, and for centuries the hermitage of monks clinging to the religious life and clinging (literally) to the cliff faces on which they dwelt. Today a paved road takes one to the immense parking lot where tourists from all nations eat in the cafeteria, shop in the gift shops, and take the tramways to the higher locations where monks formerly devoted their lives to God. Curious onlookers crowd the ledges where monks once sought isolation in the service of God. Young people camp boisterously in the campgrounds not far from the parking area and gift shops. The silence of God no longer permeates these astonishing mountains and gorges.

What does it mean to devote one's life to God today? What does it mean to commit oneself to the realization of Buddha nature today? What does it mean to be a human being today? How can I become healthy and whole and promote a decent world-order that is also healthy and whole? For the issue of my wholeness cannot be divorced from that of my world. Stupid, brutal, and fragmented persons mirror our stupid, brutal, and fragmented institutions. These questions are no longer the theoretical domain of philosophers but must be concretely addressed in every human life. In one way or another, we all bow down and worship this system of death.

The statue of Columbus overlooking the busy Barcelona harbor (where tourists dine at the seaside restaurants, take the aerial tram over the harbor, or play the video games in the amusement arcades) commemorates the Christian life of Columbus, who accepted the gift offered by Satan to Christ commemorated in the Basilica of Tibidado that overlooks the great city: "All this I will give to you if you bow down and worship me." The world system arising out of Columbus's genocidal massacre of the Arawak Indians in pursuit of gold is the global system of which we are all a part. The lust for gold has not abated but has become institutionalized and legalized in a system today claiming its own eternity and divinity (Brueggemann, 1988). Few today escape it, and no one in the first world entirely escapes it.

Today we are at a crossroads. Human consciousness has moved from a stage of primitive unity through emergent ages of magic, mythology, and subject-object duality during a two-million-year process of transformation that looks forward to a fulfillment and fullness of life beyond the fractured ego of limited perspectival awareness. Each of us, without undue effort, is in a position to activate self-awareness and a process of growth toward planetary maturity. Each of us can announce to the world the imperative to enter this process.

Once the awakening process begins, we can lead a revolutionary and self-conscious life, engaging in a *great refusal* to participate without revolutionary resistance in the bowing and worshiping of Mammon. Such a truly revolutionary life expresses a great affirmation of life itself, of the cosmogonic process, and of the eschatological fulfillment of our human destiny. It involves a life of ecstatic journeying toward transformation and fulfillment. It is a life in which the process itself becomes an ever-renewed fulfillment and celebration.

Or we can remain tourists in a world of oppression, injustice, and ecological devastation, enjoying the cuisine at fine French or Spanish restaurants while the poor of the world rot in hell. We can take a Mediterranean Cruise from the Barcelona harbor with a port of call at the fascinating ancient Roman ruins in Taragona, enhancing our personal "education," while our tax-dollars fund torture, murder, and repression in South America, Asia, and Africa. We can visit the Basilica of Tibidado (and let the kids play in the amusement park nearby), wonder at the architecture in Parc Guell, and gaze at the spires and statuary of *Sagrada Familia* while the future of our children is crushed beneath the ecological devastation of a planet that will no longer support human life by the end of the twenty-first century.

The greatest crossroads in human history confronts us – as we stroll down the boulevard *La Rambla* beginning at the Barcelona harbor with its monument to Columbus and pause to allow a street artist to sketch our cartoon portrait. A few dollars for the portrait and we have a souvenir of our visit to Barcelona, the same few dollars that serves as the weekly income of a large portion of the Earth's population. It is possible to live out our lives on the surface of existence, touching no depths, and remaining tourists amid the spectacles maintained and promoted for us by government and business. One can see all the sights of Barcelona without ever encountering the cry of a poor person: "I am hungry; I need something to eat." It is possible to live one's entire life like the walking dead, never experiencing the immense death and suffering on this planet, and never caring for the sacred Earth and her creatures.

Or one can activate a life in which the fullness of existence flows at every moment and in which the ecstasy of wakefulness vivifies each second of the day. Such a life is a life enlivened by an ecstatic, deep nonviolence, by the integration of critical theory, compassion, and active nonviolence. It is a life in which the ethical, the mystical, and the eschatological meet in the fullness of the present moment. In such a life, even solidarity with the poor and the praxis of struggle involving a compassionate suffering with the suffering of others cannot break the deep joy and celebration of the fullness, wonder, and beauty of existence infusing all of life. Ultimately, this joy is the eschatological destiny and right of all persons on Earth, and this ecstatic joy must be the foundation of a transformed world.

Such a life is a life of solidarity and revolutionary praxis. In the Bible, God tells the people of Israel, "I have set before you life and death, blessing and curse; therefore choose life" (Deut. 30:19). With the exception of a few rare persons and societies, up to the present time in history we have by and large chosen death. We have chosen to relate to the world through the distortions and falsifications of the human ego-imagination. We have chosen what is "unreal": materialism and money, systems of power, and a magical, symbolic relation to existence. At the dawn of the new millennium, we are at what may be the final crossroads in human history. It may be our final chance to choose life and to realize at last our true human destiny on this planet.

The destiny of the Earth and its creatures has been delegated to us. On our present choice hangs the future of the world. We can accept our true vocation as wayfarers on the immense and sacred journey of cosmogenesis, or we can once again refuse and remain mere tourists outside of the struggle for the fullness of life on this planet, to become ever more complicit in the death of nature and of future generations. At this daybreak of the twenty-first century, the choice is still ours. Soon it will be too late, and the choice may be revoked. Will we descend in the years ahead into ever greater darkness and nightfall? Or will we now choose, for ourselves and future generations, a glorious millennium dawn?

Works Cited

Abe, Masao (1985). *Zen and Western Thought*. Honolulu: University of Hawaii Press.

Abhayananda, S. (1996). *A History of Mysticism. The Unchanging Testament*. Third (Revised) Edition. Olympia, WA.: Atma Books.

Adler, Mortimer J. (1991). *Haves Without Have Nots. Essays for the 21st Century on Democracy and Socialism*. New York: Macmillan.

Ahmed, Nafeez Mosaddeq (2002). *The War on Freedom. How and Why America was Attacked September 11, 20002*. Joshua Tree, CA: Tree of Life Publications.

Alan-Leach, Richard (2000). "Agent Orange: Better Killing Through Chemistry," *Z Magazine*, 13:11 (November), pp. 43-47.

Allen, Terry J. (1999). "What Are Indonesia's Special Forces Doing in Vermont?," *In These Times*, 23: 24 (October 31), pp. 14-16.

Allen, Terry J. (2000). "Chemical Cops: Tear Gas and Pepper Spray Can Be Deadly," *In These Times*, 24: 9 (April 3), pp. 14-17.

Allot, Philip (1990). *Eunomia: New Order for a New World*. Oxford: Oxford University Press.

Almand, Eugenia and Martin, Glen T., eds. (2005). *Emerging World Law: Key Documents and Decisions of the Global Constituent Assemblies and Provisional World Parliament*. Sun City, AZ: Institute for Economic Democracy Press.

Alston, William P. (1991). *Perceiving God. The Epistemology of Religious Experience*. Ithaca, NY: Cornell University Press.

Amin, Samir (1997). *Capitalism in the Age of Globalization*. New York & London: Zed Books.

Amin, Samir (1998). *Spectres of Capitalism. A Critique of Current Intellectual Fashions*. New York: Monthly Review Press.

Aronson, Ronald (1995). *After Marxism*. New York: The Guilford Press.

Athanasiou, Tom (1996). "Divided Planet – An Interview with Tom Athanasiou" by Derrick Jensen. *Z Magazine*: December, 1996.

August, Arnold (1999). *Democracy in Cuba and the 1997-98 Elections*. Havana: Editorial José Marti.

Aurobindo, Sri (1974). *The Essential Aurobindo*. Robert McDermott, ed. New York: Schocken Books.

Aurobindo, Sri (1997). *The Human Cycle, The Ideal of Human Unity, War and Self-Determination*. Pondicherry, India: Sri Aruobindo Ashram.

Barbé, Dominique (1987). *Grace and Power. Base Communities and Nonviolence in Brazil*. John Pairman Brown, trans. Maryknoll, NY: Orbis Books.

Barbé, Dominique (1989). *A Theology of Conflict and Other Writings on Nonviolence*. Robert R. Barr, et al, trans. Maryknoll, NY: Orbis Books.

Barry, Tom (1987). *Roots of Rebellion: Land and Hunger in Central America*. Boston: South End Press.

Basu, Samar (1999). *The UNO, The World Government, and The Ideal of World Union: As Envisioned by Sri Aurobindo*. Pondicherry, India: World Union, Sri Aurobindo Ashram.

Bateson, Gregory (1972). *Steps to an Ecology of Mind*. New York: Ballantine

Books.
Brecher, Jeremy, Childs, John Brown, and Cutler, Jill (1993). *Global Visions: Beyond the New World Order.* Boston: South End Press.
Benoit, Hubert (1959). *The Supreme Doctrine. Psychological Studies in Zen Thought.* New York: The Viking Press.
Berdyaev, Nicholas (1936). *The Meaning of History.* George Raevey, trans. New York: Charles Scribner's Sons.
Berdyaev, Nicholas (1952). *The Beginning and the End.* R. M. French, trans. New York: Harper Brothers.
Berdyaev, Nicholas (1960). *The Destiny of Man.* Natalie Duddington, trans. New York: Harper & Row.
Berdyaev, Nicholas (1962). *Dream and Reality -- An Essay in Autobiography.* Katharine Lampert, trans. New York: Collier Books.
Berdyaev, Nicholas (1969). *The Fate of Man in the Modern World.* Donald A. Lowrie, trans. Ann Arbor: University of Michigan Press.
Berdyaev, Nicholas (1972). *Freedom and the Spirit.* Oliver Fielding Clarke, trans. New York: Arno Press, Inc.
Bernstein, J. M. (2001). *Adorno: Disenchantment and Ethics.* Cambridge: Cambridge University Press.
Bernstein, Richard J. (1978). *The Restructuring of Social and Political Theory.* N.P.: University of Pennsylvania Press.
Berry, Thomas (1990). *The Dream of the Earth.* San Francisco: Sierra Club Books.
Betto, Frei (1987). *Fidel and Religion. Castro talks on Revolution and Religion with Frei Betto.* Cuban Center for Translation, trans. New York: Simon and Schuster.
Bidmead, Harold S. (1992). *A Parliament of Man: The Federation of the World.* Swimbridge, England: Patton Publications.
Bloch, Ernst (1970). *A Philosophy of the Future.* John Cumming, trans. New York: Herder and Herder.
Bloch, Ernst (1986). *The Principle of Hope.* Neville Plaice, Stephen Plaice, and Paul Knight, trans. Three volumes. Cambridge, MA: MIT Press.
Blum, William (1995). *Killing Hope: U.S. Military and CIA Interventions Since World War II.* Monroe, ME: Common Courage Press.
Blum, William (2000). *Rogue State. A Guide to the World's Only Superpower.* Monroe, ME: Common Courage Press.
Bologh, Roslyn Wallach (1979). *Dialectical Phenomenology: Marx's Method.* Boston: Routledge & Kegan Paul.
Borge, Tomas (1992). *The Patient Impatience – From Boyhood to Guerilla: A Personal Narrative of Nicaragua's Struggle for Liberation.* Russell Bartley, Darwin Flakoll, and Sylvia Yoneda, trans. Willimantic, CT: Curbstone Press.
Boswell, Terry and Chase-Dunn, Christopher (2000). *The Spiral of Capitalism and Socialism – Toward Global Democracy.* Boulder, CO: Lynne Rienner Publishers.
Boucher, Douglas H. (1999). *The Paradox of Plenty: Hunger in a Bountiful World.* Oakland, CA: Food First Books.
Brecher, Jeremy and Costello, Tim (1994). Global Village or Global Pillage: Economic Reconstruction from the Bottom Up. Boston: South End Press.
Brenkert, George G. (1983). Marx's Ethics of Freedom. London: Routledge &

Kegan Paul.

Brown, Lester R., Renner, Michael and Halweil, Brian (1999). *Vital Signs, 1999: The Environmental Trends That Are Shaping Our Future.* New York: W. W. Norton & Co.

Brown, Lester R. (2001). *Eco-Economy: Building an Economy for the Earth.* New York: W. W. Norton & Co.

Brown, Robert McAfee (1986). *Unexpected News.* Philadelphia: The Westminster Press.

Brown, Robert McAfee (1987). *Religion and Violence.* Second Edition. Philadelphia: The Westminster Press.

Brown, Robert McAffee (1988). *Religion and Spirituality: Overcoming the Great Fallacy.* Louisville: The Westminster Press.

Brueggemann, Walter (1988). *The Prophetic Imagination.* Philadelphia: Fortress Press.

Buber, Martin (1958). *Paths in Utopia.* R. F. C. Hull, trans. Boston: Beacon Press.

Bucke, Richard Maurice, M.D.(1974). *Cosmic Consciousness: A Study in the Evolution of the Human Mind.* New York: Causeway Books.

Bugbee, Henry G., Jr. (1961). The Inward Morning. A Philosophical Exploration in Journal Form. New York: Collier Books.

Caldicott, Helen (1992). *If You Love This Planet.* New York: W.W. Norton & Co.

Caldicott, Helen (1994). *Nuclear Madness.* Revised Edition. New York: W. W. Norton & Co.

Capra, Fritjof (1975). *The Tao of Physics – An Exploration of the Parallels Between Modern Physics and Eastern Mysticism.* Berkeley: Shambhala.

Carlson, Peter "The American Way of Murder" (1994). *Washington Post Magazine,* June 19, 1994, pp.12-29.

Carmody, Denise Lardner and Carmody, John Tully (1996). *Mysticism. Holiness East and West.* Oxford: Oxford University Press.

Carter, Robert E. (1989). "Zen and Ontotheology via Heidegger" in Henry Ruf, ed. *Religion, Ontotheology, and Deconstruction.* New York: Paragon House.

Carter, Robert E. (1992). *Becoming Bamboo. Western and Eastern Explorations of the Meaning of Life.* Montreal: Mc-Gill-Queen's University Press.

Caufield, Catherine (1996). *Masters of Illusion. The World Bank and the Poverty of Nations.* New York: Henry Holt and Company.

Chomsky, Noam and Herman, Edward S. (1979). *The Washington Connection and Third World Fascism.* Boston: South End Press.

Chomsky, Noam (1989). *Necessary Illusions -- Thought Control in Democratic Societies.* Boston: South End Press.

Chomsky, Noam (1993). *Year 501 – The Conquest Continues.* Boston: South End Press.

Chomsky, Noam (1994). *Manufacturing Consent – Noam Chomsky and the Media.* Documentary film by Mark Achbar and Peter Wintonick. Toronto: Zeitgeist Films.

Chomsky, Noam (1996a). *What Uncle Sam Really Wants.* Berkeley: Odonian Press.

Chomsky, Noam (1996b). *Powers & Prospects. Reflections on Human Nature and the Social Order.* Boston: South End Press.

Chossudovsky, Michel (1999). *The Globalization of Poverty: Impacts of IMF and*

World Bank Reforms. London: Zed Books LTD.

Churchill, Ward (1998). "Perversions of Justice" in James Sterba, ed. *Social and Political Philosophy.* Second Edition. New York: Wadsworth Publishing Company, pp. 259-274.

Club Humaniste (1977). *Mundialist Summa, Volume One: One World of Reason.* Paris: Club Humaniste.

Cohen, J. M. and Phipps, J-F. (1979). *The Common Experience.* New York: St. Martin's Press.

Cohen, Joel E. (1996). *How Many People Can the Earth Support?* New York: W. W. Norton & Co.

Coicaud, Jean-Marc (2002). *Legitimacy and Politics: A Contribution to the Study of Poltical Right and Political Responsibility.* David Ames Curtis, trans. Cambridge: Cambridge University Press.

Commission on Global Governance (1995). *Report of the Commission on Global Governance.* Oxford: Oxford University Press.

Connick, C. Milo (1974). *Jesus, the Man, the Mission, and the Message.* Second Edition. Englewood Cliffs, NJ: Prentice-Hall.

Constitution for the Federation of Earth (1991). Written by world citizens in four Constituent Assemblies. Lakewood, CO: World Constitution and Parliament Association. On the web at: http://www.worldproblems.net

Corson, Walter H. (1990). *The Global Ecology Handbook: A Guide to Sustaining the Earth's Future with the Latest Information on Air, Water, Climate Change, Energy, Toxic Waste, Tropical Forests, Population and Much More.* Boston: Beacon Press.

Cort, John (1988). *Christian Socialism.* Maryknoll, NY: Orbis Books.

Crick, Bernard (1987). *Socialism.* Minneapolis: University of Minnesota Press.

Dalai Lama (Gyatso, Tenzin) (1995). *The Power of Compassion.* Geshe Thupten Jimpa, trans. London: Thorsons.

Dalai Lama (Gyatso, Tenzin) (1994). *A Flash of Lightning in the Dark of Night: A Guide to the Bodhisattva's Way of Life.* The Padmakara Translation Group, trans. Boston: Shambala.

Dalai Lama (Gyatso, Tenzin) (1985). *Kindness, Clarity, and Insight.* Jeffrey Hopkins, trans. Ithaca, NY: Snow Lion Publications.

Dalai Lama (Gyatso, Tenzin) (1990). "Love, Compassion, and Tolerance" in Benjamin Shield and Richard Carlson, eds., *For the Love of God.* San Rafael, CA: New World Library, 1990, pp.3-6.

Daly, Herman E. (1996). *Beyond Growth: The Economics of Sustainable Development.* Boston: Beacon Press.

Daly, Herman E. and Cobb, John B. (1994). *For the Common Good. Redirecting the Economy Toward Community, the Environment, and a Sustainable Future.* Boston: Beacon Press.

Dear, John (1994). *The God of Peace: Toward a Theology of Nonviolence.* Maryknoll, NY: Orbis Books.

De Martino, Richard (1960). "Zen Buddhism and the Human Situation" in Erich Fromm, D.T. Suzuki, and Richard De Martino, *Psychoanalysis and Zen Buddhism.* New York: Harper & Row.

Descartes, Rene (1975). *The Philosophical Works of Descartes.* Elizabeth S. Haldane and G. R. T. Ross, trans. Cambridge: Cambridge University Press.

Dewey, John (1993). *The Political Writings.* Debra Morris and Ian Shapiro, eds.

Indianapolis: Hackett Publishing Co.

Dogen, Eihei (1997). *The Wholehearted Way*. Shohaku Okumura and Taigen Daniel Leighton, trans. Boston: Tuttle Publishing.

Domhoff, G. William (1967). *Who Rules America?* Englewood Cliffs, NJ: Prentice Hall.

Dussel, Enrique (1990). *A Philosophy of Liberation*. Aquilina Martinez and Christine Morkovsky, trans. Maryknoll, NY: Orbis Books.

Dussel, Enrique (1995). *The Invention of the Americas. Eclipse of "the Other" and the Myth of Modernity*. Michael D. Barber, trans. New York: Continuum.

Dussel, Enrique (1993). *Ethics and Community*. Robert R. Barr, trans. Maryknoll, NY: Orbis Books.

Eagleton, Terry (1996). *The Illusions of Postmodernism*. Oxford: Blackwell Publishers.

Eck, Diana (1993). *Encountering God – A Spiritual Journey from Bozeman to Banaras*. Boston: Beacon Press.

William Eckhardt (1972). *Compassion: Toward a Science of Value*. Oakville, Ontario: Canadian Peace Research Institute.

Eckhart, Meister (1980). *Breakthrough: Meister Eckhart's Creation Spirituality in New Translation*. Matthew Fox, trans. Garden City, NY: Doubleday & Company.

Edwards, David (1996). *Burning All Illusions. A Guide to Personal and Political Freedom*. Boston: South End Press.

Ehrlich, Paul R. and Ehrlich, Anne H. (1990). *The Population Explosion*. New York: Simon and Schuster.

Einstein, Albert (1950). *Out of My Later Years*. New York: Philosophical Library.

Ellul, Jacques (1978). *Violence: Reflexions From a Christian Perspective*. Oxford: Mowbrays, p.118. Quoted in Ken Jones, *The Social Face of Buddhism*, Wisdom Publications, 1989, pp.297-298.

Emerson, Ralph Waldo (1965). *Selected Writings of Ralph Waldo Emerson*. William H. Gilman, ed. New York: New American Library.

England, F. E. (1968). *Kant's Conception of God*. New York: Humanities Press.

Evans, Donald (1993). *Spirituality and Human Nature*. Albany: SUNY Press.

Fahey, Joseph J. and Armstrong, Richard, eds. (1992). *A Peace Reader: Essential Readings on War, Justice, Non-Violence and World Order*. New York: Paulist Press.

Falk, Richard (1992). *Explorations at the Edge of Time. Prospects for World Order*. Philadelphia: Temple University Press.

Falk, Richard (1993). "The Making of Global Citizenship" in *Global Visions: Beyond the New World Order*. Jeremy Brecher, John Brown Childs, and Jill Cutler, eds. Boston: South End Press, pp. 39-50.

Farley, Margaret A. and Jones, Serence, eds. (1999). *Liberating Eschatology: Essays in Honor of Letty M. Russell*. Louisville: Westminster John Knox Press.

Ferlinghetti, Lawrence (1958). *A Coney Island of the Mind*. New York: New Directions Publishers.

Feyerabend, Paul (1975). *Against Method*. London: Verso.

Finch, Henry Leroy (1977). *Wittgenstein -- The Later Philosophy. An Exposition of the "Philosophical Investigations."* Atlantic Highlands, NJ: Humanities

Press.

Finch, Henry Leroy (1995). *Wittgenstein.* Rockport, MA: Element Books.

Findlay, J. N. (1985). "The Variety of Religious Knowing" in *Knowing Religiously.* Leroy S. Rouner, ed. Notre Dame, IN: University of Notre Dame Press, pp. 64-75.

Flavin, Christopher, et al. (2002). *State of the World 2002.* New York: W. W. Norton & Co.

Forcey, Linda Rennie, ed. (1989). *Peace: Meanings, Politics, Strategies.* Westport, CT: Praeger.

Forgacs, David, ed. (2000). *The Antonio Gramsci Reader: Selected Writings 1916-1935.* New York: New York Univesity Press.

Foster, John Bellamy (1998). "Malthus' Essay on Population at Age 200: A Marxian View." *Monthly Review:* Vol. 50, No. 7, pp. 1-18.

Fowler, James W. (1981). *Stages of Faith. The Psychology of Human Development and the Quest for Meaning.* San Francisco: Harper & Row.

Fox, Matthew (1990). *A Spirituality Named Compassion.* San Francisco: Harper & Row.

Fox, Matthew (1988). *The Coming of the Cosmic Christ.* San Francisco: Harper & Row.

Frankfort, Henri, et al. (1973). *Before Philosophy. The Intellectual Adventure of Ancient Man.* Baltimore: Penguin Books.

Franklin, Jane (1997). *Cuba and the United States: A Chronological History.* Melbourne, Australia: Ocean Press.

Freire, Paulo (1974). *Pedagogy of the Oppressed.* Myra Bergman Ramos, trans. New York: Seabury Press.

Fromm, Erich (1947). *Man for Himself – An Inquiry into the Psychology of Ethics.* New York: Holt, Rhinehart, and Winston.

Fromm, Erich (1962). *Beyond the Chains of Illusion. My Encounter with Marx and Freud.* New York: Simon & Schuster.

Fromm, Erich (1974). *The Revolution of Hope: Toward a Humanized Technology.* New York: Harper & Row.

Fromm, Erich (1992). *Marx's Concept of Man.* New York: Continuum.

Fromm, Erich (1996). *To Have Or To Be?* New York: Continuum.

Fukuyama, Francis (1989). *The End of History and the Last Man.* New York and Toronto: BARD Trade Paperbacks.

Gadamer, Hans-Georg (2002). *Truth and Method.* Joel Weinsheimer and Donald G. Marshal, trans. New York: Continuum, pp. 378-379.

Galeano, Edwardo (1973). *The Open Veins of Latin America – Five Centuries of the Pillage of a Continent.* Cedric Belfrage, trans. New York: Monthly Review Press.

Gallik, Daniel, ed. (1997). *World Military Expendures and Arms Transfers, 1996.* Washington, DC: U.S. Arms Control and Disarmament Agency.

Gandhi, M. K. (1927). *An Autobiography or The Story of My Experiments with Truth.* Mahadev Desai, trans. Ahmedabad: Navajivan Publishing House.

Gandhi, M. K. (1957). *Socialism of My Conception.* Anand T. Hingorani, ed. Bombay: Bharatiya Vidya Bhavan.

Gandhi, M. K. (1972). *All Men are Brothers.* Krishna Kripalani, ed. New York: UNESCO and Columbia University Press.

Gandhi, M. K. (1987). *The Mind of Mahatma Gandhi.* R. K. Prabhu and U.

R.Rao, eds. Ahmedabad: Navajivan Publishing House.

Gardner, John W. (1963). *Self-Renewal: The Individual and the Innovative Society.* New York: Harper & Row.

Gebser, Jean (1985). *The Ever-Present Origin.* Noel Barstad with Algis Mickunas, trans. Athens, OH: Ohio University Press.

George, Henry (1935). *Progress and Poverty: An Inquiry into the Cause of Industrial Depressions and of Increase of Want with Increase of Wealth.* New York: Robert Schalkenbach Foundation.

Geov Parish (2001). "The Pentagon's Trojan Horse." *In These Times,* July 23, 2001, pp. 14-16

Gier, Nicholas F. (1981). *Wittgenstein and Phenomenology. A Comparative Study of the Later Wittgenstein, Husserl, Heidegger, and Merleau-Ponty.* Albany: State University of New York Press.

Glossop, Ronald J. (1993). *World Federation? A Critical Analysis of Federal World Government.* Jefferson, NC: McFarland & Company.

Goldsmith, Joel (1990). *Contemplative Life.* New York: Citadel Press.

Gottlieb, Roger S. (1987). *History and Subjectivity. The Transformation of Marxist Theory.* Philadelphia: Temple University Press.

Green, Lucile W. (1991). *Journey to a Governed World: Thru 50 Years in the Peace Movement.* Berkeley, CA: The Uniquest Foundation.

Guevara, Che and Castro, Fidel (1989). *Socialism and Man in Cuba.* No translator listed. New York: Pathfinder.

Guevara, Ernesto Che (1996). *Episodes of the Cuban Revolutionary War, 1956-58.* No translator listed. New York: Pathfinder Press.

Gutierréz, Gustavo (1973). *A Theology of Liberation: History, Politics, and Salvation.* Sister Caridad Inda and John Eagleson, trans. Maryknoll, NY: Orbis Books.

Gutierréz, Gustavo (1993). *Las Casas.* Robert R. Barr, trans. Maryknoll, NY: Orbis Books.

Gutkind, Eric (1937). *The Absolute Collective – A Philosophical Attempt to Overcome our Broken State.* Marjorie Gabain, trans. London: The C.W. Daniel Company, LTD.

Gutkind, Eric (1969). *The Body of God: First Steps Toward an Anti-Theology -- The Collected Papers of Eric Gutkind.* Lucie B. Gutkind and Henry LeRoy Finch, eds. New York: Horizon Press.

Habermas, Jürgen (1975). *Legitimation Crisis.* Thomas McCarthy, trans. Boston: Beacon Press.

Habermas, Jürgen (1979). *Communication and the Evolution of Society.* Thomas McCarthy, trans. Boston: Beacon Press.

Habermas, Jürgen (1984). *The Theory of Communicative Action, Volume One: Reason and the Rationalization of Society.* Thomas McCarthy, trans. Boston: Beacon Press.

Habermas, Jürgen (1987). *The Theory of Communicative Action, Volume Two: Lifeworld and System: A Critique of Functionalist Reason.* Thomas McCarthy, trans. Boston: Beacon Press.

Habermas, Jürgen (1991). *Moral Consciousness and Communicative Action.* Christian Lenhardt and Shierry Weber Nicholsen, trans. Cambridge, MA: MIT Press.

Habermas, Jürgen (1992). *Postmetaphysical Thinking: Philosophical Essays.*

William Mark Hohengarten, trans. Cambridge, MA: MIT Press.

Habermas, Jürgen (1994). "Struggles for Recognition in the Democratic Constitutional State" in Charles Taylor, et al., *Multiculturalism*. Princeton, NJ: Princeton University Press, pp. 107-148.

Habermas, Jürgen (1998). *On the Pragmatics of Communication*. Edited by Maeve Cooke. Cambridge, MA: MIT Press.

Habicht, Max (1987). *The Abolition of War: Autobiographical Notes of a World Federalist and Collected Papers on Peace and World Federalism*. Paris: Club Humaniste.

Habito, Ruben, L. F. (1989). *Total Liberation: Zen Spirituality and the Social Dimension*. Maryknoll, NY: Orbis Books.

Habito, Ruben, L. F. (1993). *Healing Breath: Zen Spirituality for a Wounded Earth*. Maryknoll, NY: Orbis Books.

Happold, F. C. (1975). *Mysticism. A Study and an Anthology*. New York: Penguin Books.

Happold, F. C. (1981). *Religious Faith and Twentieth-Century Man*. New York: Crossroad.

Harris, Errol E. (1987). *Formal, Transcendental and Dialectical Thinking: Logic & Reality*. Albany, NY: SUNY Press.

Harris, Errol E. (1991). *Cosmos and Anthropos. A Philosophical Interpretation of the Anthropic Cosmological Principle*. London: Humanities Press International.

Harris, Errol E. (1992). *Cosmos and Theos. Ethical and Theological Implications of the Anthropic Cosmological Principle*. London: Humanities Press International.

Harris, Errol E. (1993). *One World or None: Prescription for Survival*. Atlantic Highlands, NJ.

Harris, Errol E. and Yunker, James A., eds. (1999). *Toward Genuine Global Governance: Critical Reactions to "Our Global Neighborhood."* Westport, CT: Praeger.

Harris, Errol E. (2000a). *The Restitution of Metaphysics*. Amherst, NY: Prometheus Books.

Harris, Errol E. (2000b). *Apocalypse and Paradigm: Science and Everyday Thinking*. London: Praeger.

Harris, Jonathan M., ed. (2000). *Rethinking Sustainability: Power, Knowledge, and Institutions*. Ann Arbor: University of Michigan Press.

Hartshorne, Charles (1967). *A Natural Theology For Our Time*. LaSalle, IN: Open Court.

Haus, Charles (1989). "A Rational Basis for Hope" in Linda Rennie Forcey, ed. *Peace – Meanings, Politics, Strategies*. Westport, CT: Praeger, pp. 203-217.

Heidegger, Martin (1971). *Poetry, Language, Thought*. Albert Hofstadter, trans. New York: Harper & Row.

Held, David (1980). *Introduction to Critical Theory: Horkheimer to Habermas*. Berkeley: University of California Press.

Hendley, Stephen (1996). "From Communicative Action to the Face of the Other: Habermas and Levinas on the Foundations of Moral Theory." *Philosophy Today*. Vol. 40, No. 4, pp. 504-530.

Herman, Edward S. (1982). *The Real Terror Network: Terrorism in Fact and Propaganda*. Boston: South End Press.

Herrigel, Eugen (1971). *Zen in the Art of Archery.* R. F. C. Hull, trans. New York: Random House.

Hewitt, Marsha Aileen (1995). *Critical Theory of Religion: A Feminist Analysis.* Minneapolis: Fortress Press.

Hinkelammert, Franz J. (1986). *The Ideological Weapons of Death. A Theological Critique of Capitalism.* Philip Berryman, trans. Maryknoll, NY: Orbis Books.

Hinsley, F. H. (1986). *Sovereignty.* Second Edition. Cambridge: Cambridge University Press.

Holland, Joe and Henriot, Peter, S. J. (1993). *Social Analysis: Linking Faith and Justice.* Maryknoll, NY: Dove Communications and Orbis Books.

Hopkins, Jeffrey (2001). *Cultivating Compassion – A Buddhist Perspective.* New York: Broadway Books.

Horkheimer, Max and Adorno, Theodore (1996). *Dialectic of Enlightenment.* John Cumming, trans. New York: Continuum.

Horkheimer, Max (1995). *Critical Theory – Selected Essays by Max Horkheimer.* Matthew J. O'Connell et al., trans. New York: Continuum.

Hudson, Michael (2003). *Super Imperialism: The Origin and Fundamentals of U.S. World Dominance.* Second Edition. London: Pluto Press.

Imboden, Roberta (1987). *From the Cross to the Kingdom.* New York: Harper & Row.

Ingram, David and Simon-Ingram, Julia, eds. (1992). *Critical Theory – The Essential Readings.* New York: Paragon House.

International Philosophers for Peace (2001). *IPPNO Document on World Peace.* Radford, VA.: Radford University Printing.

Isely, Philip (2000). *Immediate Economic Benefits of World Government.* Lakewood, CO: Emergency Earth Rescue Administration of the World Constitution and Parliament Assoc.

Iyer, Ragavan N. (1973). *The Moral and Political Thought of Mahatma Gandhi.* New York: Oxford University Press.

Jacobson, Nolan Pliny (1982). "A Buddhistic-Christian Probe of Our Endangered Furture." *The Eastern Buddhist.* Vol. XV, No. 1, Spring 1982, pp. 38-55.

Jacobson, Nolan Pliny (1983). *Buddhism and the Contemporary World – Change and Self-Correction.* Carbondale and Edwardsville, IL: Southern Illinois University Press.

Jäger, Willigis (1994). "Mysticism: Flight from the World or Responsibility for the World" in Christian Duquoc and Gustavo Gutierréz, eds., *Mysticism and Institutional Analysis.* London: Concilium.

James, William (1958). *The Varieties of Religious Experience.* New York: New American Library.

Jay, Martin (1984). *Marxism & Totality: The Adventures of a Concept from Lukacs to Habermas.* Berkeley: University of California Press.

Jerome, V. J. (1966). *The Paper Bridge.* New York: Citadel Press.

Jesudasan, Ignatius, S. J. (1984). *A Gandhian Theology of Liberation.* Maryknoll, NY: Orbis Books.

Johnson, Chalmers (2004). *The Sorrows of Empire. Militarism, Secrecy, and the End of the Republic.* New York: Henry Holt and Company.

Jones, Ken (1989). *The Social Face of Buddhism. An Approach to Poltical and Social Activism.* London: Wisdom Publications.

Jones, Richard H. (1993). *Mysticism Examined. Philosophical Inquiries into Mysticism.* Albany, NY: State University of New York Press.

Jung, Carl Gustav (1970). *C.G. Jung: Psychological Reflections, A New Anthology of His Writings, 1905-1961.* Jolande Jacobi, ed. Princeton, NJ: Princeton University Press.

Kafatos, Menas and Nadeau, Robert (1990). *The Conscious Universe: Part and Whole in Modern Physical Theory.* Berlin: Springer-Verlag.

Kahler, Erich (1967). *The Tower and the Abyss: An Inquiry Into the Transformation of Man.* New York: Viking Press.

Kant, Immanuel (1951). *Critique of Judgment.* J. H. Bernard, trans. New York: Collier Macmillan.

Kant, Immanuel (1956). *Critique of Practical Reason.* Lewis White Beck, trans. New York: Bobbs-Merrill Company.

Kant, Immanuel (1957). *Perpetual Peace.* Louis White Beck, trans. New York: Macmillan.

Kant, Immanuel (1964). *Groundwork of the Metaphysic of Morals.* H. J. Paton, trans. New York: Harper & Row.

Kant, Immanuel (1965). *Critique of Pure Reason.* Norman Kemp Smith, trans. New York: St. Martin's Press.

Karliner, Joshua (1997). *The Corporate Planet: Ecology and Politics in the Age of Globalization.* San Francisco: Sierra Club Books.

Kellner, Douglas (1984). *Herbert Marcuse and the Crisis of Marxism.* Berkeley: University of California Press.

Kiang, John (1984). *One World: The Approach to Permanent Peace on Earth and the General Happiness of Mankind.* Notre Dame, IN: One World Publishing Co.

Kierkegaard, Soren (1959). *The Journals of Kierkegaard.* Alexander Dru, ed. New York: Harper & Row.

King, Uusula (1980). *Towards a New Mysticism. Teilhard de Chardin and Eastern Religions.* New York: Seabury Press.

Kitaro, Nishida (1987). *Last Writings: Nothingness and the Religious Worldview.* David A. Dilworth, trans. Honolulu: University of Hawaii Press.

Klare, Michael T. and Arnson, Cynthia (1981). *Supplying Repression: U.S. Support for Authoritarian Regimes Abroad.* Washington, D.C.: Institute for Policy Studies.

Klare, Michael T. (2002). *Resource Wars. The New Landscape of Global Conflict* New York: Henry Holt & Company.

Kohlberg, Lawrence (1984). *The Psychology of Moral Development, Volume Two: The Nature and Validity of Moral Stages.* San Francisco: Harper & Row.

Koont, Sinan (2004). "Food Security in Cuba." *Monthly Review,* Vol. 55, No. 8, pp. 11-20.

Korb, Lawrence J. (2001). "10 Myths About the Defense Budget." *In These Times,* Vol. 25, No. 9, pp. 10-12.

Korten, David C. (1999). *The Post-Corporate World. Life After Capitalism.* West Hartford, CT: Kumarian Press, Inc.

Korten, David C. (2001). *When Corporations Rule the World.* Second Edition. Bloomfield, CT: Kumarian Press.

Krieger, David J. (1991). *The New Universalism. Foundations for a Global*

Theology. Maryknoll, NY: Orbis Books.

Krishnamurti, Jiddu (1970). *Talks and Dialogues.* New York: Avon Books.

Krishnamurti, Jiddu (1972). *You Are the World.* New York: Harper & Row.

Krishnamurti, Jiddu (1973). *The Flight of the Eagle.* New York: Harper & Row.

Krishnamurti, Jiddu (1977). *The Urgency of Change.* New York: Harper & Row.

Krishnamurti, Jiddu (1978). *Truth and Actuality.* New York: Harper & Row.

Krishnamurti, Jiddu (1982). *Krishnamurti's Journal.* San Francisco: Harper & Row.

Krishnamurti, Jiddu (1989). *Think on These Things.* New York: Harper & Row.

Kuhn, Thomas S. (1970). *The Structure of Scientific Revolutions.* Second Edition, enlarged. Chicago: University of Chicago Press.

Laing, R. D. (1968). *The Politics of Experience.* New York: Ballantine Books.

Lawrence, D. H. (1976). *Apocalypse.* New York: Penguin.

Leonard, George B. (1972). *The Transformation. A Guide to the Inevitable Changes in Humankind.* New York: Delta Books.

Levin, Michael David (1985). *The Body's Recollection of Being. Phenomenological Psychology and the Deconstruction of Nihilism.* London: Routledge & Kegan Paul.

Levin, Michael David (1989). *The Listening Self. Personal Growth, Social Change and the Closure of Metaphsics.* London: Routledge & Kegan Paul.

Levinas, Emmanuel (1969). *Totality and Infinity. An Essay on Exteriority.* Alphonso Lingis, trans. Pittsburgh: Duquesne University Press

Levinas, Emmanuel (1985). *Ethics and Infinity.* Richard A. Cohen, trans. Pittsburgh: Duquesne University Press.

Levinas, Emmanuel (1994). *Outside the Subject.* Michael B. Smith, trans. Stanford: Stanford University Press.

Levine, Steven (1982). *Who Dies? An Investigation of Conscious Living and Conscious Dying.* New York: Anchor Books.

Lifton, Robert Jay (1993) *The Protean Self: Human Resilience in an Age of Fragmentation.* New York: Basic Books.

Locke, John (1963). "Second Treatise on Civil Government" in *Social and Political Philosophy.* John Somerville and Ronald Santoni, eds. New York: Doubleday, pp. 169-204.

Lowy, Michael (1997). "Che's Revolutionary Humanism." *Monthly Review.* Vol. 49, Number 5, pp. 1-7.

Lula da Silva, Luiz Inacio (1993). "The Transformations Must Be Deep and Global" in *Global Visions: Beyond the New World Order.* Jeremy Brecher, John Brown Childs, and Jill Cutler, eds. Boston: South End Press, pp. 171-174.

Luntley, Michael (1990). *The Meaning of Socialism.* La Salle, IL: Open Court.

Macpherson, C. B. (1971). "The Social Bearing of Locke's Political Theory" in *Perspectives on Political Philosophy.* Vol. II. David Hart and James Downton, Jr. eds. New York: Holt, Rinehart, and Winston, pp. 147-169.

Macpherson, C. B. (1973). "Rawl's Models of Man and Society." *Philosophy of Social Sciences Journal,* No. 3, 1973, pp. 341-347.

Maheshvaranda, Dada (2003). *After Capitalism: Prout's Vision for a New World.* New Delhi: Proutist Universal Publications.

Maitra, S. K. (2000). *The Meeting of The East and The West in Sri Aurobindo's*

Philosophy. Pondicherry, India: Sri Aurobindo Ashram.

Mander, Jerry and Goldsmith, Edward (1996). *The Case Against the Global Economy: And for a Turn Toward the Local.* San Francisco: Sierra Club Books.

Mansueto, Anthony E., Jr. (1995). *Towards Synergism – The Cosmic Significance of the Human Civilizational Project.* Lanham, MD: University Press of America.

Marchand, Guy (1979). *One or Zero: The World Will Be Mundialist or Will Be No Longer.* Paris: Club Humaniste.

Marcuse, Herbert (1960). *Reason and Revolution. Hegel and the Rise of Social Theory.* Boston: Beacon Press.

Marcuse, Herbert (1962). *Eros and Civilization. A Philosophical Inquiry into Freud.* New York: Vintage Books.

Marcuse, Herbert (1969). *One Dimensional Man: Studies in the Ideology of Advanced Industrial Society.* Boston: Beacon Press.

Marcuse, Herbert (1992). "Philosophy and Critical Theory" in David Ingram and Julia Simon-Ingram, eds., *Critical Theory.* New York: Paragon House.

Margenau, Henry and Varghese, Roy Abraham, eds. (1994). *Cosmos, Bios, Theos. Scientists Reflect on Science, God, and the Origins of the Universe, Life and Homo Sapiens.* Chicago: Open Court.

Martin, Glen T. (1986). "Review of John A. Tabor, Transformative Philosophy. A Study of Sankara, Fichte, and Heidegger." *Metaphilosophy* Vol. 17, No. 4, October 1986, pp. 363-370.

Martin, Glen T. (1988a) "A Critique of Nietzsche's Metaphysical Skepticism." *International Studies in Philosophy*, Vol. XIX, No. 2, Summer, 1988, pp. 51-59.

Martin, Glen T. (1988b). "The Religious Nature of Wittgenstein's Later Philosophy." *Philosophy Today*, Fall 1988, pp. 207-220.

Martin, Glen T. (1989). *From Nietzsche to Wittgenstein. The Problem of Truth and Nihilism in the Modern World.* New York: Peter Lang Publisher.

Martin, Glen T. (1991). "Deconstruction and Breakthrough in Nietzsche and Nārgārjuna." in Graham Parkes, ed., *Nietzsche and Asian Thought.* Chicago: University of Chicago Press, pp. 91-111.

Martin Glen T. (1997). "Eschatological Ethics and Positive Peace: Western Contributions to the Critique of the Self-Centered Ego and Its Social Manifestations" in Laura Duhan Kaplan & Laurence F. Bove, eds., *Philosophical Perspectives on Power and Domination.* Amsterdam: Rodopi, pp. 79-92.

Martin, Glen T. (1998). "Freedom, Ethics, and Compassion" in Santi Nath Chattopadhyaya, ed., *Freedom.* Calcutta: Naya Prokash Publisher, pp. 187-201.

Martin, Glen T. (1999a). "A Buddhist Response to Institutional Violence" in Deane Curtin and Robert Litke, eds., *Institutional Violence.* Amsterdam: Rodopi, pp. 363-380.

Martin, Glen T. (1999b). "A Planetary Paradigm for Global Government" in Errol E. Harris and James A. Yunker, eds., *Toward Genuine Global Governance: Critical Reactions to "Our Global Neighborhood."* London: Praeger, pp. 1-18.

Martin, Glen T. (1999c). "Three Stages in the Dialectical Realization of Democracy and the Constitution for the Federation of Earth." Part One, *Across Frontiers – A WCPA/GREN Publication for Humanity*, March-April, 1999, pp. 19-20. Part Two, *Across Frontiers,*

May-June, 1999, pp. 20-22.

Martin, Glen T. (2002). "Unity in Diversity as the Foundation of World Peace" in Alison Bailey and Paula J. Smithka, eds., *Community, Diversity, and Difference: Implications for Peace.* Amsterdam: Rodopi, pp. 309-325.

Martin, Glen T. (2003). *Century Twenty-One: Manifesto of the Earth Federation.* Radford, VA: Institute on World Problems. Website: http://www.worldproblems.net

Martin, Glen T., ed. (2005). *World Revolution Through World Law: Basic Documents of the Emerging Earth Federation.* Sun City, AZ: Institute for Economic Democracy Press.

Marx, Karl and Engels, Friedrich (1978). *The Marx-Engels Reader.* Second Edition. Robert C. Tucker, ed. New York: W. W. Norton & Co.

Marx, Karl (1990). *Capital. Volume One.* Ben Fowkes, trans. London: Penguin Books.

Marx, Karl (1991). *Capital. Volume Three.* David Fernbach, trans. New York: Penguin Books.

Matthews, Clifford N. and Varghese, Roy Abraham, eds. (1995). *Cosmic Beginnings and Human Ends: Where Science and Religion Meet.* Chicago: Open Court.

Mayne, Richard and Pinder, John (1990). *Federal Union: The Pioneers. A History of Federal Union.* New York: St. Martin's Press.

McChesney, Robert W. (1997). *Corporate Media and the Threat to Democracy.* New York: Seven Stories Press.

McTavish, Hugh (1994). *Ending War in Our Lifetime: A Concrete, Realistic Plan.* St. Paul, MN: West Fork Press.

Merton, Thomas (1967). *Mystics and Zen Masters.* New York: Dell Publishing Company

Metz, Johann-Baptist and Moltmann, Jürgen (1995). *Faith and the Future – Essays on Theology, Solidarity, and Modernity.* Maryknoll, NY: Orbis Books.

Milgram, Stanley (1974). *Obedience to Authority: An Experimental View.* New York: Harper & Row.

Miranda, José Porfirio (1974). *Marx and the Bible: A Critique of the Philosophy of Oppression.* John Eagleson, trans. Maryknoll, NY: Orbis Books.

Miranda, José Porfirio (1986). *Marx Against the Marxists. The Christian Humanism of Karl Marx.* John Drury, trans. Maryknoll, NY: Orbis Books.

Mohanty, J. N. (1960). "Integralism and Modern Philosophical Anthropology" in. Haridas Chaudhuri and Federic Spiegelberg, eds., *The Integral Philosophy of Sri Aurobindo.* London: George Allen and Unwin, LTD, pp. 155-164.

Moltmann, Jürgen (1996). *The Coming of God -- Christian Eschatology.* Margaret Kohl, trans. Minneapolis: Fortress Press.

Morales, Frank (2001). "Electromagnetic Crowd Dispersal Weapon." *Z Magazine,* 14: 5, May, pp. 12-14.

Mundialist Summa (1977). *Mundialist Summa: One World of Reason – One Hundred World Citizens and World Federalist Authors.* Paris: Club Humaniste.

NACLA report (1998). "Militarized Democracy in the Americas." *Journal of the North American Congress on Latin America,* Vol. XXXII No. 3, Nov/Dec. 1998.

Nader, Ralph (2002). *Crashing the Party. How to Tell the Truth and Still Run for President.* New York: St. Martin's Press.

Nathanson, Jerome (1951). *John Dewey: The Reconstruction of the Democratic*

Life. New York: Unger Publishing Co.

Needleman, Jacob (1986). *The Heart of Philosophy.* New York: Harper & Row.

Nielsen, Kai (1976-77). "On Justifying Revolution" in *Philosophy and Phenomenological Research.* Vol 37, pp. 516-532.

Nietzsche, Friedrich (1969). *On the Geneaology of Morals and Ecce Homo,* Walter Kaufmann, trans. New York: Vintage Books.

Nietzsche, Friedrich (1967). *The Will to Power.* Walter Kaufmann, trans. New York: Random House.

Nietzsche, Friedrich (1974). *The Gay Science.* Walter Kaufmann, trans. New York: Vintage Books.

Nishitani, Keiji (1982). *Religion and Nothingness.* Jan Van Bragt, trans. Berkeley: University of California Press.

O'Connor, James (1996). "The Second Contradiction of Capitalism" in Ted Benton, ed., *The Greening of Marxism.* New York: The Guilford Press, pp. 187-221.

Palast, Greg (2003). *The Best Democracy Money Can Buy.* New York: Plume Books of Penguin Publishers.

Panikkar, Raimundo (1989). *The Silence of God. The Answer of the Buddha.* Robert R. Barr, trans. Maryknoll, NY: Orbis Books.

Panikkar, Raimundo (1991). Quoted in Krieger, David J. *The New Universalism. Foundations for a Global Theology.* Maryknoll, NY: Orbis Books.

Panikkar, Raimon (1993). *The Cosmotheandric Experience -- Emerging Religious Consciousness.* Maryknoll, NY: Orbis Books.

Parenti, Michael (1993). *Inventing Reality. The Politics of News Media.* Second Edition. New York: St. Martin's Press.

Parenti, Michael (1994). *Land of Idols. Political Mythology in America.* New York: St. Martin's Press.

Parenti, Michael (1995). *Democracy for the Few.* Sixth Edition. New York: St. Martin's Press.

Peffer, R. G. (1990). *Marxism, Morality, and Social Justice.* Princeton, NJ: Princeton University Press.

Perry, Renee Marie Crouse (1998). "A Call for Today's Sciences." *The Human Quest,* Vol. CCXII, No. 4, Nov.-Dec. 1998, pp. 16-17.

Picard, Max (1952). *The World of Silence.* Stanley Godman, trans. South Bend, IN: Regnery/ Gateway.

Pike, Nelson (1992). *Mystic Union. An Essay in the Phenomenology of Mysticism.* Ithaca, NY: Cornell University Press.

Pines, Christopher L. (1993). *Ideology and False Consciousness. Marx and His Historical Progenitors.* Albany: SUNY Press.

Pollack, Andy (1997). "Information Technology and Socialist Self-Management." *Monthly Review,* Sept. 1997, Vol. 49, No. 4, pp. 32-50.

Popora, Douglas V. (1990). *How Holocausts Happen: The United States in Central America.* Philadelphia: Temple University Press.

Provisional World Parliament (2003). *Bangkok Declaration on Legitimate Government for the Earth.* Institute On World Problems website: http://www.worldproblems.net

Pusey, Michael (1993). *Jürgen Habermas.* London: Routledge.

Radhakrishnan, Sarvepalli (1955). *Recovery of Faith.* New York: Harper & Brothers.

Rahner, Karl (1985). *Foundations of Christian Faith. An Introduction to the Idea of Christianity.* William V. Dych, trans. New York: Crossroad.

Rawls, John (1971). *A Theory of Justice.* Cambridge, MA: Harvard University Press.

Reardon, Betty (1985). *Sexism and the War System.* New York: Teacher's College Press.

Renner, Michael (1996). *Fighting for Survival: Environmental Decline, Social Conflict, and the New Age of Insecurity.* New York: W. W. Norton & Co.

Resnick, Stephen A. and Wolff, Richard D. (1987). *Knowledge and Class: A Marxian Critique of Political Economy.* Chicago: University of Chicago Press.

Reves, Emery (1946). *The Anatomy of Peace.* New York: Harper & Brothers.

Ricceur, Paul (1967). *The Symbolism of Evil.* Emerson Buchanan, trans. New York: Harper & Row.

Rich, Bruce (1994). *Mortgaging the Earth. The World Bank, Environmental Impoverishment, and the Crisis of Development.* Boston: Beacon Press.

Richards, Glyn (1991). *The Philosophy of Gandhi: A Study of His Basic Ideas.* Atlantic Highlands, NJ: Humanities Press.

Rifkin, Jeremy (1989). *Entropy: Into the Greenhouse World.* Revised Edition. New York: Bantam Books.

Roemer, John (1994). *A Future for Socialism.* Cambridge, MA: Harvard University Press.

Rogers, Carl R. (1961) *On Becoming a Person: A Therapist's View of Psychotherapy.* Boston: Houghton Mifflin.

Rowthorn, Anne (1989). *Caring for Creation.* Wilton, CT: Morehouse Publishing.

Rubel, Maximilien and Manale, Margaret (1976). *Marx Without Myth. A Chronological Study of his Life and Work.* New York: Harper & Row.

Ruf, Henry, ed. (1989). *Religion, Ontotheology and Deconstruction.* New York: Paragon House.

Russell, Peter (1995). *The Global Brain Awakens: Our Next Evolutionary Leap.* Palo Alto, CA: Global Brain, Inc.

Sartre, Jean-Paul (1956). *Being and Nothingness.* Hazel Barnes, trans. New York: Philosophical Library.

Sartre, Jean-Paul (1968). *Search for a Method.* Hazel E. Barnes, trans. New York: Vintage Books.

Sartre, Jean-Paul (1976). *Critique of Dialectical Reason.* Alan Sheridan-Smith, trans. London: New Left Books.

Sartre, Jean-Paul and Levy, Benny (1996). *Hope Now: The 1980 Interviews.* Adrian van den Hoven, trans. Chicago: University of Chicago Press.

Schneider, Stephen H. (1989). *Global Warming: Are We Entering the Greenhouse Century?* San Francisco: Sierra Club Books.

Segundo, Juan Luis, S. J. (1985). *Theology and the Church: A Response to Cardinal Ratzinger and A Warning to the Whole Church.* John W. Diercksmeier, trans. Minneapolis, MN: Winston Press.

Seligson, Mitchell A. and Passe-Smith, John T. (1993). *Development and Underdevelopment: The Political Economy of Inequality.* Boulder, CO: Lynne Rienner Publishers.

Shalom, Stephen Rosskamm (1993). *Imperial Alibis: Rationalizing U.S.*

Intervention After the Cold War. Boston: South End Press.

Sells, Michael A. (1994). *Mystical Languages of Unsaying*. Chicago: University of Chicago Press.

Shield, Benjamin and Carlson, Richard, eds. (1990). *For the Love of God: New Writings by Spiritual and Psychological Leaders*. San Rafael, CA.: New World Library.

Shiva, Vandana (1997). *Biopiracy: The Plunder of Nature and Knowledge*. Boston: South End Press.

Shiva, Vandana (2000). *Stolen Harvest: The Hijacking of the Global Food Supply*. Boston: South End Press.

Shiva, Vandana (2002). *Water Wars: Privatization, Pollution, and Profit*. Boston: South End Press.

Shorr, Ira (1999). "The Phantom Menace: The Pentagon Budget Shoots for the Stars." *In These Times*, Vol. 23, No. 7, 7 March 1999, pp. 14-16.

Singer, Peter (2002). *One World: the Ethics of Globalization*. New Haven: Yale University Press.

Siu, R. G. H. (1957). *The Tao of Science: An Essay on Western Knowledge and Eastern Wisdom*. Cambridge, MA: MIT Press.

Sivard, Ruth (1996). *World Military and Social Expenditures*. 16th Edition. Washington, DC: World Priorities, Inc.

Smart, Ninian (1985). "On Knowing What Is Uncertain" in Rouner, Leroy S., ed., *Knowing Religiously*. Notre Dame, Indiana: University of Notre Dame Press, pp. 76-86.

Smith, Huston (1977). *Forgotten Truth. The Primordial Tradition*. New York: Harper & Row.

Smith, J. W. (1994). *The World's Wasted Wealth 2*. Cambria, CA: Institute for Economic Democracy Press.

Smith, J. W. (2002). *Why? The Deeper History Behind the September 11, 2001, Terrorist Attack on America*. Sun City, AZ: Institute for Economic Democracy Press.

Smith, J. W. (2003a). *Economic Democracy – The Political Struggle of the Twenty-first Century*. Sun City, AZ: Institute for Economic Democracy.

Smith, J. W. (2003b). *Cooperative Capitalism: A Blueprint for Global Peace and Prosperity*. Sun City, AZ: Institute for Economic Democracy & Institute for Cooperative Capitalism.

Spencer, Sidney (1963). *Mysticism in World Religion*. South Brunswick, NY: A. S. Barnes and Co.

Stace, Walter T. (1960a). *Mysticism and Philosophy*. London: Macmillan.

Stace, Walter T. (1960b). *The Teachings of the Mystics*. New York: New American Library.

Swidler, Leonard, ed. (1987). *Toward a Universal Theology of Religion*. Maryknoll, NY: Orbis Books.

Swimme, Brian and Berry, Thomas (1992). *The Universe Story – From the Primordial Flaring Forth to the Ecozoic Era, A Celebration of the Unfolding of the Cosmos*. San Francisco: Harper San Francisco.

Tabor, John A. (1983). *Transformative Philosophy. A Study of Śankara, Fichte, and Heidegger*. Honolulu: University of Hawaii Press.

Taylor, Charles (1989). *Sources of the Self: The Making of the Modern Identity*. Cambridge, MA: Harvard University Press.

Taylor, Charles (1991). *The Ethics of Authenticity.* Cambridge, MA: Harvard University Press.

Teilhard de Chardin, Pierre (1959). *The Phenomenon of Man.* Bernard Wall, trans. New York: Harper and Brothers.

Teilhard de Chardin, Pierre (1970). *Activation of Energy.* René Hague, trans. New York: Harcourt Brace Jovanovich.

Thoreau, Henry David (1967). "Life Without Principle" in Joseph Wood Krutch, ed., *Walden and Other Writings.* New York: Bantam Books, pp. 353-373.

Thoreau, Henry David (1967). *Selected Journals of Henry David Thoreau.* Carl Bode, ed. New York: New American Library.

Tillich, Paul (1957). *Dynamics of Faith.* New York: Harper Torchbooks.

Tillich, Paul (1963). *The Eternal Now.* New York: Charles Scribner's Sons.

Tillich, Paul (1987). *The Essential Tillich: An Anthology of the Writings of Paul Tillich.* F. Forrester Church, ed. Chicago: University of Chicago Press.

Tillich, Paul (1991). Quoted in Krieger, David J. *The New Universalism. Foundations for a Global Theology.* Maryknoll, NY: Orbis Books.

Tokar, Brian (1997). *Earth for Sale: Reclaiming Ecology in the Age of Corporate Greenwash.* Boston: South End Press.

Tucker, Robert C. (1970). *The Marxian Revolutionary Idea.* New York: W. W. Norton & Company.

Underhill, Evelyn (1961). *Mysticism. A Study in the Nature and Development of Man's Spiritual Consciousness.* New York: E. P. Dutton.

Van Der Linden, Harry (1988). *Kantian Ethics and Socialism.* Indianapolis: Hackett Publishing Co.

Veblen, Thorstein (1919). "Why Is Economics Not an Evolutionary Science" in *The Place of Science in Modern Civilization and Other Essays.* New York: B. W. Huebsch. Quoted in Erich Fromm, *The Revolution of Hope: Toward a Humanized Technology.* New York: Harper & Row, 1968, p. 41.

Vetlesen, Arne Johan (1997). "Worlds apart? Habermas and Levinas." *Philosophy & Social Criticism.* Vol. 23, no. 1.

Vidal, Gore (2002). *Perpetual War for Perpetual Peace: How We Got To Be So Hated.* New York: Thunder's Mouth Press/Nation Books.

Wagar, W. Warren (1989). "Structuralism and World Peace" in *Peace: Meanings, Politics, Strategies.* Linda Rennie Forcey, ed. Westport, CT: Praeger, pp. 197-202.

Ward, Barbara and Dubos, René (1972). *Only One Earth – The Care and Maintenance of a Small Planet.* New York: W.W. Norton & Co.

West, Cornell (1993). *Prophetic Thought in Postmodern Times.* Boston: Common Courage Press.

White, John, ed. (1995). *What Is Enlightenment? Exploring the Goal of the Spiritual Path.* New York: Paragon House.

Wilber, Ken (1993). *The Spectrum of Consciousness.* Second Edition. Wheaton, IL: Quest Books.

Wilber, Ken (1995). "The Ultimate State of Consciousness" in John White, ed., *What Is Enlightenment? Exploring the Goal of the Spiritual Path.* New York: Paragon House.

Wilshire, Bruce (1990). *The Moral Collapse of the University: Professionalism, Purity, and Alienation.* Albany, NY: State University of New York Press.

Wilshire, Bruce (2002). *Fashionable Nihilism – A Critique of Analytic Philosophy.*

Albany, NY: State University of New York Press.

Wittgenstein, Ludwig (1965). "Wittgenstein's Lecture on Ethics," *Philosophical Review* (January 1965), pp. 3-17.

Wittgenstein, Ludwig (1968). *Philosophical Investigations*. Third Edition. G. E. M. Anscombe, trans. New York: Macmillan.

Wittgenstein, Ludwig (1972a). *Lectures & Conversations on Aesthetics, Psychology and Religious Belief.* Cyril Barrett, ed. Berkeley: University of California Press.

Wittgenstein, Ludwig (1972b). *On Certainty.* Dennis Paul and G. E. M. Anscombe, trans. New York: Harper & Row.

Wittgenstein, Ludwig (1974). *Tractatus Logico-Philosophicus.* D. F. Pears and B. F. McGuinness, trans. Atlantic Highlands, NJ: Humanities Press.

Wittgenstein, Ludwig (1978). *Philosophical Grammar.* Anthony Kenny, trans. Berkeley: University of California Press.

Wittgenstein, Ludwig (1979). *Wittgenstein's Lectures – Cambridge, 1932-1935.* Alice Ambrose, ed. Chicago: University of Chicago Press.

Wittgenstein, Ludwig (1980). *Culture and Value.* Peter Winch, trans. Chicago: University of Chicago Press.

Wittgenstein, Ludwig (1981). *Ludwig Wittgenstein: Personal Recollections.* Rush Rhees, ed. Totawa, NJ: Rowman and Littlefield.

Wolff, Robert Paul (1989). *About Philosophy.* Fourth Edition. Englewood Cliffs, NJ: Prentice Hall.

Young, Arthus M. (1976). *The Reflexive Universe: Evolution of Consciousness.* San Francisco: Delacorte Press.

Zaehner, R. C. (1978). *Mysticism: Sacred and Profane.* London: Oxford University Press.

Zinn, Howard (1991). *Declarations of Independence. Cross-examining American Ideology.* New York: Harper-Collins.

Zukav, Gary (1979). *The Dancing WuLi Masters: An Overview of the New Physics.* New York: William Morrow and Company.

Sources for the Epigraphs

Chapter One

Eric Gutkind. *The Absolute Collective.* London: The C. W. Daniel Company, 1937, p. 9.

Eric Fromm. *To Have Or To Be?* New York: Continuum, 1996, pp. 9-10.

Chapter Two

Henry Leroy Finch. *Wittgenstein.* Rockport, MA: Element Books, 1995, pp. 5-6.

Errol E. Harris. *Cosmos and Theos: Ethical and Theological Implications of the Anthropic Cosmological Principle.* Atlantic Highlands, NJ: Humanities Press, 1992, pp. 2 and 13-14.

Chapter Three

William Eckhardt. *Compassion: Toward a Science of Value.* Oakville, Ontario: Canadian Peace Research Institute, 1972, pp. 241-242.

Enrique Dussel. *Philosophy of Liberation.* Aquilina Martinez and Christine Morkovsky, trans. Maryknoll, NY: Orbis Books, p. 4.

Chapter Four

Søren Kierkegaard. *The Journals of Kierkegaard.* Alexander Dru, ed. New York: Harper & Row, 1959, p. 172.

Bugbee, Jr., H. G. *The Inward Morning: A Philosophical Exploration in Journal Form.* New York: Collier Books, 1961, p. 83.

Chapter Five

D. H. Lawrence. *Apocalypse.* New York: Penguin, 1976, pp. 125-126.

Henry. G. Bugbee, Jr. *The Inward Morning: A Philosophical Exploration in Journal Form.* New York: Collier Books, 1961, pp. 154-155.

Chapter Six

Eric Fromm. *The Essential Fromm: Life Between Having and Being.* Rainer Funk, ed. New York: Continuum, 1995, p. 95.

Nicolas Berdyaev. *The Destiny of Man.* Natalie Duddington, trans. New York: Harper & Row, 1960, p. 135.

Chapter Seven

Jiddu Krishnamurti. *Truth and Actuality.* New York: Harper & Row, 1978, p. 60.

Nicolas Berdyaev. *The Fate of Man in the Modern World.* Donald A. Lowrie, trans. Ann Arbor: University of Michigan Press, 1969, pp. 130-131.

Chapter Eight

Karl Marx. *Theses on Feuerbach* in *The Marx-Engels Reader,* Second Edition. Robert C. Tucker, ed. New York: W. W. Norton & Co., 1978, pp. 144-45.

Ernst Bloch. *A Philosophy of the Future.* John Cumming, trans. New York: Herder and Herder, 1970, p. 91.

Chapter Nine

Jung, Carl Gustav. *C.G. Jung: Psychological Reflections, A New Anthology of His Writings, 1905-1961.* Jolande Jacobi, ed. Princeton, NJ: Princeton University Press. p. 304 (Quoted in Matthew Fox, *Original Blessing.* Sante Fe, NM: Bear & Co., 1983, p. 25).

Dominique Barbé. *Grace and Power*, trans. John Pairman Brown. Maryknoll, NY: Orbis Books, 1987, pp. 83-84.

Glen T. Martin. *Personal Journal* (unpublished). 16 May 1996.

Chapter Ten

H. G. Bugbee. *The Inward Morning: A Philosophical Exploration in Journal Form.* New York: Collier Books, 1961, pp. 158-159 & 162.

Paul Tillich. *The Eternal Now.* New York: Charles Scribner's Sons, 1963, pp. 130-131.

Glen T. Martin, *Personal Journal* (unpublished). 10 January 2000.

Chapter Eleven

Pierre Teilhard de Chardin. *Activation of Energy.* René Hague, trans. New York: Harcourt Brace Jovanovich, 1971, p. 212.

Errol E. Harris. *Cosmos and Theos: Ethical and Theological Implications of the Anthropic Cosmological Principle.* London: Humanities Press International, 1992, pp. 22-23.

Chapter Twelve

Pierre Teilhard de Chardin. *Activation of Energy.* René Hague, trans. New York: Harcourt Brace Jovanovich, 1971, pp. 14-15 & 18-19.

Albert Einstein. *Out of My Later Years.* New York: Philosophical Library, 1950, p. 138.

Chapter Thirteen

Enrique Dussel. *Ethics and Community.* Robert R. Barr, trans. Maryknoll, NY: Orbis Books, 1993, pp. 52-53.

Martin Buber. *Paths in Utopia.* (Quoted in Richard Falk, *Explorations at the Edge of Time: The Prospects for World Order.* Philadelphia: Temple University Press, 1992, p.7.)

Chapter Fourteen

Nicholas Berdyeav, *Freedom and the Spirit.* Oliver Fielding Clarke, trans. New York: Arno Press, 1972, pp. 319 & 321.

Eric Gutkind, *The Absolute Collective – A Philosophical Attempt to Overcome our Broken State.* Marjorie Gabain, trans. London: The C.W. Daniel Company, LTD, 1937, p. 18.

Index of Names of Persons

Abe, Masao, 339
Abhayananda, S., 121-122
Adler, Mortimer, J., 179, 338
Adorno, Theodore, 205, 216
Afghanistan, 172,
Africa, 17
Alam, Sarwar, 325
Alexander, Samuel, 5, 343
Almand, Eugenia, 325
Alott, Philip, 351
Alston, William P., 120-121
Amerasinghe, Terence, 325
Amin, Samir, 228-230
Anaximander of Miletus, 295
Anaximenes of Miletus, 295
Aquinas, Thomas, 18, 50, 277, 295
Aristotle, 15, 19, 50, 207, 295, 296, 297
Aronson, Ronald, 283
Athanasiou, Tom, 251
Augustine, St., 286
Aurelius, Marcus, 157
Aurobindo, Sri, 276, 288, 291, 292, 304, 314, 354

Bacon, Francis, 35
Barbe, Dominique, 67, 70, 198, 206, 257
Barlow, Hugh D., 65
Bateson, Gregory, 26, 28, 36-37
Benjamin, Walter, 82, 205
Benoit, Hubert, 113
Berdyaev, Nicholas, 5, 15, 16, 139-140, 160, 166, 175, 207, 259, 260-263, 291, 343
Bernstein, Richard J., 215
Berry, Thomas, 20, 69, 103, 172
Berry, Wendell, 131
Bloch, Ernst, 82, 205, 207, 224, 262, 291
Bologh, Roslyn Wallach, 211, 219, 224, 350
Boswell, Terry, 32
Brenkert, George C., 180, 252, 253, 280
Bruno, Giordano, 122
Buber, Martin, 341, 345
Bucke, Richard Maurice, 57, 101, 169
Buddha, Gautama, 4, 39, 157, 173, 270, 292, 313
Bugbee, Henry G., 91, 104, 110, 112, 137, 265, 288
Bultmann, Rudolph, 96-97

Bush, George, 248

Caldicott, Helen, 172, 247, 248-249
Campbell, Joseph, 98
Capra, Fritjof, 27, 28
Carlson, Peter, 65
Carmody, Denise Lardner, 118, 124
Carmody, John Tully, 118, 124
Carter, Robert E., 79-80, 141, 143, 150-160, 162-164, 166, 169-171, 193
Caufield, Catherine, 358
Chase-Dunn, Christopher, 32
Chomsky, Noam, 172, 238, 241, 247, 351
Chossudovsky, Michel, 359, 365, 370, 371
Christ, Jesus, 96, 157
Chrysostom, St. John, 277
Chuang Tzu, 4
Churchill, Ward, 30
Clark, Ramsey, 172
Cohen, J. M., 130
Columbus, Christopher, 30, 240, 384-385, 391-393
Constantine, Emperor, 91
Copernicus, Nicholas, 91, 132, 202, 344
Confucius, 4
Crick, Bernard, 176-177

Dalai Lama (Tenzin Gyatso), 78, 389
Daly, Herman E., 35, 346, 370, 371
Darwin, Charles, 93, 96
De Martino, Richard, 57, 60, 172
Democritus of Abdera, 221
Descartes, Rene, 51, 73
Dewey, John, 178-179, 207, 351, 372
Dionysus the Areopagite (Pseudo-Dionysus), 295, 296
Dogen, Eihei, 200
Dubos, Rene, 317, 318
Dussel, Enrique, 15, 18, 63, 64, 183, 195, 206, 207, 235, 272, 280, 282, 286-287, 291, 341, 342, 348, 378

Eck, Diana, 299
Eckhardt, William, 63, 64, 77
Eckhart, Meister, 15, 16, 122, 270, 277, 278, 282, 296
Edwards, David, 172
Einstein, Albert, 61, 154, 300, 320, 328

Index of Subjects